Colloquial
Ukrainian

The Colloquial Series

The following languages are available in the Colloquial series:

- Albanian
- Amharic
- Arabic (Levantine)
- Arabic of Egypt
- Arabic of the Gulf and Saudi Arabia
- Bulgarian
- Cambodian
- Cantonese
- Chinese
- Czech
- Danish
- Dutch
- English
- Estonian
- French
- German
- *Greek
- Gujarati
- Hungarian
- Indonesian
- Italian
- Japanese
- Malay
- Norwegian
- Panjabi
- Persian
- Polish
- Portuguese
- Romanian
- *Russian
- Serbo-Croat
- Somali
- *Spanish
- Spanish of Latin America
- Swedish
- Thai
- Turkish
- Ukrainian
- Vietnamese
- Welsh

Accompanying cassettes are available for the above titles.
*Accompanying CDs are available.

Colloquial
Ukrainian

Ian Press and Stefan Pugh

ROUTLEDGE

London and New York

First published 1994
by Routledge
11 New Fetter Lane, London EC4P 4EE

Simultaneously published in the USA and Canada
by Routledge
29 West 35th Street, New York, NY 10001

Reprinted 1995

Typeset in Times by Transet Typesetters Ltd, Coventry, England
Printed and bound in England by Clays Ltd, St Ives plc

British Library Cataloguing in Publication Data
A catalogue record for this book is available from the British Library

Library of Congress Cataloguing in Publication Data
A catalogue record for this book is available from the Library of Congress

ISBN 0–415–09202–7 (book)
ISBN 0–415–09203–5 (cassettes)
ISBN 0–415–09204–3 (book and cassettes course)

Contents

About this book

The aim of the authors has been to provide a complete introductory course in the Ukrainian language, but one which can still be used by someone who needs only to 'survive'; it can be used for study on one's own or in a classroom setting. This course was written with all English speakers in mind as potential users; to this end, definitions of Ukrainian words include occasional American English variants alongside typically British English forms (e.g. *lorry*, Amer. *truck*). The variant of Ukrainian presented here is essentially rather neutral. One of the problems facing a grammarian of Ukrainian, however, is that there is widespread disagreement as to just what the 'standard' is, whether this concerns the lexicon or the grammar. Connected with this there is substantial regional variation in Ukrainian; where particular variants are widely used, we have supplied them alongside the 'standard' forms. As an introduction to Ukrainian, especially the spoken language, our approach is meant to be casual and fun without disregarding grammar: the structure of the Ukrainian language. You are certain to find some gaps in the subject matter treated in this work, as not all topics can be covered in a book of this nature. But *Colloquial Ukrainian* will, if you are conscientious, put you on course for reasonable competence in Ukrainian, and give you a solid basis for more advanced work in the language.

Two 60-minute cassettes are available to accompany *Colloquial Ukrainian.* If you are really serious about learning Ukrainian, then we would urge you to use them. Pronunciation and listening skills can only really be properly practised by listening to and following the example of native Ukrainian speakers. The material recorded includes dialogues and examples from the book as well as additional matter. The learner should note that where the cassette symbol appears throughout the book, not every example is recorded.

How to go further

When you have completed this course and are ready to expand your knowledge of Ukrainian, there are several avenues you can pursue. It is always a good idea, if you live in an area where there is a Ukrainian community, to contact their club: for instance the Federation of Ukrainians, or the Association of Ukrainians in Great Britain. You should have no problem in the United States or, especially, in Canada, where there are large Ukrainian communities. You can also contact any university where there is a department of Slavonic ('Slavic' in America) languages and literatures, and enquire about classes. In the United Kingdom university classes are well established at the School of Slavonic and East European Studies (University of London, Senate House, Malet Street, London WC1E 7HU). Try also to tune into Ukrainian on the radio. In the United States, the Harvard Ukrainian Research Institute (HURI, 1581–3 Massachusetts Avenue, Cambridge, Mass. 02138, USA) is a strong centre of Ukrainian studies; the American Association of Ukrainian Studies is quite active, and can be reached through HURI. In Canada you can contact the Canadian Institute of Ukrainian Studies (CIUS, Department of Slavic Languages and Literatures, University of Toronto, 21 Sussex Avenue, Toronto, Ontario, Canada M5S 1A1). Travel to Ukraine is now much easier and, although the situation in the country remains difficult, being in the country (and possibly following an organized course at the same time) would be invaluable. A non-Ukrainian using Ukrainian, however hesitantly, will be greatly appreciated by Ukrainians.

As for bookshops, try those attached to universities that have Slavonic departments. In London we would particularly recommend the Ukrainian Bookshop at 49 Linden Gardens, Notting Hill Gate, London W2 4HG, 071-229-0140; the nearest tube station is Notting Hill Gate. Both HURI (617-495-3692) and CIUS (416-978-8240), in the USA and Canada, respectively, can be contacted for Ukrainian book orders.

Acknowledgements and dedication

We hope you enjoy learning Ukrainian. It is a beautiful language, in both its sounds and its grammar, the language of a generous people smothered by political, social, and cultural oppression for far too many years. They at last have an independent state, but years of deprivation have made the creation of real democratic structures extremely difficult and beset by risks. Learning their language will demonstrate to the Ukrainians our commitment to the achievement of stability in Central and Eastern Europe.

We have received quite extraordinary and generous assistance from a number of individuals. Our thanks go to Professor Michael Branch, Director of the School of Slavonic and East European Studies (SSEES), University of London, for putting us in touch with Routledge; to

James Dingley, also of SSEES, for his help and encouragement; to Marta Jenkala for her vigorous and invaluable criticism; to Olena Bekh of Kyiv University for her time, her considerable help and her advice; to Professor Roksoliana Zorivchak of L'viv University for her extraordinary patience and for the boundless help she gave us; to Professor Evgenij Dobrenko of Duke University for his invaluable assistance and enthusiasm, as well as to William H. Pugh for his proofreading skills and comments. We have followed their advice where we could: what is good in this course is in large part thanks to them, what is bad is down to us. During a few days in Kyiv in December 1993 one of us received extraordinary help from Miron Petrovskii, Svetlana Petrovskaia, Vadim Skuratovskii, Irina Panchenko, and the Petrovskiis' neighbour, Tania. Special thanks are due to the young policeman at the metro station 'Heroyiv Dnipra', who, having listened patiently to the co-author's pleas, decided not to arrest him for taking photographs in the station. Thanks also to Ursula Griffiths of the British Council in Kyiv. For some invaluable last-minute help and advice we are deeply grateful to Valentyn Yehorov and Lesya Palka. Finally, our thanks to Simon Bell, Martin Barr, and Louisa Semlyen of Routledge for their tireless help.

We wish to dedicate this course to the memory of Viktor Svoboda of the School of Slavonic and East European Studies, University of London. His untimely death in 1992 deprived Ukraine and Ukrainian studies of one of its most knowledgeable and committed scholars. His friendship and encouragement, and his outstanding knowledge and immaculate practice of the Ukrainian language, are deeply missed.

Introduction

The Ukrainian language is spoken by around 45 million people, most of them, over 36 million, resident in Ukraine. There are Ukrainians in neighbouring states, especially in Russia and Belarus'. In addition, there are well-established Ukrainian communities in more distant lands, such as Australia, Argentina, Brazil, the countries of Western Europe, and, most notably, the United States and Canada. This is the Ukrainian diaspora, which comes mainly from the west of the Ukrainian linguistic area.

Ukraine declared its independence on 24 August 1991, a declaration that marked a stage in the dissolution of the Soviet Union. At the beginning of 1991 the official population was a little over 52 million. Ukraine's territory amounts to over 603,000 square kilometres, and its capital is Kyiv ('Kiev' is the Russian variant of this name, and will not be used in this book). The country has a highly varied landscape, from the fertile black-earth zone and the steppes and considerable heavy industry and coal mining of the east of the country, to the mountainous south-west and forested and marshy north-west. It is bounded in the east and much of the north by Russia, in the north-west by Belarus', in the west by Poland and Slovakia, in the south-west by Hungary, Romania, and Moldova and in the south by the Black Sea.

Political and subsequent cultural diversity and division inhibited standardization of the language. Moves towards this goal emerged within the context of Romanticism in the eighteenth and nineteenth centuries, advanced further (in circumstances at first exhilarating and subsequently tragic) in the 1920s and 1930s, and are almost certainly coming to final fruition at the time of writing. Ukrainian specialists have no illusions about the importance and difficulty of this task: Palamar and Bekh (1993:3) write of the 'healing of the language situation in Ukraine', and of establishing the 'free functioning of the Ukrainian language in all spheres of the life of society', now that Ukrainian is the official state language.

Ukrainian language, literature and history

Ukrainian is a Slavonic language, like Polish, Czech, Slovak, the two Sorbian languages, Bulgarian, Macedonian, Serbo-Croat, Slovene and, most closely related to it, Belarusian and Russian; the last two, together with Ukrainian, make up the East Slavonic branch of the family. In numbers of speakers Ukrainian is the second largest Slavonic language.

Around 988 AD Christianity came to the East Slavs, whose centre was Kyiv, now the capital of Ukraine. With it came a written form of Slavonic, originally based on a Balkan Slavonic (Bulgaro-Macedonian) dialect, which began to acquire East Slavonic features once established in Kyiv. The spoken language of the East Slavonic region was still East Slavonic, however. It is only later, as a result of non-linguistic developments, including the destruction of Kyiv by the Mongols/Tatars in 1240, that we can begin to talk of the planting of the seeds of separate languages in the East Slavonic area. As things have turned out, three seeds germinated, those of Ukrainian, Belarusian, and Russian, though the first two were held back for many centuries for political reasons.

The sack of Kyiv in 1240 had the dramatic effect of removing the ancient centre, a hub of East–West trade endowed at its height with an exceptionally high level of civilization, from the state of Rus'. Political power moved north-east, eventually to a relative newcomer on the scene, Muscovy (with its capital, Moscow). Until the seventeenth century much of Ukraine, including Kyiv, was ruled by the Lithuanian Grand Duchy and Poland; during this period dialect divisions between East and West Ukrainian were strengthened. In the eighteenth century the division of Ukraine (the name means 'borderland') between Russia and Austria-Hungary (1793–5) led to the increased importance of the south-eastern dialects, centred around Kyiv, Poltava and Kharkiv. We can see them as important because this period coincided with both the rise of Romanticism and the emergence in that area of very gifted writers, e.g. Ivan Kotliarevs'kyi (1769–1838) and Petro Hulak-Artemovs'kyi (1790–1865). For Ukraine the Romantic period begins around 1820 and has as its supreme figures Panteleimon Kulish (1819–97) and, above all, Taras Shevchenko (1814–61). These writers gave shape to the Ukrainian literary language by taking the dialect of the south-east and raising it to 'the status of a language by the adoption of elements from folklore and of styles bequeathed by tradition' (Shevelov 1980:152–3). The deteriorating political situation in 'Russian' Ukraine, however, meant that western Ukraine, in Austria-Hungary, began to exert an influence. Political circumstances created linguistic imbalance and discontent: which Ukrainian was 'purer'? Though there were moments of great progress, moments which indeed may have saved the language for the future, it is probably only now that Ukraine is really shaking off the shackles of centuries of dependence and subordination.

The divisions of Ukraine among Poland, Lithuania, Russia and Austria-Hungary have led to its present diverse and rich cultural heritage. In spite of all the travails of their history, the Ukrainians have an extraordinary sense of national identity, an identity of which the language is a most significant component. The creation of the language during the period of Romanticism occupies an unassailable and deeply-felt place in the hearts of Ukrainians. As a language of millions and yet about which so few have heard, Ukrainian is now entering a period of healing and of standardization, when it should acquire the prestige taken for granted by so many other European languages.

There is far more to Ukrainian literature and culture than the writers whom we have mentioned. From the second half of the nineteenth century and early twentieth century we might just mention the names of Ivan Nechui-Levyts'kyi, Panas Myrnyi, Ivan Franko, Mykhailo Kotsiubyns'kyi and Lessia Ukrainka. From the Soviet period Ostap Vyshnia, Volodymyr Gzhyts'kyi, Mykola Zerov, Pavlo Tychyna, Maksym Ryl's'kyi and Volodymyr Sosiura deserve mention, among many others.

Among writers of the 1980s, we might mention Vassyl' Stus, Ihor Kalynets', Lina Kostenko, Ivan Drach, Vassyl' Horoborod'ko, Sofia Maidans'ka, Natalka Bilotserkivets', Mykola Riabchuk, Ihor Rymaruk, and others. An outstanding translator is Mykola Lukash.

How to use this course

In the first five lessons we transcribe many of the Ukrainian words, so that it is possible for you to concentrate on the sounds. You should, however, work on the alphabet from the very start, carefully writing out letters individually and in complete words. Here, in the introduction, you will be presented with the Ukrainian alphabet; become familiarized with it before going on to the first lesson. Practise writing: like reciting aloud, this will do wonders for what is one of the real tasks in learning any language, namely the acquisition of vocabulary. If you have them, use the cassettes to grasp the pronunciation of the sounds and to help the patterns imprint themselves on your mind. A friendly Ukrainian, or an enthusiastic fellow learner, will be of great help: listen carefully, imitate, create – you must speak, even if to yourself. The dialogues in every lesson should be read and re-read; put yourself in the position of one or both speakers (if you are going through the course on your own, of course!), and try to read them, with the aid of the word-lists, before looking at the English translation (provided in the first few lessons only!). Activate your understanding of the basic patterns used in the dialogues and throughout the lessons by using them constantly.

The reference section is indispensable, if only for a quick overview of particular grammatical information: in this section you will find, in outline form, a short grammar of Ukrainian. Consult it often, and you will quickly realize how much you are learning as you progress through the book. We have also provided a list of terms used in the book. Work your way through the lessons carefully and at your own speed. If there is a cross-reference to the reference section or to another lesson, follow it up: this is very much an open-plan course, progressive but flexible. We have not crammed the course with exercises; there are plenty, but just enough to persuade you to attempt them.

One of the most difficult things about being a learner of a second language is that your developed intellect pushes you to short-circuit the years of apprenticeship you had as a child learning your native language. So be patient! Do attempt to learn by heart the words you come across; writing them out in a vocabulary book can be a great help. You may not think you have learned them, but just that action of writing them out will help imprint them on your mind. Also, though Ukrainians do not insert the stress (that is, a mark on the accented syllable) when they write, you should insert it, at least in your vocabulary book. It can be very irritating having a vocabulary book that gives no grammatical and stress information. At times it may seem that we have given you too many words. Don't despair: decide for yourself which ones seem necessary or useful to you, but attempt to use as many of them as you can when you do the exercises. As soon as you feel ready, obtain a dictionary. Using a dictionary will both get you used to the order of the letters in the Ukrainian alphabet and give you the opportunity to come across yet more words and expressions.

Ukrainian and English

Ukrainian and English are both members of the family of Indo-European languages and, as such, are related, but this relationship becomes close only if we go back very many years into the past. Strong similarities between some words, e.g. **brat** and *brother*, **máty** and *mother*, and **dva** and *two* (dual), give a misleading impression of closeness. Perhaps related words like **désyat'** and *ten* or **zolotýy** and *gold* illustrate the relationship better: they ultimately have a common source, but the process of sound change over the millennia has almost completely obscured the ties between them.

The Ukrainian alphabet consists of 33 letters, as compared with 26 Latin letters used in English. Here we present the alphabet (along with approximate English equivalents) in outline form, upper case and lower case, with approximate sound values. The sets of words that follow the alphabet can be heard on the accompanying cassette, if you have it; listen carefully and repeat, the more often the better.

Украї́нська абе́тка: Лі́тери та зву́ки
The Ukrainian alphabet: its letters and sounds

Printed	Handwritten	Name	Transcription	Approximate pronunciation
А а	А а	а	[a]	*a* as in Amer. *want* (or as *a* in *alike* (clearly) pronounced, not as in 'uh-like')
Б б	Б б	бе	[b]	*b* as in *bed*
В в	В в	ве	[v]	*v* as in *vet*
Г г	Г г	ге	[h]	close to *h* in *house*, but with more voice and less aspiration (see list of grammatical terms)
Ґ ґ	Ґ ґ	ґе	[g]	*g* as in *get*; quite a rare sound in native Ukrainian words
Д д	Д д	де	[d]	*d* as in *debt*
Е е	Е е	е	[e]	*e* as in *get*
Є є	Є є	є	[ye]	*ye* as in *yet*
Ж ж	Ж ж	же	[zh]	*s* roughly as in *pleasure* (keep your voice low and push out your lips)
З з	З з	зе	[z]	*z* as in *zen*
(И) и	(И) и	и	[y]	similar to *i* in *sit*; usually transliterated as *y*
І і	І і	і	[i]	*ee* as in *seen* or *i* as in *machine*
Ї ї	Ї ї	ї	[yi]	*yea* as in *yeast*
Й й	Й й	йот	[y]	*y* as in *boy*, *yard*

К к	*К к*	ка	[k]	*k* as in *skit* (with minimal aspiration)
Л л	*Л л*	ел	[l]	*l* as in *look*
М м	*М м*	ем	[m]	*m* as in *money*
Н н	*Н н*	ен	[n]	*n* as in *near*
О о	*О о*	о	[o]	clear *o* as in *got*, but with lips more rounded; or as in Amer. *o*h! (without the final ‘w’ sound)
П п	*П п*	пе	[p]	*p* as in *spot* (with minimal aspiration)
Р р	*Р р*	ер	[r]	*r* as in Spanish *caro* (not too many taps)
С с	*С с*	ес	[s]	*s* as in *sit*
Т т	*Т т*	те	[t]	*t* as in *stop* (minimal aspiration)
У у	*У у*	у	[u]	*oo* as in northern English *look*, or *u* in *put*
Ф ф	*Ф ф*	еф	[f]	*f* as in *fan*
Х х	*Х х*	ха	[kh]	*ch* as in Scottish English *loch* (but pronounced without too much rasping)
Ц ц	*Ц ц*	це	[ts]	*ts* as in *bits*
Ч ч	*Ч ч*	че	[ch]	*ch* as in *church* (push out your lips)
Ш ш	*Ш ш*	ша	[sh]	*sh* as in *shoot* (push out your lips)
Щ щ	*Щ щ*	ща	[shch]	*sh ch* as in *fresh chicken* (without a pause).
(Ь) ь	*ь*		[']	the ‘soft sign’ (**м’який знак**); it follows consonants and indicates that they are to be pronounced palatalized (see Notes below).
Ю ю	*Ю ю*	ю	[yu]	*you* as in *you*
Я я	*Я я*	я	[ya]	*ya* as in *yam*, but lower the tongue more

It must be noted that the transcription, i.e. the portrayal of the approximate sounds, chosen is very informal, and based to a great extent on English pronunciation. The dual function of [y] may seem confusing at first: it represents the vowel **и** (as in *sit*) when between consonants, or the consonant **й** (as initial 'y' as in *yard*) when before or after a vowel. Where we have the Cyrillic sequence -**ий**, this must be rendered in transcription as -*yy*, the first y representing a vowel and the second a consonant.

'True friends' and 'false friends'

True friends are letters that look the same in a foreign alphabet as the corresponding Latin letters; in the case of Ukrainian, they are **к**, **м**, **т**, **а**, **е**, **і**, **о** and cursive **з**. False friends are: **в**, **н**, **р**, **с**, **х**, **у**, **ь**: although they look like letters that we have, they correspond to English *v*, *n*, *r*, *s*, Scots *ch* in *loch*, *u* and the soft sign (which looks like a small *b*). If you are familiar with the Greek alphabet, four of these will cause you no trouble. All but **н** are written much as in English; **н** is written 'as a capital', whether upper case or lower case; it is just a question of size. All remaining letters are 'newcomers', and need to be learned through practice. Here are some examples; listen to the tape, if you have it, and practise reading them aloud:

кит	**том**	**мак**	**вона́**	**син**	**дух**
[kyt]	[tom]	[mak]	[voná]	[syn]	[dukh]
ра́са	**три**	**крок**	**но́са**	**схе́ма**	**сон**
[rása]	[try]	[krok]	[nósa]	[skhéma]	[son]

Notes on palatalization

The letters **я**, **ю**, **є**, **ї** have the value [y+a = ya, y+u = yu, y+e = ye, y+i = yi] when beginning a word or following another vowel, e.g. **я́сно** [yásno] *clear*, **моя́** [moyá] *my* (feminine). When the first three of them follow consonants they (as well as the soft sign **ь** and **і**) indicate that the preceding consonant is 'soft' or 'palatalized'. This means that a slight 'y' sound (as in *yet*) immediately follows the main sound of the consonant: **дя́дя** [dyádya] or [d'ád'a] *uncle* in our transcription (note that this is still two syllables, and not [diadia] or [di-adi-a]; **мить** [myt'] *moment*, where [t'] sounds like the [t] in 'tea' minus the vowel; **сіль** [s'il'] *salt*. Good English equivalents (British and southern US) are words with the sequence [tu], [du]: *tune, dew*. In these examples a slight 'y' sound is also heard after [t] and [d], which would be transcribed as [t'] and [d']. This does not apply, of course, if these two words are pronounced [toon] and [doo] in your variety of English!

The Ukrainian apostrophe

When the letters **п**, **б**, **м**, **ф**, **в**, **р** are followed by an apostrophe (') and **я**, **ю**, **є** or **ї**, this means that the consonant is not palatalized, and is followed by *ya*, *yu*, *ye* or *yi*. This may also happen when a prefix ending in a hard consonant is added to a word beginning in **я**, **ю**, **є** or **ї**.

Practise reading and writing a few examples with palatalized consonants. Note the instances where a soft consonant precedes a hard consonant (no change in pronunciation); a soft consonant will soften an immediately preceding consonant. Note also the ["] symbol for the Ukrainian apostrophe:

сядь	**сіль**	**ти́ждень**	**які́**	**ву́лиця**	**гро́ші**
[s'ad']	[s'il']	[týzhden']	[yak'í]	[vúlyts'a]	[hrósh'i]
м'я́кості	**бі́ла**	**пляж**	**п'ять**	**дорі́жка**	**до́нька**
[m"yákos't'i]	[b'íla]	[pl'azh]	[p"yat']	[dor'ízhka]	[dón'ka]
ри́мський	**ла́гідний**	**уночі́**	**ті**	**у́смішка**	**коли́шній**
[rýms'kyy]	[láh'idnyy]	[unoch'í]	[t'i]	[ús'm'íshka]	[kolýsh'n'iy]
об'є́кт	**п'ю**	**м'яки́й**	**здоро́в'я**	**з ма́тір'ю**	**від'їзд**
[ob"yékt]	[p"yú]	[m"yakyy]	[zdoróv"ya]	[z mát'ir"yu]	[v'id"yízd]

Now practise pronouncing the following words containing the consonants **п**, **б**, **т**, **д**, **к**, **г** and **ґ**. When pronouncing 'stop' consonants (*p*, *b*, *t*, *d*, *k*, *g*), keep aspiration (the puff of air) to a minimum, unless they are followed by **і** or **ь**, which makes them 'soft' or 'palatalized': listen carefully to the tape (if you have it)!

Петро́	**пи́ти**	**по́ле**	**спа́ти**	**прийти́**	**вступ**
Бори́с	**би́ти**	**боротьба́**	**бра́ти**	**жбан**	**дуб**
ти́ждень	**стоя́ти**	**от**	**тра́нспорт**	**сті́льки**	**тво́рчість**
доба́	**дитя́**	**дільни́ця**	**від**	**здоро́в**	**дріб**
кит	**кіт**	**лак**	**ле́кція**	**ско́рий**	**які́**
ґа́ва	**ґвалт**	**ґедзь**	**джиґу́н**	**ґрунт**	**дзи́ґа**
горо́д	**драглі́**	**дру́гий**	**ага́**	**Бог**	**годи́на**

Pronunciation of ф, в, с, з and х

Note especially the palatalized consonants when you practise these forms:

фóрма	**фінáнси**	**графи́ти**	**грáфік**	**жирáфа**	**жирáфі**
[fórma]	[f’inánsy]	[hrafýty]	[hráf’ik]	[zhyráfa]	[zhyráf’i]
хýтір	**хазя́йка**	**хвали́ти**	**дах**	**хи́трий**	**хібá**
[khút’ir]	[khaz’áyka]	[khvalýty]	[dakh]	[khýtryy]	[x’ibá]
сад	**сядь**	**вісь**	**вість**	**лосóсь**	**сьóмга**
[sad]	[s’ad’]	[v’is’]	[v’is’t’]	[losós’]	[s’ómha]
зави́дка	**злíва**	**зіни́ця**	**Áзія**	**мазь**	**мазки́й**
[zavýdka]	[z’l’íva]	[z’inýts’a]	[áz’iya]	[maz’]	[mazkýy]

Pronunciation of ш, ж and щ

Remember to push out your lips (make them rounder), except when these letters are palatalized (as in **жíнка** below):

пóшепки	**душá**	**кóштувати**	**мáєш**	**Швéція**	**Шíллер**
жаль	**ніж**	**кни́жка**	**нóжиці**	**жíнка**	**живéш**
щорóку	**ще**	**хрущ**	**Хоти́нщина**	**пощасти́ло**	**щíтка**

The letter в

The standard pronunciation of the letter **в** is [v], [u] or [w], depending on its position in relation to other sounds.

1 [v] at the very beginning of a word or phrase immediately before a vowel, and between vowels. 2 [u] at the very beginning of a word or phrase immediately before a consonant, or between consonants. 3 [w] between a vowel and a consonant, and after a vowel at the end of a word.

It must be noted that one does sometimes hear [v] or [f] before consonants, the latter before voiceless consonants; one may even hear [v] or [f] at the end of a word. We recommend that you stick to the standard pronunciation, as in the following:

вокзáл	**відпýстка**	**авáрія**	**Шевчéнко**	**áвто**	**автóбус**
[vogzál]	[v’idpús(t)ka]	[avár’iya]	[shewchénko]	[áwto]	[awtóbus]

в о́пері	**в Андрі́я**	**все**	**навча́льний**	**ви́йти**	**увійти́**
[v óper'i]	[v andr'íya]	[usé]	[nawchál'nyy]	[výyty]	[uv'iytý]

The pronunciation of groups of consonants

A sequence of more than two consonants tends to be simplified. Most common is a sequence of three consonants; in this case the middle of the three consonants is dropped. This is sometimes reflected in the spelling, and sometimes not. Examples illustrating the loss of consonants include:

ти́ждень	gen. **ти́жня**	week	
черне́ць	gen. **ченця́**	monk	
ко́рисць	adj. **кори́сний**	profit	useful
ра́дість	adj. **ра́дісний**	joy	joyful
ща́стя	adj. **щасли́вий**	happiness	happy, fortunate
серде́чний	noun **се́рце**	hearty	heart

It is not reflected in the spelling in **шістна́дцять** 'sixteen' (**шість** 'six'), **хвастли́вий** 'boastful' (**хваст** 'braggart'), or foreign words such as **контра́стний** 'contrasting' (**контра́ст** 'contrast'), though the middle consonant is still not pronounced.

Note especially the hushing consonants **ш**, **ч** and **ж** when followed by the soft hissing consonants **ць**, **зь** and **сь**: the hushing consonants become hissing consonants, though the voiced **ж** retains its voice, namely as [z']. Thus:

кни́жка [knýzhka]	dat. **кни́жці** [knýz'ts'i]	book
одяга́єш [od'aháyesh]	**одяга́єшся** [od'aháyes's'a]	you dress
ка́чка [káchka]	dat. **ка́чці** [káts'ts'i]	duckling

Stress

In most words with more than one vowel, only one of the vowels is stressed ('accented'), that is, is more prominent than the others. There is no general rule, so you must learn which vowel is stressed whenever you come across a new Ukrainian word. In the texts we shall indicate the stressed vowel with an acute accent; this is for your convenience, and is a convention of many Ukrainian courses, but Ukrainians themselves do not normally write in the accent. In a very few words you will find two stresses: in such instances there is a choice.

Here are some examples; practise them aloud, putting more emphasis on the stressed syllable:

самá	**сáма**	**дóбре**	**менé**	**до мéне**
[samá]	[sáma]	[dóbre]	[mené]	[do méne]
вýхо	**кінь**	**кінéць**	**кожýх**	**ідý**
[vúkho]	[k’in’]	[k’inéts’]	[kozhúkh]	[idú]
ї́жа	**ї́хати**	**пúти**	**здáлéкá**	**пóшта**
[yízha]	[yíkhaty]	[pýty]	[zdáléká]	[póshta]

Practise writing them out as well in order to continue your progress with the alphabet, and pronounce them as you write them.

Now take a look at the following forms, and try, using the alphabet table above, to render each in English (some place-names may not correspond exactly to what you expect, so be ready for a few minor adjustments!):

1 Атланта 2 Москва 3 Лондон 4 Вашингтон 5 Стокгольм 6 Метро 7 Петербург 8 Флорида 9 Африка 10 Україна 11 Нью-Йорк 12 Київ 13 Індія 14 Трансільванія 15 Кравчук 16 Андропов 17 Чарлз Диккенз 18 Джаз 19 Каліфорнія

Becoming comfortable with a new alphabet is not as difficult as it may seem; if you spend time on it at the very beginning of your course, then you will be able to concentrate more on learning the material presented in the lessons than on deciphering. Play with the alphabet, transliterating as many familiar names (of places and people) as possible.

Tips on writing

In the table on pp. 8–9 we show you how to form the Cyrillic letters in cursive; you must be careful with some of these letters, because often there is only one small feature that differentiates one from another. Here are some tips.

Four letters begin with a small downstroke hook: **ґ**, **л**, **м**, **я**, written *ґ л м я*; if you don’t make the hook, the second will be confused (in connected writing especially) with **г**, while the third and fourth will not be recognized.

ґанок	*аґрус*	*ґава*	*ґрунт*
голова	*бачили*	*хотіли*	*джерело*
мама	*мотив*	*громада*	*джемпер*
вдячні	*як*	*пом’януті*	*тяжка*

Likewise, do not forget the little hooks that extend below the line on **ц**, **щ**; otherwise the first will look like cursive **и** and the second will be identical to **ш**. Finally, place a horizontal line below **ш** in order to differentiate it from cursive **т** (*т*), which frequently looks like *ш* (you may also place a horizontal line over **т**).

Compare:

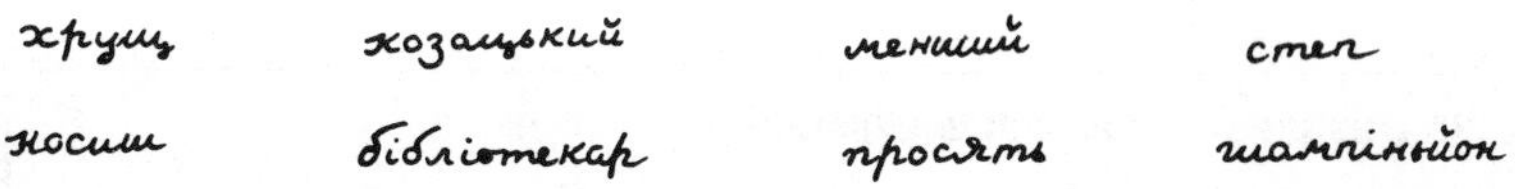

Although most Cyrillic letters can in fact be joined together in cursive, in particular, don't try to join two letters if they resist, that is, if it seems like too large a leap to get from one to the next. Most important: get the shapes of the individual letters right, and let the rest just happen.

Grammar

Ukrainian is an inflected language: thus, as in Latin and German (but unlike French, Spanish, or English), nouns, adjectives, and pronouns must have 'case endings' in order to indicate their function (subject, object, indirect object) in a sentence. Nouns are listed in the word lists and vocabulary in the subject form, that is, the 'nominative' or 'naming' case; we also provide extra information for each noun (such as another case form) that will tell you what noun type they belong to. Verbs also have endings to tell the reader/listener who is doing the action and when, much as in English; conjugating verbs may be easier in English because we have few forms in the present ('he says', 'I/you/we/they say'), but other aspects of the English verb can also be complicated (e.g. the English past tense: sing–sang–sung, go–went, etc.). Verbs are cited in the dictionary form, the infinitive (cf. Eng. *to sing*), together with information on how they conjugate. All of this will become clear as you progress, so there is no need to go into greater grammatical detail at this point. From the very beginning, you will be able to assimilate everything you need if you concentrate on the Ukrainian examples and patterns. Avoid 'thinking English'; that is, try to understand Ukrainian and to avoid the temptation to translate everything into English, because that slows down the learning process. And now, on to your first Ukrainian encounter!

1 Нови́й знайо́мий

A new acquaintance

In this lesson you will learn about:

- greetings
- the lack of articles in Ukrainian
- the verb 'to be'
- the personal pronouns
- cases and prepositions
- the present tense verb forms

The meeting

John (written **Джон** *in Cyrillic) is an English student visiting Ukraine for the first time, and upon arrival in the southern Ukrainian city of Odessa he meets a Ukrainian student named* **Мико́ла** *[mykóla]*

Мико́ла: До́брий день!
Джон: До́брий день!
Мико́ла: Я Мико́ла, студе́нт. А ви?
Джон: Я Джон, тако́ж студе́нт.
Мико́ла: Ду́же прие́мно.

Mykola: *Hello!*
John *Hello!*
Mykola: *I am Mykola, (I'm) a student. And (how about) you?*
John *I am John, (I'm) also a student.*
Mykola: *Very pleased (to meet you).*

Note: The learner can substitute any profession for **студе́нт** to suit his/her situation. You will come across some common ones in this course.

Vocabulary

дóбрий день	[dóbryy den']	hello! (lit. 'good day')
я	[ya]	I
Микóла, -и	[mykóla]	Mykola
студéнт, -а	[studént]	university student (male)
а	[a]	and, but; and how about . . .?
ви	[vy]	you (plural, polite)
Джон, -а	[dzhon]	John
такóж	[takózh]	also
дýже	[dúzhe]	very
приéмно	[pryyémno]	pleased (lit. 'it is pleasant')

The definite and indefinite articles of English

There are no articles (indefinite *a*, definite *the*) in Ukrainian. **Студéнт** means either 'a student' or 'the student', or even just 'student'. Ukrainian has quite a flexible word order, and you will often notice that where a noun like **студéнт** comes later in a sentence, it means '*a* student', whereas when it comes first or nearly so, it means '*the* student'. In context you will always be able to establish which is which. Thus:

Джон *студéнт*	John is *a* student
***Студéнт* тут.**	*The* student is here.

The verb 'to be'

As you can tell from the examples given above, the verb *to be* is normally absent in the present tense. So 'I am a student' is simply:

Я студéнт [ya studént].

Personal pronouns and gender

Personal pronouns are used in Ukrainian much as they are in English. They are:

Singular			Plural		
я	[ya]	I	**ми**	[my]	we
ти	[ty]	you (sg., familiar)	**ви**	[vy]	you (pl.)
ви	[vy]	you (sg., polite)			

він	[v'in]	he, it	**вони́**	[voný]	they
вона́	[voná]	she, it			
воно́	[vonó]	it			

You

In the singular **ви** is used when speaking to someone with whom one is not yet well acquainted and is obligatory when addressing persons in positions of authority, teachers, older people, and the like. **Ти** is used among friends, within the family and when addressing children. Other languages make the same distinction, for instance Spanish *tú/vosotros* and *usted*, French *tu* and *vous*, and German *du/ihr* and *Sie*. You may find that a Ukrainian acquaintance (of approximately the same age) or colleague will suggest that you change from **ви** to **ти** soon after meeting, as a mark of friendship. It is also perfectly acceptable for you to make the first move! Note that **ви**, when it refers to one person, and for many Ukrainians **ти**, are written with a capital initial letter in letters and certain texts.

After you and your acquaintance have entered into a **ти** relationship, you will also use more informal greetings:

Джон:	Приві́т! Як спра́ви?
Мико́ла:	Приві́т! До́бре, дя́кую. А в те́бе?
Джон:	Тако́ж до́бре.

Vocabulary

приві́т!	[pryv'ít]	Hi!
як спра́ви?	[yak správy]	How are you? (**як**, how; **спра́ви** things, affairs)
до́бре	[dóbre]	fine, good (adv.)
дя́кую	[d'ákuyu]	thanks (the word **спаси́бі** [spasýb'i] is less common, but means the same as **дя́кую**
в те́бе	[v tébe]	you (the form of **ти** used in response to **як спра́ви?**)

The move to a **ти**-relationship may be signalled by the suggestion **Дава́ймо на ти!** or **Перейдемо на ти!**

He/she/it

Nouns are differentiated by grammatical gender, for example:

студе́нт is masculine

сло́во (word) and **мі́сце** (place) are neuter
кни́жка (book) and **А́нглія** are feminine

The marker of gender is the final sound of the word:

- for masculines it is usually a bare consonant
- for neuters it is typically **-о**/**-е**
- for feminines it is typically **-а/-я** (as in Spanish and Italian)

When a noun in the singular is replaced by a pronoun, the gender of the two must agree:

студе́нт becomes **він**
сло́во becomes **воно́**
кни́жка becomes **вона́**

A man's name like **Мико́ла** is still masculine: it will decline like a feminine because it ends in **-а**, but will be replaced by **він**, as you would expect. Note that masculine and feminine pronouns will be understood as *he/she* in reference to persons, but as *it* in reference to things. We shall encounter more neuter nouns in the next chapter. For practice, when you encounter a noun in the vocabulary lists, replace it with **він**, **вона́** or **воно́**.

The words **знайо́мий** 'acquaintance' and **нови́й** 'new' are adjectival forms; **знайо́мий** functions as a noun and is masculine. The adjective is discussed in the third lesson.

Where are you from?

Мико́ла:	Ви з Аме́рики?
Джон:	Ні, з А́нглії. А ви живете́ тут?
Мико́ла:	Так, тут. Я украї́нець.
Джон:	А я англі́єць. Не америка́нець.

Mykola:	*(Are) you from America?*
John:	*No (I'm) from England; and do you* [emphasis] *live here?*
Mykola:	*Yes, I do* (lit. '*yes, here*'); *I am a Ukrainian.*
John:	*And I* (emphasis: contrast) *am an Englishman. I'm not an American.*

Vocabulary

з	[z]	*from, of*
Аме́рика, -и	[améryka]	*America*

ні	[n'i]	*no*
Áнглія, -ї	[ánhl'iya]	England
жи́ти, -вé-	[zhýty]	live
живетé	[zhyveté]	you (pl., polite) live
тут	[tut]	here
так	[tak]	yes

Cases and prepositions

The noun shows its function in a sentence by its grammatical form, or case ending. The basic form of a noun, as listed in glossaries and dictionaries, is the *nominative* (naming) case, e.g. **студéнт**, **Áнглія**; this is the form of the subject of a sentence. In Ukrainian, as in many other languages, a prepositional phrase (from England, in the city, etc.) consists of

preposition + [stem + case ending]

The preposition determines which case ending to use with the following noun. In 'Where are you from?' we see the preposition **з** 'from'; this preposition calls for the use of the *genitive* case, which can generally be described as the case of possession (of, from). As in that dialogue, we shall for the time being look only at the genitive of feminine nouns; compare the following examples carefully, since the variant spellings of case endings are always determined by the preceding consonant sound (not letter!):

Амéрика	[améryk-a]	→	**Амéрики**	[améryk-y]: hard *k*
Лéся	[Les'-a]	→	**Лéсі**	[Lés'-i]: soft *s'*
Áнглія	[ánhl'iy-a]	→	**Áнглії**	[ánhl'iy-i]: *y* only soft

Note how [y] and [i] combine in the letter **ї**.

Exercise 1a

The following forms are, or are declined as, feminine nouns and where possible the stem is identified: **студентк-**. Be careful with **Марі́я**! Use each form in the genitive in a phrase together with **кни́жка** [knýzhka], **кімнáта** [k'imnáta] 'room' or **кварти́ра** [kvartýra] 'apartment', e.g. **істóрія Украї́ни** 'history of Ukraine':

студéнтк-а	[studéntk-a]	university student (female)
Мáрт-а	[Márt-a]	Marta (Martha)
Марі́я	[Mar'íy-a]	Marija (Mary)
Микóл-а	[Mykól-a]	Mykola
жі́нк-а	[zh'ínk-a]	woman

The present tense of verbs

Ukrainian verbs belong to one of two conjugations; in this chapter we shall get to know the first conjugation, the endings of which are:

I	**-у**	[u]	we	**-емо**	[emo]
you (sg.)	**-еш**	[esh]	you (pl.)	**-ете**	[ete]
he/she	**-е**	[e]	they	**-уть**	[ut']

The first conjugation has the theme (stem) vowel [e] in all forms but the *I* form and the *they* form; the [e] is the theme, which will be realized either as Cyrillic **е** or **є** (see the verbs below).

There is no secret to learning the workings of the Ukrainian verb, but a good rule of thumb is to learn the *I* and one other form, either the *you* (**ти**) form or the *they* form, because the shape of the present tense of many verbs is not revealed by the infinitive.

Note that in grammars *I* is described as 1st person singular (1sg.), *you* (sg.) as 2sg., *he/she/it* as 3sg., *we* as 1st person plural (1pl.), *you* (pl.) as 2pl., and *they* as 3pl.

Knowledge of two of these forms will usually allow you to deduce the remaining forms of any verb type:

ЖИ́ТИ		**ЧИТА́ТИ**	
живу́	**живемо́**	**чита́ю**	**чита́ємо**
живе́ш	**живете́**	**чита́єш**	**чита́єте**
живе́	**живу́ть**	**чита́є**	**чита́ють**
zhyv-ú	zhyv-emó	chytáy-u	chytáy-emo
zhyv-ésh	zhyv-eté	chytáy-esh	chytáy-ete
zhyv-é	zhyv-út'	chytáy-e	chytáy-ut'

Thus, the infinitive *to live* is **жи́ти**, but the present tense has a form **живе́-** [zhyvé-] common to four of the persons; compare the infinitive **чита́ти** 'to read' with its common form **чита́є-** [chytáye-]. The infinitive form is that form by which the verb is cited in a dictionary. It corresponds to *to do* in 'I want to do', or *do* in 'I can do'. Note how, in verbs like [chytay-], which are extremely common, the stem-final consonant [y] combines with the ending [u] to yield the Cyrillic **ю**, [y] + [e] = **є** and so on. Each verb also has a particular stress pattern; in the verbs above we see two examples of a fixed or unchanging stress, on the ending in [zhyvú] etc., and before the ending in [chytáyu] etc. In the vocabulary verbs like **чита́ти** will be described as being of the **-а́є-** type, and verbs like **жи́ти** as of the **-вé-** type: every verb so designated is conjugated in the same way. The inclusion of a stress mark in the type designation of these two verbs indicates that the stress is fixed on that same spot.

Exercises 1b

Write out the present tense forms of the following first conjugation verbs. Insert the stress as well. The stem of the verb is supplied:

(a)	**жи́ти**	[zhýty]	stem **живé-**	live
(b)	**чита́ти**	[chytáty]	stem **чита́є-**	read
(c)	**пита́ти**	[pytáty]	steam **пита́є-**	ask
(d)	**ду́мати**	[dúmaty]	stem **ду́має-**	think
(e)	**зна́ти**	[znáty]	stem **зна́є-**	know

Exercise 1c

Construct a mini-dialogue between yourself and **Га́нна** [hánna]. Ask where she is from and tell her you are a student. To start with, use the formal **ви** greeting. Then ask her how she is, using the dialogue pattern given to you in this lesson. Incorporate the following phrases:

Vocabulary

віта́ю!	hello! (lit. 'I welcome')
добри́день	hello! (very common, but considered by some as less standard than **до́брий день**)
ра́дий вас/тебе́ ба́чити	glad to see you (a man speaking)
ра́да вас/тебе́ ба́чити	glad to see you (a woman speaking)
я також́	me too
які́ нови́ни?	what's new? (lit. 'what sort of news?')
нія́ких	nothing (response to **які́ нови́ни?**)
що ново́го?	what's new?
нічо́го/все по-старо́му/все гара́зд	nothing/as before/all OK
А у вас/ А в те́бе?	And you? (lit. 'and with you?' resp. **ви/ти**), when asking back.

Exercise 1d

See if you can read and identify the following names of cities. Some, in their Ukrainian forms, are not exactly the same as they are in English once you have transliterated them; in those cases, take an educated guess!

Пари́ж	Рим	Ка́діс	Москва́	Мінськ	Брюссе́ль
Бонн	Стокго́льм	Мю́нхен	Ло́ндон	Ві́день	Будапе́шт
Хе́льсінкі	Амстерда́м	Берлі́н	Мадри́д	Пра́га	Варша́ва
Ліо́н	Ма́нчестер	О́сло	Копенга́ген	Лісабо́н	Е́дінбург
Чіка́го	Жене́ва	Пі́тсбург	Манха́ттан	Плі́мут	Бра́йтон

2 Де ти живе́ш?

Where do you live?

In this lesson you will learn how to use:

- 'please' ('you're welcome')
- more greetings
- 'do'
- 'place where' expressions and the locative case
- suffixes to build your vocabulary

Where do you live?

As they get to know each other, Mykola and John discuss where they live. Note that they are now using the familiar ***ти*** *form*

МИКО́ЛА: Чи ти живе́ш у Ло́ндоні?
ДЖОН: Так, в Ізлінґтоні.
МИКО́ЛА: Де ти там живе́ш?
ДЖОН: Я там живу́ в кімна́ті, в університе́ті. А ти?
МИКО́ЛА: Я живу́ в кварти́рі.
ДЖОН: В Украї́ні?
МИКО́ЛА: Так, в Оде́сі.
ДЖОН: Твоя́ сім'я́ теж живе́ там?
МИКО́ЛА: Так. А де ти живе́ш в Оде́сі?
ДЖОН: Тут, у готе́лі «Украї́на».

MYKOLA: *Do you live in London?*
JOHN: *Yes, in Islington (Yes, I do).*
MYKOLA: *Where do you live there?*
JOHN: *I live in a room there, at (lit. 'in') the university. And you* [emphasis]?
MYKOLA: *I live in an apartment.*
JOHN: *In Ukraine?*
MYKOLA: *Yes, in Odessa.*

JOHN:	*Does your family live there as well?*
MYKOLA:	*Yes. And where are you staying (lit. 'living') in Odessa?*
JOHN:	*Here, in the hotel "Ukraine".*

Vocabulary

у/в	[u/v]	in (sometimes equivalent to 'at'; suggestions on ways of choosing between the two forms of this preposition are given later in the lesson)
де	[de]	where
Ізлінґтон, -а	[íz'l'ington]	Islington
там	[tam]	there
квартúра, -и	[kvartýra]	apartment
Одéса, -и	[odésa]	Odessa
Лóндон, -а	[lóndon]	London
університéт, -у	[un'iversytét]	university
кімнáта, -и	[k'imnáta]	room
теж	[tezh]	also (less common than **такóж**)
сім'я́, -ї́	[s'im"yá]	(immediate) family (compare **родúна** (extended) 'family')
готéль, -лю	[hotél']	hotel

'Please' and 'you're welcome'

'Please' and 'you're welcome' are expressed by the same word(s) in Ukrainian, as they are in many European languages (German *bitte*, Italian *prego*, etc.). In the short exchange given here, we see that **прóшу/будь лáска** are also used in polite speech when one is offering something to someone, expressing 'here you are':

МИКÓЛА:	Будь лáска/Прóшу! От вам/тобí кнúжка «Одéса»!
ДЖОН:	Дя́кую!
МИКÓЛА:	Прóшу!

будь лáска	[bud' láska]	please; you're welcome
прóшу	[próshu]	please; you're welcome
от	[ot]	here is
вам/тобí	[vam/tob'í]	for you (formal/familiar)

Будь лáска is heard all over Ukraine, but is standard in Kyiv (Eastern Ukraine); **прóшу**, while also common and understood in Kyiv, is more current in Western Ukraine. You will find the phrase **скажі́ть, будь ла́ска** [skazh'ít, bud' láska] 'tell me, please' extremely useful:

Скажі́ть, будь ла́ска, деготе́ль «Украї́на».	Tell me, please, where the hotel 'Ukrayina' is.

Other places you may be looking for could include:

вокза́л [vogzál] 'railway station' (notice that **к** is pronounced like a hard 'g' before voiced z!)
ста́нція метро́ [stán'ts'iya metró] 'underground (subway) station'
по́шта [póshta] 'post office'
таксі́ [taks'í] 'taxi'
теа́тр [teátr] 'theatre'
кінотеа́тр [k'inoteátr] 'cinema, movie theatre'
це́рква [tsérkva] 'church'
книга́рня [knyhárn'a] 'bookshop'

Just substitute them for **готе́ль «Украї́на»**. Of course, you have to be able to understand the response. At this early stage, gesture may have to do the trick, or a map drawn on some paper. A city plan might come in handy.

Some useful words to listen for or use might be: **бли́зько** [blýz'ko], **по́руч** [póruch] 'near', **дале́ко** [daléko] 'far', **іді́ть**, [id'ít'] 'go!', **ї́дьте** [yíd'te] 'drive', **пря́мо** [pr'ámo] 'straight on', **ліво́руч** [l'ivóruch] 'left', **право́руч** [pravóruch] 'right', **по́тім** [pót'im] 'then'.

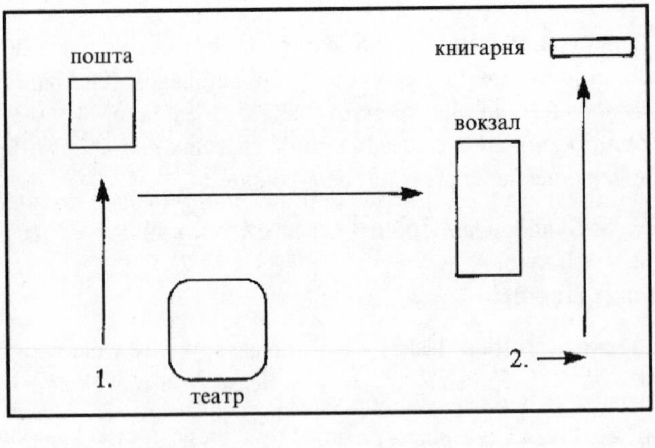

Exercise 2a

Using the words supplied above, describe (following the arrows) very simply in dialogue style how one must go to get to the places indicated at the end of the arrows. Start from 1. and answer the question **де вокза́л?** Then go to 2. and answer the question **де книга́рня?** Use greetings, 'thank you', **там/тут**, whatever you can.

More greetings

So far we have met **до́брий день** and **добри́день**, which are by far the most common Ukrainian greetings, particularly the first. We have also encountered **віта́ю** and the familiar **приві́т**. If you wish to emphasize the morning or the evening, then you can use:

До́брого ра́нку!	[dóbroho ránku]	Good morning!
До́брий ве́чір!	[dóbryy véch'ir]	Good evening!
Добри́вечір!	[dobrývech'ir]	Good evening!

or you may use the following expression:

До́брого здоро́в'я	[dóbroho zdoróv"ya]	Hello, lit. '[I wish you] good health' (often in response to someone's greeting)

Do

You may have noticed the use of *do* in 'Where do you come from?' and 'Where do you live?' where Ukrainian just has the focus verb (e.g. 'to live') or some other word, for example an adverb (e.g. 'here'); the same is true of other European languages, which only use *do* in the literal sense of 'making' or 'accomplishing', e.g. 'what are you doing?' Avoid the temptation to use the Ukrainian verb for 'to do' in such instances, as it would not be understood.

Place where: the locative case

The case which we encounter in this lesson is the *locative* case, so called because it is most commonly used to indicate 'place where' or 'location' (it is also always accompanied by a preposition). The preposition **у/в** [u/v] governs this case, and usually refers to location within the confines of a building, city, book, and the like; the preposition **на** (also + locative) on the other hand, refers to location on a surface (street etc.). Several different locative endings exist, depending on the noun in question; the ending found in the dialogue is quite common, and it can occur with nouns of all genders:

готе́ль – у готе́лі	[hotél' – u hotél'i]	hotel – in the hotel
Ні́жин – у Ні́жині	[n'ízhyn – u n'ízhyn'i]	Nizhyn – in Nizhyn
вікно́ – у вікні́	[v'iknó – u v'ikn'í]	window – in the window
Оде́са – в Оде́сі	[odésa – v odés'i]	Odessa – in Odessa

Notes:

1 In feminine nouns with soft final consonants (including -y- in words like **ста́нція** [stánts'iy-a] the genitive and locative case forms are identical.
2 The preposition meaning 'in' is spelled either **у** or **в**, depending on the sounds surrounding it (some consider that the choice is determined exclusively by what follows it). A general guide is to use **в** at the beginning of a phrase before a vowel and between vowels (remember that words beginning with the letters **я**, **ю**, **є** and **ї** begin with consonant sounds).

Exercise 2b

Translate the following short dialogue between yourself, a stranger, and a bystander (identify the speakers):

Скажі́ть, будь ла́ска, де кінотеа́тр «Оде́са».
Кінотеа́тр «Оде́са»? Я не зна́ю.
Чи ви не зна́єте?
Ні. Я не з Оде́си, я з Черні́гова.
Я зна́ю: він на ву́лиці Шевче́нка.
Дя́кую!
Про́шу.

The town mentioned in this dialogue is **Черні́гів**. **На ву́лиці Шевче́нка** = 'on Shevchenko St.'

Exercise 2c

Make sentences using the following sets of words and the grammar seen so far, following the order in which the elements are given; prepositions and conjunctions have been omitted and must be supplied where appropriate.

(a) Я, жи́ти, Оде́са.
(b) Ви, жи́ти, кварти́ра, Ло́ндон?

(c) Університéт, ми, дýмати, читáти, питáти
(d) Він, студéнт; вонá, студéнтка.
(e) Так, я, Áнглія; роди́на, жи́ти, Лóндон.
(f) Вони́, Фрáнція; жи́ти, Пари́ж.
(g) Я, читáти, кімнáта.
(h) Ти, жи́ти, тут?

Exploiting your knowledge of 'international' vocabulary, that is, words that are common to many of the world's languages, read and translate the following passages (other essential new words are supplied below):

Хто президéнт, і де він/вонá живé?

Президéнт Украї́ни живé в Ки́єві, а Президéнт Росíї живé в Москвí; Президéнт Амéрики живé в Вашингтóні, а прем'є́р-мінíстр Áнглії живé в Лóндоні. Алé де живé Президéнт Фрáнції? Дýмаю, що він живé в Пари́жі. Чи Президéнт Амéрики республікáнець чи демокрáт? Чи прем'є́р-мінíстр Áнглії чоловíк чи жíнка? Ми знáємо, що Президéнт Фрáнції чоловíк; алé хто прем'є́р-мінíстр Фрáнції?

Кімнáта

Це кімнáта. У кімнáті є телевíзор і телефóн. Чи це фотогрáфія? Так, це фотогрáфія мáми; вонá дипломáт, вонá живé в Лóндоні. А кни́жка? Чи це худóжня кни́жка? Ні, це не худóжня кни́жка: це істóрія Украї́ни й Одéси.

Vocabulary

хто	[khto]	who?
що	[shcho]	that; what?
не	[ne]	not (compare with **ні** 'no')
і	[i]	and (used after a consonant or pause, and at the beginning of a sentence; it appears as **й** between vowels and between a vowel and a consonant)
алé	[alé]	but
чи	[chy]	(a) 'is it the case that . . .?' (compare French '*est-ce que* . . .?' (b) or (N.B. both can occur in one sentence!)

це	[tse]	this is . . ./ these are . . . (pointing to something)
є	[ye]	there is, there are (existence). Can be used as 'to be' when stressing a point: **він є студент**, (he really *is* a student!).
худóжня	[khudózhn'a]	literary (text), belletristic (the feminine of the adjective **худóжній**)

By reading for meaning, and not necessarily knowing all the details, you begin to progress the way a young native speaker does.

Vocabulary building: the noun

Ukrainian is a very rich language, especially in word formation. Expanding your Ukrainian vocabulary will therefore be easier than expected, because you don't have to learn each new word: instead you can learn a basic form and then build (or analyse) new ones. New words can be built from any noun or verb using a suffix, which is not the same thing as a grammatical ending: the former builds new words, while the latter shows the function of the word in a sentence. Here we shall examine some suffixes which may be orientated towards the identity or activities of people (do bear in mind that this is an incomplete sketch, in that these suffixes may have other functions):

-**(н)ець** [-(n)ets']: masculine, person from a particular place; stress shifts to the syllable right before the suffix:

Áнглія [ánhl'iy-a: anhl'íy- + ets']	**англíєць** 'Englishman'
Амéрика [améryka + n + ets']	**америкáнець** 'American (male)' (compare **республікáнець** above)
Укра́їна [ukrayín-a: ukrayín + ets']	**украї́нець** 'Ukrainian (male)'

-**(н)ка** [-(n)ka]: feminine, person from a place, or feminine 'doer of X':

студéнт [studént + ka]	**студéнтка** 'female student'
англомáн [anhlomán + ka]	**англомáнка** 'anglophile (female)'
Áнглія [ánhl'iy-a: anhl'íy + ka]	**англíйка** 'Englishwoman'
Укра́їна [ukrayín-a: ukrayín + ka]	**украї́нка** 'Ukrainian (female)'
Амéрика [améryka + n + ka]	**америкáнка** 'American (female)'

-**íст** [-íst]: masculine, one who is occupied with an apparatus or a discipline (compare *machin-ist*):

телефóн + íст [telefón + íst]	**телефонíст** 'telephone operator'

Украї́на [ukrayín-a: + íst] — **украї́ні́ст** ‘Ukrainianist, one who studies Ukraine and things Ukrainian’

This suffix may also appear as -**ист**, e.g. **тури́ст** ‘tourist’.

-**тель** [-tel’]: ‘a male doer of X’ (formed from verbs); in the next lesson we meet **вчи́телька**, the feminine form of:

вчи́ти ‘to teach’ (stem [wchy-]) — [wchýtel’] **вчи́тель** ‘teacher, one who teaches

More than one suffix can be appended to a base form to produce a more elaborate word: -**і́ст** + **ка** [-íst + ka]:

телефон + **і́ст** + **ка** — **телефоні́стка** ‘female telephone operator

україн + **і́ст** + **ка** — **україні́стка** ‘feminine Ukrainianist’

One also finds -**истка** (see -**іст** in this section above).

Exercise 2d

Supply the missing word or words in each of the following sentences; you will find all the grammar and vocabulary in this lesson.

(a) Мико́ла . . . в кварти́рі.
(b) . . . університе́т Мико́ли? У Ки́єві.
(c) Джон студе́нт, а Марі́я . . . .
(d) Мико́ла . . . , Джон англі́єць.
(e) Це бібліоте́ка; тут ми . . . .
(f) Ви не . . . , що Украї́на респу́бліка?
(g) Де ти живе́ш? . . . в кімна́ті.
(h) Джон америка́нець? Ні, . . . англі́єць.
(i) Що є в кімна́ті? Телефо́н і . . . .
(j) Це худо́жня кни́жка? Ні, це істо́рія . . . .

Exercise 2e

Explain the meaning of the following words, breaking down each word into its constituent parts:

(a) ло́ндонець
(b) італі́йка
(c) американі́ст
(d) вчи́телька

Exercise 2f

Express these sentences in Ukrainian (J = John, M = Mykola):

(a) (J) Hello! I am a student from England.
(b) We live in London.
(c) There is a university there. ('There there is . . .')
(d) (M) I am Mykola, from Odessa.
(e) In Odessa there is a university also.
(f) Do you (polite) know where it is?
(g) (J) No, I do not know.
(h) But I know where the hotel 'Ukraine' is.
(i) (M) Do you live in a room here?
(j) (J) Yes, I do (lit. 'in a room').
(k) (M) I live in an apartment here; my family also lives here.

Exercise 2g

Make up dialogues in which you greet people and ask how they are. To help you, here are some new 'how are you?' expressions:

Як ви почувáєтеся? [yak vy pochuváyetes'a]	How are you? (lit. 'How do you feel?') (polite singular or familiar/polite plural)
Як ти почувáєшся? [yak ty pochuváyes's'a]	How are you? (lit. 'How do you feel?') (familiar)

Or, although this is seen by some as a more western Ukrainian or diaspora enquiry these days:

Як ся мáєте? [yak s'a máyete]	How are you? (lit. 'How do you feel?') (polite singular or familiar/polite plural)
Як ся мáєш? [yak s'a máyesh]	How are you? (lit. 'How do you feel?' (familiar)

Instead of saying you are well all the time, you might find the following phrases and responses helpful:

не все гарáзд [ne wse harázd]	not so good
погáно [poháno]	bad
непогáно [nepoháno]	not bad
не зóвсім . . . [ne zóws'im]	not so (good, bad, etc.)
дýже . . . [dúzhe]	very (good, bad, etc.)
на жáль [na zhál']	unfortunately

Exercise 2h

What opposites do you already know in Ukrainian? Start with the above list (the 'how are you' responses) and go back to such words as 'here'. Write them down in your vocabulary book.

3 Сім'я́

The family

In this lesson you will learn about:

- possessives: 'my, our, . . .'
- some more verb forms
- adjectives
- a few more greetings
- saying 'goodbye'
- the genitive and locative cases

Сім'я́ Мико́ли

Mykola shows John a photograph of his family's apartment in Odessa. It shows his parents, brother and sister as well. His brother is called **Васи́ль** *[vasýl'] and his sister is called* **Ната́лка** *[natálka]*

МИКО́ЛА: Ось фотогра́фія. Це на́ша кварти́ра. Там стоя́ть ма́ма й та́то.
ДЖОН: А хто стої́ть на фо́то бі́ля вікна́?
МИКО́ЛА: Брат і сестра́. Брат чита́є, а сестра́ пи́ше листа́.
ДЖОН: Як ім'я́ бра́та?
МИКО́ЛА: Васи́ль. Він ще́ хо́дить до шко́ли.
ДЖОН: А як ім'я́ сестри́?
МИКО́ЛА: Ната́лка. Вона́ тако́ж хо́дить до шко́ли; вона́ ду́же розу́мна ді́вчина!
ДЖОН: Чи ми пі́демо до ва́шої кварти́ри за́втра?
МИКО́ЛА: Пі́демо, звича́йно.

MYKOLA: *Here's a photograph. This is our flat. There are mum (mom) and dad.*
JOHN: *In the photo who's standing by the window?*
MYKOLA: *My brother and sister. My brother is reading and my sister is writing a letter.*
JOHN: *What's your brother's name?*

MYKOLA: *Vasyl'. He still goes to school.*
JOHN: *And what's your sister's name?*
MYKOLA: *Natalka. She too goes to school; she's a ve*
JOHN: *Shall we go to your flat tomorrow?*
MYKOLA: *Yes of course.*

Vocabulary

фотогра́фія, -ї	[fotohráf'iya]	photograph (also the indeclinable neuter noun **фо́то**)
ось	[os']	here is, there is (like French *voici*, *voilà*)
на́ша	[násha]	our (from **наш**)
стоя́ть	[stoyát']	(they) stand (from **стоя́ти, -і́-**)
та́то, -а	[táto]	father, dad (also **ба́тько, -а**)
стої́ть	[stoyít']	(he/she/it) stands (from **стоя́ти, -і́-**)
бі́ля	[b'íl'a]	near (+ genitive case)
брат, -а	[brat]	brother
сестра́, -и́	[sestrá]	sister
пи́ше	[pýshe]	(he/she/it) writes (from **писа́ти, -ше-**)
лист, -а́	[lyst]	letter (the genitive may be used for the accusative here)
як	[yak]	how
ім'я́, і́мені	[im"yá]	(first) name (this is a neuter noun)
хо́дить	[khódyt']	(he/she/it) goes (from **ходи́ти, -и-**)
до	[do]	to (+ genitive case)
розу́мна	[rozúmna]	clever (from **розу́мний**)
ді́вчина, -и	[d'íwchyna]	girl
пі́демо	[p'ídemo]	we shall go (from **піти́, -де-**)
ва́шої	[váshoyi]	your (from **ваш**)
за́втра	[záwtra]	tomorrow
звича́йно	[zvycháyno]	of course

Possessives

In the dialogue there are only two possessives, **на́ша** 'our' and **ва́шої** 'your'. However, in the translation there are more, because Ukrainian may omit them where there is no risk of ambiguity. In the first lesson we learned that Ukrainian nouns are differentiated by gender and that they change for case (they also have plural forms, to come in 5); possessives must agree in gender and case with the noun they qualify. The exceptions are **його** 'his/its' (masculine and neuter) and **її́** 'her/its' (feminine), which never change. Thus:

Table 3.1

Personal pronoun	Possessive (nominative singular)						Meaning
	Masculine		*Neuter*		*Feminine*		
я	**мій**	[m'iy]	**моє́**	[moyé]	**моя́**	[moyá]	my
ти	**твій**	[tv'iy]	**твоє́**	(tvoyé)	**твоя́**	[tvoyá]	your (sg., familiar)
ви	**ваш**	[vash]	**ва́ше**	[váshe]	**ва́ша**	[vásha]	your (sg., polite)
він/воно́	**його́**	[yohó]	**його́**	[yohó]	**його́**	[yohó]	his, its (masc./neut.)
вона́	**її́**	[yiyí]	**її́**	[yiyí]	**її́**	[yiyí]	her, its (fem.)
ми	**наш**	[nash]	**на́ше**	[náshe]	**на́ша**	[násha]	our
ви	**ваш**	[vash]	**ва́ше**	[váshe]	**ва́ша**	[vásha]	your (pl.)
вони́	**ї́хній**	[yíkhn'iy]	**ї́хнє**	[yíkhn'e]	**ї́хня**	[yíkhn'a]	their

Note that the nominative endings (**-й/ш**, **-я/а**, **-є/е**) resemble the noun endings of the different genders. **Мій/твій** decline identically, as do **наш** and **ваш**. **Ї́хній** declines like a soft adjective (see later in this lesson). They all also have the meaning 'mine, yours', etc., in which case they must still reflect the gender and number of the noun to which they refer. The interrogative possessive is **чий**, **чия́**, **чиє́** 'whose'. Thus:

Чия́ це кімна́та?	Whose room is this?
Це моя́/ї́хня кімна́та.	It's my/their room.
Чий брат живе́ в Ки́єві?	Whose brother lives in Kyiv?
Мій/Наш	mine/ours
Чия́ це кни́жка?	Whose is this book?
Його́/Її́	his/hers
Чий це брат?	Whose brother is this?
Його́/Її́	his/hers

Note that **це** 'this, that' is invariable and falls between the interrogative and the noun it qualifies.

Exercise 3a

Here is a list of nouns. Using the forms **мій**, **ваш**, **її́**, **ї́хній**, etc., say whose brother etc., they are. Begin with the word **це** (for example: **Це моя́ ма́ма**.)

ма́ма	**та́то**	**брат**	**сестра́**	**готе́ль**	**знайо́мий**
ім'я́	**кімна́та**	**кни́жка**	**лист**	**президе́нт**	**роди́на**
університе́т	**фотогра́фія**	**шко́ла**			

Next, ask (or pretend to ask) a fellow student 'whose this and that is', using the **Чий це** . . . construction (for example **Чия́ це кни́жка**)?

Verbs

In the dialogue we encountered forms of four new verbs, of which two introduce us to the second of the two Ukrainian conjugations; its theme vowel is -**и**-, and in the 3pl. form we now find the letter -**а**- (instead of -**у**-, as in the first conjugation). The endings of the present tense of this conjugation are as follows (note especially the *they* form):

I	**-у/ю**	[u]	we	**-имо**	[ymo]
you (sg., familiar)	**-иш**	[ysh]	you (sg., polite; pl.)	**-ите**	[yte]
he/she/it	**-ить**	[-yt']	they	**-ать/ять**	[at']

Here is the complete present tense of the two verbs met in this dialogue and of the four verbs met in the other two dialogues. (Note that the stem is a useful form, which gives you a base from which to form the tenses; it bears a stress mark only if the stress is fixed on the ending):

ходи́ти 'walk, go' (habitual)
stem: **ходи**- [khody-]

ходжу́	[khodzhú]
хо́диш	[khódysh]
хо́дить	[khódyt']
хо́димо	[khódymo]
хо́дите	[khódyte]
хо́дять	[khód'at']

стоя́ти 'stand, be standing'
stem: **стоя́-/стої́**- [stoyá-/stoyí-]

стою́	[stoyú]
стої́ш	[stoyísh]
стої́ть	[stoyít']
стоїмо́	[stoyimó]
стоїте́	[stoyité]
стоя́ть	[stoyát']

Note in the second of these verbs that [stoy- + theme vowel -y-] becomes [stoyi-]; in Cyrillic, of course, [yi] is expressed as **ї**.

роби́ти 'do, make'		**люби́ти** 'like, love'	
stem: **роби-** [roby-]		stem: **люби-** [l'uby-]	
роблю́	[robl'ú]	**люблю́**	[l'ubl'ú]
ро́биш	[róbysh]	**лю́биш**	[l'úbysh]
ро́бить	[róbyt']	**лю́бить**	[l'úbyt']
ро́бимо	[róbymo]	**лю́бимо**	[l'úbymo]
ро́бите	[róbyte]	**лю́бите**	[l'úbyte]
ро́блять	[róbl'at']	**лю́блять**	[l'úbl'at']

сиді́ти 'sit, be sitting'		**зна́чити** 'mean, signify'	
stem: **сиді́-/сиди́-** [syd'í-/sydý-]		stem: **зна́чи-** [znáchy-]	
сиджу́	[sydzhú]	–	
сиди́ш	[sydýsh]	–	
сиди́ть	[sydýt']	**зна́чить**	[znáchyt']
сидимо́	[sydymó]	–	
сидите́	[sydyté]	–	
сидя́ть	[syd'át']	**зна́чать**	[znáchat']

- The consonant can change in the 1sg. form; here we see **д** become **дж** and **б** become **бл**: **сиджу́**, **люблю́**. If the consonant is **б** or one of the other lip consonants, a change will occur in the 3pl. form too: **вони́ ро́блять**.
- The vowel of each ending may vary slightly, depending on the preceding consonants. -**у**, -**ать** spellings occur after **ч**, **ш**, **щ** and **ж**; otherwise, the 1sg. and 3pl. forms are far more commonly -**ю** and -**ять**.
- We also observe that the 3sg. forms end in -**ть**, while there is no such ending in the first conjugation.
- As the meaning of the verb implies, to give six forms for **зна́чити** would be rather artificial, as it is only used in the 3rd person (singular and plural):

  Що зна́чить сло́во «до́бре»? Сло́во «до́бре» зна́чить «fine, well».

Now let us note the forms of the three first conjugation verbs met in the three dialogues (we saw the first in its related form **піти́**; we only give the 1sg., 2sg., and 3pl. forms, since you can now generate the remaining forms yourself!):

іти́/йти́ 'go, be going/walking'		**писа́ти** 'write'	
stem: **іде́-** [idé-]		stem: **пише-** [pyshe]	
іду́	[idú]	**пишу́**	[pyshú]
іде́ш	[idésh]	**пи́шеш**	[pýshesh]
іду́ть	[idút']	**пи́шуть**	[pýshut']

працюва́ти 'work'
stem: **працюва́-/працю́є-** [prats'uvá-/prats'úye-]

працю́ю	[prats'úyu]
працю́єш	[prats'úyesh]
працю́ють	[prats'úyut']

Stress

There are a few rules of thumb that will help you remember how verbs are stressed. For now, don't memorize them, just observe the patterns as you learn new verbs: you will then have a feel for the system and you won't have to memorize.

1 If the stem type 'key' carried a stress mark, then there is fixed stress on that syllable (or ending):

-áє-	**чита́ю, чита́єш, чита́ти**
-ýє-/ю́є-	**працю́ю, працю́єш**; but infinitive always **-юва́ти**!
-дé-	**іду́, іде́ш, ідемо́, іти́**; stress on last syllable throughout
-í-	**сиджу́, сиди́ш, сидимо́, сиді́ти**

2 If the 'key' carries no stress mark, stress may or may not be mobile and you will have to look at the infinitive: if the stress is on the ending there, then stress is mobile; if it is to the left of that ending, it is not. Compare:

-и-	**роби́ти, роблю́** (stress as in infinitive), but **ро́биш** etc.
-ше-	**писа́ти, пишу́** (stress as in infinitive), but **пи́шеш** etc.
-ає-	**ду́маю, ду́маєш**, etc.

A few exceptions exist (naturally!), and these will be pointed out when they occur. Read the following simple sentences in which we use the verbs presented above; they are not translated, so read carefully!

Де Ната́лка? Вона́ сиди́ть вдо́ма й чита́є.
Його́ ба́тько працю́є на заво́ді в Оде́сі.
Брат лю́бить працюва́ти в університе́ті; він не студе́нт, він вчи́тель.
Ми сидимо́ й пи́шемо, а вони́ стоя́ть і чита́ють.

Spelling

We noticed in the second lesson that the letter **у** sometimes interchanges with **в**. The same thing happens with **і** and **й**. There is a certain amount of fluctuation in Ukrainian here, but we might simply state the rule as follows:

- **і** is written **і**, unless it is preceded by a vowel, when it is written **й** (between a vowel and a consonant **і** 'and' may be replaced by **та**)
- **у** is written **у**, unless it is preceded by a vowel, when it is written **в**
- They are often written **І** and **У** when they come as the very first letter/word in a sentence, unless a vowel follows.

Thus:

Він живé в Кúєві	He lives in Kyiv.
У Кúєві є велúкий готéль	In Kyiv there is a big hotel.
Васúль ідé до шкóли	Vasyl' is going to school.
Натáлка йдé до шкóли	Natalka is going to school.
В Одéсі	In Odessa.

(some Ukrainians prefer **у Кúєві** no matter what goes before)

The form **йдé** is commonly encountered even when it begins a sentence, however. In a few words there is no variation: thus **Украї́на** is always **Украї́на** and **університéт** is always **університéт** (there is no variation in most foreign words).

Exercise 3b

Fill in the blanks using the verbs you have learned. Supplementary words: **кудú?** 'where to, whither? (movement)', **чомý?** 'why' (**томý що** 'because'), **додóму** '(to) home'. Placing **не** immediately before the verb negates it: 'he does *not* work here'.

Де ти . . . ?	Я . . . на завóді.
Чи ти . . . в Украї́ні?	Ні, я не . . . в Украї́ні.
Чомý ти . . . ?	Томý що я . . . .
Чомý ви . . . тут?	Томý що це стáнція метрó.
Я не . . . метрó.	Я . . . ходúти.
Що ти . . . (do)?	Я . . . (write).
Кудú . . . ?	Я . . . додóму.

Розмóва

Mykola talks about his family.

Джон: Де працю́є твій бáтько?
Микóла: Він працю́є на вели́кому завóді. Він інженéр.
Джон: А мáма?
Микóла: Вонá вчи́телька, вонá працю́є в шкóлі у цéнтрі мі́ста. Мáма й тáто із Хáркова. Хáрків – вели́ке украї́нське мі́сто.
Джон: Чи твої́ брат і сестрá ще хóдять до шкóли?
Микóла: Так. Васи́ль ду́же лю́бить читáти й писáти. Натáлка, мені́ здає́ться, бі́льше лю́бить спорт, хочá вонá ду́же дóбре вчи́ться.
Джон: Тепéр трéба йти́ в університéт. До побáчення.
Микóла: На все дóбре.

John: *Where does your dad work?*
Mykola: *He works at a big factory. He's an engineer.*
John: *And mum/mom?*
Mykola: *She's a teacher, she works in a school in the centre of town. Mum/mom and Dad are from Kharkiv. Kharkiv is a big Ukrainian town.*
John: *Do your brother and sister still go to school?*
Mykola: *Yes, Vasyl' very much likes to read and write. But Natalka, I think*, likes sport more, though she studies very well.*
John: *Now I must go to the university. Good-bye.*
Mykola: *So long.*

*In English we are more likely to say 'I think' than 'it seems to me'; in Ukrainian, however, we on the whole say **мені́ здає́ться**, because **я ду́маю** literally means 'I am thinking, engaged in the thinking process'.

Vocabulary

працю́є	[prats'úye]	(he/she/it) works (from **працювáти, -ю́є-**)
на	[na]	at, in (prep. + locative)
вели́кому	[velýkomu]	big (loc. sg. masc.; from **вели́кий**)
завóд, -у	[zavód]	factory, works
інженéр, -а	[inzhenér]	engineer
вчи́телька, -и	[wchýtel'ka]	teacher (woman)
центр, -у	[tsentr]	centre

вели́ке	[velýke]	big (nom. sg. neut,; from **вели́кий**)
так	[tak]	yes
мені́ здає́ться	[men'í zdayéts'ts'a]	it seems to me
бі́льше	[b'íl'she]	more
спорт, -у	[sport]	sport
хоч(á)	[xoch(á)]	although (note that it is preceded by a comma)
вчи́тися, -и-	[wchýtys'a]	study
тепе́р	[tepér]	now
тре́ба	[tréba]	one must, it is necessary
йти́ (іти́), -дé-	[yt´y] ([itý])	go
до поба́чення	[do pobáchen'n'a]	goodbye
на все до́бре	[na wse dóbre]	so long, all the best

Adjectives

Adjectives, like most possessives, must agree with the noun they qualify in gender, case, and number. In the first two chapters we encountered the following phrase:

худо́жня **кни́жка**

To this we have added, among others:

вели́ке украї́нське **мі́сто**

We learned in *1* how to identify gender in most nouns; below we see that the nominative singular forms of adjectives fit in with that pattern:

Masculine		Neuter		Feminine	
украї́нський	[-yy]	**украї́нське**	[-e]	**украї́нська**	[-a]
вели́кий	[-yy]	**вели́ке**	[-e]	**вели́ка**	[-a]
ї́хній	['iy]	**ї́хнє**	[-'e]	**ї́хня**	[-'a]

Another useful adjective at this stage is the interrogative **яки́й**, **яка́**, **яке́** 'what sort of . . .'. It can be used in a construction similar to that used with **чий** 'whose?' Thus:

Яка́ це кни́жка?	What sort of book is this?
Це ціка́ва кни́жка.	It's an interesting book.
Яке́ це мі́сто?	What kind of city is this?
Це ду́же вели́ке мі́сто.	It's a very large city.

A few more greetings

There are a few more expressions of greeting; note those that are used by your friends and acquaintances, because they are not all current everywhere in Ukraine:

Здоро́в! (rather familiar, and usually only between men)
Будь здоро́в! (masc.), **Будь здоро́ва!** (fem.) and **Бу́дьте здоро́ві** (formal, sg. pl.) are also used in the sense of 'goodbye', lit. 'be healthy!'; **будь** and **бу́дьте** are commonly replaced respectively by **бува́й, бува́йте**. (**Будь здоро́в(а)!** is also a response to someone sneezing: 'Bless you!')
З приві́том is very common
Слу́хаю lit. 'I'm listening', **алло́** and **га́лло́** are the most common greetings when answering the phone; the first is not rude in Ukrainian, even though you would never pick up the phone in English and say 'I'm listening'!

Sometimes you want your greetings to be passed on to someone else. A simple way of doing this is to use the word **приві́т** or **віта́ння** followed by the dative case (*6, 7*) of the 'someone else'.

Goodbye

Now that you can greet people in a variety of ways, you have to be able to say 'goodbye', too! The standard Ukrainian expression for 'goodbye' is **до поба́чення** [do pobáchen'n'a], literally 'until the "seeing"' (compare *Auf wiedersehen*). It can be used in all circumstances, much as **До́брий день** 'Hello!' More informal is **на все до́бре**. Rather familiar, and perhaps best to avoid until you hear it used, is **папа́,** roughly equivalent to 'bye', 'see you (later)'; this is especially common among young Ukrainians.

The following will also be heard:

бува́й (здоро́вий/здоро́ва)! (familiar, respectively masculine and feminine singular)
бува́йте (здоро́ві)! (plural or polite singular)
прощава́й(те)! 'farewell!' (familiar, or plural or polite singular)
до зу́стрічі! 'until we meet again!'
(на) добра́ніч! 'good night!'
усього́ найкра́щого! 'all the best!'

Genitive

The genitive case usually expresses possession (*of the city*, *John's*, etc.). This is an indispensable case, so make an effort to learn the genitive forms of nouns as you go. Overall, the genitive singular of feminine and neuter nouns is quite straightforward; that of masculine nouns is somewhat less so.

First, neuter nouns ending in **-о** replace **-о** with **-а**, and those ending in **-е** replace **-е** with **-я**:

вікнó becomes **вікнá**
мíсце becomes **мíсця**

Second, feminine nouns: those with an **-а** ending replace it with **-и**, while those ending in **-я** replace it with **-і** (**-ї** if **-я** immediately follows a vowel or apostrophe; remember the locative in the first chapter); note that **-жа**, **-ша**, **-ща** and **-ча** become **-жі**, **-ші**, **-щі** and **-чі**. Thus:

кімнáта becomes **кімнáти**
пíсня 'song' becomes **пíсні**
лéкція becomes **лéкції**
кáша 'porridge' becomes **кáші**

Third, feminine nouns ending in a consonant and in **-ь** add **-і** and replace **-ь** with **-і**, respectively. Thus:

ніч 'night' becomes **нóчі**
сіль 'salt' becomes **сóлі**
Русь 'Rus' becomes **Русí**
твóрчість 'creativity' becomes **твóрчості**

Fourth, masculine nouns ending in hard consonants add **-а** or **-у**; those ending in **-ь** replace **-ь** with **-я** or **-ю**. There is no simple rule as to whether **-а/-я** or **-у/-ю** should be chosen. It is best to learn them as you come across them, to accept that variation is a problem that besets native speakers too, and to bear in mind that nouns denoting living beings tend to have **-а/-я**. Thus:

університéт becomes **університéту**
Васúль becomes **Василя́**
край 'region' becomes **крáю**
ніж 'knife' becomes **ножá**

We always give the genitive singular in the word lists and the vocabulary. For those of you who would like to have some general idea of which masculine nouns take which ending, here are a few guidelines:

-а/-я

• people, machines, structures	**товáриш/а**, **трáктор/а, коридóр/а** 'comrade', 'tractor', 'corridor'
• weights and measures	**гектáр/а**, **кілогрáм/а** 'hectare', 'kilogram'
• scientific terms	**áтом/а** 'atom'
• most names of towns	**Кúїв/Кúєва** 'Kyiv'

-у/-ю

• substances	**азóт/у**, **мéд/у** 'nitrogen', 'honey'
• natural phenomena	**сніг/у, морóз/у** 'snow', 'frost'
• indefinite areas	**ліс/у**, **гай/гáю** 'forest', 'grove'
• generalized, abstract concepts and processes	**ýспіх/у, рóзвиток/-тку** 'success', 'development'
• names of rivers, mountains, countries	**Дунáй/Дунáю**, **Крúм/у** 'Danube', 'Crimea'

Acknowledgement: Rusanivskyi et al. (1991:99)

The genitive singular forms of adjectives and possessives may be illustrated by the following four examples:

Masculine, Neuter		Feminine	
украї́нського	[-oho]	**украї́нської**	[-oyi]
ї́хнього	[-'oho]	**ї́хньої**	[-'oyi]
моґó	[-oho]	**моє́ї**	[-yeyi]
нáшого	[-oho]	**нáшої**	[-oyi]

Read the following short passage and identify all genitives, in nouns and adjectives (look up unfamiliar words in the vocabulary):

> Істóрія украї́нського нарóду – це істóрія дуже цікáвої нáції. Столúця нáшої краї́ни старá; алé колú був* почáток нáшої столúці Кúєва? Хто знáє? Мені́ здає́ться, що істóрія Áнглії та Амéрики теж цікáва; чи ви знáєте, колú був почáток вáшого нарóду, вáшої столúці?

*'was'; the past tense is introduced in the next lesson.

The locative of adjectives and possessives

The forms are as follows:

Masculine, Neuter		Feminine	
украї́нському	[-omu]	**украї́нській**	[-iy]
ї́хньому	[-'omu]	**ї́хній**	[-'iy]
моє́му	[-yemu]	**мої́й**	[-yiy]
на́шому	[-omu]	**на́шій**	[-iy]

Now we can say such things as:

Ми живемо́ в мале́нькій кварти́рі.	We live in a small apartment.
У ї́хньому мі́сті живе́ брат на́шого старо́го знайо́мого.	In their town lives the brother of our old acquaintance.

Alternations: o – i and e – i; 'fleeting' o/e

1 We have come across a few words in which there is a vowel alternation. In *1* it was the third person pronoun, which was **вона́**, **воно́**, **вони́**, but **він**. We have also come across **Ки́їв**, with its locative **у Ки́єві**, and the town name **Ха́рків**, with its locative **у Ха́ркові**. Among our examples for the genitive singular masculine we had **ніж** (which becomes **ножа́**) and **з Черні́гова** 'from Chernigiv'. Compare also **ніч** (genitive **но́чі**) and the city **Львів** (**у Льво́ві**). Clearly, within some words we have either [i], preceded by a soft consonant, or [o] or [e] preceded by a hard consonant. Putting it simply, **і** [i] very often becomes **о** or **е** when the consonant following it is itself followed by a vowel.

2 Note masculines with the suffixes **-ець**, **-ок**: when a case ending is added to these suffixes (in this instance the genitive), the vowel *e* or *o* will drop. This is called a 'fleeting' vowel: **украї́нець** becomes **украї́нця** and **дімо́к** 'little house' becomes **дімка́**.

Exercise 3c

Use the locative case preceded by the preposition **у/в** or **на** 'on, in, at' to say where Mykola and Natalka are in the preceding picture (use **на** with **пóшта** 'post office' and **вýлиця** 'street'; learn which nouns take **на** as you go along). You should be able to guess what the other words mean. Include the adjectives or possessive pronouns **вели́кий, наш, стари́й, твій**.

Mykola's father is 'at the factory': how would you say that?

4 Кварти́ра й мі́сто

The flat and the city

In this lesson you will learn about:

- reflexive verbs
- more prepositions
- introducing yourself and others
- questions and answers
- conjunctions
- the vocative case
- the past tense

У кварти́рі

Мико́ла: Тепе́р ми у кварти́рі. Вона́ зати́шна́. Тут приє́мно.

Джон: Так. Вона́ наспра́вді ду́же приє́мна.

Мико́ла: Тут телеві́зор, а там газе́та. Уве́чері лю́бимо сиді́ти й чита́ти. Брат і сестра́, коли́ вони́ не працю́ють удо́ма, тако́ж лю́блять диви́тися телеві́зор.

Джон: Зна́чить, це віта́льня. А де ж ку́хня, і де ва́нна?

Мико́ла: Он ку́хня, ліво́руч. Це мала́ кімна́та. А ва́нна тут бі́ля ку́хні, право́руч.

Mykola: *Now we are in the flat (apartment). It's cosy. It's pleasant here.*

John *Yes. It really is very nice.*

Mykola: *Here's the television and there is a newspaper. In the evening we like to sit and read. My brother and sister, when they aren't working at home, like to watch TV.*

John *So, this is the sitting room. Where is the kitchen then, and where is the bathroom?*

Mykola: *The kitchen is over there, on the left. It's a small room. And the bathroom is over there near the kitchen, on the right.*

Vocabulary

затишний	[zatýshnýy]	cosy; **зáтишно** ‘it’s cosy’ (neut. impers.)
приємно	[pryyémno]	it’s pleasant/nice (neut. impers.)
насправді	[naspráwd’i]	really, indeed
а	[a]	and, but
газéта, -и	[hazéta]	newspaper
увéчері	[uvécher’i]	in the evening
люби́ти, -и-	[l’ubýty]	to like
коли́	[kolý]	when, if
вдóма	[udóma/wdóma]	at home
диви́тися, -и-	[dyvýtys’a]	to watch
знáчить, -и-	[znáchyt’]	so, that is, that means (literally)
ж	[zh]	and, but (suggests a contrast, or introduces new information, and comes straight after the first stressed word in the sentence or phrase; after a consonant we have **же** [zhe])
вітáльня, -і	[v’itál’n’a]	sitting room, drawing room
кýхня, -і	[kúxn’a]	kitchen
вáнна, -ої	[vánna]	bathroom (declined like an adjective)
он	[on]	over there
лівóруч	[l’ivóruch]	on/to the left
мали́й	[malýy]	little, small
правóруч	[pravóruch]	on/to the right

Reflexive verbs

Reflexive verbs differ in no way from ordinary verbs apart from the attachment of the particle **-ся** to them (**-сь** is also possible). Thus, for the second conjugation:

диви́тися ‘to watch’		**учи́тися/вчи́тися** ‘to study’	
дивлю́ся	[dywl’ús’a]	**вчýся**	[vchús’a]
ди́вишся	[dývys’s’a]	**вчи́шся**	[vch´ys’s’a]
ди́виться	[dývyts’ts’a]	**вчи́ться**	[vchýts’ts’a]
ди́вимося	[dývymos’a]	**вчимóся**	[vchymós’a]
ди́витеся	[dývytes’a]	**вчитéся**	[vchytés’a]
ди́вляться	[dýwl’ats’ts’a]	**вчáться**	[vcháts’ts’a]

Note the pronunciation of the second person singular, where [sh + s’] gives way to a long [s’]. As for **диви́тися**, we see that it conjugates like

робúти and **любúти**: whenever a 2nd conjugation verb has a stem-final **п, б, в, м** or **ф** (all involving the lips), -**л**- appears in the 1sg. and 3pl.

For the first conjugation we may note the present tense of the verb **зустрічáтися** 'to meet', which we encounter in the second text for reading below (see if you can manage without the transcription!). Pay particular attention to the third person singular:

зустрічáтися 'to meet'

зустрічáюся
зустрічáєшся
зустрічáє*ться*
зустрічáємося
зустрічáєтеся
зустрічáються

In the third person singular of reflexive first-conjugation verbs the ending -**ть**- shows up as it does in the second conjugation. Read the following sentences using this new verb:

Де ви зустрічáєтеся?
В університéті.
Ми зустрічáємося на завóді.
Чи трéба зустрічáтися на завóді?
Ні! Мóжна зустрічáтися на вýлиці, бíля завóду.

Prepositions

In *1* we met the prepositions **у/в** and **на**, which govern the locative case, and the preposition **з**, which governs the genitive case. In this lesson we have met two more prepositions, which govern the genitive case: **бíля** 'near' and **до** 'to'. Remember that they always precede the noun (or 'adjective + noun' etc.) that they govern, and that any adjective qualifying the noun will agree fully with the noun. Thus:

кýхня – бíля кýхні – бíля велúкої кýхні
kitchen – near the kitchen – near the big kitchen
шкóла – бíля шкóли – бíля нáшої шкóли
school – near the school – near our school

Exercise 4a

There follow a few jumbled sentences. See if you can unjumble them (there may be some punctuation to include!). Remember that the word order of Ukrainian is quite flexible in certain respects.

(a) шко́ли, хо́дить, Ната́лка, до
(b) Ло́ндоні, Джон, в, живе́
(c) кварти́рі, прие́мна, ';', ми, в, ду́же, вона́
(d) ва́нної, віта́льня, бі́ля
(e) йде́, сього́дні, Мико́ла, університе́т
(f) в, знайо́мий, чита́є, віта́льні, мій

Що ти сього́дні роби́в?

Mykola and John arranged to meet in the evening; Mykola would like to know how John spent the day, so he asks a lot of questions

МИКО́ЛА: Джо́н(е)! До́брий ве́чір!
ДЖОН: Мико́ло! До́брий ве́чір!
МИКО́ЛА: Як спра́ви?
ДЖОН: Дя́кую, до́бре; а в те́бе як?
МИКО́ЛА: Непога́но. Що ти сього́дні роби́в? Де був?
ДЖОН: Сього́дні я був у мі́сті.
МИКО́ЛА: Де? Чи ти про́сто гуля́в по мі́сті, чи захо́див і в магази́ни?
ДЖОН: Так, я і по мі́сті гуля́в й до магази́нів захо́див.
МИКО́ЛА: Чи ти щось купува́в?
ДЖОН: Ні, нічо́го.
МИКО́ЛА: Що ж ти шука́в?
ДЖОН: Я шука́в словни́к украї́нської мо́ви, але́ . . .
МИКО́ЛА: Невже́ нема́є словника́ в Оде́сі?
ДЖОН: Нема́є. Але́ я ще шука́тиму.
МИКО́ЛА: Можли́во, зна́йдеш у Ки́єві.

MYKOLA: *John! Good evening!*
JOHN: *Mykola! Good evening!*
MYKOLA: *How are you ('things')?*
JOHN: *Fine, thanks; and you?*
MYKOLA: *Not bad. What did you do today? Where have you been?*
JOHN: *Today I was in the city/in town.*
MYKOLA: *Where? Did you just walk around the town, or also go to the shops?*
JOHN: *Yes, I went both walking and shopping.*

MYKOLA: *Did you buy anything?*
JOHN: *No, nothing.*
MYKOLA: *What were you looking for?*
JOHN: *I was looking for a Ukrainian dictionary (lit.: of the Ukrainian language), but . . .*
MYKOLA: *Is it possible there isn't one in Odessa?*
JOHN: *There isn't, but I'll carry on looking.*
MYKOLA: *Perhaps you'll find one in Kyiv.*

Vocabulary

ве́чір, -чора	[véch'ir]	evening
непога́но	[nepoháno]	not bad(ly) (adverb)
бу́ти	[búty]	be
мі́сто, -а	[m'ísto]	city
гуля́ти, -я́є-	[hul'áty]	walk, go for a walk
по	[po]	around, all over (prep. + loc., in this meaning)
захо́дити, -и-	[zakhódyty]	call in at, drop in at (followed by **у/в** + acc. or **до** + gen.)
магази́н, -а	[mahazýn]	store, shop (in this dialogue we find the genitive plural after **до**; a popular alternative (especially in West Ukraine) is **крамни́ця**, -і [kramnýts'a])
про́сто	[prósto]	simply, only
надво́рі	[nadvór'i]	outside (adverb)
щось	[shchos']	something, anything: [shcho] + [s']
купува́ти, -у́є-	[kupuváty]	buy (imperfective; see *5* for a presentation of verbal aspect)
шука́ти, -а́є-	[shukáty]	look for (the form **шука́тиму** is an example of the synthetic future, which we meet in *6*)
словни́к, -а́	[slownýk]	dictionary (derived from **сло́во,** -a 'word')
невже́	[newzhé]	'Is it possible that', 'Are you serious that?' (interrogative particle)
нема́є	[nemáye]	there is no, is not (any/a . . .), + genitive (also **нема́** + gen.)
можли́во	[mozhlývo]	perhaps, maybe, possible

знайти́, -де-	[znaytý]	find (more colloquial is **натра́пити, -и-** 'find by chance, come across', (followed by **на** + acc. when it has an object))

Introducing yourself and others

The following conversational patterns are used when introducing yourself to someone else or introducing someone (or being introduced) to a third party. Some are more complex or formal than others, so start out by working on the simplest patterns.

До́брий день!	Hello!
Добри́день!	Hello! (choice of 'hello' up to you)
Мене́ зва́ти Сте́фан. А вас?	My name is Stefan. And you?
(Мене́ зва́ти) Оле́кса.	(My name is) Oleksa.
Ра́дий з ва́ми познайо́митися	Pleased/happy to meet you ('make your acquaintance')

If you join a group of people of the same age or status (that is, people with whom you are already on **ти** terms), you could of course replace **до́брий день** with **приві́т!**, even when addressing someone you don't yet know. A female speaker would say **ра́да** and more than one person **ра́ді** 'happy (to meet you)'. Now for some more examples:

Дава́йте познайо́мимося; мене́ зва́ти Мико́ла Петро́вич.	Let's get acquainted. I'm called Mykola Petrovych.
Ду́же прие́мно; мене́ зва́ти Ма́йкал Джефферсон.	Very pleased (to meet you); I'm called Michael Jefferson.
Ду́же прие́мно.	Very pleased (to meet you).
Дозво́льте предста́витися/ відрекомендува́тися: Гончаре́нко, Мико́ла Петро́вич.	Allow me to introduce myself: Honcharenko, Mykola Petrovych.
Познайо́мся, це Іва́н.	Get acquainted, this is Ivan. (**ти**)
Приві́т! Ра́дий познайо́митися.	Hi!/glad to meet you.
Приві́т. А як тебе́ зва́ти?	Hi. And what's your name?
Познайо́мтеся, це Профе́сор Молоді́д.	Get acquainted, this is Professor Molodid. (**ви**)
До́брий день.	Hello.
До́брий день. А як вас зва́ти?	Hello. And what's your name?

In addition to using **тебе́ зва́ти** + name (familiar) or **вас зва́ти** + name (polite), you can ask for a person's first name, patronymic, and family name, respectively **ім'я́, по ба́тькові** or **патроні́мі́чне ім'я́** and **прі́звище** (names are examined in detail in *18*). If you ask someone one of their names, then the expressions are:

Як тебе́/вас зва́ти? (respond with either first name, first name and patronymic or last name)
Як твоє́/ва́ше ім'я́?
Як тебе́/вас по ба́тькові?
Як твоє́/ва́ше прі́звище?

The use of first name and patronymic is extremely common between acquaintances (rather than close or good friends) and in polite address. We discuss this more thoroughly in *18*; look ahead by all means!

Questions and answers

Questions introduced by What? Where? When? and Why? are as easily answered in Ukrainian as they are in English (**Де? – У магази́ні/** Where? – In a shop.). 'Yes–no' questions, on the other hand, require some comment. When the answer is 'no', we simply say **ні** and supply some information:

Чи ти був про́сто надво́рі?	Were you just outside?
Ні, я був і надво́рі й у магази́ні	No, I was both outside and in a shop

This, again, is very much like what we do in English. When the answer is 'yes', however, we can use or leave out **так**, but the general principle is that the word or phrase that is the focus of the question is repeated:

Нема́є?	**(Так,) нема́є**
Чи ти був у магази́ні?	**(Так,) у магази́ні.**
Чи вона́ чита́ла?	**(Так,) чита́ла.**

Conjunctions

You have now seen three conjunctions. In the first chapter we saw that **а** serves to contrast two things or situations ('but, on the other hand'), whereas **і** is purely a joining element; this is especially clear in the use of **і . . . і** as '*both . . . and*' in the dialogue. **Та** combines a string of similar elements (it may also occasionally be seen as a synonym of **і**). Sometimes the conjunction is omitted. Compare:

Opposition	*Agreement*
Микóла студéнт, а я вчи́тель.	Микóла студéнт, і я студéнт.
Олéкса читáє, а Óльга дýмає.	Олéкса читáє, і Óльга читáє.
	Олéкса і читáє, і дýмає.
	Олéкса читáє та дýмає.

A string of similar elements

Росíя, Пóльща, Білорýсь, Угóрщина, Словáччина. Трíшки дáлі є Itáлія та Німéччина; та ще дáлі Фрáнція й Іспáнія. Russia, Poland, Belarus', Hungary, and Slovakia. A little further off there is Italy and Germany; and even further France and Spain.

If we want to express 'but' when there is only one subject, or when the sense of contrast is stronger, then we must use the form **алé**:

Я говорю́ украї́нською (мóвою), алé не дóсить дóбре.
I speak (in) Ukrainian, but not well enough.

Він украї́нець, алé дóбре говóрить англíйською (мóвою).
He is Ukrainian, but speaks (in) English well.

The vocative case

'What did you do today?' introduced a new case, the vocative, which indicates that a person is being addressed by someone. Thus, a form like **Микóло** by itself expresses something like 'Hey Mykola!' or 'Excuse me, Mykola'. 'John' may or may not have this ending here (depending on the speaker), as it is a foreign name; Ukrainian names can be used in the nominative but that is not usual. The endings of this case are essentially used only with first names and patronymics (not obligatorily last names!), and with nouns referring to people; they depend, as usual, on the final consonant of the name or noun:

Masculines with a hard final consonant (including most names ending in -**о**)

-**е** **Богдáн – Богдáне! Степáн – Степáне!**
(**Михáйло - Михáйле!** is possible, but simply **Михáйло!** is common)

- When the final -**о** is stressed, the stress shifts in the vocative: **Петрó** becomes **Пéтре!**, **Павлó** becomes **Пáвле!** (Again, just **Петрó!** is perfectly acceptable)
- Final -**к**/-**ц**- becomes **ч**: **чоловíк** becomes **чоловíче!**, **хлóпець** becomes **хлóпче!**

- **Пан** 'Mr' will appear in the vocative, as will titles used with it: **пáне профéсоре!**, **пáне Кравчýк!**

Feminines with a hard final consonant (and masculines of the 'Mykola' type)

-о: **Мáрта! – Мáрто!**, **Натáлка! – Натáлко!**, **Вíра! – Вíро!**

Masculines ending in ч, a soft final consonant and names ending in -ко

-у/-ю **Петрóвич** becomes **Петрóвичу!**, **Васúль** becomes **Васúлю!**, **Андрíйко** becomes **Андрíйку!**, **Íгор** becomes **Íгорю!** (Note that this final **-р** is a disguised soft consonant: it appears hard when no ending follows.)

Feminines ending in a soft final consonant

-е, -є, -ю: **Гáля! – Гáлю! Марíя! – Марíє!**, **Óля! – Óле!**, **Óлю!**

A few forms of address involving the vocative (or nominative in the case of plurals) can be tacked on to **Дóбрий день** etc.; the forms with special vocative endings are in italic. And so, **Дóбрий день!**

пáне [páne], **добрóдію** [dobród'iyu]	sir
пáні [pán'i], **добрóдійко** [dobród'iyko]	madam (plural 'ladies' is the same)
панóве [panóve], **добрóдії** [dobród'iyi]	sir and madam, sir (and ladies)
пáнно [pánno]	miss
товáришу [továryshu]	comrade (close to 'friend') (masculine)
товáришко [továryshko]	comrade (close to 'friend') (feminine; plural **товáришки** [továryshky])
товаришí [tovarysh'í]	comrades (close to 'friends') (masculine or mixed)
дрýже [drúzhe]	friend (masculine)
пóдруго [pódruho]	friend (feminine; plural **пóдруги** [pódruhy])
дрýзі [drúz'i]	friends (masculine or mixed)

The past tense

The formation of the past tense is extremely straightforward. To the infinitive stem of any given verb (most often the infinitive minus **-ти**) we simply add three endings in the singular to indicate the gender of the subject; there is only one form in the plural, no matter who or what the subjects are:

роби́ти	**він**	**роби́-в**	**чита́ти**	**чита́-в**
	вона́	**роби́-ла**		**чита́-ла**
	воно́	**роби́-ло**		**чита́-ло**
	вони́	**роби́-ли**		**чита́-ли**

When the pronouns **я/ти** are used, the gender of the verb must always correspond to the gender of the speaker: **я/ти чита́в**, **я/ти чита́ла**. But always use the plural form of a verb when using **ви**. Of the verbs you have seen thus far, the past tense is regular in all but **іти́**, **іду́**, where we find **ішо́в**, **ішла́**, **ішло́**, **ішли́** or **йшов**, etc. Like all exceptions, these simply have to be seen and heard, used and memorized; as this is such a common verb, you will indeed read and hear it often. Reflexive verbs are treated in exactly the same way in the past tense as they are in the present, the particle **-ся** being appended to the past tense forms: **учи́в+ся**. Thus:

диви́вся	**вчи́вся**	**зустріча́вся**
диви́лася	**вчи́лася**	**зустріча́лася**

Taking a telephone message

In *3* we referred to saying ‘hello’ on the telephone. Often you may have to write down a message; this may give you an opportunity to use the past tense. If someone simply asks you to tell another person to phone back, you might write:

Проси́в/Проси́ла [. . .] зателефонува́ти [NAME]: 295–53–28 . . .
[NAME] asked [you] to phone; his/her number is 295–53–28

(Choose the form of **просúв** according to whoever asked you to phone. Note that when it comes to saying telephone numbers, it is usual to read each component as a compound, i.e. 295 + 53 + 28. You should be able to do this after *9*. Until then, and even after then, you may read it as a list of single units, i.e. 2 + 9 + 5 + 5 + 3 + 2 + 8, for which see the reference section or *9*).

Exercise 4b

Below are present tense forms of some verbs you have met thus far; give the past tense **він** and **вона́** forms for each.

(a) **стою́**
(b) **чита́єш**
(c) **ідемо́**
(d) **живе́**
(e) **роблю́**
(f) **ходжу́**
(g) **зна́ють**
(h) **працю́ю**
(i) **зна́чить**
(j) **дивлю́ся**

'Ukrainian' etc.

Be very careful when using adjectives of nationality: in English we can say 'a Ukrainian person', 'a Ukrainian book', 'a Ukrainian lesson', but in Ukrainian we differentiate between something dealing with Ukrainian and something that is Ukrainian (that is, of Ukrainian provenance). Thus, we say **профéсор украї́нської мóви**, which means 'professor of Ukrainian' (he/she might be Ukrainian, but can in fact be of any nationality), but **украї́нський профéсор** would be understood to mean that he/she is Ukrainian **(профéсор-украї́нець** would be more frequently encountered). Likewise, we distinguish between a book on Ukrainian (say, a dictionary) and a book from Ukraine (here both constructions are possible). Note that when one talks of a Ukrainian textbook, exercise book or exercises, one uses the preposition **з**: **підрýчник/зóшит/впрáви з украї́нської мóви**. This seems to be optional with **словни́к** 'dictionary'.

Readings

Снідáнок

Щодня́ Президéнт сні́дає рáно й дýмає. Жі́нка сні́дає такóж. Коли́ вони́ сні́дають, нічóго не кáжуть. Це типóвий англі́йський снідáнок. Газéта цікáва; у газéті пи́шуть: «Президéнт і жі́нка гáрна пáра і багáто працю́ють». «Це дóбре. Сьогóдні мóжу відпочивáти», кáже Президéнт. «Краї́на в дóбрих рукáх.»

Vocabulary

снідáнок, -нку	breakfast (masc.)
щодня́	every day (adv.)
сні́дати, -ає-	have breakfast
рáно	early (adv.)
сьогóдні	today (adv.)
цікáвий	interesting (adj.)
нічóго не	nothing (direct object of verb)
казáти, -же-	say
типóвий	typical
гáрний	fine, beautiful, nice
пáра, -и	pair
багáто	much, many
могти́, мóжу, мóжеш	to be able (unusual infinitive)
відпочивáти, -áє-	to rest
краї́на, -и	country
в дóбрих рукáх	in good hands

Львів

Сього́дні ми у Льво́ві. Львів вели́ке мі́сто в Галичині́, части́ні За́хідної Украї́ни. Рані́ше він був у скла́ді А́встро-Уго́рщини, а по́тім По́льщі; тепе́р він, наре́шті, в Украї́ні. Є й і́нші вели́кі міста́ в Украї́ні, а са́ме Ки́їв (це столи́ця Украї́ни), Ха́рків, Оде́са, Жито́мир, Полта́ва, Дніпропетро́вськ, Доне́цьк то́що. Зна́чить, Украї́на там, де за́хід і схід зустріча́ються; по́руч розташо́вані Росі́я, По́льща, Білору́сь, Уго́рщина, Молдо́ва та Слова́ччина. Тро́шки да́лі є Іта́лія та Німе́ччина; та ще да́лі Фра́нція й Іспа́нія.

Vocabulary

Галичина́, -и́	Halychyna, Galicia
части́на, -и	part
за́хідний	western
рані́ше	earlier, formerly, before
був	was (masculine past tense)
А́встрія, -ї	Austria
Австро-Уго́рщина, -и	Austro/Austria–Hungary
По́льща, -і	Poland
наре́шті	at last, finally
і́нший	other (nominative plural **і́нші**)
вели́кий	large (nominative plural **вели́кі**)
міста́	towns, cities (nominative plural of **мі́сто**)
а са́ме	namely, that is
столи́ця, -і	capital (city)
то́що	and so on
за́хід, за́ходу	west
схід, схо́ду	east
зустріча́тися, -а́є-	to meet (each other)
розташо́ваний	situated
по́руч	close by, nearby
Молдо́ва, -и	Moldova
тро́шки	a little
да́лі	further
Іта́лія, -ї	Italy
Німе́ччина, -и	Germany
та	and, but
Іспа́нія, -ї	Spain

Vocabulary building: the adjective – nationalities

In our vocabulary we encountered the adjective **украї́нський** 'Ukrainian'. This ending **-(н)ський** [-(n)s'kiy] is extremely common, very often complementing -**(н)ець** [-(n)ets'], which we met in the first chapter. Thus (note the absence of a capital letter at the beginning of all adjective and person forms!):

Place	*Adjective*	*Person*
Украї́на	**украї́нський**	**украї́нець/украї́нка**
А́нглія	**англі́йський**	**англі́єць/англі́йка**
Іта́лія	**італі́йський**	**італі́єць/італі́йка**
Іспа́нія	**іспа́нський**	**іспа́нець/іспа́нка**
Аме́рика	**америка́нський**	**америка́нець/америка́нка**
А́встрія	**австрі́йський**	**австрі́єць/австрі́йка**
Уго́рщина	**уго́рський**	**уго́рець/уго́рка**
Німе́ччина	**німе́цький**	**ні́мець/ні́мка** or **німке́ня**

The adverbs corresponding to 'in the X fashion or manner' may have two different forms:

по-украї́нському, по-украї́нськи 'in the Ukrainian manner'

These (the first variant more often than the second) are also used in conjunction with **розмовля́ти (розмовля́ю розмовля́єш)** 'to chat, talk', **говори́ти (говорю́, гово́риш)** 'to speak', **писа́ти** and **чита́ти**. For example:

Ми щодня́ розмовля́ємо по-італі́йському 'Every day we talk Italian'.

However, another construction is far more commonly used with these verbs: **украї́нською (мо́вою)** 'in Ukrainian'. This (using the instrumental case, to be presented later) only means 'in Ukrainian' in relation to language, and does not express 'in the Ukrainian fashion/manner'.

The noun

The suffix **-(н)ець** [-(n)ets'] is not the only one used to denote people from a particular country:

Place	*Adjective*	*Person*
Росі́я	**росі́йський**	**росія́нин/росія́нка**
По́льща	**по́льський**	**поля́к/по́лька**
Фра́нція	**францу́зький**	**францу́з/францу́женка**
Че́хія	**че́ський**	**чех/че́шка**
Слова́ччина	**слова́цький**	**слова́к/слова́чка**

For example:

Росія́нин гово́рить росі́йською (мо́вою).

Францу́з гово́рить францу́зькою (мо́вою), . . .
Поля́к пи́ше по́льською (мо́вою), . . .

Exercise 4c

Fill in the gaps in the following sentences:

(a) Мико́ла . . . до шко́ли.
(b) У К. . . є вели́ка бібліоте́ка.
(c) Кварти́ра, де . . . О́льга й Андрі́й, ду́же пр. . . .
(d) Ма́ма й та́то розм . . . у ку́хн . . . .
(e) . . . не зна́єте, де працю́ють брат і сестра́?
(f) Олекса́ндр . . . бі́ля вікн . . . й чита́є.
(g) Ната́лка не пише́, вона́ . . . телеві́зор.
(h) Сього́дні ми не працю́ємо, а від . . . .
(i) Її́ кни́жка ду́же ці. . . .
(j) Джон ст. . . у кімна́т . . . й ду́. . . .

Exercise 4d

Here are the names of a few countries; using the preposition **з** + genitive 'from', say you are from 'X' place (some are not exactly as they are in English: try to figure them out without the aid of a dictionary first!). For example;

Я з Украї́ни. I am from Ukraine.

Євро́па	А́нглія	Фра́нція
Іспа́нія	Португа́лія	Іта́лія
Бе́льгія	Голла́ндія	Вірме́нія
Німе́ччина	Да́нія	Норве́гія
Шве́ція	Фінля́ндія	Ісла́ндія
Есто́нія	Ла́твія	Литва́
По́льща	Білору́сь	Ро́сі́я
Слова́ччина	А́встрія	Че́хія
Уго́рщина	Молдо́ва	Руму́нія
Хорва́тія	Болга́рія	Алба́нія
Македо́нія	Се́рбія	Гре́ція
Слове́нія	Туре́ччина	Кана́да
Об'є́днане Королі́вство	Ірла́ндія	Аме́рика
Австра́лія	Нова́ Зела́ндія	Шотла́ндія
Аргенти́на	Брази́лія	Гру́зія

Here are two travel agent street advertisements. See what sense you can make of them before looking at the translations. They include lots of geographical names in the genitive case!

Advertisement 1

«ІНТУРТРАНСКОМ»
МІЖНАРОДНА ТУРИСТИЧНА
ТА ТРАНСПОРТНА КОМПАНІЯ

ПОДОРОЖІ
З ВІДПОЧИНКОМ,
ЛІКУВАННЯМ,
ШОПІНГОМ
ДО КРАЇН ЄВРОПИ,
БЛИЗЬКОГО СХОДУ,
ЦЕНТРАЛЬНОЇ АЗІЇ
АМЕРИКИ, СНД

вул. ПУШКІНСЬКА, 14
тел. 228–38–35
факс 228–38–76, телекс 631777

Translation of Advertisement 1: ' *"INTURTRANSKOM" – International Tourist and Transport Company – Journeys offering rest, treatment, and shopping to the countries of Europe, the Near East, Central Asia, North America, and the CIS – 14, Pushkin St., tel. 228–38–35, fax 228–38–76, telext 631777* '

Advertisement 2

УКРЗАРУБІЖТУРСЕРВІС

запрошує вас у захоплюючі подорожі до

АВСТРІЇ	**МОНГОЛІЇ**
БЕЛЬГІЇ	**НІМЕЧЧИНІ**
БОЛГАРІЇ (відпочинок)	**ПАКИСТАНУ**
БОЛГАРІЇ-ТУРЕЧЧИНИ	**США**
БОГЛГАРІЇ-СІРІЇ	**СІРІЇ**
УГОРЩИНИ	**САУДІВСЬКОЇ АРАВІЇ**

ГРЕЦІЇ	СІНГАПУРУ – МАЛАЙЗІЇ
ГОЛЛАНДІЇ	ФРАНЦІЇ
ЄГИПТУ	ФІНЛЯНДІЇ
ІСПАНІЇ	ЧЕХО-СЛОВАЧЧИНИ
ІНДІЇ	ШВЕЙЦАРІЇ
ІТАЛІЇ	ЮГОСЛАВІЇ
КАНАРСЬКИХ ОСТРОВІВ	ПІВДЕННОЇ КОРЕЇ
КІПРУ	КРУЇЗИ ПО СЕРЕДЗЕМНОМУ
КИТАЮ	МОРЮ

НАША АДРЕСА: ВУЛ. ЛЕНІНА, 26 229–84–13, 224–75–72

Translation of Advertisement 2: '*UKRZARUBIZhTURSERVIS [Ukrainian Foreign Tour Service] invites you on exciting journeys to Austria, Belgium, Bulgaria (relaxation), Bulgaria – Turkey, Bulgaria – Syria, Hungary, Greece, Holland, Egypt, Spain, India, Italy, the Canary Islands, Cyprus, China, Mongolia, Germany, Pakistan, the USA, Syria, Saudi Arabia, Singapore – Malaysia, France, Finland, Czechoslovakia, Switzerland, Yugoslavia, South Korea, a cruise in the Mediterranean. Our address: 26, Lenin St. [Tel.:] 229–84–13, 224–75–72*'

Exercise 4e

Translate the following sentences into Ukrainian:

(a) Natalka lives in the centre of town.
(b) We don't speak Polish; we speak Ukrainian.
(c) Every day I have breakfast and read.
(d) I don't know why she still goes to school.*
(e) My friend works in London University.†
(f) The book is over there, by the kitchen.
(g) Petro is from Poltava.
(h) Lida is sitting on the right, near the window.
(i) Where are the president and his wife?
(j) Where are you going?

*__Чому__ is subject to the same punctuation rule as **хоч(á)** see **Розмóва**, *3*).
†Don't be afraid, forming an adjective from **Лóндон** is quite straightforward.

5 Я хо́чу купи́ти кни́жку

I want to buy a book

In this lesson you will learn about:

- shopping in Ukrainian
- the verb 'to like'
- the cases: nominative plural, accusative, and more locatives
- verbal aspect
- reported speech

Окса́на, по́друга Джо́на

During John and Mykola's conversation they are joined by Oksana, born in England but of Ukrainian descent, and a member of John's tour group

Джон:	Окса́но! Ми тут!
Окса́на:	Джон(е)! Ви́бачте, я не ба́чила вас.
Джон:	Це ніч́ого! Мико́ло, це́ Окса́на: познайо́мтеся!
Мико́ла:	Ду́же прие́мно, Окса́но.
Окса́на:	Прие́мно, Мико́ло.
Мико́ла:	Ви украї́нка?
Окса́на:	Ні, але́ так за́вжди́ ду́мають!
Мико́ла:	Ви ма́єте украї́нське ім'я́.
Окса́на:	Пра́вда: бабу́ся украї́нка, її́ ім'я́ теж Окса́на.
Мико́ла:	А, розумі́ю. Чи вам подо́бається на́ше мі́сто?
Окса́на:	О, яке́ га́рне мі́сто! Ву́лиці, буди́нки, па́рки . . .
Джон:	А магази́ни? Чи ти шука́ла словни́к?
Окса́на:	Шука́ла.
Мико́ла:	Джон не знайшо́в. А ви?
Окса́на:	Я знайшла́, звича́йно. На Францу́зькому бульва́рі, бі́ля університе́ту; там є мали́й магази́н.
Джон:	Яки́й магази́н? Я не ба́чив його́.
Окса́на:	Це книга́рня; вона́ назива́ється «Книжки́».
Джон:	До́бре. За́втра я піду́ туди́ й куплю́ словни́к.

JOHN:	*Oksana! We're (over) here!*
OKSANA:	*John! Excuse me, I didn't see you* (plural)
JOHN:	*It's OK ('nothing')! Mykola, this is Oksana; get to know one another.*
MYKOLA:	*Very pleased (to meet you), Oksana.*
OKSANA:	*Pleased (to meet you), Mykola.*
MYKOLA:	*Are you Ukrainian?*
OKSANA:	*No, but people ('they') always think that ('thus').*
MYKOLA:	*You have a Ukrainian name.*
OKSANA:	*True: my grandmother's a Ukrainian, (and) her name is also Oksana.*
MYKOLA:	*Ah, I understand. Do you like our city?*
OKSANA:	*Oh, what a beautiful city! The streets, buildings, parks . . .*
JOHN:	*And the shops? Were you looking for the dictionary?*
OKSANA:	*Yes.*
MYKOLA:	*John didn't find (it). How about you?*
OKSANA:	*I found (it), of course. On French Boulevard near the university; there's a small shop there.*
JOHN:	*What shop? I didn't see it.*
OKSANA:	*It's a bookshop. It's called 'Books'.*
JOHN:	*OK. Tomorrow I'll go there and I'll buy the dictionary.*

Vocabulary

по́друга, -и	[pódruha]	friend (female)
ви́бачте	[výbachte]	excuse me, pardon
ба́чити, -и-	[báchyty]	see
вас	[vas]	you (pl./polite; acc.)
за́вжди́	[záwzhdý]	always
ма́ти, -а́є-	[máty]	have
бабу́ся, -і	[babús'a]	grandmother
розумі́ю	[rozum'íyu]	I understand (**розумі́ти, -і́є-**)
подо́бається	[podóbayets'ts'a]	it is pleasing, 'to like' + dat. (see note below)
буди́нки	[budýnky]	buildings (**буди́нок, -кну**)
па́рки	[párky]	parks (**парк, -у**)
знайшо́в, -шла́	[znayshów]	found, masc./fem. (**знайти́, -де-**, cf. **іти́**)
її́	[yiyí]	it (fem., acc.)
назива́ється	[nazyváyets'ts'a]	it is called (**назива́тися, -а́є-**)
туди́	[tudý]	(to) there, to that place
куплю́	[kupl'ú]	I'll buy (**купи́ти, -и-**)

Shopping

At this point in the course we give just the very basics for looking around shops, asking for things and paying. Self-service shops and departments (**ві́дділ самообслуго́вування**) are emerging, but the typical Ukrainian way of shopping is to find what you want to buy (**купи́ти**, **-и-**) and its price (**ціна́**, **-и́**), then go off to a till (**ка́са**, **-и**), pay, and obtain a receipt (**чек**, **-а**). The phrase **вибива́ти**, **-а́є**, perf. **ви́бити**, **ви́б'є чек** is used in the sense 'provide with a receipt' (lit. 'beat out a receipt on the till'). Finally, you return to the counter to produce your receipt and receive your goods. Use the following phrases:

Покажі́ть, будь ла́ска, XXX!	Show (me) XXX, please!
Скі́льки це ко́штує?	How much does this cost?
Скажі́ть, будь ла́ска, до котро́ї ка́си я ма́ю плати́ти?	Tell (me), please, at which (lit. to which) till I have to pay
Скажі́ть, будь ла́ска, ви ма́єте . . .?	Tell (me), please, do you have . . .?
Я куплю́/Я візьму́ . . .	I'll buy/I'll take . . .

Ukrainian currency

Note that the currency situation in Ukraine at the moment of writing is extremely uncertain. Traditionally the price is marked, so you may just have to look or be shown. Just now the **купо́н, -а** ‘coupon’ is used as currency, but the **гри́вня**, **-і** is supposed to be introduced eventually; the **карбо́ванець**, **-нця** ‘karbovanets’ (rouble), divided into 100 **копі́йка**, **-и** ‘copeck(s)’ was used during the Soviet period, and is currently maintained. For the moment, pointing and looking, or a request to write the price out: **Напиші́ть, будь ла́ска, ціну́!** ‘Write down, please!’, may have to suffice.

Cash (especially foreign) is always welcome: you will have no trouble using the **до́лар**, **-а** ‘dollar’ or the **фунт**, **-а** ‘pound’; **акредити́ви** are ‘travellers cheques’ (singular **акредити́в**, **-а**). A credit card is called **креди́тна ка́ртка**, **-ої -и**. In certain shops, a bank, or a hotel, you will be understood if you mention the actual name of the more well-known credit and charge cards: **Я ма́ю креди́тну ка́ртку/Ві́зу**, for example. Such cards are likely to become more usable. When changing money, the following phrases will be useful:

Я хо́чу розміня́ти гро́ші/ до́лари/фу́нти/акредити́ви.	I want to change money/dollars/ pounds/travellers cheques.
Де я мо́жу/Де мо́жна розміня́ти . . .?	Where can I change . . .?

Instead of saying **скажі́ть, будь ла́ска**, you might also use any one of the following expressions for ‘excuse me’; the last two are more often used in the sense of ‘I’m sorry’:

ви́бачте, проба́чте, про́шу проба́чення, перепро́шую

For example:

Ви́бачте, чи ви ма́єте підру́чники з украї́нської мо́ви?
Так, ось вони́.
Покажі́ть, будь ла́ска.
Про́шу.
Я візьму́ оце́й. Скі́льки він ко́штує? (оце́й, ‘this one’; see 9)
Подиві́ться, тут ціна́.
До котро́ї ка́си я ма́ю плати́ти?
До пе́ршої/дру́гої/тре́тьої/четве́ртої . . .
Дя́кую.
(Customer goes to pay and gets the ‘check’.)
Про́шу, ось чек.
Про́шу, візьмі́ть (take!) підру́чник. До поба́чення.
До поба́чення.

Saying you like something

In addition to expressing 'to love', **любúти** is also used to convey matters of taste, or preference:

Я люблю́ молоко́ й ма́сло, але́ не люблю́ си́ру.	I like milk and butter, but I don't like cheese.

A common way of saying 'like' in Ukrainian is to use the verb **подо́батися**. It actually means 'to please, to be pleasing', so it will almost always be found in the third person singular or plural, and what pleases you is the subject of the sentence. 'You', or the one who likes, appears in the dative case (the 'to/for' case): in other words, literally 'X is pleasing to Y'. We study this case later, but for now just give the forms appropriate to 'you', 'I', and 'we':

Чи тобі́ подо́бається це мі́сто?	Do you (**ти**) like this town?
Так, воно́ мені́ ду́же подо́бається.	Yes, I like it very much.
Чи вам подо́бається ця кни́жка?	Do you (**ви**) like this book?
Так, вона́ мені́/нам ду́же подо́бається.	Yes, I/we like it very much.

The nominative plural

In the dialogue we have the plurals **ву́лиці, буди́нки** and **па́рки**. The **-и** ending is the most common ending in masculine and feminine nouns, alternating with the rarer **-і**, which occurs as follows:

Masculines and feminines

The final letter in the nominative singular is **-ь** or **-я**:

вчи́тель – вчителі́ **віта́льня – віта́льні** 'front room'

The stem-final consonant is **ж, ш, ч** or **щ**:

ніж – ножі́ **ка́ша – ка́ші** 'porridge, *kasha*'

(-yi [-ї] where the stem-final consonant is **-у**: **край – краї́, ле́кція – ле́кції**)

A few nouns in **-ар** or **-яр** (in other words, with hidden soft r!):

ма́ля́р – малярі́ 'painter'

Neuters change **-o** to **-a**, **-e** and most **-я** to **-я** (after **ж**, **ш**, **ч**, **щ** and **-e** usually to **-a**); the special **-м'я** becomes **-мена́** for the few neuters in **-м'я**. This form usually looks just like the genitive singular, but the place of stress may differentiate the two forms. To illustrate the neuters you know, plus an example of the very plentiful neuters in **-я**, we have;

вікно́ becomes **ві́кна**
заняття́ becomes **заняття́** 'lesson'
і́м'я becomes **імена́**
мі́сце becomes **місця́**
прі́звище becomes **прі́звища**
пита́ння becomes **пита́ння** 'question, issue'

The nominative plural of adjectives is very simply **-i**: **до́брі**, **вели́кі**, etc.

Exercise 5a

Give the following plurals in Ukrainian, keeping in mind that stresss can shift from its place in the singular! All the words below are found in the first four lessons:

students, hotels, apartments, universities, rooms, families, theatres, bookstores, brothers, sisters, letters, (first) names, factories, engineers, teachers, shops, evenings, cities, dictionaries, comrades, friends, countries

The accusative case

The accusative is the case of the direct object: in other words, if you buy a book, see a person or read a newspaper, then 'book', 'person' and 'newspaper' are in the accusative case. As you may have already noticed in the passage above, sometimes a form does not change when it is the direct object. In fact, only one set of nouns has a unique accusative ending: feminines in **-a** or **-я**:

кни́жка becomes **кни́жку**
Окса́на becomes **Окса́ну**
Аме́рика becomes **Аме́рику**
Украї́на becomes **Украї́ну**
голова́ 'head' becomes **го́лову**
фотогра́фія becomes **фотогра́фію**
Росі́я becomes **Росі́ю**
віта́льня becomes **віта́льню**
ку́хня becomes **ку́хню**
нога́ 'leg, foot' becomes **но́гу**

Notice the possible backward shift of stress when the nominative case has a stressed **-á**. Nouns that do not change include: feminines ending in a consonant, for example **ніч** (**ніч**), **Білору́сь** (**Білору́сь**), neuter nouns, for example **вікно́**, **ім'я́** and **мі́сто**; and usually masculine nouns denoting things or non-living beings, for example **лист**, **університéт**, **парк**, **Лóндон**, **телевíзор**, **телефóн**, etc. Masculines denoting living beings (we call such nouns 'animate') do change in the accusative, but this ending is the same as in the genitive case: **Івáн** becomes **Івáна**, **профéсор** becomes **профéсора** and so on. Sometimes we find this same ending with inanimates as well: **я пишý листá**. So the only truly new case ending to learn here is still the feminine **-у/-ю**.

Adjectives modifying nouns in the accusative must agree: the nominative for neuters and inanimate masculines, the genitive for animate masculines and the feminine ending exactly the same as the noun ending, namely **-у/-ю**. Note that although a noun like **ніч** may not change, it has feminine gender, which will be reflected in an accompanying adjective, e.g. **тúха ніч** but **я люблю́ тúху ніч**.

In the plural, of course, nominative plurals of inanimates are also the accusative plurals! Compare:

Nominative	*Accusative*
Там є телевíзор	**Чи ти бáчиш телевíзор?**
Там є телевíзори	**Чи ти бáчиш телевíзори?**

The accusative and genitive of personal pronouns are identical

я	**лю́биш *мене́***
ти	**люблю́ *тебе́***
ви	**бáчу *вас***
він/вонó	**бáчу *йогó***
вонá	**бáчу *її́***
ми	**бáчать *нас***
ви	**бáчу *вас***
воні́	**бáчу їх**

Note that the forms 'him, her, it' are identical to the possessives 'his, her, its'. When these pronouns are used with prepositions there are some slight changes that take place in all but **нас** and **вас**. Compare the use of the pronouns with the preposition **до** (+ gen.) 'to':

мене́:	**до мéне**	(stress)
тебé:	**до тéбе**	(stress)
йогó:	**до ньóго**	(stress and initial **н-**)
її́:	**до нéї**	(stress, vowel and initital **н-**)
їх:	**до них**	(vowel and initial **н-**)

Зага́дка (Riddle)

Хто за́вжди́ пра́вду ка́же?
[The solution will be found after the exercise.]

Exercise 5b

Read the following sentences and identify the accusative nouns and adjectives and the pronouns in the accusative (remember, even if a word doesn't change when it is the object of a verb, it is grammatically still in the accusative case!). Not every sentence has an accusative.

(a) Що ти чита́єш? Я чита́ю пе́рше занятта́ ('lesson one') кни́жки.
(b) Сього́дні ми ба́чили профе́сора-украї́нця.
(c) Чи ти тако́ж його́ ба́чив?
(d) Мій ба́тько пише́ листи́ до нього́.
(e) О́льго, де твій нови́й телеві́зор?
(f) Я люблю́ ва́ші га́рні міста́.
(g) Я її́ не зна́ю, але́ зна́ю Петра́.
(h) Чи це кварти́ра ва́шого си́на?
(i) Зда́ється, що мій ба́тько лю́бить Ки́їв, Оде́су, і Львів.
(j) Ната́лка лю́бить ти́хий день, а я люблю́ ти́ху ніч.

Відга́дка (Solution): **Дзе́ркало** 'the mirror'

Aspect

One of the most characteristic features of the Ukrainian verb is 'aspect'. Instead of having a large number of different tenses, such as the 'imperfect' and 'perfect' (among others), almost each verb is a member of an 'aspectual' pair; compare French or Spanish, both of which do have a large number of tenses, and therefore a large number of forms to learn. The two aspects are called imperfective and perfective, and they express different kinds of action (do not confuse them with the tenses named above!). In general, an *imperfective* action is one that is ongoing (at present or over a period of time) or not completed or habitual; most of those that you have seen thus far have been imperfective. A perfective action is a completed or limited action; this can refer to a large-scale action, such as reading through a whole book, or to short actions, e.g. leading to a change. Both aspects can have past and future tenses, but the completedness of perfective action means that it doesn't express something happening in the present; the present tense proper can only be expressed by imperfective verbs. Thus, the 'present' forms of perfective verbs are future in meaning.

The aspectual pairs can be differentiated in three ways:

- by the presence of a prefix in the perfective
- by the stem type to which the verbs belong
- by being unrelated in form

A prefix added to the imperfective can often change the meaning of the verb (sometimes just a little, at other times radically), so that the two do not make up a true (synonymous) pair any more. Below we give a few verbs which come close to being pairs.

Imperfective		*Perfective*	
ба́чити	see	**поба́чити**	catch sight of
бра́ти	take	**узя́ти**	take
диви́тися	watch	**подиви́тися**	take a look
ду́мати	think	**поду́мати**	think
зустріча́ти	meet	**зустрі́ти**	meet
люби́ти	love	**полюби́ти**	fall in love
писа́ти	write	**написа́ти**	write
пита́ти	ask	**спита́ти**	ask
роби́ти	do, make	**зроби́ти**	do, make
учи́тися	study	**навчи́тися**	study
чита́ти	read	**прочита́ти**	read through, read all

Most of these perfectives differ from the imperfectives only by the presence of a prefix; one pair consists of two unrelated forms (find them!) and the members of another pair conjugate differently (identify them as well!). The addition of prefixes in the following verbs changes the meaning to a greater extent:

Imperfective		*Perfective*	
жи́ти	live	**дожи́ти**	live to see, reach the age of
зна́ти	know	**призна́ти**	grant, admit
писа́ти	write	**переписа́ти**	rewrite
писа́ти	write	**підписа́ти**	sign
писа́ти	write	**дописа́ти**	add, finish writing
писа́ти	write	**записа́ти**	note down

сиді́ти	sit	**поси́діти***	sit for a while
стоя́ти	stand	**посто́яти***	stand for a while
чита́ти	read	**дочита́ти**	read through, up to
чита́ти	read	**перечита́ти**	reread

*Note the change in place of stress

Some of the perfectives in this table may need an imperfective partner: the meaning has changed, and the new action (e.g., to 'sign' instead of 'to write') may also take place 'imperfectively'. A new imperfective verb is then formed from the perfective, e.g. perfective **записа́ти** becomes imperfective **запи́сувати** and **призна́ти** becomes **признава́ти**; we shall see more such new imperfectives later.

Overall, it may be best to think of the perfective as a limitation of sorts: so the perfective of 'sit' is to 'have a sit' or 'to have sat' (i.e., for a while), 'stand' is 'to stand for a while' or 'to have stood for a while', etc. In some cases, of course, the meaning of both members of the pair seems to be identical, and only context shows the true difference: usually it is completion of a change that is central to the perfective member. Don't worry about getting your choice of aspect right every time. As you will see, certain meanings lend themselves to one aspect rather than another, e.g. 'work' is more naturally imperfective, while 'forget', 'find', 'tell' and 'decide' are more naturally perfective. Study the use of the verbs in the following dialogue (note especially those in italics), and remember that the present tense almost always requires an imperfective.

Окса́на була́ в бібліоте́ці

Mykola, John, and Oksana continue their conversation; Mykola is especially interested in what Oksana did after she bought her dictionary

МИКО́ЛА: Окса́но, де ти була́ пі́сля магази́на?
ОКСА́НА: Пі́сля магази́на я була́ в бібліоте́ці.
МИКО́ЛА: Наві́що?
ОКСА́НА: Я хоті́ла дізна́тися, де студе́нти й професори́ працю́ють.
МИКО́ЛА: Що ти *роби́ла* там? *Чита́ла?*
ОКСА́НА: Так; я *подиви́лася* кни́жку, *прочита́ла* статтю́.
МИКО́ЛА: А в статті́ було́ щось ціка́ве?
ОКСА́НА: Нічо́го; була́ ціка́ва стаття́ в і́ншій кни́жці, але́ я її́ не чита́ла.

Джон:	Шкодá; а пóтім?
Оксáна:	Пóтім я *сиділа* в кав'ярні, *пилá* кáву, *написáла* листá до брáта.
Джон:	Алé скажи́: як же ти нас *знайшлá*?
Оксáна:	Я знáла, що ви *чекáєте* в пáрку ім. Шевчéнка, алé я не *знáла*, де він; óтже, я *побáчила* якóгось хлóпця на ву́лиці й *спитáла* йогó.
Микóла:	Вáжко *знайти́* такé мі́сце в новóму мі́сті. Ну, слáва Бóгу, що ти *знайшлá*. Тепéр ідемó до нáшої кварти́ри: на нас чекáють.

Mykola:	*Oksana, where did you go ('were you') after the store?*
Oksana:	*After the store I was in the library.*
Mykola:	*Why?*
Oksana:	*I wanted to find out where students and professors work.*
Mykola:	*What did you do there? (Did you) read?*
Oksana:	*Yes; I took a look at a book and read (through) an article.*
Mykola:	*And was there anything interesting (of interest) in the article?*
Oksana:	*Nothing; there was an interesting article in another book, but I didn't read it.*
John:	*Pity; and then?*
Oksana:	*Then I sat in a café, drank some coffee, (and) wrote (my) brother a letter.*
John:	*But tell (us); how did you find us?*
Oksana:	*I knew that you were waiting in Shevchenko park, but I didn't know where it was, so I saw a boy in the street and asked him.*
Mykola:	*It is hard to find such a place in a new city. Well, thank goodness (that) you found (us). Now we shall go to our apartment: we are expected ('they are waiting for us').*

Vocabulary

пі́сля	[p'ís'l'a]	after; prep. + gen.
наві́що	[nav'íshcho]	why, for what purpose? (**чому́** [chomú] 'why, for what reason?'); **тому́ що** [tomú shcho] 'because'
дізнáтися, -áє-	[d'iznátys'a]	find out, perf.; imperf. **дізнавáтися, -aє́-**
хоті́ти, хóче	[xot'íty]	want; stem: irregular

статтй, -í	[stat't'á]	article
шкодá	[shkodá]	too bad! (what) a pity
пóтім	[pót'im]	then, next, afterwards
кав'ярня, -і	[kav"yarn'a]	café (also **кафé** neuter, indeclinable)
пи́ти, п'є	[pýty]	drink; imperf.
кáва, -и	[káva]	coffee
скажи́!	[skazhý]	tell! (imperative)
чекáти, -áє- [на]	[chekáty (na)]	wait (for: **на** + acc.)
óтже	[ódzhe]	and so, consequently
яки́йсь	[yakýys']	some, a
на	[na]	on, at; prep. + loc.
вáжко	[vázhko]	(it is) difficult
мíсце	[m'ístse]	place
слáва Бóгу	[sláva bóhu]	thank God, thank goodness
тепéр	[tepér]	now

Aspect

In the dialogue **Оксáна булá в бібліотéці** we find several ways in which aspect can make a clear difference to the meaning of a sentence. In questions such as 'what did you do' or 'did you read', it is the imperfective we need because the question is a general one: Mykola was not asking Oksana what she had accomplished or whether she had finished reading, but whether what she had been doing was reading (as opposed to some other action). Oksana then answered by enumerating several things that she did; note that they are all perfective, because first she did one thing, then another, then another (they were all completed, in other words; they were consecutive actions). In reference to the article which she didn't manage to read, the verb is imperfective, meaning perhaps that she didn't manage to read any of it, or that she didn't mean to read it (for whatever reason); were this verb perfective, it would have to mean that she had begun reading it but didn't finish.

Next, in the café, the first verb (imperfective **сиді́ти**) sets the stage: while she was sitting, and drinking coffee, she wrote (finished) a letter; this last verb could also be imperfective, if she had been writing a letter (and hadn't finished it). Note that the use of an English verb with an *-ing* ending ('I was writing') usually calls for a Ukrainian imperfective. We find more consecutive actions in Oksana's last statement: she caught sight of a boy, then she asked him how to find the park.

Mykola's last statement is also instructive: 'Thank goodness you found (perfective) us'. More examples of this type are found in the reading at the end of this lesson; there you will find that key words or phrases ('once', 'every day', etc.) often indicate which aspect is preferable.

Reported speech

Tenses in reported speech ('he said that he X-ed') reflect the tense used in the original speech (or thought) in Ukrainian. At the time she was looking for Mykola and John, Oksana was thinking 'they are waiting'; when she relates this thought later, it can only be expressed using the present tense in Ukrainian and Oksana says literally 'I knew you are waiting', instead of 'were waiting', which we would have in English. Reported speech in Ukrainian is separated from any introductory words by a comma, and the word 'that' (**що**) is as a rule obligatory; read the following examples, and think Ukrainian, not English, tenses!

Окса́на сказа́ла, що ти чека́єш. (She said 'you are waiting')	Oksana said (that) you were waiting.
Мико́ла сказа́в, що О́льга чека́ла (He said 'Ol'ha was waiting')	Mykola said (that) Ol'ha was/had been waiting.
Я ду́мав, що Іва́н чита́є (I was thinking 'Ivan is reading')	I thought (that) Ivan was reading.

More alternations

In *2* we found that there can be vowel alternations in some Ukrainian words (**о** and **е** can alternate with **і**), as well as consonant alternations (**д** to **дж** and **б** to **бл** in the verb, for example). In the dialogue we note another set of alternations: in nouns with a final consonant **к**, **г** or **х** these consonants will become **ц**, **з** or **с** before the locative ending **-і**:

кни́жка – у кни́жці	**бік – на бо́ці** (side)
О́льга – О́льзі	**ріг – на ро́зі** (corner)
му́ха – му́сі (a fly)	**рух – у ру́сі** (movement)

The alternation is most common in feminine nouns. There is another locative ending for masculines, namely **-у**, before which the alternation cannot take place; this ending occurs with some nouns you already know, which have the suffixes:

-ик:	**істо́рик – істо́рику**
-ник:	**словни́к – словнику́**
-ок:	**буди́нок – буди́нку**

The alternation is also excluded in some (but not all!) one-syllable nouns which also have the genitive ending **-у**. Here stress differentiates the two case forms: the locative ending is stressed, the genitive is not. This is a general rule of thumb; just observe as you learn, and note exceptions:

	Nominative	*Genitive*	*Locative*	
	сніг	**сні́гу**	**на снігу́**	snow
But	**рік**	**ро́ку**	**у ро́ці**	year
And	**парк**	**па́рку**	**у па́рку**	park

Exercise 5c

Write out every noun in Dialogue 2; modify with an appropriate adjective or pronoun from the following: **га́рний**, **молоди́й**, **вели́кий**, **наш**, **твій**, and put the new phrase into the locative (with the correct preposition). Pay attention to gender!

Vocabulary building

The adjective

Many adjectives, as you will notice, have a stem-final **н**; that is, adjectives frequently end in **-ний**. This means that they have, for the most part, been derived from another form (usually a noun). Here are a few examples:

хо́лод	(the) cold	**холо́дний**	cold
го́лос	voice	**голосни́й**	loud (note end stress)
мільйо́н	million	**мільйо́нний**	millionth
наро́д	people, nation	**наро́дний**	folk, national
во́ля	will, freedom	**ві́льний**	vacant, free

Sometimes we note a change in the final root consonant, either in the form of palatalization ([l] to [l']) or as a mutation (if that consonant is **к**, **г** or **х**):

смак	taste	**смачни́й**	tasty
проща́ла	she bade farewell	**проща́льний**	farewell, parting

рука́	hand	**ручни́й**	of/for the hand(s)
вага́	weight	**ва́жни́й**	serious, important
ру́х	movement	**рушни́й**	agile, brisk

Reading

Окса́на й Джон живу́ть у готе́лі, але́ вони́ лю́блять готува́ти сніда́нок по-дома́шньому. Учо́ра ви́рішили готува́ти сніда́нок в кімна́ті: їм потрі́бно було́ хлі́ба, ча́ю, та цу́кру. Вони́ пішли́ в ду́же вели́кий магази́н, але́ там знайшли́ ті́льки хліб та чай. Продаве́ць сказа́в, що, на жаль, цу́кру нема́є; о́тже, вони́ цу́кру не купи́ли. По́тім вони́ пішли́ в і́нший магази́н (цим ра́зом він був мали́й!) на ву́лиці Іва́на Франка́: там було́ бага́то цу́кру! Вони́ купи́ли його́, приготува́ли сніда́нок, та відпочи́ли. Коли́ вони́ подиви́лися на годи́нник, то засмія́лися: вони́ так до́вго шука́ли цу́кор, що було́ вже пі́зно йти́ в університе́т! Насту́пного дня вони́ поясни́ли причи́ну своє́ї відсу́тності.

Vocabulary

готува́ти, -у́є-	[hotuváty]	prepare, cook; imperf. Perf. **при-/з-готува́ти**
по-дома́шньому	[podomásh'n'omu]	just like at home (adv.)
учо́ра	[uchóra]	yesterday
ви́рішити, -и-	[výr'ishyty]	decide; perf.
потрі́бно (бу́ти)	[potr'íbno]	need (an impersonal expression; note that what is needed appears in the genitive case)
хліб, -а	[khl'ib]	bread; in gen. = 'some bread'
чай, -ю	[chay]	tea
цу́кор, -ру	[tsúkor]	sugar
у/в + acc.	[u/v]	into (motion)
продаве́ць, -вця́	[prodavéts']	salesman
на жаль	[na zhal']	unfortunately
цим ра́зом	[tsym rázom]	this time
годи́нник, -а	[hodýnnyk]	clock
то	[to]	'then' (it balances **коли́**, earlier in the sentence)

засмія́тися, -іє-	[zas'm'iyátys'a]	burst out laughing, began to laugh
до́вго	[dóvho]	for a long time
пі́зно	[p'ízno]	(it is/was) (too) late (adv.)
насту́пного дня	[nastúpnoho dn'a]	the next day (adv.)
поясни́ти, -и́-	[poyasnýty]	explain; perf.; imperf. **поясня́ти**, **-я́є-** or **поя́снювати**, **-ює-**
причи́на, -и	[prychýna]	reason
свій	[s'v'iy]	their (see *8*)
відсу́тність, -ості	[v'idsútn'is't']	absence

Exercise 5d

Put the nouns in the list below into the accusative:

Оле́кса ба́чить . . .

будинок
брат
лист
маши́на 'car'
кни́жка
О́льга
дире́ктор
вчи́телька
ба́тько
Петро́
ву́лиця
чита́ч 'reader'
ніч
син
день
лі́кар 'physician'
NB: final **-р** here is 'soft'!

Exercise 5e

Now add the correct form of either **мій** or **наш** to the answers above.

Exercise 5f

Give the vocative of the following names (look back at *4* for the vocative and, if you have not already done so, take a look at *18* for the formation of the patronymic):

Наді́я Сергі́ївна, Марко́, пан профе́сор, Миха́йло Володи́мирович, Ю́рій, Петро́ Семе́нович, Оле́кса Григо́рович, Марі́я Бори́сівна, Га́ля, Тара́с, Ната́лка, Ле́ся.

Exercise 5g

Choose the verb that you think is right for the sentences below. Where the sentence appears to be neutral (i.e., where either aspect is possible) circle both aspectual forms.

(a) Учо́ра він (чита́в/прочита́в) кни́жку.
(b) Вона́ до́вго (сиді́ла/поси́діла).
(c) Оле́кса (писа́в/написа́в) листа́, по́тім (чита́в/прочита́в) статтю́.
(d) Ми за́вжди (ду́маємо/поду́маємо) про нього́.
(e) Вони́ (диви́лися/подиви́лися) фі́льми ці́лий день (all day).
(f) Ма́ма вже (купи́ла/купува́ла) хліб.
(g) Вони́ щодня́ (зустріча́лися/зустрі́лися) тут.
(h) Тепе́р я (працю́ю/попрацю́ю) на по́шті.

Exercise 5h

Translate the above sentences. Try to make your translations reflect the aspect you selected.

6 Вече́ря у сім'ї́ Мико́ли

Supper with Mykola's family

In this lesson you will learn about:

- tag questions: 'Isn't it?'
- verbs: future time and irregulars
- more words relating to shopping (the post office and the market)
- cases: dative of personal pronouns and more uses of the genitive
- collectives
- 'to have'

Розмо́ва й вече́ря

Mykola arrives at his flat (apartment) with John. Everyone meets, and the meal begins

ДЖОН: Яки́й вели́кий буди́нок! Чи тут знахо́диться ва́ша кварти́ра?

МИКО́ЛА: Так, наре́шті ми добра́лися до не́ї. Таки́й буди́нок назива́ється «багатоповерхо́вий». До́бре, що ма́ємо ліфт.

ДЖОН: До́бре, звича́йно.

МИКО́ЛА: Де ж ключ? Чи я не дав його́ тобі́? А, я знайшо́в його́. Про́шу до нас.

ДЖОН: Дя́кую. Це я впе́рше в украї́нській кварти́рі. Я сподіва́юся, що ти бу́деш допомага́ти мені́.

МИКО́ЛА: Звича́йно, та й наві́що допомага́ти тобі́? Ма́мо, ми вже тут! Диви́сь, Джо́н(е), як за́тишно в на́шій кварти́рі.

МА́МА: До́брий день, Мико́ло. Добри́день, Джо́н(е), про́шу до віта́льні. Ми всі вже чека́ємо на вас, сидимо́, розмовля́ємо. Познайо́мтеся: це на́ша до́ня Ната́лка та моло́дший син Васи́ль. Ма́бу́ть ви голо́дні. У їда́льні на́шого університе́ту ма́бу́ть несма́чно готу́ють.

ДЖОН:	Ні, там до́сить сма́чно готу́ють, мені́ здає́ться, але́ так до́бре бу́ти в спра́вжньому украї́нському до́мі.
МА́МА:	Про́шу до сто́лу. Сього́дні бу́демо ї́сти украї́нські стра́ви. Це Ната́лка купи́ла проду́кти й накри́ла на стіл. Будь ла́ска, сіда́йте.

JOHN:	*What a big building! Is this your flat/apartment?*
MYKOLA:	*Yes, we've got to it at last. This kind of building is called 'multistoreyed.' It's a good thing we have a lift, isn't it?*
JOHN:	*Yes, certainly.*
MYKOLA:	*Where's my key? Didn't I give it to you? Ah, I've found it. Please come into our flat.*
JOHN:	*Thanks. This is the first time I've been in a Ukrainian flat. You'll help me, I hope.*
MYKOLA:	*Of course, but why should you need help! Mum/Mom, we're here. Look, John, how cosy it is in our flat.*
MOTHER:	*Hello, Mykola. Hello, John, do come into our sitting room. We're all already waiting for you, sitting and chatting. Meet our daughter, Natalka, and our second son, Vasyl'. You're probably hungry. I don't think they cook well in the refectory of our university.*
JOHN:	*No, they do cook quite well, it seems to me, but it's so good to be in a real Ukrainian home.*
MOTHER:	*Come to the table, please. Today we'll eat Ukrainian dishes. Natalka did the shopping and set the table. Please, (do) sit down.*

Vocabulary

вече́ря, -і	supper, dinner (evening meal; the midday meal is usually **обі́д, -у**)
розмо́ва, -и	conversation
добра́тися, -бере́- до + gen.	get to, reach
багатоповерхо́вий	multi-storeyed
ліфт, -а	lift, elevator
бу́демо	we shall
ключ, -а́	key
да́ти, дам, дасть; irreg.	give
тобі́	to/for you (dat. of **ти**)
впе́рше	for the first time
допомага́ти, -а́є-; imperf.	help (perf. **допомогти́**, -же-
мені́	to/for me (dat. of **я**)
сподіва́тися, -а́є-; imperf.	hope (also **наді́ятися**, -і́є-)

ув́есь	all, everyone (nom. plural **всі**)
вже	already
до́ня, -і	daughter
моло́дший	younger
син, -а	son
ма́бу́ть	perhaps, probably, I think
голо́дний	hungry
їда́льня, -і	refectory, canteen
несма́чно	not good/well, not tasty/tastily (of food)
здає́ться	it seems ('to . . .' = dative case)
до́сить	quite, enough
сма́чно	well, tastily (note this way of forming many adverbs from adjectives)
спра́вжній	real, genuine
дім, до́му	house, home
ї́сти, їм, їсть; irreg.	to eat (used in the future here; irregular verb)
стра́ви	dishes, food (plural of **стра́ва, -и**)
накри́ла	laid/set (the table); followed by **стіл** or, better, **на стіл**

Tag questions

In 'Yes-No' questions in English we often attach 'isn't it' or something similar to the end of the sentence, just as the French use *n'est-ce pas?*, the Spanish *¿verdad?*, and the Germans *nicht wahr?* Such 'tags' are rare in Ukrainian. There have been several opportunities for them in the dialogues, but often Ukrainian uses a statement rather than a question, e.g.

У їда́льні на́шого університе́ту ма́бу́ть несма́чно готу́ють.

taken from the first dialogue. Note that the crucial word (**ма́бу́ть**) tells us that the speaker wants information or confirmation about what follows (here: cooking 'not tastily'). If you wish to append a tag, you can use **(не) пра́вда?** 'is(n't) that true?', or **чи не так?** 'isn't it so?'

Verbs: future tense

In *5* reference was made to the future tense in the section on aspect. In **бу́демо відпочива́ти** 'we shall rest' we have a form of the future tense of an imperfective verb. To obtain it, we take the future tense of the verb **бу́ти** 'to be', and follow it with the imperfective infinitive. Thus:

я бу́ду	**ми бу́демо**		
ти бу́деш	**ви бу́дете**	+	**відпочива́ти**
він бу́де	**вони́ бу́дуть**		

Another way of doing the same thing is to add a set of endings to the imperfective infinitive (this is used with reflexives too):

відпочива́тиму	**відпочива́тимемо**
відпочива́тимеш	**відпочива́тимете**
відпочива́тиме	**відпочива́тимуть**

The future tense of a perfective verb, which means 'shall do, shall have done something' and is very frequent in everyday situations, is simply the 'present tense' form of the perfective verb:

Сього́дні я бу́ду чита́ти/ чита́тиму кни́жку.	Today I shall be reading the book.
Сього́дні я прочита́ю його́ листі́вку.	Today I shall read (completely) his postcard.

Verbs: 'irregulars' and other forms

In our dialogue we met the forms **дав**, **ї́сти**, **знайшо́в**, **здає́ться** and **сіда́йте**. The first two of these bring us to two of the three irregular Ukrainian verbs. Note that **да́ти** is perfective (imperf. **дава́ти**) and **ї́сти** is imperfective (perf. **з'ї́сти**):

	Future perfective	*Present*	*Past*
я	**дам**	**їм**	**дав, дала́ . . .**
ти	**даси́/даш**	**їси́**	
вона́	**дасть**	**їсть**	**ї́в, ї́ла . . .**
ми	**дамо́**	**їмо́**	
ви	**дасте́**	**їсте́**	
вони́	**даду́ть**	**їдя́ть**	

The third irregular verb is **-вісти**, which only occurs with prefixes; in this lesson we meet **відпові́сти́** 'to reply, answer', a perfective verb with the regular imperfective **відповіда́ти**. The forms of **відпові́сти́** (its past is **відпові́в**, **відпові́ла** . . .) are:

Future perfective		*Present imperfective*	
відпові́м	**відповімо́**	**відповіда́ю**	**відповіда́ємо**
відповіси́	**відповісте́**	**відповіда́єш**	**відповіда́єте**
відпові́сть	**відповідя́ть**	**відповіда́є**	**відповіда́ють**

Of the other three verbs, **знайшо́в** is the past tense of **знайти́** (perf.), which we have already encountered. This verb forms the past tense in the same way as **іти́/йти́**:

	знайти́	Compare іти́
він	знайшо́в	ішо́в/йшо́в
вона́	знайшла́	ішла́/йшла́
воно́	знайшло́	ішло́/йшло́
вони́	знайшли́	ішли́/йшли́

In the verb **іти́** and compounds containing it, **і** is generally replaced by **й** when a vowel precedes. Thus: **він ішо́в** 'he was going', but **вона́ йшла** 'she was going', and, of course **знайшо́в** etc.

Здає́ться has the infinitive **здава́тися**. In '**-ава-**' verbs **-ва-** disappears in the present tense and the stress is fixed on the ending. Thus:

	Present of **дава́ти** 'give'	**здава́тися**
я	даю́	–
ти	дає́ш	–
ві́н/вона́	дає́	здає́ться
ми	даємо́	–
ви	даєте́	–
вони́	даю́ть	–

Given its meaning 'to seem', **здава́тися** tends only to be found in the third person singular (neuter in the past: **здава́лося**). The person to whom something 'seems' is in the dative case.

Last, **сіда́йте** is the polite or plural command form (imperative). The command forms of other verbs will be dealt with later. Do note that **сіда́ти** means 'to sit down, have a seat', i.e. to move into a sitting position; **сиді́ти** means 'to be in a sitting position'.

Зага́дка

Не ї́сть, не п'є, а хо́дить і б'є.
(**би́ти, б'є-** 'beat, strike')
[The solution will be found before the section on the dative case.]

Пошта́мт

The post office

Ви́бачте, де пошта́мт?
Він там, зо́всім блі́зько.
Дя́кую.
Про́шу.

Чи ви зна́єте, де продаю́ть ма́рки/конве́рти/листі́вки?

Так, те вікóнце лівóруч.

Я хóчу відіслáти листá й листíвку (авіапóштою) до Áнглії.
Скíльки з мéне?
З вас XXX (купóни, *etc.*).
А рекомендóваний лист? Скíльки кóштує?
Такóж до Áнглії ? Так . . . це кóштує XXX.
Спасúбі. Скажíть, будь лáска, де мóжна одéржати пакýнок.
Пакýнок ви одéржите з íншого бóку приміщення.
Дякую.

Useful vocabulary for the post office

адрéса, -и	address
авіапóшта, -и	air mail (**авіапóштою** 'by air mail')
бандерóль, -і	postal wrapper
відправлЯти, -Яє-	to send (perf. **відпрáвити -и-**)
вікóнце, -я	window (for service)
висилáти, -áє-	to send (perf. **відіслáти, відішлю́, -шлé**)
вітáльна листíвка, -ої -и	greetings card
вíдділ, -у	department, section
до Áнглії	to England
до запитáння	poste restante, general delivery (Amer.); mail to be claimed at the post office
дістáти, дістáне-	to receive (perf.; imperf. **діставáти**, -áє-)
з íншого боку + gen.	on the other side of
примíщення, -я	hall, large room
запóвнювати бланк	to fill in a form (-**юе**-: perf. **запóвнити**, **-и-**)
конвéрт, -а	envelope
лист, -á	letter
листíвка, -и	postcard
(поштóва) мáрка, (-ої) -и	stamp
одéржати, -и-	to receive (perf.; imperf. **одéржувати, -ує-**)
пакýнок, -чка	parcel
папíр, -éру (для листíв)	writing paper
перéказ, -у	transfer
посúлка, -и	package
поштáмт, -у; пóшта, -и	post office (large; the latter word also means 'post')
поштóве віддíлення, -ого, -я	small, local, village post office
працíвниця, -і поштáмту	post office worker (woman)
працíвник, -а поштáмту	post office worker (man)
рекомендóваний	registered
скíльки кóштує . . .?	how much does . . . cost?
скíльки з мéне?	how much do I owe? (answer **з вас** + amount)

Addressing a letter

ДЖОН: Окса́но, скажи́, як написа́ти цю адре́су.
ОКСА́НА: Це лист для Оле́кси; він живе́ в Ки́єві. Адре́су ми пи́шемо так:
252001, Київ,
вул. В. Хмельницького, 4, к. 215,
Кравцю Олексі Анатолійовичу

Note how, in the fictitious address of O.A. Kravets', we start with a code, then give the country or go straight to the city, town or village (a code may be tacked on, e.g. **Львів-8**), then to the street name, followed by the number of the building (this may be preceded by the abbreviation **буд**. for **буди́нок** 'building'), then **к**. or **кв**. for **кварти́ра** and the number of the flat; last, the name of the addressee starting with the surname and followed by the first name and patronymic, all in the dative case (see below and also the next lesson).

Відга́дка:	**Годи́нник** 'a watch, clock'

The dative: verbs and personal pronouns

The most familiar meaning of the dative case is implied by its name, which derives from the Latin verb 'give'. In English it is typically translated as 'to' or 'for', most often relating to a person, and linked with verbs of giving, sending, saying, replying, showing, lending, recounting, relating, explaining, writing to and buying for, and the like; rather similar are verbs of promising (making a promise to), returning (giving back), and wishing (e.g. success to someone). Sometimes this is concealed in English, e.g. 'he gave me a book', but the dative is revealed by the synonymous 'he gave a book to me'.

Common verbs requiring the dative

	Imperfective	*Perfective*
buy	**купува́ти, -у́є-**	**купи́ти, -и-**
explain	**поя́снювати, -ює-**	**поясни́ти, -и́-**
give	**дава́ти, -ає́-**	**да́ти, дам** . . .
give back	**поверта́ти, -а́є-**	**поверну́ти, -не-**
lend	**позича́ти, -а́є-**	**пози́чити, -и-**
recount	**розповіда́ти, -а́є-**	**розпові́сти́, розпові́м** . . .
reply	**відповіда́ти, -а́є-**	**відпові́сти́, відпові́м** . . .
say	**каза́ти, -же-**	**сказа́ти, -же-**
send	**відсила́ти, -а́є-**	**віді́сла́ти, -шлю́, -шле́ш**
show	**пока́зувати, -ує-**	**показа́ти, -же-**
wish	**бажа́ти, -а́є-**	**побажа́ти, -а́є-**
write	**писа́ти, -ше-**	**написа́ти, -ше-**

These Ukrainian verbs correspond well to the equivalent constructions in English. There are also verbs which are not obviously 'dative', e.g. **допомага́ти/допомогти́** 'to help', **по-ра́дити (ра́джу, ра́диш)** 'advise' and **зава(д)жа́ти/зава́дити, (зава́джу, зава́диш)** 'pester, prevent, get in the way of'; one way to remember that these take the dative is to think in terms of 'giving help to', 'giving advice to'. The dative is very little used after prepositions. In this section we give perhaps the most important datives, those of the personal pronouns and the interrogative **хто** 'who'. In the next chapter we extend our coverage to the nouns and adjectives.

Nominative	*Dative*
хто?	**кому́?**
я	**мені́**
ти	**тобі́**
ви	**вам**
він	**йому́**
вона́	**їй**
воно́	**йому́**
ми	**нам**
ви	**вам**
вони́	**їм**

Read and make sure you understand the following sentences using the dative personal pronouns and the new verbs introduced above.

Ми дамо́ їй нову́ кни́жку.
Ви дає́те йому́ стару́ статтю́.
Ми відповімо́ тобі́, коли́ ти запита́єш про на́ше здоро́в'я.
Коли́ ти дає́ш нам хлі́ба, ми залюбки́ їмо́ його́.
Коли́ ти даси́ нам хлі́ба, ми залюбки́ з'їмо́ його́.

Залюбки́ 'with pleasure'; **запита́ти, -а́є-** 'ask' (imperf. **пита́ти, -а́є-**).

Exercise 6a

Formulate questions and answers using a different dative personal pronoun with each of the following: **купува́ти**, **поя́снювати**, **да́ти**, **пози́чити**, **розпові́сти́**. For example:

Коли́ вона́ відісла́ла йому́ кни́жку?
Учо́ра вона́ відісла́ла йому́ кни́жку.

Як ми купува́ли проду́кти

During and after supper the conversation turns to the preparations for the meal

Джон: Усе́ так сма́чно. Зна́чно кра́ще, ніж в університе́ті. Я ніко́ли не їв тако́го смачно́го борщу́.

Мико́ла: До борщу́ до́бре ї́сти чо́рний хліб. У цьо́му борщі́ буряки́, помідо́ри, капу́ста й часни́к. От чому́ він таки́й смачни́й.

Мама: На дру́ге бу́дуть варе́ники з си́ром, капу́стою і смета́ною. Ната́лка зготува́ла їх сього́дні вра́нці. Чи ви лю́бите украї́нське вино́?

Джон: Ду́же люблю́.

Ната́лка: На десе́рт компо́т. У нас є да́ча, де на горо́ді ма́ємо ви́шні, гру́ші та я́блуні. Ми ча́сто ї́здимо туди́. А цю садовину́ я купи́ла вчо́ра на база́рі. Ми хо́димо на база́р ма́йже щодня́. Він до́сить дале́ко. Бли́зько є магази́н, де купу́ємо м'я́со, сир, ка́ву, цу́кор, молоко́ то́що.

Мико́ла: Так прие́мно, що ти у нас сього́дні. Бу́демо пи́ти за твоє́ здоро́в'я та й за здоро́в'я твоє́ї роди́ни в А́нглії.

ДЖОН: Ду́же дя́кую. А я бу́ду пи́ти за ва́ше здоро́в'я. Так до́бре сиді́ти у вас у го́стях.

JOHN: *It's all so delicious, far better than in the university. I've never eaten such delicious borshch.*

MYKOLA: *It's good to eat some black bread with borshch. In this borshch there's beetroot, tomatoes, cabbage and garlic. That's why it's so delicious.*

MOTHER: *For the second course there'll be varenyky with cheese, cabbage and smetana. Natalka cooked them this morning. Do you like Ukrainian wine?*

JOHN: *Yes, very much.*

NATALKA: *For dessert there's stewed fruit (compote). We have a dacha, where we have cherry, pear and apple trees in the kitchen garden. We often go there. But I bought this fruit yesterday at the market. We go to the market almost every day. It's quite far away. Nearby there's a shop, where we buy meat, cheese, coffee, sugar, milk and the like.*

MYKOLA: *It's so nice to have you with us today. We shall drink to your health and to that of your family in England.*

JOHN: *Thank you very much. And I shall drink to your health. It's so good to be with you.*

Vocabulary

зна́чно	(it is) much, significantly (+ comparative)
кра́ще	better
ніж	than
ніко́ли не	never (followed by a verb form)
таки́й	such (a)
борщ, -у́	borshch, borsht (genitive: see below)
до + gen.	to, up to, until, into (here used with the sense 'as an accompaniment to')
цей	this (loc. sing. masc.)
буряки́, -ів	beet(root)
поміді́р, -а	tomato
капу́ста, -и	cabbage(s) (collective)
часни́к, -у́	garlic
от чому́	that's why
на дру́ге	for the second (main) course (**на заку́ску** 'as starters, hors d'œuvres', **на пе́рше** 'for the first course, e.g. soup, **на**

трéтє or **на десéрт** 'for the third course (dessert); **на** + accusative

варéники, -ів dumplings with fillings (plural of **варéник, -а**)

си́р, -у cheese (**з**, in its meaning 'with, accompanied by', requires the instrumental: **си́ром**)

сметáна, -и smetana, sour cream

капу́ста, -и cabbage

врáнці in the morning (adverb)

винó, -á wine

компóт, -у compote, stewed fruit

у нас we have (see 'to have' below)

дáча, -і dacha, summer house, secondary residence

горóд, -у kitchen garden (note **на** + loc. 'in')

ви́шня, -і (gen. pl. **ви́шень**) cherry tree, cherry

гру́ша, -і pear tree, pear

я́блуня, -і apple tree (**я́блуко, -а** 'apple')

чáсто often

ї́здити, -и- go (by some means of transport; indet.)

садовинá, -и́ fruit

базáр, -у market (also very common is **ри́нок, -нку**, which suggests a 'market place/square')

мáйже almost

дóсить quite

далéко far (away)

бли́зько near(by)

чáсом sometimes (adverb)

проду́кти, -ів products (used with **купувáти** to mean 'to do the shopping'; from **проду́кт, -у-**)

м'я́со, -а meat

молокó, -á milk

у/в + gen. here (at a person's home)

так so

пи́ти, п'є- за + acc. to drink (a toast) to (someone)

здорóв'я, -я, neut. health

у гóстях 'as guests, on a visit' (used with verbs of 'being somewhere'

In this dialogue we have once again met the prepositions **до** + genitive and, though it will be dealt with properly later, **з** + instrumental. The former is a very important preposition, used both temporally and spatially; it very often translates 'to' after verbs of motion. Note also that **горóд**, **базáр** and **ри́нок** are accompanied by **на** rather than by **у/в**.

Here we also meet the feminine-looking neuter **здоро́в'я**. There are a considerable number of such nouns in Ukrainian; be careful to keep them apart from the much smaller group of neuter nouns in **-м'я** (e.g. **ім'я́**).

Wishes before eating

Смачно́го!	Bon appétit!
Дя́кую/Спаси́бі! (вам/тобі́ тако́ж!)	Thanks! (To you too!)
Прие́много апети́ту!	Bon appétit! (slightly more formal)
Дя́кую/Спаси́бі! (Вам/тобі́ тако́ж!)	Thanks! (To you too!)

And thanks after

Дя́кую/Спаси́бі	Thanks (for the dinner)!
На здоро́в'я!	Literally: 'to your health!' (no toasting involved)

На база́рі

The market usually has the widest range of produce, though it can be rather expensive these days. As regards **м'я́со, -а** 'meat', you might find at least:

свини́на, -и 'pork'
теля́тина, -и 'veal'
ку́рка, -и 'chicken'
я́ловичина, -и 'beef'

As for **о́вочі, -ів** or **горо́дина, -и** 'vegetables', you will have a wide range, including:

карто́пля, -і 'potatoes'
буря́к, -у́ 'beetroot' (Amer. beets)
капу́ста, -и 'cabbage'
цибу́ля, -і 'onions'
мо́рква, -и 'carrots'
квасо́ля or **фасо́ля, -і** 'beans'

Note that these are all collective nouns, which decline as if singular. **Буря́к** can decline in the plural, however. And you can find dairy products, for example:

молоко́, -**á** 'milk'
смета́на, -**и** 'smetana; sour cream'
кефі́р, -**у** 'buttermilk'
сир, -**у** 'cheese'
вершки́, -**і́в** 'cream, "top of the milk" ' (pl. only)

Fruits will include at least **я́блуко**, -**а** 'apple' and **гру́ша**, -**і** 'pear'. The various berries include **полуни́ця**, -**і** 'strawberry', **мали́на**, -**и** 'raspberries', **чо́рна смoро́дина**, -**ої** -**и** 'blackberries' and **порі́чка**, -**и** '(red) currant'. **Мали́на** and **чо́рна смoро́дина** are collectives. One should not forget the mushroom, namely **гриб**, -**á**. John wants to know how to shop at the market:

ДЖОН: Що ти роби́в сього́дні, Мико́ла?
МИКО́ЛА: Я купува́в проду́кти на база́рі.
ДЖОН: Я тако́ж хо́чу піти́ на база́р; як тре́ба зверта́тися до продавщи́ці?
МИКО́ЛА: Це ду́же про́сто: «дайте, будь ла́ска . . .», і «чи ви ма́єте . . .?»
ДЖОН: Дя́кую!

Note that Mykola's use of aspect depends on whether he simply 'went shopping' or actually managed to buy something at the market.

Apart from the general phrases for requesting things, you will need to use weights, e.g. **грам**, -**а** (nominative and genitive plural **гра́ми/гра́мів**) 'gram', **кіло́**, -**á** (nominative and genitive plural **кі́ла/кіл**, though it may be considered indeclinable) or **кілогра́м**, -**а**, -**и**, -**ів** 'kilogram'. We will use numerals in *8*. For now, concentrate on asking for a kilogram of produce! For example:

ДЖОН: Про́шу, чи ви ма́єте свини́ну?
ПРОДАВЕ́ЦЬ: Так, ма́ємо. Скі́льки вам?
ДЖОН: Оди́н кілогра́м.
ПРОДАВЕ́ЦЬ: Про́шу.
ДЖОН: Дя́кую!

In the foodstore **універма́г, -у** sections have the following names:

напівфабрика́ти (-ів)	prepared foodstuffs
бакалі́я (-ії)	groceries
моло́ко (-а́) сир (-у)	milk – cheese
гастроно́мія (-ії)	delicatessen
хліб (-у)	bread
кондви́роби (-ів)	pastries, confectionery
м'я́со (-а) ковба́си (ковба́с)	meat – sausages
ри́ба (-и)	fish
пти́ця, -і	fowl

Bread: particular types of bread include **бато́н, -а** 'long loaf, stick (white)', **паляни́ця, -і** 'oval, smallish loaf (white)', **хліб да́рницький** 'somewhat like a brown *palianytsya*', **хліб формови́й** 'shaped (squarish) loaf, "tin" '. The last cost 1080 krb. in December 1993 (a monthly salary for an experienced secondary education teacher would be around 150000 krb.).

Other prices noted at the time include:

кофемо́лка, -и	coffee grinder (electric)	75000 крб.
ча́й, -ю	tea	10500 крб. (1/100 г.)
моро́зиво, -а	ice cream	600 крб. (1/100 г.)
пломбі́р глазуро́ваний, -у -ого	sugar coated ice cream	2160 крб.
оселе́дці атланти́чні (оселе́дець, -дця, -дців)	Atlantic herring	51300 крб. (1/1 кг.)
тріска́, -и́	cod	42000 крб. (1/1 кг.)
ку́рка, -и	chicken	26000 крб.
цу́кор, -кру (за спи́ском)	sugar (if a local)	4660 крб.
ара́хіс, -у	peanuts	24410 крб. (1/1 кг.)
пе́чиво, -а «зоологі́чне»	"Zoological (!)" biscuits	5680 крб. (1/1 кор. = коро́бка, -и 'box')
пирі́г, -ога́ «ювіле́йний»	"Jubilee" tart	5140 крб.
па́ста зубна́, -и -о́ї	toothpaste	10625 крб.

Note how the prices are marked.

Breakfast cereals (the prices were not noted) included **кі́льця глазуро́вані, -лець -их** 'sugar-coated rings', a **нови́нка, -и** 'new item', and **кукуру́зні пластівці́, -их, -вців** 'corn flakes', described as **сма́чно, шви́дко, пожи́вно** 'tasty, quick, nourishing' on the packet.

Ukrainian vodka

white wine

red wine

Genitive (1): case after negative verb

While a positive verb is usually followed by the accusative case, after a negative verb one often has the genitive. One may still use the accusative, however, if the object is 'definite'. Thus:

я купи́в кни́жку	I bought a book
я не купи́в кни́жки	I didn't buy a book

But:

я не купи́в *цю* кни́жку	I didn't buy *this* book
я не купи́в *ва́шу* кни́жку	I didn't buy *your* book

Зага́дка

> **Не ма́є ні поча́тку, ні кінця́.**
> (**поча́ток, -тку** 'beginning'; **кіне́ць, -нця́** 'end')
> [The solution will be found after the section on collectives.]

Genitive (2): the 'partitive'

Where the object of a verb refers to a part of the whole, equivalent to English 'some', then the genitive may be used instead of the accusative, which is more definite. Compare:

Дай мені́ води́!	Give me some water!
Я п'ю во́ду	I drink water

Check the list of foods sold at the **база́р**, and practise this construction; say 'give (me), please, some pork, some onions, some carrots, some cheese, some cabbage'.

Collectives

Many nouns typically refer to uncountable masses, e.g. tea, coffee. Sometimes, however, if one wishes to specify 'one', a special form is needed. We can take the example of **капу́ста**, in our text, and add two more for illustration:

капу́ста	cabbage	**капусти́на**	one cabbage
цибу́ля	onions	**цибули́на**	one onion
карто́пля	potatoes	**картопли́на**	one potato

Such forms should be learned as they are encountered. Note that the stress is always on -**и́на**.

Відга́дка:	**Колесо́** 'a wheel'

To have

This verb can be rendered in a straightforward way for speakers of English by using the verb **ма́ти**, which is quite regular and takes an accusative object (or genitive, as above):

Ми ма́ємо ду́же га́рне мі́сто	We have a very nice town
Чи ти ма́єш нову́ кни́жку?	Do you have a new book?

In the present tense there is a special negative form with the meaning 'there is/are not': **нема́** or more often **нема́є**. This form must be accompanied by the genitive case of whatever is absent (this is an extremely frequent and hence an important construction!). Thus:

Сього́дні в магази́ні нема́є хлі́ба	There's no bread in the shop today

In other words, it is the negative form of **є** 'there is/are'. Note that in the future and past **бути** is used: **не бу́де**, **не було́** (the **воно́** forms). An alternative way of expressing 'to have' is to use the preposition **у/в** + genitive (of the person) plus the verb 'to be' in a suitable form:

У ме́не є вели́ка кварти́ра	I have a big flat/apartment
У те́бе бу́де до́брий словни́к	you will have a good dictionary
У не́ї була́ ціка́ва кни́жка	she had an interesting book

The construction with **ма́ти** is preferred by many:

Я ма́ю вели́ку кварти́ру	I have a big flat
Ти ма́тимеш до́брий словни́к	you will have a good dictionary
Вона́ ма́ла ціка́ву кни́жку	she had an interesting book

The negative forms of **є** (+ gen.) are a completely acceptable alternative to **ма́ти**, however:

У ме́не нема́є вели́кої кварти́ри	I don't have a big flat
У те́бе не бу́де до́брого словника́	you won't have a good dictionary
У не́ї не було́ ціка́вої кни́жки	she didn't have an interesting book

Exercise 6b

Practise using positive and negative verbs and the expression for 'to have', in order to establish firmly how these constructions work and get used to the genitive case. For example:

(a) Ма́ємо/У нас нема́є (кварти́ра, да́ча, університе́т, ка́ва, чай)
(b) Чи ти не купу́єш (газе́та, кни́жка, цу́кор, словни́к)?
(c) Я ба́чу/Не ба́чу (знайо́мий, жі́нка, демокра́т, вино́)

Exercise 6c

Make sentences using the following words (verbs in any tense); remember to use the dative, and accusative with a direct object:

він, дава́ти, я, кни́жка
що, вона́, каза́ти, вона́
ти, відповіда́ти, ми
ви, відсила́ти, він, лист
вона́, писа́ти, ми, листі́вка
я, показа́ти, вони́, маши́на

Exercise 6d

You (in the person of John) are at the market, asking the stallholders for meat and vegetables. Note: **шмато́к**, **-тка́** 'piece', **бага́то** 'much, many, a lot of' (+ genitive singular or plural as appropriate), **небага́то** and **тро́шки** 'a little' (+ genitive singular); all these words can also be used on their own. Fill in the blanks in the following dialogue as appropriate:

Джон: Добри́день!
Продаве́ць: Добри́день, па́не! Слу́хаю вас.
Джон: Чи ви . . . ку́рки?
Продаве́ць: Ні, на жаль ку́рки . . . ; але́ сього́дні є . . . .
Джон: Так; зна́чить, візьму́ . . . .
Продаве́ць: До́бре; а ще . . . ?
Джон: А ще тро́шки . . . .
Продаве́ць: Кілогра́м . . . 18 XXX.
Джон: Да́йте, . . . , кілогра́м
Продаве́ць: І ще шмато́к . . . ?
Джон: Ні, дя́кую; це вже до́сить!
Продаве́ць: Дя́кую, па́не! До поба́чення!
Джон: До поба́чення!

7 Гуля́ємо по мі́сті

We walk about the town

In this lesson you will learn about:

- verbs of motion
- prepositions and the dative case of nouns and adjectives
- expressions of time
- impersonal expressions
- describing people

The number of new words (especially for describing people) is quite large. You will need to recognize and produce many of these vocabulary items, so try to familiarize yourself with the ones that you feel apply to you.

Йдемо́ гуля́ти

Dinner's over, so a walk in the streets of Odessa precedes John's return to his hotel

МИКО́ЛА: Мені́ так приє́мно ходи́ти по цьо́му мі́сті, особли́во ко́ло О́перного теа́тру.

ДЖОН: Так. Оде́са чудо́ве мі́сто. Сього́дні вве́чері мені́ зо́всім не хо́лодно; а тобі́?

МИКО́ЛА: Мені́ тако́ж. А он та люди́на йде́ шви́дко по ву́лиці. Ма́бу́ть їй хо́лодно; або́ вона́ про́сто поспіша́є додо́му. Чи ти ма́єш (авто)маши́ну в А́нглії?

ДЖОН: Так. Я ду́же люблю́ ї́здити маши́ною по мі́сті. Тут, в Украї́ні, я наре́шті зрозумі́в, як приє́мно ходи́ти пі́шки.

МИКО́ЛА: Мо́же ми ско́ро ві́зьмемо мою́ маши́ну й пої́демо

	у Ки́їв. Уже́ час нам пої́хати туди́ й побу́ти там ти́ждень. За́втра я напишу́ листа́ дідусе́ві, дя́дькові й ті́тці. Мину́лого ро́ку батьки́ каза́ли, що мо́жна зупини́тися в них, коли́ ми бу́демо у Ки́єві. Я пообіця́в ба́тькові й ма́мі, що я ува́жно й обере́жно бу́ду ї́хати і по доро́зі і в Ки́єві.
Джон:	Як ти ду́маєш, чи мо́жна бу́де пої́хати до Льво́ва пі́сля Ки́єва?
Мико́ла:	Так, ма́бу́ть. Мо́жемо пої́хати.

Mykola:	*I so like walking around this town.*
John:	*Yes. Odessa's a wonderful town. This evening I'm not cold at all, what about you?*
Mykola:	*Me neither. But that person over there is walking quickly along the street. Perhaps he's cold; or he's simply rushing home. Do you have a car in England?*
John:	*Yes I really like driving around town by car. Here in Ukraine I've at last realized how pleasant it is to go on foot.*
Mykola:	*Perhaps we'll soon take my car and set off to Kyiv. It's already time we went there and spent a week there. Tomorrow I'll write a letter to my grandfather, uncle and aunt. Last year they told my father that we could stay with them when we would be in Kyiv. I'll promise my father and mother to drive attentively and carefully both when we're going to Kyiv and when we're in the city.*
John:	*Do you think we'll be able to go to L'viv after Kyiv?*
Mykola:	*Yes, probably. We can go.*

Vocabulary

ко́ло	near (prep. + gen.)	**той**	that (demonstrative)
о́перний теа́тр, -ого -у	opera (theatre) (**о́пера, -и** 'opera')	**поспіша́ти, -а́є-**	rush (imperf.; perf. **поспіши́ти, -и́-**)
чудо́вий	wonderful		
вве́чері, уве́чері	in the evening (adverb)	**додо́му**	home(wards) (i.e. movement towards home)
зо́всім не	not at all		
хо́лодно	cold ('it is . . .', adverbial form)	**(авто)маши́на, -и**	car; also **автомобі́ль**

маши́ною	by car (adverb; instrumental case of **маши́на**)
зрозумі́ти, -і́є-	understand (perf.)
взя́ти, візьму́, ві́зьмеш	take (perf.; imperf. **бра́ти, бере́-**)
час нам	it's time for us to . . . (+ infinitive)
зупини́тися, -и-	to stay, spend some time (perf.; imperf. **-я́є-**)
ти́ждень	for a week (also a noun, gen. **ти́жня**)
діду́сь, -я́	grandfather
дя́дько, -а	uncle
ті́тка, -и	aunt
мину́лого ро́ку	last year
ба́тько, -а	father (parents: **батьки́**)
пообіця́ти, -я́є-	promise (perf.; imperf. **обіця́ти, -я́є-**)
ува́жно	attentively (adv. from **ува́жний**)
обере́жно	carefully, cautiously (adv. from **обере́жний**)
і . . . і . . .	both . . ., and . . .
мо́жна бу́де	it will be possible/ OK

The verbs of motion

In the previous chapter we met the verbs **ї́здити** and **ходи́ти**, the former referring to movement by some means of transport and the latter referring to movement under one's own power, usually walking. **Ходи́ти** is related to **іти́/йти́**, and **ї́хати** stands in the same relationship to **ї́здити**. This is not an aspectual relationship, as both are imperfective. In the simplest terms, **ходи́ти** and **ї́здити** refer to habitual movement, movement in various directions or natural ability: they are called 'indeterminate' or 'multidirectional'. The verbs **іти́** and **ї́хати** refer to movement in a specific direction at a specific time, and tend to correspond to the progressive forms of English, e.g. 'I am going'; they are called 'determinate' or 'unidirectional'. The present tenses are:

ї́здити	**ї́хати**	**ходи́ти**	**іти́/йти́**
ї́жджу	**ї́ду**	**ходжу́**	**іду́/йду́**
ї́здиш	**ї́деш**	**хо́диш**	**іде́ш/йде́ш**
ї́здить	**ї́де**	**хо́дить**	**іде́/йде́**
ї́здимо	**ї́демо**	**хо́димо**	**ідемо́/йдемо́**
ї́здите	**ї́дете**	**хо́дите**	**ідете́/йдете́**
ї́здять	**ї́дуть**	**хо́дять**	**іду́ть/йду́ть**

Be careful to differentiate **ї́ду** from **іду́/йду́**, as they are very close in sound; note also that the determinates are conjugation I (**е**), while the indeterminates are conjugation II (**и**). The nearest equivalents to perfectives are **піти́** and **пої́хати**, often with a sense of 'to set off'. Now examine again how these verbs are used in the preceding dialogue: 'walk around the city' (**ходи́ти**), 'drive around the city' (**ї́здити**), 'set off for (by vehicle)' (**пої́хати**), emphasis on the process of getting to a place (here by vehicle) (**ї́хати**): here Mykola is saying 'when I am in the process of going (future) to Kyiv'. Compare the following examples:

Я люблю́ ходи́ти пі́шки.
Куди́ йде́ш, Окса́но? Йду́ додо́му.
Де Іва́н, Мико́ло? Він пішо́в до робо́ти ('work').
Коли́ ї́деш до робо́ти, ти чита́єш газе́ту? Так, в поїзді.

A diagram can help fix the use of these verbs in your memory:

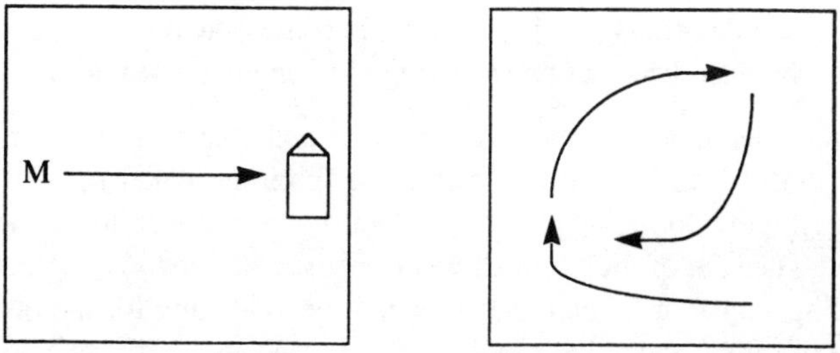

Мико́ла йде́ додо́му
Мико́ла ї́де додо́му.

Він/вона́ хо́дить по мі́сті.
Він/вона́ ї́здить по мі́сті.

Dative of nouns and adjectives

The dative singular of adjectives and possessive and demonstrative pronouns is straightforward: it is identical with the locative for the feminines and with the **-ому** form of the locative for the masculines and neuters:

Masculine and neuter	*Feminine*
украї́нському	**украї́нській**
спра́вжньому	**спра́вжній**
ї́хньому	**ї́хній**
моє́му	**мої́й**
на́шому	**на́шій**
тому́	**тій** (from **той** 'that')
цьому́	**цій** (from **цей** 'this')

As regards the noun, the dative of feminines is identical with the locative, but there is no such identity in the masculines and neuters. So, for the feminines:

ма́ма becomes **ма́мі**	**стаття́** becomes **статті́**
Аме́рика becomes **Аме́риці**	**столи́ця** becomes **столи́ці**
А́нглія becomes **А́нглії**	**ка́ша** becomes **ка́ші**
о́сінь 'autumn' becomes **о́сені**	**піч** 'oven' becomes **пе́чі**

You can generalize from these examples; note that **ка́ші** and **пе́чі** cover all feminines where the stem-final consonant is **ш**, **ж**, **щ** or **ч**.

For the neuters the ending is not complicated. Nouns ending in **-о** take the ending **-у**, as do those ending in **-ше**, **-ще**, **-же** and **-че**. All others ending in **-е**, and those ending in **-я**, take **-ю**. Thus:.

вікно́ becomes **вікну́**	**мі́сце** becomes **мі́сцю**
плече́ 'shoulder' becomes **плечу́**	**здоро́в'я** becomes **здоро́в'ю**

The masculines may have the same endings as the neuters (but remember that those ending in **-а**, **-я** follow the feminine pattern), with the important qualification that there is another more or less optional ending available. The rule of thumb in choosing between the two is to take the new ending, **-ові**, for human animates and the **-у** ending for the others. Some authorities generalize **-ові** (and its variants **-еві**, **-єві**) to all instances where there would be a choice. Some examples:

ба́тько becomes **ба́тькові**	**ніж** 'knife' becomes **ножу́ (-є́ві)**
учи́тель becomes **учи́телеві**	**край** becomes **краю́ (-є́ві)**
студе́нт becomes **студе́нтові**	**Мико́ла** becomes **Мико́лі**
маля́р becomes **маляре́ві**	

Nouns in **-ар/-яр** have some 'soft endings'

Exercise 7a

Form sentences from the words below without looking back at the previous chapter; do so only if you need reminding (e.g. of verbs and pronominal forms).

(a) да́ти, ба́тько, ціка́вий, кни́жка, за́втра
(b) ма́ма, відповісти́, я
(c) профе́сор, студе́нт, сказа́ти, що, екза́мен, нема́є
(d) лю́ди, посла́ти, по́друга, листи́, в, Украї́на, з, А́нглія
(e) вона́, купи́ти, дити́на, ні́чо́го

(f) інженéр, покáзувати, ми, завóд
(g) хто, ти, писáти, лист
(h) мáма, зáвжди, розповідáти, він, про, дáвній, Украї́на

Prepositions

In the preceding dialogue we met the preposition **по** in the sense 'over, along, all around', followed by the locative case (in Kyiv **по мі́сту** is preferred):

Ї́здити по мі́сті **ходи́ти по мі́сті** **ходи́ти по ву́лиці**

Note that we use **ходи́ти** even when it does not mean 'walking around', but 'along'; a person might walk along a certain street habitually, as compared to being in the process of walking along a street, which would have to be expressed by means of **йти́**.

With regard to the very few dative prepositions, we can mention **к**, meaning 'to, towards' in a spatial sense and 'towards' in a temporal sense in the set phrase **Я послáв її к бі́су** 'I sent her to the devil' (**біс** 'devil') and **к кінцю́ ти́жня** 'towards the end of the week' (**кінéць** 'end'). But it is restricted to a few colloquial set phrases, and is readily replaced by other prepositions, e.g. **до** + gen. and **під** + acc., respectively, in the two expressions given here.

Expressions of time

Note how one can build up expressions of time. We have had **сьогóдні ввéчері**. On that pattern we can replace **сьогóдні** with **зáвтра** 'tomorrow' and **учóра** 'yesterday', **ввéчері** with **урáнці** and so on. Notice how indispensable the genitive case is! We can replace **мину́лого**, in **мину́лого рóку**, with **насту́пного**, giving **насту́пного рóку** 'next year', **цьогó**, giving **цьогó рóку** 'this year'. And by prefixing **що**- to a genitive we get 'every . . .', e.g. **щовéчора** 'every evening'. When an expression of time overall means 'during', one may also use the accusative on its own, thus **ти́ждень** '(for) a week':

Цьогó рóку ми прочитáли цікáву кни́жку.	This year we read (and finished) an interesting book.
Мину́лого/цьогó/насту́пного ти́жня я не (диви́вся/дивлю́ся/диви́тимуся) телеві́зора.	Last/this/next week I (didn't/don't/won't watch) television.

Я читáла цю книжку ці́лий тиждень/прóтягом тиждня, алé на жаль, не встигла прочитáти її́ до кінця́.	I read this book for a whole week, but unfortunately didn't manage to read it to the end.

(**ці́лий** 'a whole'; **прóтягом** 'during' + gen.; **встигáти**, **-áє-**, perf. **встигнути**, **-гне- встиг(ла)** 'to manage to')

More expressions of time will come up in future lessons; for the moment you should learn them as you come across them, in the senses they have in the dialogues and texts.

Impersonal expressions

One of the most important uses of the dative case in Ukrainian is in 'impersonal' constructions. In such constructions there is no obvious subject. If a verb is present, it will be in the third person singular; if there is no verb, an adverbial form is present and expresses some physical or psychological state. The person in such constructions is in the dative case. Compare:

мені́ здає́ться	it seems to me (Eng. 'I think')
Івáнові хóлодно	Ivan is cold (lit. 'it is cold to Ivan')
їй тéпло	she is warm (lit. 'it is warm to her')
нам мóжна?	are we allowed? (lit. 'is it possible/ permissible for us?')
йомý трéба . . .	he has to . . . (lit. 'it is necessary for him . . .')

In this dialogue we encountered three impersonal expressions, in each of which the 'subject' may be expressed in the dative case. Thus:

їй хóлодно	she's cold, lit. 'to her it is cold'
нам час	it's time for us . . .
сестрі́ мóжна	my sister can/may, lit. 'to sister it is possible/ OK'

To express future or past time, we simply add **бýде** or **булó**, often after the impersonal expression, e.g. **Сестрі́ мóжна бýде** . . . . Impersonal expressions with a sense of 'can, may, might, must, ought to' are often referred to as modals (see *12*). These phrases are also frequently used without reference to a particular individual (i.e. without the use of a pronoun or person), in which case the English will contain a 'dummy *it*':

хóлодно	it's cold
трéба піти́ додóму	(I) have to go home (it is necessary)
там не мóжна кури́ти	there one may not (it is not allowed to) smoke
Чи в Одéсі тéпло?	is it warm in Odessa?

These constructions are extremely common in Ukrainian. Don't 'think English' in such cases, as an English phrase of the kind 'I am cold' translated directly into Ukrainian could mean something like 'I am a cold person', having nothing to do with the temperature.

Exercise 7b

Now for a few jumbled sentences. It's useful to know that, because the word order of Ukrainian is quite flexible, there are often several possibilities. However, there are some things that are less, or even not at all, flexible (e.g. placing of prepositions and adjectives).

(a) мíсті, ї́здить, Натáлка, чáсто, по, маши́ною
(b) дя́дько, дáчі, живу́ть, ті́тка, на, та
(c) стіл, ку́хні, накривáв, булá, коли́, Микóла, Оксáна, на, в
(d) товáришеві, що, Івáн, вели́ку, здаéться, мáє, маши́ну, йогó
(e) квартúрі, булó, бáткові, Натáлки, приє́мно, в

You may wish to add a comma to (c) and (d).

Vocabulary building

The adjective

In *6* we met the adjective **багатоповерхóвий** 'multistoreyed'. The word **багáт**- 'much, many' is linked by -**о**- to **пóверх** 'floor, storey', to which is suffixed -**ов**- (extremely common in the formation of adjectives) and the ending. Compare:

випадкóвий 'accidental, chance'	**ви́пад(о)к + -ов-** 'accident, chance'
добросéрдий 'good-hearted'	**дóбр(ий) + -о- + серд-** (**сéрце** 'heart')
довгобoрóдий 'long-bearded'	**дóвг(ий) + -о- + бород-** (**бородá** 'beard')

Describing people

Here we concentrate on people's physical appearance; in the next chapter we look at what people wear. The verb 'to describe' is **опи́сувати**, **-ує-**, perf. **описа́ти**, **-ше-**. One form used if you want to request a description of someone is:

Опиши́, будь ла́ска, (Миха́йла/ Окса́ну . . .)!	(if you are on **ти**-terms)
Опиши́, будь ла́ска, (твого́ дру́га/твою́ по́другу)!	(if you are on **ти**-terms)
Опиши́ його́/її́, будь ла́ска!	(if you are on **ти**-terms)

If you are **ви** terms, replace **опиши́** with **опиші́ть!** Note that the object pronoun comes immediately after the verb.

In case this might seem rather direct, you can increase the politeness of your request by using a negative question or by using the verb **вигляда́ти** 'to look like' (see p. 335 for the constructions). For example:

Чи ви не могли́ б його́ описа́ти?	(lit. Wouldn't you be able to describe him?
Як Ната́лка вигляда́є?	What (lit. how) does Natalka look like?

The form **могли́ б** is a conditional, made up simply of the past tense and the particle **б** (after a vowel) or **би** (after a consonant). For the moment just learn it as a formula. Should you be so polite with someone with whom you are on **ти**-terms, then the form would be **міг би (ти)** (masculine) or **могла́ б (ти)** (feminine). To all these requests you can simply respond by saying 'He/She is . . .' **Він/Вона́** . . .

вродли́вий	**вродли́ва**	handsome, beautiful
краси́вий	**краси́ва**	handsome, beautiful
симпати́чний	**симпати́чна**	nice, likeable
ми́лий	**ми́ла**	nice, pleasant
прива́бливий	**прива́блива**	attractive
непоказни́й	**непоказна́**	plain-looking
висо́кий	**висо́ка**	tall
невисо́кий	**невисо́ка**	not tall, short
мале́нький	**мале́нька**	small, short
по́вний	**по́вна**	stout
дебе́лий	**дебе́ла**	plump
худи́й	**худа́**	thin

стрункий	**стрункá**	slim
тендітний	**тендітна**	soft, gentle, fine

Note **висóкий** and **невисóкий**. If you cannot think of the antonym, prefixing **не-** will usually work – **не-** does often give a particular nuance (as does 'not' in English!), but your message should get across. There is, too, the possibility of using nouns and fixed expressions instead of adjectives, e.g. **крáсень** 'a handsome man', **красýня** 'a beautful woman', **висóкого зрóсту** 'tall' (lit 'of high stature'), **низькóго зрóсту** 'short, small' (lit. 'of low stature') (these last two could also be in response to the questions **Якúй він/Якá вонá на зріст?** or **Якóго він/вонá зрóсту?**).

We also need to know the words for a few of the parts of the body and their grammatical gender. Here, with gender noted where necessary, are a few such words:

Vocabulary

головá, -ú (acc. **гóлову,** pl. **-и**)	head	**ніс, нóса**	nose
волóсся, -я, neut.	hair	**рот, -а**	mouth
облúччя, -я, neut.	face	**плечé, -á** (pl. **плéчі, -éй**)	shoulder
óчі, очéй (instr. **очúма**)	eyes (sing. **óко, -а**)	**рукá, -ú** (acc. **рýку,** pl. **-и**)	arm, hand
щокá, -ú (pl. **щóки**)	cheek	**ногá, -ú** (acc. **нóгу,** pl. **-и**)	leg, foot

To ask 'what sort of . . . does she have?', we use an appropriate form of **якúй** 'what sort of . . .?' and one of the now familiar expressions for 'to have'. Thus:

Якé вонá мáє волóсся? or **Якé в нéї волóсся?**	What sort of hair does she have?

Here we have **якé**, because **волóсся** is neuter and singular (cf. **якúй**, **якá**, **які**). To answer the questions, we just remove **якúй** and supply an adjective:

Вонá мáє . . . волóсся or **У нéї . . . волóсся**	She has . . . hair.

So

Які́й він ма́є ніс? **Він ма́є до́вгий ніс.**

Які́й у не́ї рот? **Вона́ ма́є краси́вий рот.**

Here are a few more useful adjectives, in addition to those you have already seen:

Vocabulary

руди́й	red (hair)	**рум'я́ний**	red, rosy (cheeks)
си́вий	grey (hair)	**бруна́тний**	brown (hair)
біля́вий	blond, light-coloured	**те́мний**	dark
		вузьки́й	narrow
широ́кий	broad	**квадра́тний**	square
кру́глий	round	**бліди́й**	pale
смагля́вий	tanned	**зеле́ний**	green
блаки́тний	blue	**сі́рий**	grey (eyes)
чо́рний	black	**вто́млений**	tired
ка́рий	brown (eyes)	**орли́ний**	aquiline
прями́й	straight	**коротки́й**	short
до́вгий	long	**го́стрий**	sharp
кирпа́тий	flat, snub-nosed		

Exercise 7c

Your Ukrainian friend asks «як вигляда́є твій ба́тько?». How would you describe your father (or your parents, a sibling or a spouse) using these three sets of vocabulary? Try it!

Reading

Вече́ря в ку́хні

Оле́на й Миха́йло лю́блять ра́зом готува́ти ї́жу в ку́хні. Вони́ ма́ють просто́ру ку́хню. Там вони́ сні́дають, і́нколи обі́дають (коли́ не працю́ють), і ма́йже за́вжди вече́ряють. Але́ коли́ в них дру́зі, вони́ ї́дя́ть у віта́льні. У ку́хні вони́ ма́ють га́зову плиту́, холоди́льник, та ша́фу для по́суду. У ша́фі лежа́ть ножі́, виде́лки, ло́жки́ й ложечки́, стоя́ть тарі́лки́, підста́вочки, склянки́ й філіжа́нки. Вве́чері стіл покривáють чи́стою скатерти́ною. Врáнці, коли́ трéба поспішáти на робóту, їдя́ть нашвидкýрýч. На снідáнок Олéна їсть чóрний хліб і сир; Михáйло – вáрене яйцé і білий хліб. Він п'є чай без цýкру із філіжáнки; Олéна п'є кáву з чáшки. Звичáйно вони́ обідають у їдáльні на завóді. Після робóти абó Михáйло абó Олéна купýє продýкти: салáт, помідóри, ковбасý, ри́бу, сіль, пéрець, картóплю, мóркву тóщо. Вдóма все готýють, накривáють на стіл, сідáють до стóлу й вечéряють. Як і ли́чить, зáвжди́ берýть сервéтки; чáсом паперóві, чáсом з льóну.

Алé вони́ не зáвжди́ вечéряють удóма. Íнколи хóдять до ресторáну, чáсом батьки́, дрýзі абó діти запрóшують їх на вечéрю. Їм приє́мно побýти чи ресторáні чи помéшканні близьки́х людéй. Назáвтра їх запроси́ли в гóсті, алé вони́ ще не ви́рішили, чи підуть пішки чи поїдуть автомаши́ною. Оцé так проблéма!

Vocabulary

ра́зом	together; (all) at once (adv.)
просто́рий	spacious
дру́зі, -ів	friends (non-standard nom. pl.; from **друг**, **-а**)
га́зова плита́, -ої -и́	gas cooker (Amer. stove)
холоди́льник, -а	refrigerator
ша́фа, -и	cupboard (for dishes and cutlery: **для по́суду**)
ніж, но́жа	knife
виде́лка, -и	fork
ло́жка, -и	(table)spoon
ло́жечка, -и	(tea)spoon
тарі́лка, -и	plate
підста́вочка, -и	small plate, saucer
скля́нка, -и	glass
філіжа́нка, -и	cup
ча́шка, -и	cup
покрива́ти, -а́є-	cover (imperf.)
скатерти́на, -и (or **ска́терть, -і**, fem.)	tablecloth
тре́ба	it is necessary (impers.; + dat.)
робо́та, -и	work (**пра́ця** 'labour')
ва́рений	boiled (agreeing with **яйце́, -я**)
яйце́, -я́	egg
бі́лий	white (adj.)
без цу́кру	without sugar (**без** + gen. 'without', **цу́кор**)
сала́т, -у	salad
ковбаса́, -и́	sausage
ри́ба, -и	fish
сіль, со́лі fem.	salt
пе́рець, -рцю masc.	pepper
все	everything (nom./acc. sing. neut. of **(у)весь**, **вся**, **все**, **всі** 'all')
як і ли́чить	as is appropriate, proper, befitting
серве́тка, -и	napkin
паперо́вий	(made of) paper
з льо́ну	(made of) linen (gen. of **льон**)
рестора́н, -у	restaurant
батьки́, -і́в	parents (pl. of **ба́тько**)
запро́шувати, -ує-	invite (imperf.; perf. **запроси́ти**, **-и-**)
ді́ти, -е́й	children (singular **дити́на**, **-и**)
поме́шкання, -я	flat, apartment of several rooms; dwelling
нашвидку́ру́ч	hastily (adv.)
близькі́ лю́ди, -и́х, -е́й	people close to them
наза́втра	for tomorrow
в го́сті	'to stay, as guests' (with verbs of motion invitation; cf. **у го́стях**)
пробле́ма -и	problem

Зага́дки

Без чо́го жо́дна річ не мо́же бу́ти?
(**річ, ре́чі** 'thing'; **жо́ден** 'no, not a' (note the 'double negative'))
Де є міста́ без буді́вель і рі́ки без води́?
(**буді́вля, -влі** 'building'; **рiка́, -и́** 'river')
[The solutions will be found after the exercises.]

Exercise 7d

Fill in the gaps in the following sentences:

(a) Ната́лка . . . стіл.
(b) За́втра вони́ . . . у К. . . .
(c) . . . тре́ба з'ї́сти щось; я таки́й . . . .
(d) Ма́рта за . . . мене́ на обі́д.
(e) Ма́ма живе́ дале́ко, на д. . . , але́ ми ча́сто . . . до не́ї.
(f) . . . здає́ться, що він наре́шті зн. . . ключ.
(g) Я купи́в карто́плю й цибу́лю, але́ на база́рі не . . . си́ру.
(h) Я вважа́ю, що вже до́сить до́бре . . . укр. . . .

(**вважа́ти**, **-а́є-** 'consider, think'; better in this context than **ду́мати**)

Exercise 7e

Express these sentences in Ukrainian:

(a) Oksana found her key when she was walking along the street.
(b) We've decided to set off to Kyiv by car tomorrow.
(c) Petro lives nearby, in the centre of the town.
(d) It's time to eat, because soon I must go to the factory.
(e) It seems to them that they may do nothing; they simply lie in the park.
(f) This evening I want to go to the new restaurant.
(g) She was writing a letter when he decided to have some supper.
(h) What is the point of my sitting at home?
(i) I'm cold!
(j) We have to go home now.

Exercise 7f

Tell a Ukrainian friend about an evening out; you arrived at a flat/apartment, said 'hello' to the people living there, sat down in the lounge (Amer. den), then went to the table to eat. Remember your etiquette: what did you say when beginning to eat and what did you say when you finished? What did your host say in response? What did you eat and drink?

Відга́дки: Без на́зви 'without a name'; **На ка́рті** 'on a map'

8 Ї́демо до Ки́єва

We go to Kyiv

In this lesson you will learn about:

- 'one's own'
- more expressions of time and impersonals
- the instrumental case
- more nominative plurals
- clothing
- the use of the numerals 1–4 (and multiples thereof)

Please note that from this lesson onwards, we do not translate the dialogues. You are now 'on your own'!

Пої́дьмо!

John and Mykola continue to discuss their trip to Kyiv; John is now in a hurry and has some doubts as to the mode of travel

Джон: Ну, коли́ ми пої́демо до Ки́єва? Мо́же за́втра?

Мико́ла: Чи ти хо́чеш ї́хати так ско́ро?

Джон: Так, якнайскорі́ше. Я вже закінчи́в свою́ робо́ту тут.

Мико́ла: А коли́ ти поверта́єшся до Англії?

Джон: За мі́сяць тре́ба поверну́тися.

Мико́ла: Так. Розумі́ю. Зна́чить, пої́демо за́втра. Між і́ншим, моя́ маши́на гото́ва.

Джон: Слу́хай, а мо́же ї́демо не маши́ною, а по́їздом?

Мико́ла: По́їздом!? Чому́?

Джон: Якщо́ пої́демо по́їздом, змо́жемо розмовля́ти, диви́тися се́ла . . .

Мико́ла: Ну я не зна́ю.

Джон: До́бре, до́бре. А авто́бусом? Літако́м?

Мико́ла: Що!? Ти не хо́чеш зі мно́ю маши́ною?

Джон: Хо́чу, хо́чу! Я ду́мав ті́льки, що мо́же тобі́ бу́де

	ле́гше, якщо́ ми не пої́демо а́втом. Але́, звича́йно, я хо́чу з тобо́ю!
Мико́ла:	Зна́чить маши́ною. А Окса́на тако́ж ї́де з на́ми. Вона́ гото́ва?
Джон:	Так, ми з не́ю говори́ли про доро́гу в Ки́їв сього́дні вра́нці.
Мико́ла:	Ду́маю, що нам бу́де ду́же ве́село, як ти гада́єш?
Джон:	Пе́вно, що так!

Vocabulary

ско́ро	soon (adverb)	**пої́зд, -у**	train (also **по́тяг, -а**)
якнайскорі́ше	as soon as possible: **як-най-скорі́ше**	**якщо́**	if
		село́, -а́	village
закінчи́ти, -и́-	finish (perf.; imperf. **кінча́ти, -а́є-**	**авто́бус, -а**	bus
		літа́к, -а́	aeroplane (airplane)
свій	one's (own)	**ле́гше**	easier, more easily
поверта́тися, -а́є-, поверну́тися, -не-	return (imperf. and perf., respectively)	**доро́га, -и**	way, trip, journey
		ве́село	pleasant, fun (adv.)
за + acc.	in (time)		
мі́сяць, -я	month	**гада́ти, -а́є-**	(here) think, be of the opinion
між і́ншим	by the way		
гото́в, -а, -е	ready, prepared (cf. **готува́ти, -у́є-**)	**пра́вда, -и**	(lit.) truth; (here) it is true
слу́хай!	listen! (imperative of **слу́хати, -ає-**)	**пе́вно**	certain(ly), it's certain

Свій

To the possessives already encountered we now add **свій**, which is declined just like **мій** and **твій**; in essence it can be used in place of any possessive pronoun, but it emphasizes 'one's own'. In the dialogue, for instance, it is found instead of **мій (мою́)**; in the 1st and 2nd persons its use is purely optional, so **мою́** would have been fine. Where this possessive is critical is in the third persons, that is, where we would say 'his, her, its, their'. **Свій** always refers back to the subject of the clause, whereas **його́ ї́ї ї́хній** will refer to someone else, or at least be ambiguous. Compare the following examples:

я узя́в свою́ кни́жку is synonymous with **я узя́в мою́ кни́жку**
ти узя́в свою́ кни́жку is synonymous with **ти узя́в твою́ кни́жку**

But

вона́ взяла́ свою́ кни́жку means	*she took her (own) book*
вона́ взяла́ її́ кни́жку means	*she took her (someone else's) book*

Expressions of time: За and Че́рез + acc.

За + acc., in its meaning of 'completing something in a certain time', is very useful. **Че́рез** + acc. is extremely common: this construction allows you to say that you will do or did XY or Z after a specified length of time:

Че́рез ти́ждень/рік/мі́сяць я пої́ду додо́му.	In/after a week/ year/ month I shall go (set off) for home.
Че́рез день я поїхала додо́му.	After a day I went (set off for) home.

Ellipsis

One of the interesting things that you will no doubt notice is that words can sometimes be left out, as they are implied by other elements in the sentence. Thus, in **Поїдьмо!**, we find **Ти не хо́чеш зі мно́ю маши́ною?** answered by **Але́, звича́йно, хо́чу з тобо́ю!** What's missing? Context clearly tells us that a verb is missing, in this case a verb of motion: 'Don't you want [to go] with me by car?' 'But of course I want [to go] with you'. Such verbal economy is frequent, and English usually supplies the dummy word 'to' or verb 'do' in such instances: 'of course I do want to', 'of course I do'.

More impersonals

Here are more useful impersonal constructions with the dative case found in the dialogue:

тобі́ ле́гше	it is easier for you
нам бу́де ве́село	it will be fun for us (we will have fun)

The instrumental case

The seventh and final case used in Ukrainian is known as the instrumental. As its name implies, one of the uses of this case is to express the means by which an action is carried out, focusing on the instrument. So, in descriptions of hitting a nail with a hammer, stirring coffee with a spoon, or writing with a pencil, the instrument or implement used (hammer, spoon, pencil) will be in this case; in these examples English 'with' could be replaced by 'by means of'. The instrumental case is also used with a number of common prepositions and verbs. The singular forms of this case are as follows:

Masculine/Neuter

Nom.	**дру́г**	**мі́сто**	**лист**	**перо́**	**олівéць**
Instr.	**дру́гом**	**мі́стом**	**листо́м**	**перо́м**	**олівцéм**
Nom.	**това́риш**	**прі́звище**	**життя́**	**мі́сце**	
Instr.	**това́ришем**	**прі́звищем**	**життя́м**	**мі́сцем**	

In other words, neuter nouns add **-м** to the final vowel of the nominative, no matter what the vowel is (**-о**, **-е** or **-я**), while a vowel – **-о** or **-е**, depending on the final consonant – has to be supplied for masculines: thus, **-ом/-ем** are added to the stem. Stress follows patterns already established (when in doubt check the genitive!). The instrumental ending for the corresponding adjectives is **-им/-ім**.

Feminine

Nom.	**кни́жка**	**ву́лиця**	**голова́**	**ніч**	**-ність**
Instr.	**кни́жкою**	**ву́лицею**	**голово́ю**	**ні́ччю**	**-ністю**

In the feminine, final **-а/-я** are replaced by **-ою/-ею**. Feminines ending in a single consonant lengthen it (that is, it is doubled in writing) before the ending **-ю**; note that forms which have a vowel alternation in other cases (**ніч** – **но́чі**) do not have it in the instrumental. The adjective ending in the instrumental is the same as for the noun: **до́брою кни́жкою, си́ньою водо́ю**. Note that adjectival **-ою** occurs with soft as well as hard consonants. The instrumental of the personal pronouns is:

мно́ю
тобо́ю
ним (masc./neut.)
не́ю (fem.)
на́ми
ва́ми
ни́ми

One basic meaning of this case is 'with'; there is also a preposition **з** that means 'with', used in the preceding lesson. Right from the start, learn to keep apart the constructions with and without the preposition: **з** is required only when the meaning is 'in the company of, together with'. Compare the following sentences:

by means of (action x using object y)

Я пишу́ олівце́м	I write *with a pencil*
Оле́кса працю́є мо́лотом	Oleksa works *with a hammer*
Він узя́в кни́жку однією руко́ю	He took the book *with one hand*

together with (person/object x with person/object y)

Я п'ю чай з цу́кром	I drink tea with sugar
Окса́на була́ вдо́ма з О́льгою	Oksana was home with Ol'ha
***ми* з бра́том були́ у Ки́єві**	My brother and I were in Kyiv
***ви* з бра́том були́ у Ки́єві**	You and your brother were in Kyiv
***вони́* з бра́том були́ у Ки́єві**	*He/She* and *his/her* brother were in Kyiv

In Ukrainian the words 'my brother and I' might sound stilted; instead you should use the plural pronoun in place of the singular + **з** + instrumental of the other person: lit. 'we and my brother'. Conceptually the two people are considered to form a unit or group. In the example **ви з бра́том**, then, we would find **ви** whether you were on **ти** or **ви** terms with the other speaker; only context can tell us who is involved in the last example given. Note the example used in the dialogue: **ми з не́ю поговори́ли** 'she and I had a talk'.

The preposition **з** has the spelling variants **з, (із) зі**, depending on the following sound or combination of sounds:

з тобо́ю
з Оле́ксою
зі мно́ю
(із/з сі́ллю)

Among other common prepositions governing the instrumental are a number having to do with precise location (NB: if movement is conveyed, the accusative must be used after them):

пе́ред	in front of
за	behind, by means of, according to
між	between, among
над	above
під	under

Compare the following examples, noting especially the accusative form:

Пéред вáми вýлиця Шевчéнка.
За нáшим будúнком є велúкий парк.
Він пішóв за будúнок і побáчив парк.
Між парком і будúнком грáють дíти. (**грáти**: to play)

Finally, there are several very common verbs that can require the use of this case, of which we give two examples:

говорúти англíйською (мóвою)	to speak (in) English
цікáвитися математúкою	to be interested in mathematics

The second example expresses being interested by something (compare 'by means of what?' above) and is extremely useful when getting to know someone:

Чим ти цікáвишся?	What are you interested in?
Я цікáвлюся спóртом та мýзикою. А ти?	I am interested in sport and music. And you?

Other verbs of this nature will occur later.

Загáдка

Вéчір чим кінчáється, а рáнок чим починáється?
(**рáнок, -нку** 'morning')
[The solution can be found after the exercise.]

Exercise 8a

The following verbs and verb phrases (column 1) can be used with or require the use of the instrumental; match them up with suitable objects (column 2) and put the latter into the instrumental case (some may work with more than one):

(a) Я розмовляю	молокó
(b) Я пишý	машúна
(c) Ми займáємося	будúнок
(d) Ти цікáвишся	англíйська мóва
(e) Я їду	рýчка (pen)
(f) Я не працюю	мýзика
(g) Я стою пéред	прáця
(h) Я п'ю кáву з	зимá

Відга́дка: Бу́квою «р» 'with the letter ' "r" '

More on the nominative plural

In 5 we gave you the nominative plural endings. As we showed then in reference to neuter nouns, it is the place of stress that often differentiates the nominative plural from the genitive singular: the stress may be in the same place in the nominative and genitive singular, then shift in the nominative plural. The following are only a few of the neuter and feminine forms you have already seen that follow this pattern:

Nominative Singular	*Genitive Singular*	*Nominative Plural*
дочка́	**дочки́**	**до́чки**
мі́сто	**мі́ста**	**міста́**
мі́сце	**мі́сця**	**місця́**
вікно́	**вікна́**	**ві́кна**
тарі́лка	**тарі́лки**	**тарілки́**
скля́нка	**скля́нки**	**склянки́**
ча́шка	**ча́шки**	**чашки́**
яйце́	**яйця́**	**я́йця**
ковбаса́	**ковбаси́**	**ковба́си**

There are also many forms that are identical in the genitive singular and the nominative plural. For example:

пробле́ма: ***пробле́ми*** **· стра́ва :** ***стра́ви*** **· ву́лиця :** ***ву́лиці***

Some plural forms appear to be irregular. As it happens, these forms are often extremely common words: compare the 'child-children' and 'person-people' pairs in English. The following are among those most often found:

друг, дру́зі	friend, friends (expected **-ги**)
ба́тько, батьки́	father, fathers/parents (expected: **-а**)
люди́на, лю́ди	person, people
дити́на, ді́ти	child, children
пан, пани́	Mr, gentlemen, (but voc. **пано́ве!**)

All the words with the suffix **-анин** in the nominative singular lose the final **-ин** throughout the plural paradigm, but have the regular nominative plural **-и: росія́нин, росія́ни** 'a Russian, Russians'.

Exercise 8b

Identify the case of the following (nominative singular, genitive singular or nominative plural – some may be more than one!); try not to look back at the grammatical explanations until after you have given an answer.

вікнá; мíсця; дрýга; кни́жка; маши́ни; листá; буди́нки; ім'я́; прáця; рýчки; мíста; здорóв'я

Ми мáємо бензи́н!

The threesome are in the car, having waited a long time to fill up the car's tank; they are now on their way out of Odessa

МИКÓЛА: Нарéшті мáємо дóсить бензи́ну. Дóбре, що знайшли́ бензоколóнку. В дорóгу! Готóві?

ОКСÁНА: Так. Мені́ сподóбалася Одéса, алé тепéр я хóчу подиви́тися столи́цю.

ДЖОН: Я згóден. Микóло, я не знáю геогрáфії Украї́ни: чи до Ки́єва далéко чи бли́зько?

МИКÓЛА: На жаль дýже далéко; нам трéба бýде дóвго ї́хати, принаймні оди́н день, можли́во нáвіть ці́лу добý.

ОКСÁНА: Це нічóго! Спáти мóжна в Ки́єві; я цікáвлюся прирóдою, всім. Чи ми бýдемо ї́хати лíсом?

МИКÓЛА: Ні, по дорóзі ті́льки степ, алé в Украї́ні ще є гáрні ліси́; ви побáчите вели́кі поля́, сéла, і малéнькі і вели́кі, та містá.

ДЖОН: Які́?

МИКÓЛА: Напри́клад Вікторі́вка, У́мань, Бі́ла Цéрква, Васи́льків; Васи́льків вже бли́зько від Ки́єва.

ОКСÁНА: Чи побáчимо ми теж вели́кі містá?

МИКÓЛА: Так, Бі́ла Цéрква та У́мань – це дóсить вели́кі містá.

ДЖОН: Ой, подиви́ся, Оксáно! Ї́демо тепéр селóм! Мені́ здаéться, що там є ті́льки три абó чоти́ри буди́нки, алé я мóжу помиля́тися.

ОКСÁНА: Чим займáються люди в такóму селі́?

МИКÓЛА: Звичáйно сі́льським господáрством; алé життя́ тут ще дóсить старосві́тське.

ОКСА́НА: Гово́рять, що життя́ тепе́р особли́во важке́.

МИКО́ЛА: Це пра́вильно. Працю́ють ти́жні, мі́сяці, ро́ки́, але́ ма́ло ма́ють. Потребу́ємо те́хніки (комба́йнів то́що), а, о́тже, чима́ло гро́шей. Коли́ ї́деш таки́м село́м, почина́єш розумі́ти стан справ у суча́сній Украї́ні.

Vocabulary

до́сить	(here) enough (of)	**життя́, -я́** (neut.)	life
бензи́н, -у	petrol, (Amer.) gasoline	**старосві́тський**	old-fashioned: **старо**- 'old' + **світ**- 'world'
бензоколо́нка, -и	petrol station/pump	**особли́во**	especially
в доро́гу!	en route!	**пра́вильно**	correct (impers.)
зго́ден	agreed: **я зго́ден** 'I agree'	**мі́сяць, -я**	month
		рік, ро́ку	year
геогра́фія, -ї	geography	**те́хніка, -и**	technology
принаймні	at least	**комба́йн, -у**	combine harvester
на́віть	even (adverb)	**о́тже**	consequently
ці́лий	whole	**чима́ло**	quite a lot of, a great deal of (+ gen.)
доба́, -и́	day (period of 24 hours)		
спа́ти, спить	to sleep	**гро́ші, -ей**	money (only plural)
ввесь, все, вся (у-)	all; instr. sg. masc./neut. **всім**	**почина́ти, -а́є-**	to begin (imperf.) (perf. **поча́ти, -не́-**; note that, like **кінча́ти/закінчи́ти** 'to finish', the infinitive that follows is always imperfective)
приро́да, -и	nature		
степ, -у	steppe		
ті́льки	only (adverb)		
ліс, -а	forest, woods		
по́ле, -я	field		
помиля́тися, -я́є-	to be mistaken (imperf.; perf. **помили́тися, -и-**)		
займа́тися, -а́є-	to be occupied with (imperf.); +instr.	**стан, -у справ**	situation, state of affairs
		суча́сний	modern
звича́йно	(here) usually		
сільське́ господа́рство	agriculture		

Reminders

Several forms in the dialogue reflect grammatical points discussed recently; among these forms are:

1	**до́сить бензи́ну**	the partitive genitive, "enough of" petrol
2	**у доро́гу**	implied verb, '[let's get] to the road!'
3	**не зна́ю геогра́фії**	negated object in the genitive
4	**поля́, се́ла, міста́**	neuter plurals with stress different from the genitive singular
5	**займа́тися**	another verb requiring the instrumental: **Чим? Сільськи́м господа́рством**

6 As we saw in the previous chapter, when relating 'for how long' you are, have or will be doing something, all you do is use the verb plus the accusative of the time unit(s). There are two examples of this construction in **Ми ма́ємо бензи́н!**, namely:

ї́хати	**оди́н день, ці́лу добу́**
працю́ють	**ти́жні, мі́сяці, ро́ки́**

Most of these forms look like the nominative, until we get to **ці́лу добу́**: here we clearly have an accusative.

What people wear

When in English we say 'she wears a red coat', we mean that she wears it regularly or habitually. This is conveyed in Ukrainian by the verb **носи́ти**, **-и-**, or the verb **ходи́ти**, **-и-** followed by **у/в** + locative (lit. 'to walk in'!). Thus:

Вона́ но́сить черво́не пальто́	she wears a red coat
Вона́ хо́дить у черво́ному пальті́	

If we say 'she's wearing a red coat', then we may use the verb 'to be' in one of the following constructions:

На ній черво́не пальто́	lit. 'on her is a red coat'
Вона́ в черво́ному пальті́	lit. 'she is in a red coat'

(If it is a case of headgear, then the **на**-construction is preferable: **На ній черво́ний капелю́шок** 'she's wearing a red hat'.)

Verbs for 'dressing' include:

Vocabulary

одяга́ти, -а́є-, perf. **одягну́ти, -не-**	to dress (someone), to put (something on) (+ acc.)	**переодяга́тися**	to change clothes (perf.; as **одяга́тися**)
вдяга́ти, -а́є-, perf. **вдягну́ти, -не-**	to put (something on) (+ acc)	**взува́ти, -а́є-,** perf. **взу́ти, -у́є-**	to put (shoes) on
одяга́тися/ удяга́тися	to get dressed (perf.; as **одяга́ти** and **вдяга́ти**)	**взува́тися**	to put one's shoes on (perf.; as **взува́ти**)
роздяга́тися	to get undressed (oneself) (perf.; as **одяга́тися**)	**роззува́ти(ся),** perf. **роззу́тися, -у́є-**	to take one's shoes off (perf.; as **взува́ти**)

Read the following short passage using these verbs:

Ми за́вжди́ гово́римо на́шій дочці́, що тре́ба вдяга́ти светр, коли́ хо́лодно; на жаль, вона́ не лю́бить носи́ти све́три. Моя́ мале́нька дочка́ ще не мо́же одяга́тися, о́тже я одяга́ю її́; але́ вона́ вже мо́же роздяга́тися! Коли́ їй те́пло, і тре́ба переодяга́тися, ми (звича́йно!) допомага́ємо їй.

Buying clothes

Remember that the verb 'to buy' is **купува́ти**, -**у́є**-, with its perfective **купи́ти**, -**и**-. What you are buying goes in the accusative case, and the person you are buying it for goes in the dative case.

Купува́ти might be replaced by, among others, **бра́ти/взя́ти** 'to take', which you would use when telling the salesperson that you will 'take' the item in question. 'To sell' is **продава́ти**, -**ає́**-, perf. **прода́ти**, **прода́сть;** again, what you are selling is in the accusative case, and the person you are selling it to goes into the dative case:

За́втра я куплю́ сестрі́ светр.	Tomorrow I'll buy my sister a sweater.
Так, блу́зкаподо́бається: візьму́ її́.	Yes, I like the blouse: I'll take it.

Вона́ продала́ мені́ зимо́ве пальто́. She sold me a winter coat.

Note the following pattern:

Мені́ потрі́бен/потрі́бна/потрі́бно or **потрі́бне/потрі́бні** I need

This is literally 'to me is necessary . . .', and **потрі́бен** will agree in gender and number with whatever you need. Thus: **Мені́ потрі́бні чо́рні шкарпе́тки** 'I need a pair of black socks'. In a shop you may ask: **Що в вас сього́дні в прода́жу?** 'What do have on sale today?', and the assistant may well respond: **Що ви бажа́єте придба́ти?** 'What do you want (lit. "What do you desire to acquire?")'. In reply, you could hear: **Сього́дні в нас нема́є (XXX)** 'We don't have (XXX) today.'

Here are a few words which might come in useful:

Vocabulary

жіно́чий	women's
мо́дний	fashionable
зру́чний	comfortable
о́дяг, -у	clothes
капелю́х, -а	hat
костю́м, -а	suit
блу́зка, -и	blouse
ко́мір, -міру	collar
спідни́ця, -і	skirt
штани́, і́в	trousers
светр, -а	sweater
ко́фта, -и	women's blouse
рукави́чки, -чок	gloves (sg. **-чка**)
пальто́, -а́	overcoat
череви́ки, -ів	shoes (sg. **-ви́к**; ankle-high)
ка́пці, -ів	slippers (sg. **ка́пець**)
ме́шти, мешт	shoes (sg. **ме́шта, -и** eastern, **ту́флі, -фель,** sg. **ту́фля, -і**)
чолові́чий	men's
стари́й	old(-fashioned)
ро́змір, -у	size
головні́ убо́ри	headwear*
взуття́, я́	footwear
ку́ртка, -и	jacket
соро́чка, -и	shirt
каблу́к, -а́	heel
су́кня, -і	dress
білИ́зна, -и	underclothes
пуло́вер, -а	pullover
дже́мпер, -а	jumper
шкарпе́тки, -ток	socks (sg. **-тка**)
панчо́хи, панчо́х	stockings (sg. **-ха**)
чо́боти, чобі́т	boots (sg. **чо́біт**)†
кросі́вки, -вок	trainers (sg. **-вка**)
колго́тки, -ток	tights

*genitive **головни́х убо́рів** (from **убі́р, убо́ру** 'attire')
†the diminutive **чобіто́к, -тка́** is very common

Exercise 8c

Say briefly what you are wearing right now (compare with what you regularly wear!), using vocabulary from this list and the 'wearing' constructions given earlier.

Read the following brief sample dialogues (you can, of course, do variations on them!):

Мені́ потрі́бен светр.
Яко́го ро́зміру?
44 (со́рок четве́ртого).
Вас влашто́вує сі́рий ко́лір?
Цілко́м. Я куплю́ його́.

Покажі́ть, будь ла́ска, ту блаки́тну су́кню.
Про́шу.
Вона́ не пасу́є мені́. Да́йте, будь ла́ска, і́ншу.
На жаль у нас нема́є. Захо́дьте за́втра.

Окса́но, чи мені́ пасу́є це зимо́ве пальто́?
Звича́йно. Чи ти ку́пиш його́?
Неодмі́нно куплю́. Мені́ ду́же потрі́бно зимо́ве пальто́.

влашто́вувати, -**ує**-, imperf.	suit (perf. **улаштува́ти**, -**у́є**-)
пасу́є	'suits' + dative of person.
неодмі́нно	by all means, certainly, without fail
зимо́вий	winter (adjective)

The instrumental of place

When 'going through/along/across places' in Ukrainian we often simply put the place into the instrumental, instead of using a preposition (such as English 'through'):

Ї́демо широ́кою ву́лицею	we drive along the wide street
ходжу́ вели́ким лі́сом	I walk through the big forest
ми йшли́ по́лем	we were walking across the field

The precise meaning of the instrumental in such instances is dictated by the characteristics of the place you have in mind: whether it is enclosed (forest), an open space (field) or along a line (street). In **Ми ма́ємо бензи́н**, the pertinent phrases are **ї́хати лі́сом** and **мали́м село́м**.

Numerals 1–4 and multiples thereof

In English we are used to plural and singular, and anything over '1' must be accompanied by a simple plural. In Ukrainian all numbers ending in '1' (excepting 11) are followed by the nominative singular and '1' has all three genders:

оди́н день	1 day
два́дцять оди́н день	21 days
сто оди́н день	101 days
одна́ кни́жка	1 book
два́дцять одна́ кни́жка	21 books
одне́ вікно́	1 window

The nominative plural is used in Ukrainian, but only following the numbers 2, 3, 4 and multiples such as 22, 23, 24, 32, 33, etc. (again, 12, 13, 14 do not follow this pattern). Any adjectives occurring in such numeral phrases will also be in the nominative plural. Straightforward as this may appear, it is extremely important to remember the place of stress in such forms. As we saw above, the nominative plural of neuter and feminine nouns is usually differentiated from the genitive singular by the place of stress: when used with numerals ending in 2, 3 and 4, however, the place of stress (when there is a difference) will follow that of the genitive singular! Compare the following examples, and note that '2' has one form for masculines and neuters, another for feminines:

	Nominative Singular	*Genitive Singular*	*Nominative Plural*
два бра́ти	**брат**	**бра́та**	**брати́**
два села́	**село́**	**села́**	**се́ла**
дві голови́	**голова́**	**голови́**	**го́лови**
три мі́ста	**мі́сто**	**мі́ста**	**міста́**
чоти́ри кни́жки	**кни́жка**	**кни́жки**	**книжки́**

A look at masculine nouns confirms that it is in fact the nominative plural, not the genitive singular, that occurs with such numbers: **два дні, три буди́нки**, etc. A very few exceptions do seem to exist: words in **-анин** may optionally take the genitive singular, e.g. '**2, 3, 4 росі́янина**'. The 'teens' and all other numbers require the use of the genitive plural, which will be introduced in the next chapter.

Exercise 8d

Render the following phrases into Ukrainian, keeping in mind the role of stress:

(a) 1 book
(b) 2 books
(c) 3 windows
(d) 4 male students
(e) 1 female student
(f) 2 buildings
(g) 3 cities
(h) 4 villages

Exercise 8e

Devise sentences that make sense out of the followings sets of words/phrases:

(a) ї́хати, робо́та, люди́на, до, маши́на
(b) його́, брат (*pl.*), займа́тися, матема́тика
(c) два, рік, та́то, працюва́ти, заво́д, на
(d) в, село́, чоти́ри, вели́кий, ву́лиця
(e) ціка́витися, украї́нська мо́ва
(f) студе́нт, іти́, ву́лиця, мину́лий рік
(g) я, дава́ти, друг, три, кни́жка
(h) ми, люби́ти, писа́ти, оліве́ць

9 Колú приї́демо?

When do we arrive?

In this lesson you will learn about:

- prefixed verbs of motion
- urban transport
- the demonstratives **цей, той**
- adverbialized instrumental forms
- vocabulary: the hotel room and bathroom
- cardinal numerals: 1–100

As was the case in 7, this lesson contains a rather large list of words that you will want to know (and will have to use!) once you get to Ukraine: these are the words referring to your surroundings and personal belongings in a hotel room.

У дідуся́ Микóли

The travelling threesome are now in Kyiv, at the home of Mykola's grandfather (**діду́сь: Миха́йло Андріє́нко**).

МИКÓЛА: Діду́сю! Я хóчу познайóмити вас з Оксáною і з Джóном.

ДІДУ́СЬ: Михáйло Тарáсович. Ду́же рáдий вас бáчити. Ласкáво прóсимо!

ОКСА́НА: Дя́куємо, пáне Андріє́нко; ду́же приє́мно.

ДІДУ́СЬ: Сідáйте, сідáйте, дру́зі. Як булá пóдорож? Чи ви щóйно приї́хали?

МИКÓЛА: Так. Пóдорож булá дóсить приє́мна, алé тривáла: ми втомúлися.

ДІДУ́СЬ: Розумíю. Відпочивáйте, дру́зі! Що вам принестú? Кáви, чи чáю? Чи чогóсь трóхи міцні́шого?

МИКÓЛА: Мені́ нічóго, дя́кую, алé мóже Джóнові та Оксáні.

ДЖОН: Пра́вду ка́жучи, хо́чу пи́ти щось; чи ви ма́єте мінера́льну во́ду?
ДІДУ́СЬ: Ая́кже. А вам, Окса́но?
ОКСА́НА: Мо́же сік, або́ лимона́д?
ДІДУ́СЬ: На жаль, со́ку нема́є, але́ сього́дні я купи́в пепсі-ко́лу. За́раз принесу́ ва́ші напо́ї. (Прино́сить мінера́льну во́ду та пепсі.) На здоро́в'я!
ОКСА́НА/ДЖОН: Дя́куємо.
ДІДУ́СЬ: Коли́ ви ви́їхали з Оде́си?
МИКО́ЛА: Ми хоті́ли поі́хати вчо́ра вве́чері, але́ ви́їхали до Ки́єва ті́льки сього́дні вра́нці, і ї́хали ці́лий день. До ре́чі, я не знав, куди́ поста́вити маши́ну, і зали́шив її́ на ву́лиці пе́ред цим буди́нком.
ДІДУ́СЬ: Ні, тре́ба переста́вити її на і́нше мі́сце: переї́деш на́шу ву́лицю, по́тім доі́деш до парку і́мені Іва́на Франка́; там є зупи́нка.
МИКО́ЛА: До́бре. За́раз поверну́ся.
ДІДУ́СЬ: Окса́но й Джо́н(е), тим ча́сом ви мо́жете розповісти́, як вамподо́бається на́ша Украї́на!

Vocabulary

дідусь, -я́	grandfather	**пра́вду ка́жучи**	to tell the truth
ра́дий	glad	**мінера́льна вода́**	mineral water
ласка́во про́симо!	welcome!	**ая́кже**	of course!
		сік, со́ку	juice
сіда́йте	have a seat, sit down! (imperative)	**лимона́д, -у**	soft drink (including British 'lemonade')
по́дорож, -и, fem.	trip		
що́йно	just, just now	**за́раз**	right away; in a second
приї́хати, приї́ду, приї́деш	arrive (by vehicle)		
		напі́й, напо́ю	beverage, drink
трива́лий	lengthy	**прино́сити, -и-,** imperf.	bring (on foot)
утоми́тися, -и-	become tired, be tired out		
		ви́їхати, -де-, perf.	leave, depart from (+ **з** + gen)
принести́, -се́-, perf.	bring (on foot) (see **прино́сити** below)	**до ре́чі**	by the way
		поста́вити, -и-, perf.	place in a standing position (here: car)
тро́хи	a little		
що́сь	something		
міцни́й, -і́ший	strong, stronger		

зали́шити, -и-, perf.	leave (something somewhere)	**і́мені** + gen. of name	named for/after . . . (here: 'Ivan Franko Park')
ага́	aha!		
переста́вити, -и-, perf.	move, to put in a different place	**зупи́нка, -и**	parking place; also '(bus, trolley) stop'
перeї́хати, -ї́ду, -ї́деш, perf.	cross over (by vehicle)	**поверну́тися, -не-,** perf.	return, come back
доі́хати, -ї́ду, -ї́деш, perf.	drive up to, as far as	**тим ча́сом**	meanwhile

Prefixed verbs of motion

The verbs of motion you have learned thus far have, apart from those with the prefix **по-**, been unprefixed 'determinate' and 'indeterminate' verbs indicating motion of a very general nature: 'going', by foot and by vehicle. These verbs can be prefixed in order to specify more precisely the nature of this motion; several of these prefixed verbs are used in the preceding dialogue. Once they are prefixed, however, they are no longer determinate and indeterminate. Instead, they now join the 'mainstream' of Ukrainian verbs and become new perfective–imperfective pairs: verbs based on indeterminates are imperfective, those based on determinates are perfective. The new verbs are to be used as you would expect: imperfectives have all three tenses, perfectives only have two and the distinction between incompleted/habitual and completed/one-time actions holds here as well.

The following are paradigms of both 'foot' and 'vehicle' verbs of motion (context limited the dialogue to 'vehicle' verbs). Note that the place of stress in the new imperfectives differs in the infinitive and other forms from that of the original indeterminate (**ходжу́–прихо́джу**), and after the 1st person in the new perfectives (**йде́ш–при́йдеш**):

ходи́ти	***іти́***	***ПРИ- +***
прихо́дити	**прийти́**	*to arrive*
прихо́джу	**прийду́**	
прихо́диш	**при́йдеш**	
прихо́дять	**при́йдуть**	
прихо́див	**прийшо́в**	
прихо́дила	**прийшла́**	

The same pattern holds for the prefixes **від**- 'leave, go away from', **пере**- 'across, over', **до**- 'up to, reaching', **ви**- 'exit from, set out from', **в/у**- 'enter', and others, which we shall encounter in future lessons.

Nota bene:

1 'Leaving' is often expressed simply by using the form **ї́хати/пої́хати**.
2 'Vehicle' verbs refer to the motion of people or things using a conveyance, while the motion of many vehicles (trains, buses) themselves is considered to be 'by foot', because they themselves are doing the moving: no other object is conveying them. There is some vacillation: we find both **по́їзд ї́де** 'the train is going/coming' and **по́їзд іде́** 'the train arrives'.

One of the peculiarities of the new Ukrainian aspectual pair relating to travelling by a conveyance is the existence of two possible imperfectives, one an expected second conjugation verb, the other a new first conjugation verb:

ї́здити			***ї́хати***
приїзди́ти	*or*	**приїжджа́ти**	**приї́хати**
приїжджу́		**приїжджа́ю**	**приї́ду**
приїзди́ш		**приїжджа́єш**	**приї́деш**
приїздя́ть		**приїжджа́ють**	**приї́дуть**
приїзди́в		**приїжджа́в**	**приї́хав**
приїзди́ла		**приїжджа́ла**	**приї́хала**

When the prefix is **від**-, an apostrophe (indicating the hardness of the final **д**-) is written between the prefix and those verbs beginning in **ї-: від'ї́хати, від'їжджа́ти** or **від'їзди́ти**.

To the verbs used in previous lessons we may now add the pair 'to carry' (on foot), which is also treated as a set of motion verbs:

Indeterminate		*Determinate*	
носи́ти:	**ношу́**	**нести́:**	**несу́**
	но́сиш		**несе́ш**
	но́сять		**несу́ть**
	носи́в		**ніс**
	носи́ла		**несла́**

Note that they are conjugated as are the other motion verbs, i.e. the indeterminate is second conjugation, the determinate is first conjugation. As verbs of motion, they can also be prefixed, as seen in the dialogue: **прино́сити – принести́** 'to bring', analogously to 'arriving'. There is a change in stress here as well, as in the case of **ходи́ти** above, from **носи́ти – ношу́** to **прино́сити – прино́шу** (but **принести́, -се́-** remain ending-stressed). To this list we add **ста́вити – поста́вити** and the more precise form **переста́вити** lit. 'to place across/over', which means 'to move something from one position to another.' There are other prefixes, which will be introduced as the need arises.

Urban transport

Apart from getting around on foot, **ходи́ти пі́шки**, or perhaps by bicycle (**ї́здити на велосипе́ді**), one may get around by taxi, bus, trolleybus, tram, underground or car (**ї́здити на таксі́/авто́бусом/ троле́йбусом/трамва́єм/на метро́; ї́здити маши́ною**). Do vary the verbs of motion according to whether you are talking about specific journeys at specific times, when you would use **іти́** and **ї́хати**, or about habitual, regular movement or non-specific movement, when you would use **ходи́ти** and **ї́здити**. You will catch most public means of transport at a stop **зупи́нка, -и (на зупи́нці)**, or at an underground station: **ста́нція, -ї метро́ (на ста́нції метро́)**. If you are travelling out into the suburbs (the **примі́ські райо́ни**), you may take a suburban train, the **електри́чка, -и**.

If you want to ask how to get somewhere, the usual formulae are **Як доїхати** and **Як дійти́ до** + gen. **Як діста́тися/дібра́тися до** + gen. also mean 'How to get to . . .?' but may imply that there is some difficulty (e.g. great distance) involved in getting there. If you want to emphasize 'How do **I** get to . . .?', you insert the personal pronoun in the dative case before the infinitive: **Як мені́ дійти́ до . . .?**

The reply you receive may relate to a particular bus or tram troute. 'No. 57', for example, will literally be 'the fifty-seventh (bus)'. If one believes the joke about the woman from out of town who waited patiently for the 'fifty-seventh' bus to arrive, you can appreciate that the potential for misunderstanding is real. Sometimes you may hear the cardinal numeral, or **но́мер** + cardinal, after the words **авто́бус** or **тролейбус**. If you know which bus you want, but do not know where the stop is, ask **Де зупи́нка XXX авто́буса?** or **Де зупи́нка авто́буса (но́мер) XXX?** If you don't know the route followed by a particular bus, use the verb **зупиня́тися**, **-я́є-** 'to stop': **Де зупиня́ється (цей/п'ятий) авто́бус?**

Here are more useful words and phrases, followed by two possible situations:

Vocabulary

ви́йти, -де- з + gen.	get out/off (imperf. **вихо́дити, -и-**)
зайня́ти, -ме- мі́сце у/в + loc.	get on (imperf. **займа́ти, -а́є-**), take a seat 'in'
увійти́, -де- у/в + acc.	get on (imperf. **у/вхо́дити, -и-**)
сі́сти, ся́де- у/в + acc.	get on (slightly coll.; imperf. **сіда́ти, -а́є-**)
зроби́ти, -и- переса́дку на + acc.	change (onto) (imperf. **роби́ти, -и-**)
маршру́т, -у	route
лі́нія, -ї	line
квито́к, -тка́	ticket (for the underground and train), sometimes preceded by the adjective **проїзни́й** '(related to a) journey'
тало́н, -а	ticket (for the bus etc.; you may buy several from the driver **воді́й, водія́**, and you cancel them (**компостирува́ти, -у́є-**) in the punching machine: **компо́стер, -тра**
передава́ти, -ає́-, imperf.	hand over, pass (perf. **переда́ти**, irreg.; followed by the acc. of what you are passing, the dative for the person you are passing it to)
пропуска́ти, -а́є-, imperf.	let through (perf. **пропусти́ти, -и-**. NB **я пропущу́**. Say **Пропусті́ть!** if you need to get through a crowd of people to get on or off)
у яки́й бік?	in what direction? (the answer may be **у цей бік** or **у той бік**)

Monthly pass for all bus and metro

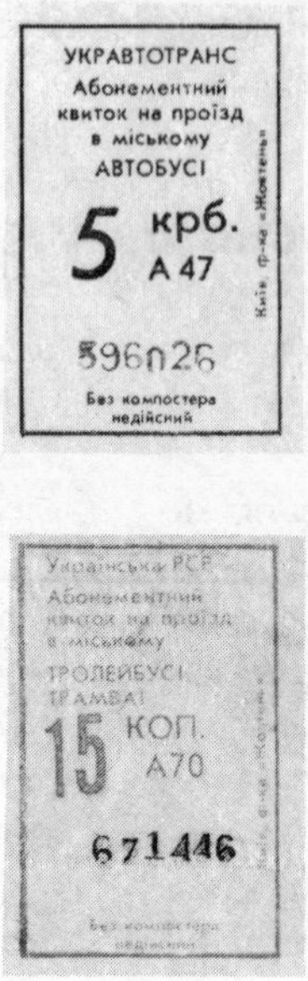

Trolley, bus and tram tickets

Київська міська Рада народних депутатів
ТРАМВАЙНО-ТРОЛЕЙБУСНЕ УПРАВЛІННЯ
Серія ТД

КВИТАНЦІЯ № 023381

про стягнення штрафу в сумі
ОДИН КАРБОВАНЕЦЬ
За неоплачений проїзд та провезення багажу
на міському електротранспорті

Квитанція не звільняє від придбання квитка

Киев. Кн ф-ка «Жовтень». Зак. 2-987—300 тыс.

Fine for travelling on tram/trolley bus without paying

In these dialogues, numbers refer to different speakers:

1: Скажі́ть, будь ла́ска, де зупиня́ється три́дцять шо́стий авто́бус?
2: Ви́бачте, я не зна́ю, я не туте́шній.
1: Про́шу . . . Бу́дьте ласка́ві, ви не зна́єте, де зупиня́ється три́дцять шо́стий авто́бус?
3: Зна́ю, он там, у кінці́ ву́лиці.
1: Щи́ро дя́кую.

1: Я не хо́чу спізни́тися на елекри́чку. Дозво́льте, будь ла́ска, пройти́.
3: На насту́пній зупи́нці й я вихо́джу.
1: Проба́чте.
2: Тобі́ здає́ться, що всти́гнемо на не́ї? Вже дру́га годи́на.
1: Всти́гнемо. Про́сто шкода́, що тре́ба було́ чека́ти де́сять хвили́н на троле́йбус. Яки́й інтерва́л ру́ху троле́йбусів?
2: Це зале́жить від маршру́ту! Але́ ми наре́шті приї́хали.

There are some useful phrases in these two dialogues that you may not know, but perhaps you can work out what they mean from the context. **Дозво́льте пройти́** is a polite substitute for one word in the list. The word **інтерва́л** might help explain **інтерва́л ру́ху; всти́гнемо**, from the perfective verb **всти́гнути, -не-**, is the antonym of **спізни́тися** (note that they are both followed by **на** + acc.). **Годи́на** 'hour'; **хвили́на** 'minute'. **Зале́жати, -и- від** + gen. means 'to depend on'.

Demonstrative pronouns: цей and той

The declension of the pronouns **цей** 'this' and **той** 'that' is like that of the possessive pronouns you have already seen, so we need not present an entire paradigm (you will find it anyway in the reference section). The forms used in the dialogue above are instr. sg. masc. **цим** and nom. sg. fem. **ця**. The main point to keep in mind is that a sharper distinction is made between 'this' and 'that' in English than in Ukrainian: **цей** can be used to express both English terms in most instances, while **той** usually imparts the notion 'over there' and will occur in situations of contrast:

Цей студе́нт чита́є до́бре, а той (студе́нт) чита́є пога́но.	This student (here) reads well, but that one (over there) reads badly.

One might note that where **той** is used without any overt contrast with **цей**, it is followed by more information ('that one, the one that/who'):

Я купи́в словни́к у тій книга́рні, де є букіністи́чний ві́дділ.	I bought the dictionary in the/that bookshop where there is a second-hand section.

Both the demonstratives may be replaced in speech by forms with the unstressed prefix **о-**, e.g. **оця́ ді́вчина, ото́й студе́нт**.

Either **той** or **цей**, expanded as **той/цей же са́мий** can convey English 'the same': **Ті же са́мі лю́ди бу́дуть там** 'The same people will be there'. Sometimes **той же** or **цей же** is sufficient. Ukrainian also has the exact literal equivalent of English 'one and the same': **Вонú мéшкають в однóму і тóму же мíсті** 'They live in one and the same town'.

Corresponding to these pronouns are the indeclinable forms **це** and **то**, of which the former is extremely common (and familiar to you), meaning 'this, it'. They do not change even if followed by a plural noun. Remember that we use **це** when pointing out something, and it again replaces both 'this is' and 'that is', unless you are pointing out something quite distant from you, in which case you should use **то**. Some examples:

Це моя́ кни́жка, і це твоя́ (кни́жка)	This/that is my book, and this/that is yours
То його́ ру́чка	That (over there) is his pen
Це Іва́н, яки́й приї́хав учо́ра	It's Ivan who arrived yesterday; Ivan is the one . . .
То ва́ші батьки́, які́ ви́рішили поїхати до Ки́єва	That's your parents who decided to go to Kyiv' (cf. *11* for 'who/which' clauses)

Do keep these separate from **ось**, **от** and **он**, which mean respectively 'here, there, over there is/are' and correspond to French *voici*, *voilà*. Pay especially close attention to the difference between the last two sentences.

Це мій олівéць, а то ваш.	This is my pencil, and that is yours
Цей олівéць мій, а той ваш	This pencil is mine, and that one is yours

Vocabulary building

Adverbs

Many adverbs or adverbial constructions (many to do with time) are simply words or phrases in the instrumental case. The following are some of the more common forms you will come across.

ча́сом	at times; the instrumental of **час** 'time'
тим ча́сом	(from the dialogue) is translated as 'meanwhile', but is in fact the instrumental of the phrase **той час** 'that time'

зима́	winter	**зимо́ю**	in winter
весна́	spring	**весно́ю**	in spring
лі́то	summer	**лі́том**	in summer

But in autumn/fall **(у) восени́**

ра́нком	(synonymous with **вра́нці**) in the morning
ми́ттю	in an instant, from **ми́ть** ‘wink, blink, moment’

We shall come across more such adverbs in future lessons.

Reading

Кімна́та

John and Oksana have left Mykola and his grandfather and are now settling into their hotel rooms. Their first task is to inspect them

Джон і Окса́на зайняли́ кімна́ти (номери́) в готе́лі «Ли́бідь». Коли́ вони́ діста́ли ключі́ та візи́тні картки́, то ви́явилося, що вони́ зо́всім недале́ко одне́ від о́дного живу́ть. На ко́жному по́версі (звича́йно там, де знахо́диться ліфт) є черговий́ або́ чергова́, яки́й (яка́) допомага́є го́стям, коли́ вони́ ма́ють пробле́ми або́ запита́ння. Чергова́ на ї́хньому по́версі показа́ла їм кімна́ти. Джон відчини́в две́рі й огля́нув свою́ кімна́ту з ціка́вістю: там він поба́чив до́сить вели́ке лі́жко, крі́сло, письмо́вий стіл, стіле́ць. На столі́ була́ насті́льна ла́мпа; на ща́стя, він знайшо́в ще одну́ ла́мпу бі́ля лі́жка, на мале́нькому сто́лику: Джон лю́бить чита́ти в лі́жку. Із задово́ленням він заува́жив телефо́н на письмо́вому столі́, і телеві́зор ко́ло стіни́; коли́ поба́чив холоди́льник, Джон зраді́в: у цій кімна́ті він бу́де як удо́ма! Але́ вже є мале́нька пробле́ма: одна́ ла́мпочка не працю́є; тре́ба ви́кликати чергову́!

Vocabulary

зайня́ти, -йму́, -йме́ш кімна́ту/но́мер	to take/rent/get a hotel room, perf.
візи́тна ка́ртка	hotel room card (usually to be shown when getting your key)
діста́ти, -не-, perf.	to obtain, get (imperf. **дістава́ти, -ає́-**)
ви́явитися, -и-, perf.	to turn out
одне́ о́дного	each other (male/female); with two males:

	оди́н о́дного, with two females **одна́ о́дну**
ко́жен (ко́жний)	every
по́верх, -у	storey, floor (not what is under your feet)
знахо́дитися, -и-, imperf.	be located
чергови́й, -а́	person on duty for the day (not just in hotels); declines as an adjective.
або́	or
яки́й	who, which/that (relative pronoun)
допомага́ти, -а́є-, imperf.	to help + dative of person helped
гість, го́стя	guest
запита́ння, neut.	question(s)
відчини́ти, -и-, perf.	to open (imperf. **відчиня́ти**, **-я́є-**)
две́рі, -е́й	door (plural form only in Ukrainian)
огля́нути, -не-, perf.	to look around (at) (imperf. **огляда́ти**, **-а́є-**)
ціка́вість, -ості	interest, curiosity
лі́жко, -а	bed
крі́сло, -а	armchair
стіл, стола́	table; **письмо́вий стіл:** writing table, desk
стіле́ць, -лця́	chair
ла́мпа, -и	lamp; **насті́льна ла́мпа**: table/reading lamp
на ща́стя	happily, luckily
ще	still, yet; **ще оди́н** 'yet another'
сто́лик, -у	small table
задово́лення, -я, neut.	satisfaction
заува́жити, -и-, perf.	to notice (imperf. **заува́жувати**, **-ує-**)
стіна́, -и́	wall
зраді́ти, -і́є-, perf.	to be(come) happy (imperf. **раді́ти**, **-і́є-**)
ла́мпочка, -и	light bulb
ви́кликати, -че-, perf.	summon, 'call out' (**виклика́ти**, **-а́є-**)

Reading

Ва́нна

У ва́нній Окса́на увімкну́ла сві́тло: вимика́ч вона́ знайшла́ бі́ля ра́ковини. Там вона́ поба́чила ва́нну, туале́т, дзе́ркало (над ра́ковиною), та ві́шалку для рушникі́в; у ва́нній був тако́ж нови́й душ. Окса́на спро́бувала все, і ви́явилося, що булá холóдна та гаря́ча водá (усе працювáло!). На ві́шалці були́ рушники́, алé не булó ні ми́ла ні туалéтного папéру: на щáстя, вонá привезлá своє ми́ло, алé папі́р трéба булó дістáти в черговóї. Íнші рéчі, котрі́ Оксáна ви́йняла із валі́зки, шампу́нь, зубну́ пáсту та щі́тку, дезодорáнт, вонá поклáла пóряд із ми́лом. У своїй кімнáті Джон теж розпакувáв валі́зку, та поклáв на поли́чку в вáнній ті сáмі рéчі, а такóж бри́тву та помазóк для голі́ння.

Vocabulary

увімкну́ти, -нé-, perf.	to turn on (a light), imperf. **вмикáти**, -áє-; turn off: **ви́мкнути**, -не-, imperf. **вимикáти**, -áє- perf. **виймáти**, -áє-)
сві́тло, -а	light
вимикáч, -á	light switch
рáковина, -и	sink, wash basin
туалéт, -у	toilet
дзéркало, а	mirror
над	over, above + instr.
ві́шалка, -и для рушникі́в	towel rod
душ, -і, fem., or **-у,** masc.	shower
спрóбувати, -ує-, perf.	try, test (imperf. **прóбувати**, -ує-)
гаря́чий	hot (as in water)
рушни́к, -á	towel
ми́ло, а	soap
туалéтний папі́р, -пéру	toilet tissue
привезти́, -зé, приво́зити, -и-	to bring by vehicle
річ, рéчі, fem.	thing
ви́йняти, ви́йме-, perf.	take out (imperf. **виймáти**, -áє-)
валі́зка, и	suitcase
шампу́нь, -я, masc.	shampoo
зубнá пáста, -ої -и	toothpaste
зубнá щі́тка, -ої -и	toothbrush
пóряд з + instr.	alongside
дезодорáнт, -у	deodorant
розпакувáти, -ýє-, perf.	unpack (something), imperf. **розпакóвувати, -ує- (пакувáти(ся)**, -ýє- 'to pack (one's luggage)')
поклáсти, -де- (він поклáв)	place, put in a lying position
поли́чка, -и	shelf
той сáмий	the same (also **цей сáмий**)
бри́тва, -и	razor (shaver)
помазóк, -зкá для голі́ння	shaving brush (**голи́ти(ся)**, -и-, imperf. 'to shave'; perf. **поголи́тися**, -и-)

Numerals

Up to this point you have seen the numbers 1–4; all other numbers not ending in 1–4 (except for the teens) require the use of the genitive plural, which will be introduced in the next chapter. For now, familiarize yourself with the numbers themselves: practise counting; whenever you come across numbers (speed limit signs, page numbers, airline flight numbers, etc., all from real life!) try to produce them in Ukrainian. Fix a few in your memory at a time (1–10; tens up to 100) and you will be able to use them as needed; you don't have to be reminded how critical it is to know numbers, so give it a try. Here are the bare numbers from 1 to 100, given to you without accompanying numerals; you will remember them better if you have to think about them a little harder. Compound numbers (21, 22, etc.) are merely combinations of – say – 20 and 1, as in English.

оди́н	одина́дцять	три́дцять
два	двана́дцять	со́рок
три	трина́дцять	п'ятдеся́т
чоти́ри	чотирна́дцять	шістдеся́т
п'ять	п'ятна́дцять	сімдеся́т
шість	шістна́дцять	вісімдеся́т
сім	сімна́дцять	дев'яно́сто
ві́сім	вісімна́дцять	сто
де́в'ять	дев'ятна́дцять	
де́сять	два́дцять	

Note: spellings, e.g. lost soft signs in the middle of the teens and upper tens and at the end of the 'upper 10s'; there are two '10s' that don't follow any patterns: which are they?

Exercise 9a

Put the following words (for the most part unknown) into the instrumental case, judging by what you know at this stage:

сад; се́рце; телеба́чення; банду́ра; ві́дповідь (*fem.*); дощ; дурни́ця; кіне́ць; карто́пля; кість; конфере́нція; геро́й; папі́р.

Exercise 9b

Choose the correct verb of motion and use it in the correct form:

(a) Ми сьогóдні (ітú/ходúти) в теáтр.
(b) Óльга вчóра (ходúла/йшла) у шкóлу.
(c) Кудú ти (ходúти/ітú/прихóдити)?
(d) Чéрез дві хвилúни (прихóдити/приї́хати) пóїзд.
(e) Я побáчив йогó, колú він (носúти/нестú/понестú) книжку додóму.

Exercise 9c

Translate **Ванна** into English, replacing the past tense with the present tense.

Exercise 9d

Translate into Ukrainain:

(a) In a month we shall have read this book; every page (**сторі́нка, и**) (of it).
(b) This bathroom is small, but pretty; I like the washbasin.
(c) Did you try the hot water?
(d) No, but I used the television; it works!
(e) Ivan said that he would come by car (lit.: 'he will come') after a week.
(f) My room is not very large: I have books, suitcases, other things too.
(g) Next to the bed is the telephone; over the bed is the light.
(h) In front of the window is a small table, and on that table I write letters.
(i) What are you interested in? Music? History? The Ukrainian language?
(j) What can (I/one) bring to you? Some coffee, some mineral water?

10 У Ки́єві

In Kyiv

In this lesson you will learn about (or increase your knowledge of):

- the genitive plural
- the dative, instrumental and locative plural
- the imperative
- expressing one’s feelings
- the indefinite personal form of the verb
- a few antonyms
- how to describe where you live

Розмо́ва про Ки́їв

Mykola, Oksana, and John discuss Kyiv with Mykola’s grandfather, Mykhailo Andriyenko

ДЖОН: От Мико́ла йде́. Сподіва́юся, він знайшо́в, де поста́вити а́вто. Мико́ло, чи все в поря́дку?

МИКО́ЛА: Так, усе́ до́бре. Там на ву́лиці сті́льки маши́н, грузовикі́в, авто́бусів. Я ду́мав, що в Ки́єві не так бага́то ру́ху, але́ ба́чу, що все змі́нюється.

ДІДУ́СЬ: Так, тепе́р всі поспіша́ють, popзайма́ються бі́знесом. Та й щове́чора сусі́ди, дру́зі залиша́ють свої́ маши́ни пе́ред буди́нком або́ за ним. Ну, поговорі́мо про на́ше мі́сто, столи́цю Украї́ни.

ОКСА́НА: Я впе́рше тут, а мені́ вже два́дцять ро́ків. Я така́ ра́да, що приї́хала сюди́. Шість мі́сяців тому́ я була́ в Аме́риці, а от упе́рше у ва́шій столи́ці.

МИКО́ЛА: Я вже був у Ки́єві де́кілька разі́в, до́бре зна́ю Дніпро́, церкви́ й рі́зні райо́ни мі́ста. Скажі́ть, діду́сю, скі́льки ро́ків ви живете́ тут.

A street sign for the Khreshchatyk, the main street in Kyiv.

Vocabulary

всé в поря́дку	everything's fine (lit. 'in order')
грузови́к, -á	lorry, truck
рух, -у	traffic; movement
змі́нювати(ся), -ює-, imperf.	to change (oneself); perf. **змінúтися, -и-**
привáтний	private
та й	and (indeed)
сусі́д, -а	neighbour
поговори́ти, -и-, perf.	to have a chat, talk for a while
томý	ago (after number + noun, just as in English)
дéкілька	several (+ gen. pl.)
Дніпрó, -á	Dnieper
цéрква, -и	church
рі́зний	various, different
райóн, -у	region, area

The genitive plural

The genitive plural of nouns is obtained by the addition of one of three endings, variously distributed among the genders of words:

1	**-ів**
2	–
3	**-ей**

The genitive plural of adjectives and pronouns is either **-их** or **-іх**; the latter is restricted to soft adjectives and the pronoun **(у)ве́сь**, or where **у** precedes the ending. Here are a few examples of adjectival and pronominal genitive plurals. Remember that there is no formal distinction of gender in the plural:

Nominative Singular	*Genitive Plural*	*Nominative Singular*	*Genitive Plural*
до́брий, -а, -е	**до́брих**	**пізні́ший, -а, -е**	**пізні́ших**
да́вній, -я, -є	**да́вніх**	**тре́тій, -я, -є**	**тре́тіх**
той, -а, -е	**тих**	**цей, -я, -е**	**цих**
мій, -оя, -оє	**мої́х**	**чий, -ия, -иє**	**чиї́х**
наш, -а, -е	**на́ших**	**ваш, -а, -е**	**ва́ших**
вони́	**їх (них)**	**(у)ве́сь, уся́, усе́**	**усі́х**

The distribution of the three genitive plural forms of nouns among the nouns is essentially straightforward, although there are always exceptions: learn them right from the start, especially as they involve many common words. We approach the noun according to gender and the nature of the final consonant:

Masculine nouns

Hard		*Soft*		*Hissing/Hushing*	
ри́нок	**ри́нків**			**ніж**	**ножі́в**
ба́тько	**батькі́в**	**день**	**днів**	**борщ**	**борщі́в**
ста́роста	**ста́рост(і́в)**	**суддя́**	**судді́в**	**кіне́ць**	**кінці́в**

ста́роста ‘chief, elder; go-between (with **-і́в**)’, **суддя́** ‘judge’.

Note the following exceptions:

росія́нин	**росія́н**	**чолові́к**	**чолові́к/чолові́ків**
раз	**разі́в/раз**	**гість**	**госте́й**

There is a difference of meaning between the two forms of **чоловік** ('people'/'men'); in the case of **разів/раз** the first form is more common.

Neuter nouns

Hard		*Soft*		*Hissing/Hushing*	
місто	**міст**	**питáння**	**питáнь**	**прізвище**	**прізвищ**
вýхо	**вух**	**ім'я́**	**імéн**	**місце**	**місць**
óко	**очéй**	**порося́**	**порося́т**	**плечé**	**пліч/ плечéй**
слóво	**слів**				
селó	**сіл**				
пóле	**піль/полів**				
мóре	**морів**				

порося́ 'piglet', **вýхо** 'ear', **óко** 'eye', **плечé** 'shoulder', **мóре** 'sea'.

The most general patterns are those of **місто/слóво** and **питáння**, with **ім'я́** and **порося́** exemplifying small groups of similar nouns. It is the zero ending which is normal overall, but there has been some penetration of **-ів** and, after hushing consonants, of **-ей**.

As we saw in *4*, if **-е-** or **-о-** is the vowel of the syllable preceding the zero ending, it may become **-і-**, as in **слів** (**слóво**) and **сіл** (**селó**); compare masculine **стіл/столів**, where the zero occurs in the nominative singular.

If a group of consonants precedes the ending, the group may have to be split when the ending is zero, usually for reasons of pronounceability. The vowel inserted will usually be **-е-**; if one of the consonants is **к** it will be **-о-**, e.g. **вікнó/вікон** (this information is supplied with entries in the glossary). We saw this in *4* as well, in the genitive singular, where we spoke of 'fleeting vowels' and the zero occurred in the nominative singular: **стілéць/стільця́**.

Feminine nouns

Hard		*Soft*		*Hushing*	
кімнáта	**кімнáт**	**столи́ця**	**столи́ць**	**кáша**	**каш**
мáма	**мам**	**земля́**	**земéль**	**ми́ша**	**мишéй**
кни́жка	**книжóк**	**лéкція**	**лéкцій**	**річ**	**речéй**
сестрá	**сестéр**	**стаття́**	**статéй**	**ніч**	**ночéй**

су́кня	**су́конь**
по́вість	**повісте́й**

По́вість 'novel, story', **су́кня** 'dress'; note that **ма́ма** tends to be used either in direct address or within the family; it is an intimate term, while **ма́ти** is more neutral.

As with the neuter nouns, the norm is a zero ending, with the same corollaries concerning inserted vowels and vowel alternations. Observe that:

1 A very few nouns with a final hard consonant have **-ів** (the very colloquial **мамі́в**) as an option
2 Those in a final soft consonant (and no final vowel in the nominative singular) have **-ей**
3 Those in a final hushing consonant on the whole have **-ей**, too
4 Nouns such as **статтю́** simplify the double consonant

With nouns that have no singular form it can be difficult, in the absence of a singular and of any clear indication of gender, to find any pointers to the likely genitive plural. Such words are quite few, and it is best to learn them as you come across them. A common one is **діте́й**, the genitive and accusative plural of **ді́ти** 'children', where the singular exists but is **дити́на**.

The genitive plural forms of human masculines (and optionally of all other animates, of whatever gender), also serve as the accusative plural, as in the singular; otherwise this form is identical with the nominative.

Apart from the already familiar use of the genitive, for example, to indicate possession, the genitive plural is to be found after expressions of quantity:

(a) **бага́то** 'many' (the genitive singular when it means 'much')
(b) **ма́ло** 'little, few', **чима́ло** 'quite a few, a good deal of'
(c) **де́кілька** 'a few', **кі́лька** 'several'
(d) **скі́льки** 'how many/much?'
(e) all numerals in the nominative or nominative/accusative except **оди́н**, **два**, **три**, **чоти́ри** (and those ending in **оди́н** etc.)

The genitive singular replaces the genitive plural when appropriate from the meaning, e.g. **бага́то/скі́льки хлі́ба** 'much/how much bread'. Compare these uses of the genitive plural to see how indispensable it is:

Скі́льки книжо́к ви ма́єте?	How many books have you got?
П'ять книжо́к, шість листі́в.	Five books, six letters.

В Украї́ні бага́то міст.	In Ukraine there are a lot of cities.
І нема́ло сіл!	And not a few villages!
Скі́льки ко́штує маши́на?	How much does the car cost?
1000 до́ларів.	1000 dollars.
Скі́льки їй ро́ків?	How old is she?
Їй сімна́дцять ро́ків.	She's seventeen.

Зага́дки

У ба́тька сім сині́в, а ко́жний син ма́є одне́ лице́ бі́ле, а дру́ге чо́рне.
Без ніг, без рук – на дах лі́зе.
(**дах, -у** 'roof'; **лі́зти, лі́зе** 'crawl, climb')
[The solutions can be found after the glossary to Dialogue 2.]

Розмо́ву продо́вжують

ДІДУ́СЬ: Ма́йже все життя́, сімдеся́т три ро́ки, я прожи́в у Ки́єві, а пе́ред тим ві́сім ро́ків у мало́му селі́ зо́всім бли́зько, біля на́шої столи́ці.

МИКО́ЛА: Зна́чить, вам вісімдеся́т оди́н рік. Ви ма́єте до́бре зна́ти кия́н, не ка́жучи вже про саме́ мі́сто, його́ буди́нки, па́рки, рі́ку, та й його́ істо́рію.

ДЖОН: Мені́ сказа́ли, що Ки́їв був столи́цею Ки́ївської Русі́, держа́ви, що існува́ла ти́сячу ро́кі́в тому́ і в які́й процвіта́ли культу́ра й архітекту́ра. Пізні́ші поді́ї привели́ до окре́много ро́звитку Украї́ни й Моско́вії, по́тім Росі́ї.

ОКСА́НА: Ми так ра́ді, що наре́шті Украї́на ста́ла незале́жною держа́вою. Ва́жко бу́де, але́ ми зна́ємо, що бу́де кра́ще.

ДІДУ́СЬ: Коли́ бу́дете огляда́ти Ки́їв, це бу́де, ма́бу́ть, за́втра, істо́рію мі́ста поба́чите в його́ пам'ятниках; їх сті́льки тут. А я тепе́р уже́ геть утоми́вся; піду́ спа́ти. До́бре бу́де й вам поспа́ти; що́йно приї́хали з Оде́си, за́втра ви бага́то бу́дете пі́шки ходи́ти по мі́сті.

МИКО́ЛА: Гара́зд, діду́сю, ско́ро пі́демо спа́ти. ... ... Ну, дру́зі, дава́йте тро́шки поговори́мо про за́втрашній о́гляд Ки́єва!

Vocabulary

продо́вжувати -(ся), -ає-, imperf.	continue (intrans. takes the form of a reflexive verb)
прожи́ти, -ве́-, perf.	live (a certain period of time)
пе́ред тим, як	before (+ verb form; note the comma)
кия́нин, а	a male Kyivan (Kievan); **-ка** female
не ка́жучи вже про	not to mention (+ acc.)
сам	itself (emphatic pron./adj.
ріка́, -и́	river
існувати, -у́є-	exist
тому́	ago (note the acc. of time preceding it)
ти́сяча, -и	thousand
процвіта́ти, -а́є	flower
культу́ра, -и	culture
архітекту́ра, -и	architecture
пізні́ший	later, subsequent
поді́я, -ї	event
привести́, -де́-, perf.	lead
окре́мий	separate
ро́звиток, -тку	development
ки́ївський	Kyivan (adj.)
Русь, Русі́	Rus’
Моско́вія, -ї	Muscovy (ancient state of Moscow)
Ро́сія, -ї	Russia (**Росі́я** is more common)
ста́ти, -не-, perf.	become (+ instr.)
незале́жний	independent
держа́ва, -и	state, country
огляда́ти, -а́є-, imperf.	to visit, see the sights (of) (+ acc.)
па́м’ятник, -а	monument
геть	completely, utterly, a great deal; away(!) (interjection)
поспа́ти, -и́-, perf.	have a (little) sleep (imperf. **спа́ти, -и́-**)
гара́зд	fine, OK, yes (also **до́бре**)
піти́, -де-, perf.	go, set off (see **іти́, іду́, іде́ш**)
поговори́ти, -и-	talk a little, have a chat
за́втрашній	tomorrow’s
о́гляд, -у	visit, sightseeing (note the following gen.)

Відга́дки: **Ти́ждень, доба́, день і ніч** ‘a week, 24 hours, day and night’; **Дим** ‘smoke’

АГЕНТСТВО НЕРУХОМОГО МАЙНА
ПРОДАЖ
ОБМІН
ОРЕНДА
АПАРТАМЕНТІВ
ТА ОФІСІВ
JANUS
SALE
EXCHANGE
LEASE OF
APARTMENTS
AND OFFICES
229·60·91
229·69·38

Estate agent's sign

The dative, instrumental and locative plural

In this chapter a few of these case forms will be encountered; they will be studied in more detail later. For the moment let us simply note that the endings in all nouns are:

Dative	*Instrumental*	*Locative*
-ам/-ям	**-ами/-ями**	**-ах/-ях**

added to the stem-final consonant.

The indefinite personal form of the verb

Ukrainian doesn't insist on the subject personal pronoun being expressed; however, when the verb is in the third person plural ('they') form and **вони́** is omitted, it may have the meaning 'one [does something]', 'people [do something]'. Note the word order (not obligatory, but typical):

Мені́ сказа́ли	One has told me, People have told me, I have been told
У газе́ті пи́шуть	In the newspaper it is written, etc.
Розмо́ву продо́вжують	The conversation is continued, They continue . . .

The imperative

The main imperative or command forms in Ukrainian most often relate to **ти** and **ви**: '(you sg./pl.) do it!' Usually one also includes the 'let us' form, i.e. when the speaker includes himself (**ми**): 'Let us do (it)!'

The formation of the imperative is quite straightforward. All you have to look at is:

(a) the stem: is there a [y] before the personal endings, as in **ає** type verbs:
чита́ю, працю́ю, розумі́ю, накри́ю
or is there another consonant?
ди́в-иться, ро́б-имо, ба́ч-иш

(b) the place of stress: is the first person 'I' form stressed on the ending or not?
дивлю́ся, ба́чу, забу́ду

There are three sets of endings depending on these two criteria. We have one sub-rule: a verb with *two* consonants at the end of the stem always follows the pattern of end-stressed verbs for ease of pronunciation. In table form, the endings are (0 = zero):

Stem	**ти**	**ви**	**ми**	*No end-stress*
vowel +y (ay, iy, uy, yy)	**-й**	**-йте**	**-ймо**	
one consonant	**-и**	**-іть**	**-ім(о)**	**-0/-ь -те -мо**
two (+) consonants	**-и**	**-іть**	**-ім(о)**	

Present		*Imperative*		
1 sg.	2 sg., 3 pl.	**ти**	**ви**	**ми**
чита́ю	**чита́єш, чита́ють**	**чита́й**	**чита́йте**	**чита́ймо**
працю́ю	**працю́єш, працю́ють**	**працю́й**	**працю́йте**	**працю́ймо**
розумі́ю	**розумі́єш, розумі́ють**	**розумі́й**	**розумі́йте**	**розумі́ймо**
стою́	**сто́їш, стоя́ть**	**сті́й**	**сті́йте**	**сті́ймо**
пишу́	**пи́шеш, пи́шуть**	**пиши́**	**пиші́ть**	**пиші́м(о)**

роблю́	**ро́биш, ро́блять**	**роби́**	**робі́ть**	**робі́м(о)**
ба́чу	**ба́чиш, ба́чать**	**ба́ч**	**ба́чте**	**ба́чмо**
забу́ду	**забу́деш, забу́дуть**	**забу́дь**	**забу́дьте**	**забу́дьмо**
підкре́слю	**підкре́слиш, -кре́слять**	**підкре́сли**	**підкре́сліть**	**підкре́слім(о)**

Thus, for stems ending in a single consonant, you have to look at stress: given no end-stress (**ба́чу**, **ба́чиш**) the **ти** form has a zero ending (nothing). If it can be palatalized, that consonant will be soft (**забу́дь**).

Note especially the following forms, which are not based on the present stem (**дава́ти**, **да́ти**, **ї́сти**):

даю́	**дає́ш, даю́ть**	**дава́й**	**дава́йте**	**дава́ймо**
дам	**даси́, даду́ть**	**дай**	**да́йте**	**да́ймо**
ї́м	**їси́, їдя́ть**	**ї́ж**	**ї́жте**	**ї́жмо**

The verb **відпові́сти́** 'to answer, reply' may take its imperative from the imperfective, namely **відповіда́ти: відповіда́й(те)**, but often one will simply say **Дай ві́дповідь!** 'Give an answer!'

The first person plural perfective on its own, e.g. **пі́демо**, may function as the **ми** form. Another possibility, found in certain verbs of motion, is the plural form of the perfective past, e.g **пішли́** 'let's go!'; this latter form is very common in spoken Ukrainian, and should be noted now! Forms with **дава́йте** + imperfective infinitive are also encountered.

When one wants a third person to do something (i.e. **він**, **вона́**, **вони́**), one simply places **хай** or **неха́й** before the appropriate form of the verb (**неха́й** is not negative!).

Here are a few examples. Note the use of aspect: basic commands are usually perfective, while negative commands are imperfective, except in warnings, which are as a rule perfective:

Джо́н(е), напиши́/напиші́ть, будь ла́ска, ва́ше пр́ізвище!	John, please write your surname! (basic command)
Не забу́дьте, де ви покла́ли зо́шит з францу́зької мо́ви!	Don't forget where you put your French exercise book! (warning)
Не перехо́дь/перейди́ ву́лиці, ї́де маши́на!	Don't cross the street, there's a car coming! (warning)
Не слу́хайте його́, він зо́всім нічо́го не знає́!	Don't listen to him, he knows nothing at all! (basic negative)
Студе́нти, прочита́йте цю статтю́!	Students, read this article! (basic command)

Слу́хай, тепе́р говорі́м(о) тільки украї́нською!	Hey, now let's speak Ukrainian Note: use imperfective in a 'general' command/suggestion.
Я не хо́чу відповіда́ти: хай О́льга відповіда́є.	I don't want to answer, let Ol'ha answer! (3rd person)
Скажі́ть, будь ла́ска, де ви живете́! Говорі́ть пові́льно!	Please tell me where you live! Speak slowly! (basic command, followed by a general command/suggestion)

Exercise 10a

Provide the genitive plural of the words in parentheses (if a genitive plural is appropriate):

(a) Бага́то (украї́нець) живе́ в се́лах.
(b) В Украї́ні є чима́ло (вели́кий, мі́сто).
(c) До (мину́лий, рік) ду́же ма́ло (англі́єць) зна́ли про краї́ни схі́дної Євро́пи.
(d) Є сті́льки (пита́ння)!
(e) Без (ві́дповідь) на ці пита́ння, ми не змо́жемо закі́нчи́ти (пра́ця).
(f) Я прочита́в цей рома́н п'ять (раз).
(g) У на́шій кварти́рі шість (кімна́та).
(h) Да́йте мені́ де́сять (ніж, виде́лка, ло́жка)!
(i) Скі́льки (сло́во) ти ви́вчила вчо́ра?
(j) Скі́льки з ме́не? З вас два́дцять п'ять (карбо́ванець).

Sentence (i) means 'How many words did you learn yesterday?'

Exercise 10b

Form the appropriate imperatives from the following words. Only one aspect form is given and it may not always be the appropriate one, so check the rules of thumb provided above before making your choice!

(a) (Показа́ти) мені́ оту́ кни́жку!
(b) Не (забу́ти) підру́чника!
(c) (Ходи́ти) до теа́тру сього́дні вве́чері!
(d) (Захо́дити), коли́ ти бу́деш у Льво́ві!
(e) Не (дава́ти) йому́ рушника́, він мені́ ще потрі́бен!
(f) (Писа́ти) до ба́тька ко́жного дня!

(g) (Одяга́тися) шви́дко, ми запізни́лися!
(h) (Прочита́ти) оце́й рома́н обов'язко́во: незаба́ром про нього розмовля́тимемо в шко́лі!
(i) (Виріشува́ти) це пита́ння, воно́ ду́же ціка́ве!
(j) (Знайти́) ба́тька, до нього телефону́ють.

Запізни́тися, **-и́-** (imperf. **запі́знюватися**, **-юєт-**) 'come too late'; **обов'язко́во** 'without fail'; **незаба́ром** 'soon'; **по-/за- телефонува́ти**, **-у́є-** 'telephone'.

Expressing desires and feelings

The basic verb 'to want' is **хоті́ти**, perfective **схоті́ти/захоті́ти**. Its infinitive gives no indication as to its conjugation in the present tense, which is that of a completely regular first-conjugation verb:

я хо́чу	**ми хо́чемо**
ти хо́чеш	**ви хо́чете**
він . . . хо́че	**вони́ хо́чуть**

Like the other verbs of 'wanting', it may be followed by an infinitive, e.g. **я хо́чу пої́хати до Ки́єва** 'I want to go to Kyiv', or by a noun in the genitive, e.g. **він хо́че моро́зива** 'he wants an icecream' (gen. of **моро́зиво** 'icecream'). Two other verbs of similar meaning are **(по)бажа́ти**, **-а́є-** 'to desire' and **пра́гнути**, **-не-** 'to yearn'. The perfective of **хоті́ти** and **бажа́ти** will have the sense 'to have, conceive a wish or desire to/for' and should only be used when that particular nuance is required, e.g. **вона́ ра́птом схоті́ла піти́ в го́сті до свого́ бра́та** 'she suddenly felt she wanted to go and visit her brother'. **Хоті́ти** is often used in the 'conditional mood', expressing 'I would like . . .', which is simply the past tense followed by the particle **би** (after a consonant; **б** after a vowel): **ми хоті́ли б про́сто сиді́ти та чита́ти** 'we'd like just to sit and read'.

Note that **хоті́ти** + infinitive is used when there is only one subject ('I want to read'); if there are two subjects (I want him to come tomorrow'), we must use the construction **хоті́ти, щоб** + and the verb in the appropriate form of the past tense. Thus:

Я хо́чу, щоб він прийшо́в за́втра. I want him to come tomorrow.

Note the obligatory comma in writing!

Emotions in Ukrainian are often conveyed by the association of the dative case with the impersonal form of a verb or of an adjective. Where a verb is concerned, this can soften the expression, giving a sense of 'to feel like'. Thus, if we transform **хоті́ти** into the reflexive **хоті́тися** and use it in the third person singular (neuter if past), we achieve the nuance of 'to feel like':

Мені́ хо́четься моро́зива.	I feel like an icecream.
Мені́ хоті́лося ї́сти.	I felt hungry.

We can do this with lots of other verbs to convey the sense of 'feeling disposed towards . . .', e.g. **Мені́ сього́дні не працю́ється** 'I don't feel like working today', **Я не зна́ю чому́, але́ мені́ про́сто не спи́ться** 'I don't know why, but I just don't feel like sleeping/can't get to sleep'.

Some impersonal adjectival forms were mentioned in *7*. Others include **хо́лодно** 'cold', **жа́рко** 'hot', **те́пло** 'warm', **прие́мно** 'pleasant', **ра́дісно** 'joyful, gives joy', **су́мно** 'sad', **при́кро** 'unpleasant, harsh', **незру́чно** 'uncomfortable, embarrassed', **до́бре** 'fine', **пога́но** 'not so well, sick' and **байду́же** 'indifferent, not to care less'; note also the noun **шкода́** 'be sorry', which can occur alone or with a dative. Compare:

Як тут мені́ (було́) хо́лодно!	How cold I am (was) here!
Ї́м було́ так су́мно, що вони́ не вств́игли . . .	They were so sad (that) they didn't manage to . . .
Ї́й зо́всім байду́же, чи він чита́є її́ вірш, чи ні.	She couldn't care less whether he reads her poem or not.
Шкода́, Іва́не, що не ба́чив цей фільм.	What a pity, Ivan, that you didn't see this film.
Тобі́ не шкода́, Оле́ксо, що . . .?	Aren't you sorry, Oleksa, that . . .?

Note the very useful verb **встига́ти**, **-а́є-**, perfective **вст́игнути**, **-не-**; past **-г-** 'to manage to, succeed in', followed by the infinitive.

Most of these impersonal forms are derived from adjectives, e.g. **холо́дний, сумни́й, до́брий, весе́лий**. It is also possible to have a construction that is much closer to what we find in English, namely **Він холо́дний** 'He is cold'; however, this implies a quality of the person's character rather than how he may feel at a certain time.

If you are glad or happy about something, then you can use the verb **раді́ти**, **-і́є-**, followed by the dative case, e.g. **Ти так раді́єш зу́стрічі** 'you're so glad about the meeting' (also by **з** + gen). And if something makes you suffer, then the appropriate verb is **стражда́ти**, **-а́є-**, followed by the preposition **від** + genitive, e.g. **я стражда́ю від то́го, що він таки́й нетерпля́чий** 'I'm suffering from the fact that he's so impatient'.

Now we can come full circle and return to 'liking', without impersonals. Remember (cf. 5) that the easier verb to use is **люби́ти**, **-и-**, which implies a deeper feeling or preference (the perfective, **полюби́ти**, can give a sense of 'beginning/coming to like something'). The alternative, where the person who 'likes' goes in the dative, is **(с)подо́батися**, **-ає-**, which implies more of an instant reaction to a single experience. A few examples:

Чи тобі́ сподо́балася ця п'єса?	Did you like that play (that you've just seen)?
Я рані́ше ду́же люби́ла цю п'єсу.	I really used to like that play.
Вона́ лю́бить прогу́люватися.	She likes going for a walk.
Він подо́бається їй.	She likes him. (lit. 'he is pleasing to her')

Exercise 10c

Express your feelings about: your spouse/friend; tea and coffee, going for walks. Say that you are: happy, sad, cold, hot. Finally, say 'it's a pity that . . .' (about something you feel strongly about).

Vocabulary building

A few antonyms

It's always useful to learn a few opposites:

вели́кий	**мали́й**	**широ́кий**	**вузьки́й**
висо́кий	**низьки́й**	**до́вгий**	**коро́ткий**
важки́й	**ле́гкий**	**дорогий**	**деше́вий**
га́рний	**пога́ний**	**розу́мний**	**дурни́й**
струнки́й	**товсти́й**	**си́льний**	**слабки́й**

Some of them you already know; others you can look up in a dictionary. Remember that, when asking what something or someone is like, you may use **яки́й**, e.g. **Яка́ це кімна́та?** An alternative, especially as regards animates, is the expression: **Яки́й він із се́бе?** 'What's he like?'

Reading

Столи́ця Украї́ни

Ки́їв знахо́диться над Дніпро́м, се́ред па́горбів і рівни́н. До Ки́єва прибува́ють літако́м, по́їздом, паропла́вом, авто́бусом, або́ маши́ною. Головни́й аеропо́рт – Бори́спіль. Крім ньо́го є залізни́чий вокза́л, авто́бусний вокза́л і річкови́й вокза́л. Коли́ ви приї́дете до Ки́єва, тре́ба бу́де дізна́тися, де зупини́тися. Якщо́ у вас нема́є дру́га або́ коле́ги в Ки́єві, тре́ба зупини́тися в готе́лі. У це́нтрі є готе́ль «Москва́», зо́всім бли́зько є ще бага́то і́нших готе́лів, зокре́ма́ «Ли́бідь», «Ки́їв». Ки́їв – це старови́нне мі́сто водно́ча́с моде́рна, спра́вжня столи́ця вели́кої держа́ви.

(Adapted from Zhluktenko *et al*. (1978) *Ukrainian* 286–8)

Vocabulary

па́горб, -у	hill	**аеропо́рт, -у**	airport
рівни́на, -и	plain	**залізни́чий**	rail(way)
прибува́ти, -а́є-, imperf.	to come, arrive	**авто́бусний**	bus, coach
		річкови́й	river
літа́к, -а́	plane	**старови́нний**	old, ancient
паропла́в, -у	motor vessel, ship	**водно́ча́с**	simultaneously, at one and the same time
вокза́л, -у	station		
головни́й	main, principal		
крім (+ gen.)	besides, apart from	**моде́рний**	modern

Talking about where you live

We have already (particularly in 2), looked at the locative and genitive cases and seen how one says where one is from and where one lives. Here we build on what you already know by referring to particular houses, streets and floors and giving some simple information about homes. Try to follow the dialogue without referring to the main vocabulary or your dictionary, then look up words as needed and proceed to exercise 10d.

– До́брий день, Пе́тре! Як спра́ви?
– *До́бре, дя́кую, Окса́но. Ми давно́ не ба́чилися. Де ти тепе́р ме́шкаєш?*
– Я що́йно переї́хала у нову́ кварти́ру. Вона́ недале́ко від це́нтру мі́ста, точні́ше від пло́щі Перемо́ги, на ву́лиці Гжи́цького, 10 (де́сять), кварти́ра 243 (дві́сті со́рок три/тре́тя).
– *Я до́бре зна́ю той буди́нок. Чи твоя́ кварти́ра на четве́ртому по́версі?*
– Ні, вона́ на шо́стому. Там до́бре, кра́ще, ніж там, де я рані́ше жила́. Моя́ ма́ма раді́є тому́, що я в цій кварти́рі. Вона́ ма́є три кімна́ти, ку́хню, ва́нну то́що.
– *Я ба́чу, що ти задово́лена.*
– Так, я наспра́вді задово́лена, хоча́ вто́млена. Прихо́дь у го́сті.
– *Дя́кую, я залюбки́/охо́че прийду́. До поба́чення, Окса́но.*
– До поба́чення, Пе́тре.

Exercise 10d

Answer in English the following questions on the above dialogue:

(a) Have Petro and Oksana met recently?
(b) What has Oksana just done?
(c) Is her flat (apartment) near the town centre?
(d) What else is it near?
(e) What floor is it on, and what floor does Petro think it is on?
(f) Is her flat better than where she used to live?
(g) How does Oksana feel?

11 Наш день у це́нтрі мі́ста

Our day in the city centre

In this lesson you will learn about:

- who/which clauses
- telling the time
- more possessives

Наш день у Ки́єві

Mykola, Oksana, and John discuss their plans for the next day; they have decided to accept Mykola's grandfather's invitation to stay with him

МИКО́ЛА: Можли́во, ви вже хо́чете спа́ти.

ОКСА́НА: Я хо́чу спа́ти, але́ бу́де ду́же прие́мно й кори́сно ви́рішити, які́ в нас пла́ни на за́втрашній день.

ДЖОН: Я тако́ж хо́чу поговори́ти про це. Що́йно передали́ по ра́діо, що за́втра пого́да бу́де чудо́ва, спра́вжня спе́ка. Зна́чить, без пробле́м змо́жемо ходи́ти по мі́сті.

МИКО́ЛА: Якщо́ така́ бу́де пого́да, змо́жемо на́віть поі́хати до одно́го з сі́л, які́ знахо́дяться під Ки́євом.

ОКСА́НА: Ой, не зна́ю, на мою́ ду́мку, на це не ма́ємо ча́су. Щоб усе́ подиви́тись, тре́ба ці́лий ти́ждень!

ДЖОН: Не зна́ю, як ви ду́маєте, але́ я б хоті́в побу́ти за́втра в само́му мі́сті. Було́ б до́бре побу́ти в око́лицях Ки́єва після́за́втра.

ОКСА́НА: Спра́вді. Ду́же прие́мно бу́де ви́їхати по́за мі́сто, на приро́ду.

Vocabulary

корúсний	useful
план, -у	plan
передáти	transmit, broadcast; hand over (perf.; like **дáти**)
погóда, -и	weather
спéка, -и	hot weather, heatwave
змогтú, змóжу, змóже, perf.	be able; can (imperf. **могтú**)
поїхати, -їде-	go (by vehicle; perf. of **ї́хати**)
знахóдитися, -и-	be located (also: **містúтися**)
під	near (+ instr.; often used with place-names)
на мою думку	in my opinion (**дýмка, -и** 'opinion')
не мáємо чáсу	we don't have time (genitive: negative verb)
ці́лий	(a) whole, entire
я б хоті́в	I'd like (conditional mood)
побýти, -де-, perf.	be for a while; to 'spend'
окóлиця, -і	outskirts, environs (often in plural)
післязáвтра	the day after tomorrow
спрáвді	really
ви́їхати	go out (of a place) by vehicle
пóза мі́сто	out of town (movement)
прирóда, -и	nature

Who/which ('relative') clauses

In English the words 'who(m)', 'which' and 'that' are often omitted: 'There's the woman (whom) I was talking about'. Ukrainian as a rule does not allow this omission, and the word it uses in this function is **якúй, якá, якé, які́** (seen already in the meaning 'what kind?'). Its gender and number depend on the noun it relates to, but its case is selected according to its role in the clause in which it is located. So, in our sentence above we would have:

Он жі́нка, про якý я розповідáла

This corresponds to the two sentences:

Он жі́нка (and) **Про жі́нку я розповідáла**

So we just join these two sentences, replacing the second **жі́нку** with the equivalent form of **якúй (якý)**, and place a comma before **якúй** and any preposition accompanying it. The comma is necessary in written

Ukrainian, and it is important not to have a preposition stranded at the end of the sentence (as frequently happens in English).

There is another, and more frequent, way of doing this in Ukrainian, namely to use the word **що**, which is invariable in this construction. Thus:

Там сиди́ть ді́вчина, що вивча́є англі́йську мо́ву.	There sits the girl who is studying English.
Я зустрі́в чолові́ка, що з ним ти розмовля́в учо́ра.	I met the man you were talking to yesterday.

In other words: **що** alone if one would otherwise have the nominative of **яки́й**, and **що** plus a third person pronoun (**ним**, for example) if one would not use the nominative of **яки́й**. It is very important not to confuse such relatives as 'which' or 'whose' with the same sounding interrogatives (question words) **котри́й** 'which?' and **чи́й** 'whose?'; in answer to questions using these interrogatives, they are retained. Thus, in answer to **Котра́ годи́на?** 'What time is it?', **Чия́ це сестра́?** 'Whose sister is this?', one would retain **котри́й** and **чи́й**:

Я не зна́ю, котра́ годи́на.
Я не зна́ю, чия́ це сестра́.

Some proverbs simply use 'what' and 'who' to mean 'that which' and 'he/she who'; the following examples are translated literally and therefore sound a bit stilted in English:

Що посі́єш, те й пожне́ш.
What you sow, that you will also reap.

Хто пі́зно хо́дить, той сам собі́ шко́дить.
(He) who goes late, (that one) hurts himself.

Exercise 11a

Join the following pairs of sentences, using who/which clauses.

(a) Вона́ живе́ на да́чі/Да́ча знахо́диться на Полта́вщині
(b) Джон телефону́є до ді́вчини/Він познайо́мився з ді́вчиною вчо́ра
(c) Ось той чолові́к/Той чолові́к до́бре зна́є Ната́лку
(d) Я чита́ю підру́чник/Я купи́в підру́чник у цій книга́рні
(e) У саду́ стоя́ть дере́ва/Сад бі́ля рі́чки
(f) Мені́ подо́бається хло́пець/Я дав я́блуко хло́пцеві

(g) Ми знайшли́ цю статтю́/Вона́ шука́ла статтю́
(h) Покажі́ть мені́ кварти́ру/Вони́ коли́сь жили́ у кварти́рі
(i) Два хло́пці приї́хали до Ха́ркова/Два хло́пці купи́ли ба́тькові маши́ну
(j) Ви зроби́ли ма́йже всі впра́ви/Вона́ написа́ла всі впра́ви до ціє́ї ле́кції

Note the following new words and constructions:

Vocabulary

телефонува́ти, -у́є-, imperf. telephone (**до +** gen. 'to someone'; perfective **по-/за-телефонува́ти,** -**у́є**-; one may also come across **(по)-дзвони́ти**, -**и**-)

Полта́вщина, -и the Poltava region

коли́сь once (not in the sense 'once, twice . . .'), sometimes (-**сь** is an indefinite suffix; more later)

впра́ва, -и exercise

The Ivan Franko Park, Kyiv. Painted by a pupil of the Klovsky Lyceum, Kyiv

Наш день продо́вжується

Мико́ла: От наре́шті я знайшо́в план мі́ста й кни́жку про істо́рію й суча́сне життя́ Ки́єва. Звича́йно, ми бу́демо йти́ по Хреща́тику, центра́льній ву́лиці мі́ста. Там бли́зько рі́зні бульва́ри, пло́щі, теа́три, а головне́ – Університе́т і́мені Тара́са Шевче́нка, інститу́ти й цирк! Пі́демо за́втра на конце́рт або́ в теа́тр подиви́тися п'є́су. Покажи́ газе́ту, Джон(е)!

Джон: От вона́. В одні́й кни́жці я що́йно чита́в, що Пу́ща-Води́ця це ду́же га́рне мі́сце; то, ма́бу́ть, че́рез два дні, якщо́ ще бу́де спе́ка, пі́демо на оди́н з ки́ївських пля́жів.

Окса́на: Здає́ться, ми тут бу́демо бага́то ходи́ти. Я сподіва́юся, що на ву́лицях Ки́єва є й бага́то кафе́! Чи мо́жна тепер сказа́ти вам, хло́пці, що хо́чу піти́ до́бре поспа́ти; я зо́всім втоми́лася, а за́втра ду́же хо́чу огляда́ти мі́сто ра́зом з ва́ми. О котрі́й годи́ні встаємо́?

Мико́ла: І я хо́чу спа́ти. Відпочи́ньмо до́бре, вста́немо, коли́ ви́спимося. На все ма́ємо час. О пів на девя́ту, мо́же пізні́ше, бу́демо сні́дати. Зна́чить, ти вста́неш рані́ше, Окса́но, приготува́ти сніда́нок!

Оксана: На такі́ зая́ви не ва́рто відповіда́ти. О девя́тій вста́ну. Спаси́бі заздалегі́дь за сніда́нок!

Vocabulary

суча́сний	contemporary, modern
центра́льний	central
бульва́р, -у	boulevard
пло́ща, -і	square
головне́	principally, mainly, the main thing
інститу́т, -у	institute
і́мені	named after (+ gen: lit 'of the name of')
цирк, -у	circus
конце́рт, -у	concert
п'є́са, -и	play
Пу́ща-Води́ця, -і - -і	Pushcha-Vodytsia
то	then, so (conj.)
пляж, -у	beach
кафе́, indecl.	café (indeclinable neuter)
огляда́ти, -а́є-	look around, visit
ра́зом з + instr.	together with, along with
хло́пець, -пця	boy, lad, fellow

о котрі́й годи́ні	at what time?	**зая́ва, -и**	statement, declaration
устава́ти, -ає́-	to get up (imperf.; perf. **уста́ти, -не-**)	**(не) ва́рто**	it's (not) worth, it makes (no) sense to
ви́спатися, -и- (perf.)	have a good sleep (perf: 'we shall have had a good sleep')	**спаси́бі**	thanks (**за** + acc. 'for')
		заздалегі́дь	in advance
о пів на дев'я́ту	at half past eight		

Telling the time

In the text we met the forms **о пів на дев'я́ту** and **о дев'я́тій**. These are examples of the ordinal numeral, e.g. 'first', 'sixth', etc., which is essential to telling the time in Ukrainian. In form and declension ordinals are like adjectives.

1st	**пе́рший**	**пе́рша**	**пе́рше**	**пе́рші**
2nd	**дру́гий**	**дру́га**	**дру́ге**	**дру́гі**
3rd	**тре́тій**	**тре́тя**	**тре́тє**	**тре́ті**
4th	**четве́ртий**	**четве́рта**	**четве́рте**	**четве́рті**
5th	**п'я́тий**	**п'я́та**	**п'я́те**	**п'я́ті**
6th	**шо́стий**	**шо́ста**	**шо́сте**	**шо́сті**
7th	**сьо́мий**	**сьо́ма**	**сьо́ме**	**сьо́мі**
8th	**во́сьмий**	**во́сьма**	**во́сьме**	**во́сьмі**
9th	**дев'я́тий**	**дев'я́та**	**дев'я́те**	**дев'я́ті**
10th	**деся́тий**	**деся́та**	**деся́те**	**деся́ті**
11th	**одина́дцятий**	**одина́дцята**	**одина́дцяте**	**одина́дцяті**
12th	**двана́дцятий**	**двана́дцята**	**двана́дцяте**	**двана́дцяті**
(13–19 follow the same pattern)				
20th	**двадця́тий**	**двадця́та**	**двадця́те**	**двадця́ті**

21st **два́дцять пе́рший** and so on, the first component remaining invariable.

The feminine form (**пе́рша**, **дру́га** . . .) is the relevant one here: it agrees with the word **годи́на** 'hour'. To ask what time it is, one uses the interrogative adjective **котри́й** 'which?' Thus:

Котра́ годи́на?	What time is it?
Чи ви не ска́жете, котра́ годи́на?	(more polite)

To express 'At what time . . .', one uses **коли́?** 'when?' or **о котрі́й годи́ні?** (locative case). Thus:

Колú вонú приїздя́ть до Кúєва? **О котрíй годúні вонú приїздя́ть до Кúєва?**	When/At what time will they arrive in Kyiv?

One answers these questions by a simple exercise of substitution, except that the word **годúна** may be omitted (past tense: **булá**, again to agree with **годúна**):

Трéтя	**3.00**	It's three o'clock
Четвéрта	**4.00**	It's four o'clock
Одинáдцята	**11.00**	It's eleven o'clock
Булá одинáдцята	**11.00**	It was eleven o'clock
О трéтій	**0 3-ій**	At three o'clock
О четвéртій	**0 4-ій**	At four o'clock
Об одинáдцятій	**0б 11-ій**	At eleven o'clock

Notice that before a numeral beginning with a vowel, the preposition is **об**. Not everything happens on the hour, of course, so we need also to specify 'past/after' and 'to'. '1–29 minutes past' and 'a quarter (**чверть**, fem.) past' are rendered in one of the following two ways (past tense no longer involves **годúна**, so 'it was' is rendered by the neuter **булó**):

minutes/**чверть + по** + loc. of preceding hour
minutes/**чверть + на** + acc. of following hour

Thus:

П'ять по сьóмій	Five past/after seven
Деся́ть по дев'я́тій	Ten past/after nine
Чверть на деся́ту	A quarter past/after nine
Двáдцять сім на дванáдцяту	Twenty-seven minutes past eleven

The word **хвилúна** 'minute' may be inserted, as **хвилúна** with 1 and 21, as **хвилúни** with 2–4, 22–4, and as **хвилúн** with the others, plus 30 ('second' **секýнда** is probably not needed here):

П'ять хвилúн по сьóмій	Five past/after seven
Деся́ть хвилúн по дев'я́тій	Ten past/after nine
Двáдцять однá хвилúна на деся́ту	Twenty-one past/after nine
Три хвилúни на дванáдцяту	Three minutes past eleven

These forms convey both 'it's . . .' and 'at . . .'; in other words, **о(б)** is not needed. The word used for 'half' is **пів**; it is invariable and may or may not be preceded by **о(б)** to render 'at' a particular time. 'Half past X (X-thirty)' is conveyed by one of the following constructions:

пів + **на** + acc. of following hour
пів + **до** + gen. of following hour

Thus:

(О) пів на дру́гу ми пої́демо туди́	At half past one we'll set off there
(О) пів до тре́тьої вона́ прийшла́	She arrived at half past two

For the second half of the clock (i.e. after the half hour) we use

за + minutes/**чверть** (acc.) + following hour (nom.)

За чверть деся́та ми вста́немо	We'll get up at a quarter to ten
Уже́ за два́дцять сьо́ма. Ми спізни́лися.	It's twenty to seven. We're late.

О(б) is not needed to render 'at' here either. You may also hear the preposition **без** 'without' + gen. instead of **за** + accusative to convey 'to (the hour)'; see the reference section for the genitive case of the numerals.

It is also possible to tell the time in a more 'English' way, e.g. **во́сьма два́дцять** 'eight twenty' (this is regarded as colloquial), or even the rather official-sounding **п'ятна́дцять п'ять** 'fifteen five', using the 24-hour clock (note that the cardinal, not the ordinal, number is used here). In contrast to the English 24-hour clock (as used in the military or in radio broadcasts), Ukrainian does not use the word 'hundred', as in 'twenty-two hundred hours' ('2200'); this will simply be **два́дцять два нуль нуль**, lit. 'twenty-two zero zero'. The 24-hour clock is used in official timetables such as train schedules and in radio/TV programming.

The genitive of the various divisions of the day is used to convey 'a.m.' and 'p.m.':

но́чі	0100–0400
ра́нку	0400–1200
дня	1200–1700
ве́чора	1700–2400

For example: **Тре́тя но́чі; одина́дцята ра́нку; п'я́та дня; сьо́ма ве́чора**

Since, until, before

If we wish to say 'since/from 7 o'clock', then we use the preposition **з** + genitive (so 'from' spatially and temporally); both 'until' and 'before' are conveyed by the preposition **до** + genitive:

У Льво́ві вони́ були́ з сьо́мої годи́ни.	They had been in L'viv since seven o'clock.
Зу́стріч трива́тиме до одина́дцятої годи́ни.	The meeting will last until eleven o'clock'. (**трива́ти**, **-а́є-** 'last')
Вони́ приї́хали до пе́ршої.	They arrived before one o'clock.

A few constructions used with expressions of time

Among verbs often encountered in expressions of time we find 'to take place': **відбу́тися**, -де-, imperf. **відбува́тися**, **-а́є-**. Thus:

Коли́ відбу́дуться збо́ри?	When is the meeting? (Note that this word for 'meeting' is a plural noun!)

Usually one arranges meetings for a certain time or agrees to meet at a certain time. For this, where there is a sense of 'purpose', a look to the future, we need **на** + accusative:

Вона́ домо́вилася зустрі́тися з ним на дру́гу.	She agreed/arranged to meet him at two.
Бе́сіду з дире́ктором призна́чено на во́сьму годи́ну ра́нку.	The interview with the director was arranged for eight o'clock in the morning.

Note here that 'arranged' **призна́чено** is an invariable impersonal form (you learn more about this construction in *18*), with the object in the accusative, as if we had used the standard, personal form **признача́ти**, **-а́є-**, perf. **призначи́ти**, **-и-** or **-и́-** 'to set, fix, arrange, allocate'.

'Starting' and 'ending' are also important when talking about time. When we want to say 'the film starts . . .' or 'the concert ends . . .', we use **починá́тися**, **-а́є-** (perf. **поча́тися**, **-чне́-**) 'to start, begin' (also **розпочина́тися/розпоча́тися** following the same conjugation patterns) or **кінча́тися**, **-а́є-**, perf. **закінчи́тися**, **-и́-**. Some examples:

Мене́ турбу́є, що Мико́ла не сказа́в, коли́ фі́льм почне́ться.	What bothers me is that Mykola didn't say when the film would start.

Коли́ по́дорож наре́шті закінчи́лася, ми хоті́ли ті́льки спа́ти.	When the journey finally ended, all we wanted to do was sleep.

Do note that these verbs of ‘starting’ and ‘ending’ may also occur non-reflexively; when they do, they must either be followed by an object in the accusative or an imperfective infinitive, e.g. ‘to begin a lecture’, ‘to stop reading’:

Виклада́ч прийшо́в і поча́в ле́кцію.	The lecturer arrived and started the lecture.
Ма́ма хо́че, щоб я закінчи́ла чита́ти.	Mum wants me to stop reading.

Exercise 11b

Write out the times (all p.m.) in the following dialogue, then translate it:

О котрі́й годи́ні ти бу́деш удо́ма?
О 8.50. Тепе́р 6.00, іще́ ма́йже три годи́ни бу́ду тут.
О 9.30 ді́ти на нас чека́тимуть у теа́трі. Якщо́ ти бу́деш удо́ма о 9.00, змо́жеш повече́ряти.
Гара́зд. Я ду́же хо́чу бу́ти вдо́ма рі́вно о 10.00, бо ма́ю робо́ту.
Шкода́. Ти ніко́ли не відпочива́єш. Твоє́ життя́ таке́ важке́.

Vocabulary

теа́тр, -у	theatre
рі́вно	precisely, on the dot
бо	because, for
таки́й	so, such a (note that ‘so big’ and similar phrases are translated not by using **так**, but by using **таки́й**, which will agree in case, gender, and number with the adjective)

Note: where reference is to the future, we have the future tense after **якщо́** (and in the other half of the ‘if’ sentence).

Exercise 11c

Say and write out in full the following times:

(a)	10.40 p.m.	(b)	1.15 a.m.	(c)	2.30 p.m.	(d)	8.00 a.m.
(e)	7.00 p.m.	(f)	10.25 p.m.	(g)	5.10 a.m.	(h)	3.45 p.m.
(i)	9.05 a.m.	(j)	4.20 a.m.	(k)	12.16 p.m.	(l)	6.50 p.m.

Now repeat them, replacing 'p.m.' with 'a.m.' and 'a.m.' with 'p.m.'then recast them as 'at . . .'.

Orthodox church in Kyiv, painted by a pupil of the Klovsky Lyceum, Kyiv

Excuse me, do you have the time?

Your watch has stopped, and you have to approach someone and ask him/her the time (you have to meet a friend at the underground/subway stop). You should use the following patterns:

Скажíть, будь лáска, котрá годи́на.
Ви́бачте, пáне, чи ви не знáєте, котрá годи́на?
Прóшу сказáти, котрá годи́на; мій годи́нник зупини́вся.
Мій годи́нник поспішáє/відстáв.

годи́нник, -а 'watch'; **зупини́вся** 'has stopped'; **поспішáє** 'is fast'; **відстáв** 'is slow' (lit. 'has lagged behind')

Exercise 11d

Respond to the following questions and statements giving a precise time (use full answers where appropriate, e.g. by saying when the accompanying event happened):

(a) Мико́ло, коли́ ти бу́деш у мі́сті?
(b) Марі́є, котра́ годи́на?
(c) Мико́ло Володи́мировичу, коли́ почина́ється ле́кція?
(d) Чи він сказа́в тобі́, коли́ приїздя́ть?
(e) Будь ла́ска, скажи́, коли́ відчиня́ються магази́ни; коли́ нема́ че́рги?
(f) За́втра я бу́ду у Льво́ві, але́ не зна́ю то́чно коли́. Коли́ при́йде по́їзд?
(g) Учо́ра Окса́на прийшла́ додо́му пі́сля полу́дня?

Note: **по́лудень**, **по́лудня** 'noon', as against **пі́вдень**, **пі́вдня** 'south', while **пі́вніч**, **пі́вночі** does service for both 'midnight' and 'north'. **Че́рга́** 'queue, line'; a useful expression is **без че́рги́** 'without having to wait (long)', in other words, without a queue.

Vocabulary building

Possessives

Possessive adjectives are extremely common in Ukrainian and highly recommended for normal usage. They are formed from people's names and nouns denoting animate beings. Basically, forms in **-а** or **-я** replace these endings with **-ин** (those in **-ія** replaces this with **-їін**). Others, masculines ending in a consonant or **-о**, have the suffix **-ів** (written **-їв** after [y]). Some examples of the two patterns are:

Мико́ла	**Мико́лин, Мико́лина, Мико́лине, Мико́лині**
	Мико́лів, Мико́лова, Мико́лове, Мико́лові
Марі́я	**Марі́їн, Марі́їна, Марі́їне, Марі́їні**
О́льга	**О́льжин, О́льжина, О́льжине, О́льжині** (final **г**, **к**, **х** become **ж**, **ч**, **ш**)
ба́тько	**ба́тьків, ба́тькова, ба́тькове, ба́тькові**
Андрі́й	**Андрі́їв, Андрі́єва, Андрі́єве, Андрі́єві**
Васи́ль	**Васи́лів, Васи́лева, Васи́леве, Васи́леві**
брат	**бра́тів, бра́това, бра́тове, бра́тові**

Note the alternation in the second pattern, and observe how it works.

These are in form adjectives, with the exception of the nominative and nominative–accusative masculine singular form. In Exercise 11a (i), you read:

Два хло́пці купи́ли ба́тькові маши́ну.

Supposing you had read:

Два хло́пці купи́ли ба́тькову маши́ну.

What is the difference in meaning?

Exercise 11e

Here are a few more names and nouns. Form possessives from them:

Богда́н	**Оле́кса/Оле́ксій**	**Петро́**	**Семе́н**
Макси́м	**Валенти́на**	**Зінаї́да**	**Іри́на**
Степа́н	**Окса́на**	**Оле́на**	**Яросла́ва**
Катери́на	**син**	**дочка́**	**ма́ма**
Тетя́на	**Ва́ля**	**Сла́ва**	**Зі́на**
Катру́ся	**Дмитро́**	**Євге́н**	

Exercise 11f

Work out the meaning of the following two proverbs:

Да́лі свого́ но́са нічо́го не ба́чить.
Від своє́ї со́вісті не втече́ш.

Words to help you: **ніс** ‘nose’, **со́вість** ‘conscience’, **втекти́** ‘to flee, escape’.

12 Ве́чір у мі́сті

An evening in the city

In this lesson you will learn about:

- expressions of time referring to the week, the month and the year
- modals (normal verbs, predicative adjectives, impersonals)

Розмо́ва в рестора́ні в це́нтрі мі́ста

Mykola, John, Mykhailo Andriyenko, and Oksana talk of the sights of Kyiv

Мико́ла: Ой, так до́бре поси́діти! У ме́не но́ги боля́ть.

Джон: А в ме́не боли́ть голова́. Сті́льки вра́жень! Два дні тому́ я був в Оде́сі, мину́лого ти́жня ще́ в А́нглії. Про́сто не ві́рю тому́, що ро́биться зі мно́ю.

Окса́на: Вече́ряти бу́демо в цьо́му рестора́ні, відпочи́немо. Що вам найбі́льш сподо́балося?

Мико́ла: Мені́ найбі́льш сподо́балося ходи́ти, ї́здити по мі́сті. Бульва́ри, по яки́х ми йшли, такі́ широ́кі, ти́хі, сті́льки дере́в. Я про́сто не зна́в, що Ки́їв таке́ па́гористе, таке́ зеле́не мі́сто.

Джон: Я ду́же ра́дий, що ми сі́ли в троле́йбус і поїхали в університе́тський ботані́чний сад.

Окса́на: Та й по́тім пішли́ до ста́нції метро́ й метрополіте́ном поверну́лися до це́нтру.

Мико́ла: Я ду́же люблю́ залиша́ти маши́ну вдо́ма й походи́ти або́ поїздити по мі́сті чи на таксі́, чи авто́бусом, чи на метро́.

ОКСА́НА: Ми були́ у ботані́чному саду́, у па́рках, до́бре огля́нули рі́зні буди́нки, па́м'ятники. Здає́ться, (що) до́бре зна́ю мі́сто, і зна́ю як мені́ дійти́ до око́лиць, як доі́хати до інститу́тів, де вча́ться студе́нти з Ки́єва, з яки́ми я регуля́рно листу́юся.

Vocabulary

вече́ряти, -яє-, imperf.	to have dinner/ supper	**де́рево, -а**	tree
нога́, -и́ (acc. **но́гу**)	foot, leg	**про́сто**	simply
болі́ти, боли́ть, боля́ть	to ache (observe the pattern in the dialogue)	**па́гористий**	hilly
голова́, -и́ (acc. **го́лову**)	head	**зеле́ний**	green
сті́льки	so much, so many (+ gen. sg./pl.)	**сі́сти, ся́де-,** perf. **у/в** + acc.	to get on (a bus etc.; imperf. **сіда́ти**, **-а́є**-)
вра́ження, -я, neut.	impression	**троле́йбус, -а**	trolleybus
ві́рити, -и-, imperf.	to believe (+ dat.)	**ботані́чний**	botanical
роби́тися, -и-, imperf.	to happen (**з** + instr. 'to [me]')	**ста́нція, -ї метро́**	subway/under-ground station
сподо́батися, -ає-, perf.	to please (perf.; note the construction)	**метрополіте́н, -у** (**метро́,** indecl.)*	subway/ underground
найбі́льш(е)	most (of all)	**походи́ти, -и-,** perf.	to walk around a little
широ́кий	wide	**поі́здити, -и-,** perf.	to 'drive' around a little
ти́хий	quiet, peaceful	**регуля́рно**	regularly
		листува́тися, -у́є-, imperf.	to correspond (write letters) (**з**+ instr. 'with')

*This word is indeclinable in standard Ukrainian: thus you must say **на метро́**. In very colloquial (some might call it 'substandard') Ukrainian you may well hear an instrumental **метро́м**, however (use the standard!).

Exercise 12a

Imagine that you, too, have had a hard day's sightseeing, that various parts of your body are in need of a rest and that you would like to eat and drink something. Create a dialogue either on your own or with fellow learners. Some useful words and phrases, in addition to those you have already met and which you might find in the next dialogue, include:

замовля́ти, замо́вити	to order
Скі́льки ко́штує/ко́штують . . .?	How much is/are . . .?
Я хо́чу заплати́ти	May I have the bill ('I want to pay')
Скі́льки з ме́не?	How much do I owe?
моро́зиво, -а	ice-cream
пе́псі, ко́ка ко́ла	Pepsi, Coca Cola

Пла́ни на за́втра

ДЖОН: В А́нглії під час відпочи́нку в субо́ту та неді́лю я люблю́ ї́здити на велосипе́ді по вузьки́х сільськи́х доро́гах. Бі́ля по́лудня мо́жна, ні, обов'язко́во тре́ба зупини́тися десь у таве́рні відпочи́ти, спокі́йно ви́пити з дві га́льби пи́ва й пої́сти. Незважа́ючи на весь прогре́с, іще́ є такі́ місця́ у нас.

МИКО́ЛА: А що бу́де на за́втра, дру́зі? На мою́ ду́мку не ва́рто ще раз ходи́ти по мі́сті.

ДЖОН: Я зго́ден з тобо́ю. В А́нглії я зацікáвився старови́нними церква́ми. Я пе́вен, що є чудо́ві украї́нські церкви́ в око́лицях Ки́єва або́ на́віть у близьки́х міста́х. Ду́же до́бре було́ б побува́ти у таки́х місця́х, подиви́тися на Ки́ївщину, ті́льки не на Чорно́биль; безсумні́вно нам не мо́жна бу́де пої́хати туди́.

ОКСА́НА: Але́ споча́тку бу́дьмо реалі́стами: тре́ба повече́ряти (я так хо́чу ї́сти!), до́бре поспа́ти, а за́втра вра́нці я куплю́ фотоплі́вку й пої́демо.

Vocabulary

під час відпочи́нку	when not working, during rest-time (a synonym for the whole phrase is **уїке́нд**)
ї́здити на велосипе́ді	to cycle (**велосипе́д, -а**)
вузьки́й	narrow
бі́ля по́лудня	around midday (**полу́день, полу́дня**)
зупини́тися, -и-, perf.	stop
таве́рна, -и	inn
спокі́йно	calmly, peacefully
з + acc.	about, approximately
га́льба, -и	pint (actually 'half a litre')
пи́во, -а	beer
пої́сти, perf., irreg.	have something to eat (see **ї́сти**)
незважа́ючи на	in spite of (+ acc.)
прогре́с -у	progress
ще раз	once again
зацікáвитися, -и-, perf.	to become interested in (imperf. **цікáвитися** + instr.)
пе́вен, пе́вна	certain, sure
близьки́й	near
побува́ти, -а́є- imperf.	spend some time in, visit
безсумні́вно	without doubt
спочáтку	at first
повече́ряти, -яє-, perf.	have a little supper (or just 'to have supper')
поспа́ти, -и́-, perf.	have a little sleep, take a nap
реалі́ст, -а	realist (note the use of the instr. after **бу́ти**)
фотоплі́вка, -и	film (for a camera)

More expressions of time

	Дні ти́жня	*The days of the week*	
Su	**неді́ля**	**у неді́лю**	**по неді́лях**
Mo	**понеді́лок**	**у понеді́лок**	**по понеді́лках**
Tu	**вівто́рок**	**у вівто́рок**	**по вівто́рках**
We	**середá**	**у се́реду**	**по се́редах**
Th	**четве́р**	**у четве́р**	**по четвергáх** (NB!)
Fr	**п'я́тниця**	**у п'я́тницю**	**по п'я́тницях**
Sa	**субо́та**	**у субо́ту**	**по субо́тах**

Saint Sophia's Cathedral, Kyiv

'On Sunday, Monday', etc. is conveyed by the preposition **в/у** + acc. (one may include **цей** (masc.) or **цю** (fem.) to give 'this Saturday' etc.), while the expression 'on Tuesdays, Wednesdays etc.' (that is, on Tuesdays or Wednesday as a rule) is conveyed by **по** + loc. pl. 'Month' is **мі́сяць** (masc.):

Мі́сяці ро́ку			*The months of the year*		
Jan	**сі́чень**	**у сі́чні**	July	**ли́пень**	**у ли́пні**
Feb	**лю́тий**	**у лю́тому**	Aug	**се́рпень**	**у се́рпні**
Mar	**бе́резень**	**у бе́резні**	Sept	**ве́ресень**	**у ве́ресні**
Apr	**кві́тень**	**у кві́тні**	Oct	**жо́втень**	**у жо́втні**
May	**тра́вень**	**у тра́вні**	Nov	**листопа́д**	**у листопа́ді**
June	**че́рвень**	**у че́рвні**	Dec	**гру́день**	**у гру́дні**

All the names of the months are masculine; note that **лю́тий** is adjectival in form. Except for **лю́тий**, the genitive singular is **-я/-а**. Note that 'in January, February, etc.' is conveyed by means of the preposition **в/у** + loc. 'Season' is **пора́ ро́ку** (lit. 'time of the year'):

По́ри ро́ку		*The Seasons*	
Spring	**весна́**	**навесні́**	'in spring'
Summer	**лі́то**	**влі́тку**	'in summer'
Autumn/Fall	**о́сінь**	**восени́**	'in autumn/fall'
Winter	**зима́**	**взи́мку**	'in winter'

The instrumental of the seasons, e.g. **весно́ю** 'in spring' (*9*) must be used when specifying the year (not available for **о́сінь**); when the year is not mentioned, the two possible constructions are considered synonymous. With all of the preceding forms one may use **пі́сля** + gen. to express 'after'; 'before' is expressed (as you have seen already) by **до** + gen. Compare the following:

Пі́сля середи́ бу́демо відпочива́ти.
Не зна́ю, коли́ Петро́ поі́де в Ки́їв; здає́ться, що він хо́че поі́хати до неді́лі.
Пі́сля лі́та ді́тям тре́ба ходи́ти у шко́лу.

When asking what the date is, and on what date something happens, we use **котри́й** with the noun **число́**; note the different constructions required by (say) 'the fourteenth of February' compared with 'on the fourteenth of February':

Котре́ сьогодні число́?	What date is it today?
Сього́дні чотирна́дцяте лю́того.	Today's the fourteenth of February.
Котро́го числа́ він при́їде?	On what date will he arrive?
Він при́їде шо́стого ли́пня.	On the sixth of July.

'Of the month' is simply rendered by using the genitive, as you might have expected. Various adverbs of time will be encountered as the course progresses, and they are summarized in tabular form in the reference section. Here, for convenience, we mention the key words for:

Days and parts of the day

(Use them separately or combine a term from the first column with one from the second):

	Day	*Part of day*	
the day before yesterday	**позавчо́ра**		
yesterday	**вчо́ра**	**вра́нці**	*in the morning*
today	**сього́дні**	**пі́сля по́лудня**	*in the afternoon*

tomorrow	**зáвтра**	**ввéчері/увéчері**	*in the evening*
day after tomorrow	**післязáвтра**	**вночí**	*during the night*
day after tomorrow	**позáвтра** (coll.)		

Past, present and future of weeks and years

Use the genitive (we have already encountered examples of this) and combine and adjective with an appropriate noun:

last	**минýлого**	**тúжня**	week
this	**цьогó**	**рóку**	year
next	**настýпного**		

For the months one uses a locative construction ('in', as in English: 'in January'): **в/у** + (**минýлому/цьóму/настýпному** + the name of the month in the locative): e.g. **у бéрезні** 'in March', **у цьóму бéрезні** 'this March', etc. Note that in English we drop 'in' when we add 'this, last, next', but Ukrainian always uses the 'in + locative' construction.

Finally, a reminder about the most general expressions of time, when there is no Ukrainian preposition expressing English 'for' or 'during', e.g. 'she was there a week', 'I travelled there five days' (i.e. it took five days to get there). Remember that Ukrainian uses the accusative here:

Вонá булá там тúждень.	She was there for a week.
Я ́їхав тудú п'ять днів.	It took me five days to get there.
Ми читáли годúну.	We read for an hour.

Note the following situation when you do have a preposition for English 'for'. If you are going somewhere for a period of time (that is, you are not travelling during that time, but it is the length of your stay after you get there), then we use **на** + acc. A good rule of thumb is that if you can leave out 'for' in English, then use no preposition in Ukrainian; otherwise use **на**.

Вонá поїхала тудú на п'ять днів.
Івáн поїхав в Одéсу на ці́лу веснý.

Test the rule of thumb: you wouldn't say in English 'She went there five days' (but you would say 'she was there five days') or 'Ivan went to Odessa the whole spring'; these sentences make it sound as though 'she' and 'Ivan' spent five days/the whole spring getting to these places. If that were the case, you would have no preposition, and you would need a different verb, certainly not a perfective (these express 'set out'), in Ukrainian!

Exercise 12b

Express the following in Ukrainian:

(a) The day before yesterday in the evening I saw Ol'ha.
(b) Last year (I think in January) I read an interesting book.
(c) In July (that's in summer) we rest.
(d) What was the date yesterday?
(e) (On) what date did Oksana come to Ukraine from England?
(f) The day after tomorrow (maybe in the morning), or perhaps next week, I'll call you.

Years

None of the constructions involving years (**рік**, **póку**) feels especially 'foreign' to an English speaker. When saying 'in 1995' (for example) the numeral is cardinal and undeclined in all components save the last, which is an ordinal in the locative singular masculine agreeing with **póці**. Thus:

У ти́сяча дев'ятсо́т дев'яно́сто п'я́тому ро́ці

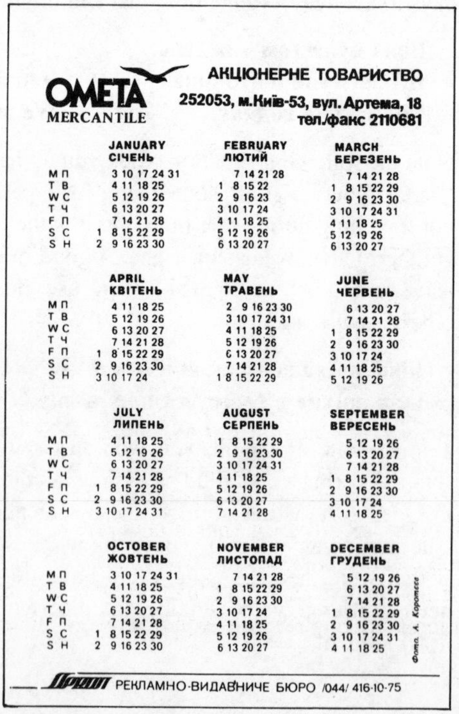

OMETA MERCANTILE

АКЦІОНЕРНЕ ТОВАРИСТВО
252053, м.Київ-53, вул. Артема, 18
тел./факс 2110681

	JANUARY СІЧЕНЬ	FEBRUARY ЛЮТИЙ	MARCH БЕРЕЗЕНЬ
M П	3 10 17 24 31	7 14 21 28	7 14 21 28
T В	4 11 18 25	1 8 15 22	1 8 15 22 29
W С	5 12 19 26	2 9 16 23	2 9 16 23 30
T Ч	6 13 20 27	3 10 17 24	3 10 17 24 31
F П	7 14 21 28	4 11 18 25	4 11 18 25
S С	1 8 15 22 29	5 12 19 26	5 12 19 26
S Н	2 9 16 23 30	6 13 20 27	6 13 20 27

	APRIL КВІТЕНЬ	MAY ТРАВЕНЬ	JUNE ЧЕРВЕНЬ
M П	4 11 18 25	2 9 16 23 30	6 13 20 27
T В	5 12 19 26	3 10 17 24 31	7 14 21 28
W С	6 13 20 27	4 11 18 25	1 8 15 22 29
T Ч	7 14 21 28	5 12 19 26	2 9 16 23 30
F П	1 8 15 22 29	6 13 20 27	3 10 17 24
S С	2 9 16 23 30	7 14 21 28	4 11 18 25
S Н	3 10 17 24	1 8 15 22 29	5 12 19 26

	JULY ЛИПЕНЬ	AUGUST СЕРПЕНЬ	SEPTEMBER ВЕРЕСЕНЬ
M П	4 11 18 25	1 8 15 22 29	5 12 19 26
T В	5 12 19 26	2 9 16 23 30	6 13 20 27
W С	6 13 20 27	3 10 17 24 31	7 14 21 28
T Ч	7 14 21 28	4 11 18 25	1 8 15 22 29
F П	1 8 15 22 29	5 12 19 26	2 9 16 23 30
S С	2 9 16 23 30	6 13 20 27	3 10 17 24
S Н	3 10 17 24 31	7 14 21 28	4 11 18 25

	OCTOBER ЖОВТЕНЬ	NOVEMBER ЛИСТОПАД	DECEMBER ГРУДЕНЬ
M П	3 10 17 24 31	7 14 21 28	5 12 19 26
T В	4 11 18 25	1 8 15 22 29	6 13 20 27
W С	5 12 19 26	2 9 16 23 30	7 14 21 28
T Ч	6 13 20 27	3 10 17 24	1 8 15 22 29
F П	7 14 21 28	4 11 18 25	2 9 16 23 30
S С	1 8 15 22 29	5 12 19 26	3 10 17 24 31
S Н	2 9 16 23 30	6 13 20 27	4 11 18 25

Фото. А. Коротєєв

РЕКЛАМНО-ВИДАВНИЧЕ БЮРО /044/ 416-10-75

1994 calendar in Ukrainian

In other words, 'in the one thousand nine hundred ninety-fifth year'. If one simply names a year ('The year is 1995'), the nominative is used: **ти́сяча дев'ятсо́т дев'яно́сто п'я́тий рік**. Colloquially, one can omit the word **рік**, **ро́ці**, in these constructions, but it is best not to.

When a date precedes a year, the last number (ordinal) and the word 'year' are in the genitive: literally, we say 'X date of the year YZ':

> **п'я́те/п'я́того лю́того ти́сяча дев'ятсо́т дев'яно́сто пе́ршого ро́ку**
> **деся́те/деся́того бе́резня ти́сяча дев'ятсо́т вісімдеся́т дев'я́того ро́ку**

Exercise 12c

Read and write out the following dates in full (note that in Ukraine, as in other European countries, the order of the date when using numerals is 'day-month-year', with the month appearing in Roman numerals):

(a)	2.ii.1994	(b)	3.viii.1978	(c)	16.i.2001	(d)	28.ix.1990
(e)	8.xii.1968	(f)	5.vii.1941	(g)	9.vi.1919	(h)	27.v.1950
(i)	18.iii.1957	(j)	21.iv.1995	(k)	7.xi.1986	(l)	31.x.1998

Exercise 12d

Now express the same dates in response to a 'when?' question.

Зага́дка

> **Яки́й рік трива́є ті́льки оди́н день?**
> [The solution will be found after the section on modals.]

Modals

By modals we understand those verbs or verb-like forms that convey a subject's attitude to something he or she does. They correspond roughly to 'can', 'be able to', 'must', 'ought to', 'should', 'have to', 'intend to', 'be inclined to', 'be supposed to', 'wish to', 'know how to', 'be glad to', 'be ready to'. In Ukrainian certain of these are conveyed by straightforward verbs, but others are rendered by impersonal expressions: as we have seen already, the person involved is not conveyed in the nominative case (and may often be omitted). Here in a literal translation into English, we would have as the subject of the verb an 'it' referring to nothing easily identifiable: 'it is necessary to sit down'.

Ukrainian modals are often followed by an infinitive. If the verb exists in both aspects, choose according to the usual criteria: namely, perfective if very specific, imperfective if rather vague, general, abstract or habitual. Below we list a few useful examples of modals, with suggestions for their use.

'Normal' verbs

могти́, змогти́	to be able to, can (physical ability mainly)
умі́ти, зумі́ти	to be able to, know how to, can (skill, knowledge)
хоті́ти, схоті́ти	to want to (the perfective implies a sudden desire)
му́сити	to have to, must (no perfective)

There is also the rather mild but very common impersonal verb **дово́дитися**, **-и-**, perf. **довести́ся**, **-дé-** 'to have to, to happen to have to, to fall to one's lot to' with the subject in the dative. Thus:

Йому́ довело́ся прийня́ти рі́шення	He had to accept the decision

The issue at hand was out of his control and he had little choice in the matter, or was even forced to accept the decision. One can also mention the verb **ма́ти**, **-áє-** 'have' which, when followed by an infinitive, has the sense of 'be supposed to, due to, intend':

Я мав йому́ переда́ти цю листі́вку.	I meant/was to give him this postcard.

Predicative adjectives

Here the adjective has a subject, with which it agrees; the construction does not always correspond literally to the equivalent English construction. Thus:

гото́вий/гото́в	ready
зго́дний/зго́ден	agree
ла́дний/ла́ден	capable of, ready, inclined
пе́вний/пе́вен	sure, certain
ра́дий/рад	glad
пови́нний/пови́нен	should, must, be obliged to
потрі́бний/потрі́бен	necessary

The feminine, neuter and plural forms are all derived regularly from the full masculine form. Note that **зго́дний** is also constructed with **з** + instr. e.g. **я зго́ден з тобо́ю** 'I agree with you'; remember that **потрі́бен** is used on the pattern 'the book is necessary to me', i.e. 'I need the book'; **Кни́жка мені́ потрі́бна** (*8*). Some of these modals may share meanings with regular verbs, e.g. **домо́витися** (perf.) 'to come to an agreement', used only in the plural and very common in the form **домо́вилися** 'OK, agreed!'. It may be followed either by an infinitive (agree to do something) or by **про** + acc. (agree about something):

Ми домо́вилися зустріча́тися о дев'я́тій.
Ми домо́вилися про цю телевізі́йну програ́му: вона́ ду́же пога́на.

'Impersonals'

We mention four very common impersonals here, of which the last two are already familiar. The first three are constructed with the dative of the subject:

слід	it is advisable to, one should, one has to
мо́жна	it is possible to, it is permissible to, one may, one must
тре́ба	it is necessary to, one has to, one must
ва́рто	it is worth (neg. 'there's no point in, it's not worth')

Examples:

Ва́рто чека́ти на ньо́го: він ду́же симпати́чний.
Мо́жна йти́ у парк пі́шки? Так, він зо́всім близьки́й.
Ви́бачте, О́льго. (Мені́) тре́ба йти́ додо́му.
Па́не профе́соре, я вже прочита́в усі́ статті́. До́бре, так слід.

Відга́дка: **Нови́й рік** 'the New Year'

Exercise 12e

Translate the following sentences into Ukrainian:

(a) I shall be able to do the shopping tomorrow.
(b) I must go to Kyiv, as it's only there that they can help me.
(c) May I borrow your city plan? I left mine at home.
(d) There's no point having dinner here; the cooking is not good.
(e) I'm really glad that you find the book interesting.

(f) I agree that he should go, but are you sure that his sister will do the work better?
(g) I don't know how to type, so I must hand the document over to our secretary.
(h) Unfortunately we had to go to the café.
(i) Tell me, can you speak Ukrainian?

Vocabulary

друкува́ти, -у́є- (на маши́нці) to type
доку́мент, -у document
секрета́рка, -и secretary

Exercise 12f

Now for a few sentences to unjumble (note that individual sequences may conceal two sentences). The words are all separated by commas and indispensable punctuation is within quotation marks (« »). Note that **кіно́** is indeclinable, so you have to work out which case it might be in!

(a) з, ба́тько, Ки́єва, приї́хав, до, ма́мою
(b) вве́чері, кі́но, за́втра, диви́тися, фі́льм, ході́мо, до
(c) О́льга, вікна́, ліво́руч, сиди́ть, від, поза́ду
(d) жо́втня, Петро́, Оде́си, трина́дцятого, з, пої́хав
(e) із, яки́й, «?», він, він, висо́кий, «,», товсти́й, се́бе
(f) у, бага́то, вона́, книга́рні, купи́ла, книжо́к
(g) батьки́, да́чі, мої́, на, тепе́р, ме́шкають
(h) її́, ми, база́рі, сесте́р, на, зустрі́ли
(i) ко́льору, «?», цей, яко́го, жо́втий, він, телефо́н
(j) що, «,» він, нас, пе́вна, я, до, за́йде

ation practice, dialogues and role-playing exercises, recorded by native speakers of Ukrainian, and will be an invaluable aid to improving your language skills.

If you have been unable to obtain the course pack, the double cassette (ISBN 0–415–09204–3) can be ordered separately through your bookseller or, in case of difficulty, send cash with order to Routledge Ltd, ITPS, Cheriton House, North Way, Andover, Hants SP10 5BE, price (1994) £16.99* including VAT, or to Routledge Inc., 29 West 35th Street, New York, NY 10001, USA, price $18.95*.

* *The publishers reserve the right to change prices without notice.*

CASSETTES ORDER FORM

Please supply one/two/ .... double cassette(s) of

Colloquial Ukrainian, Press & Pugh.
ISBN 0–415–09204–3

Price £16.99* incl. VAT
$18.95*

I enclose payment with order.
Please debit my Access/Mastercharge/Mastercard/Visa/American Express:

Expiry date ....

Name ....

Address ....

....

....

13 На ву́лицях, у магази́нах

On the streets, in the shops

In this lesson you will primarily consolidate your knowledge of the grammar and vocabulary presented in previous lessons. You will also learn about:

- the plurals of the remaining cases (dative, instrumental and locative)
- the weather and the climate
- approximate quantities
- comparatives and superlatives

Dialogue 1 Джон купу́є листі́вки

Микола:	Джо́н(е), де ви були́ сього́дні вра́нці?
Джон:	Ми ходи́ли по па́рках, по ву́лицях, були́ в магази́нах . . .
Микола:	До́бре; чи ви тако́ж розмовля́ли з людьми́?
Джон:	Звича́йно: ми розмовля́ли з продавця́ми, (з) продавщи́цями, (з) дітьми́ . . .
Микола:	Ду́же до́бре! І що ви купува́ли?
Джон:	Тільки листі́вки.
Микола:	Кому́ ти бу́деш відсила́ти ці листі́вки?
Джон:	Ну . . . дру́зям, батька́м, на́шим викладача́м . . .

продавщи́ця, -і saleswoman; **виклада́ч, -а́** teacher, lecturer

The dative, instrumental and locative plural

The dative, locative and instrumental plural endings for all regular nouns are **-ам**, **-ах** and **-ами** (**-ям**, **-ях** and **-ями**). Note that the placing of stress follows that of the nominative plural, so make sure that you know these basic forms before going on to the other cases! Compare:

	Feminine	*Masculine*	*Neuter*
Nom.	**ву́лиці**	**столи́**	**ві́кна**
Dat.	**ву́лицям**	**стола́м**	**ві́кнам**
Instr.	**ву́лицями**	**стола́ми**	**ві́кнами**
Loc.	**ву́лицях**	**стола́х**	**ві́кнах**

Of these three oblique cases, the instrumental looks a little different in a few very common nouns, and sometimes a noun can have more than one instrumental ending. Because they are so common, they need to be learned as you come across them:

the ending -**(ь)ми́**	**дітьми́, людьми́**
the ending -**и́ма**	**о́чі/очи́ма, пле́чі/плечи́ма** 'eyes, shoulders'
both	**двери́ма (двермі́), гроши́ма (гро́шми)**

Note that the ending -**и́ма** is always stressed on -**и́**, no matter what the stress is in the remaining case forms; in the last set of examples the ending -**и́ма** is preferred. But note the normal instrumental plural of **(у)ве́сь**: **усіма́**.

Accompanying adjectives and adjectival pronouns have similar endings: -**им**, -**ими** and -**их** (-**ім**, -**іми**, -**іх**, -**їм**, -**їми**, -**їх**). As a result, memorizing them is extremely simple. Just remember a few pairs of words: **нови́м листа́м**, **нови́ми листа́ми**, **нови́х листа́х** etc.

Exercise 13a

Give the dative, locative and instrumental plurals for the following noun phrases:

(a) **центра́льний бульва́р**
(b) **і́нший райо́н**
(c) **незале́жна держа́ва**
(d) **вузька́ доро́га**
(e) **суча́сне мі́сто**
(f) **за́втрашня газе́та**
(g) **цей англі́єць**
(h) **ця америка́нка**
(i) **нова́ маши́на**
(j) **четве́рта ле́кція**

The weather and the climate

To ask about the weather we use a pattern involving **який** and the word **пого́да** 'weather'. Thus:

Яка́ сього́дні пого́да?	What's the weather like today?
Яка́ була́ пого́да вчо́ра?	What was the weather like yesterday?
Яка́ бу́де пого́да за́втра?	What'll the weather be like tomorrow?

One might also wish to make the question more specific ('the weather *where*?') e.g. **в Іта́лії** 'in Italy', **у Льво́ві** 'in L'viv', **надво́рі** 'outside'. The answer could be framed as follows:

Сього́дні пого́да . . .
Вчо́ра пого́да була́ . . .
За́втра пого́да бу́де . . .

Сього́дні чудо́ва пого́да для купа́ння	Today (there is) fantastic weather for bathing/swimming.

The adjective is in the nominative singular feminine, agreeing with **пого́да**. In fairly rapid, informal, speech one may just give the adjective. Thus:

хоро́ша	**пога́на**	**мінли́ва**	**чудо́ва**
good	bad	changeable	fantastic

But an adjective is not the only option: we may say 'it's raining' or 'the sun's shining'. Here is a short selection:

Сві́тить со́нце.	The sun's shining.
Іде́ дощ/сніг/град.	It's raining/snowing/hailing.
Йшов дощ/сніг/град.	It was raining/snowing/hailing.
Бу́де дощ/сніг/град.	It'll be raining/snowing/hailing.

(світи́ти, -и-; со́нце, -я; дощ, -у́; сніг, -у; град, -у)

One may just use the noun on its own (**пого́да сього́дні**: **дощ/сніг/град**); for 'raining' and 'snowing' there are also the verbs **дощи́ти** and **сніжи́ти**:

Дощи́ть/Дощи́ло.	It's raining/It was raining.
Сніжи́ть/Сніжи́ло.	It's snowing/It was snowing.

Other words useful to know include **ві́тер**, **-тру** 'wind' (it may be used with the verb **ві́яти**, **-і́є-** 'to blow', thus **Ві́є ві́тер** 'there's a wind (blowing)'), **шторм**, **-у** 'gale, tempest', **пурга́**, **-и́** (sometimes **пурґа́**, **-и**) and **хуртови́на**, **-и** 'snowstorm', **бу́ря**, **-і** 'storm', **грім**, **гро́му** 'thunder' (**грими́ть** 'it's thundering', from **грими́ти**, **-и́-**), **блискави́ця**, **-і** '(flash of) lightning' (**бли́скає** 'there is lightning', from **бли́скати**, **-ає-**), **хма́рно** 'it's cloudy' (from **хма́ра**, **-и** 'cloud'; note, too, **безхма́рне**, **чи́сте не́бо** 'a cloudless, pure sky'), **хо́лодно** 'it's cold', **жа́рко** 'it's hot', **спеко́тно** 'it's really hot, a heatwave, sultry', **ду́шно** 'it's close, stifling', **те́пло** 'it's warm', **прохоло́дно** 'it's cool, refresh-ng', **га́рно** 'it's nice', and **припіка́є** 'it's getting scorching'.

If the weather is of a type you can't stand, use the verb **витри́мувати**, **-ує-**, perf. **ви́тримати**, **-ає-** 'to bear, hold out'. Thus:

Я не витри́мую хо́лоду/моро́зу/спе́ки.	I can't bear the cold/frost/heat.

(**хо́лод**, **-у**; **моро́з**, **-у**; **спе́ка**, **-и**)

Передаю́ть по ра́діо . . .

До́брого ра́нку, дорогі́ дру́зі! Прогно́з пого́ди на сього́дні: по Ки́єву бу́де хма́рна з проя́сненнями пого́да, вра́нці хо́лодно, бли́зько 5-8 гра́дусів моро́зу. Вдень потеплі́шає до 2-4 гра́дусів ни́жче нуля́, не́бо проясни́ться, ви́гляне со́нце. Уве́чері – можли́вий мо́крий сніг, відли́га. . . Вночі́ очі́кується поси́лення моро́зу до 8-10 гра́дусів, на доро́гах – ожеле́диця. Водії́ за кермо́м автомобі́ля ма́ють бу́ти особли́во обере́жними. На пі́вночі Ки́ївської о́бласті вночі́ можли́вий сніг, поси́лення ві́тру, хуртови́ни.

Vocabulary

передава́ти, -ає́-, imperf.	broadcast	**відли́га, -и**	thaw
гра́дус, -а	degree	**очі́куватися, -ує-**	be expected (imperf.)
моро́з, -у	frost	**поси́лення, -я**	strengthening
проя́снення, -я	clear interval	**ожеле́диця, -і**	slippery/icy (roads)
вдень	during the day (adv.)	**водíй, -я́**	driver
потеплі́шати, -ає-	become warmer (perf.)	**за кермо́м** (+ gen.)	at the wheel (of . . .)
проясни́тися, -и́-	clear up (perf.)		
ви́глянути, -не-	peep out (perf.)		

When talking in terms of degrees, the appropriate form of **гра́дус, -а, -ів** will be used after the numeral (after **нуль, -я́** 'zero' one has the genitive plural **гра́дусів**), with **моро́зу** 'of frost' (below freezing), **тепла́** 'of warmth' (above freezing) or **ви́ще/ни́жче нуля́** 'above/below zero' (freezing) added. If asking for the temperature, then the word is **температу́ра, -и**; use the **яки́й** construction as for the weather:

Яка́ сього́дні бу́де температу́ра?

When talking specifically about the climate, **клі́мат, -у**, appropriate adjectives would also include **суво́рий** 'severe', **м'яки́й** 'soft, gentle', **континента́льний** 'continental', **помі́рний** 'moderate', **сухи́й** 'dry', **воло́гий** 'damp, humid' (you might find the adverb **типо́во** 'typically' useful). Again, the **яки́й** construction may be used:

Яки́й у вас клі́мат на пі́вдні Сполу́чених Шта́тів?
Лі́том? У нас суво́рий клі́мат: там зана́дто жа́рко. (**зана́дто** 'too')

Зага́дка

Під яки́м кущéм сиди́ть зá́єць, коли́ ідé дощ?
(**кущ, -á** 'bush'; **зá́єць, зá́йця** 'hare')
[The solution will be found after the exercise.]

Exercise 13b

Write a short composition (pretend you're speaking to a curious Ukrainian friend) using the expressions for the weather encountered above. Describe what New Year (**Нови́й рік, -о́го Ро́ку**), Christmas (**Різдво́, -а́**), Easter (**Вели́кдень, Велико́дня**) or your birthday (**день, -дня (твого́) наро́дження**) are like where you live: you will be asked these questions!

Then describe how you spend your holidays (**кані́кули, кані́кул**) and what you do: use **під ча́с кані́кул** 'during the holidays' (prep. + genitive); for the feast days just mentioned the expressions are: **на Різдво́, на Нови́й Рік, на Вели́кдень** and **у день** (. . .) **наро́дження**). Verbs and expressions you can use: **купа́тися, -а́є-** 'bathe/go swimming', **пла́вати, -ає-** 'swim', **загоря́ти, -я́є-** (perf. **загорі́ти, -і́є-**) 'sunbathe, get sunburnt' (**загорі́лий** 'sunburnt'), **ката́тися, -а́є- на ли́жах/**

ковзана́х/санча́тах 'to go skiing/skating/sledge' (**ли́жа, и** 'ski', **ковза́н, -а́** 'skate', **санча́та, санча́т** 'small sledge/sled' (plural-only noun).

Відга́дка:	**Мо́крим** 'a wet one'

Ukrainian Easter card

A note on approximation

In order to express 'about, approximately' with numerals, we can use words such as the prepositions **бі́ля** + gen. and **з** + acc. 'about' or the indefinite adverb **десь** 'somewhere' in front of the quantity: **Марі́я чита́ла кни́жку бі́ля трьох годи́н** 'Mariya was reading the book for about three hours', **Він сказа́в мені́, що йому́ тре́ба з два́дцять до́ларів** 'He told me he needed about twenty dollars', **Десь чоти́ри**

гра́дуси моро́зу було́ вночі́ 'There was somewhere around four degrees of frost during the night'.

For numbers above 'one', we can simply invert the order in which the numeral and the object occur: **сантимéтрів два-три** 'about two-three centimetres', **ро́ків чоти́ри** 'about four years'. If there is a preposition involved, the number will precede the preposition+noun phrase: **він пішо́в годи́н на дві** 'he went for about two hours'. Note from these examples that the measurement will then appear in the genitive plural, no matter what the number is ('of the set of "centimeters", we have the number X'); some speakers may prefer to keep the noun in the case specified by the number (**годи́ни на дві**), but this is not standard.

Exercise 13c

Practise by inverting and changing (if necessary) the case of the noun – and write in the noun stress:

(a) два столи
(b) дві книжки
(c) п'ять домів
(d) три будинки
(e) де́сять міст

Ду́же коро́ткий діало́г

Микола́: Окса́но, чи твоя́ кварти́ра в А́нглії бі́льша чи ме́нша від на́шої?
Окса́на: Ме́нша, бо я там живу́ одна́. Але́ моя ку́хня бі́льша, ніж ва́ша.

Why did Oksana used **ви/ва́ш** while Mykola used **ти/твій**?

The comparative of the adjective

Ukrainian comparatives are formed in exactly the same manner for adjectives and adverbs:

adjective (minus **-ий** ending)	adverb (minus **-о/е** ending)
+ і́ший	**+ -і́ше**
холодні́ший	**холодні́ше**
теплі́ший	**теплі́ше**

Note that **-íший** is usually stressed.

There are many ways to express 'than' after comparative adjectives; compare the following:

(a)	**ніж**	+	thing/person compared (no change in case)
(b)	**від**	+	genitive of the thing/person compared
(c)	**за**	+	accusative of the thing/person compared
(d)	**як**	+	thing/person compared (no change in case)
(e)	**прóти**	+	genitive of the thing/person compared

Some examples:

Мій чай теплíший, ніж твій.	My tea is warmer than yours.
Мій брат розумнíший за Оксáну.	My brother is cleverer than Oksana.
У Хáркові теплíше, ніж у Кúєві.	It's warmer in Kharkiv than in Kyiv.
Гáнна вúща прóти Андрíя.	Hanner is taller than (lit. 'as against') Andriy.
Ця кнúжка цікавíша від тієї.	This book is more interesting than that one.

Note the use of the adverbial form **теплíше** to express 'it is warmer'. An alternative to forms such as **теплíший** and **холоднíший** is to use **більш** 'more' + basic adjective, e.g.

більш новúй будúнок	a/the newer (lit. 'more new') house

This is really restricted to adjectives composed of many syllables and even then is only optional, e.g. **енергíйний** 'energetic', **більш енергíйний/енергійнíший** 'more energetic'. Note that the same construction may be required in English; for instance, we simply cannot say that someone is 'energetic-er', but rather that he/she is 'more energetic'. The corresponding 'less' is of course not optional:

Він менш енергíйний ніж вонá.	He's less energetic than she.

The most commonly used adjectives and adverbs have 'irregular' comparative forms that are based on other roots (compare English 'good/better', 'bad/worse'):

Adjective	*Comparative adjective*	*Adverb (predicative)*
велúкий, -о	**бíльший**	**бíльш(е)**
гáрний, -о	**крáщий/гарнíший**	**крáще/гарнíше**
малúй, мáло	**мéнший**	**мéнш(е)**

до́брий, -е	**кра́щий, лі́пший** (but **добрі́ший** 'kinder')	**кра́ще/лі́пше**
пога́ний	**гі́рший**	**гі́рше**

Thus:

бі́льше мі́сто
ме́нша кни́жка
кра́щий буди́нок
лі́пший велосипе́д
гі́рший напі́й

Adjectives/adverbs with the suffixes **-к-**, **-ок-** and **-ек-** lose the suffixes before a simplified comparative suffix (it is with these adjectives that **-ш-** is most common):

дале́кий becomes	**да́льший**
дале́ко becomes	**да́льше**
широ́кий becomes	**ши́рший**
ши́роко becomes	**ши́рше**

If there is a consonant cluster at the end of the stem we may find the suffix further changed: for example, **бли́зько** becomes **бли́жче**. These forms will be pointed out as they occur.

Exercise 13d

Compare the weather of your home town with that of another place you have visited, using comparatives as above.

Vocabulary and grammar review (1)

A number of words/or parts of words and grammatical endings are missing from the following text. Try to fill in the gaps in such a way that the passage makes sense, then translate it.

Exercise 13e

Окса́на й Джон живу́ть у ______, але́ лю́блять вари́ти с______. Їм потріб______ бул______ хлі́ба та цу́кру. Вони́ пі______ в ду́же вели______ магази́н. Продав______ сказа́в, що цу́кру ______. Наре́шті, на ву́лиц______ Іва́на Франка́ вони́ знай______ цу́кор: вони́ куп______ його́ й звар______ чай. Але́ так ______ шук______ цу́кор, що пі́зно ______ йти́ в ______!

Suggested vocabulary item: **сам**, **самá**, **самó**, **самí** 'self, oneself, very; alone' (note the stressed ending; its declension is adjective-like, except for the nominative/accusative singular masculine and neuter).

Dialogue 2 Трéба ви́рішити!

ОКСÁНА: Микóло! Я хóчу купи́ти кни́жку про Ки́їв, алé не знáю, якá найкрáща.

МИКÓЛА: Усі гáрні, алé здаєтъся, що ця найцікавíша. Прáвда?

ОКСÁНА: Так, згíдна. Алé ця кни́жка такóж найдорóжча! Що роби́ти?

МИКÓЛА: Трéба ви́рішити: якá тобí найбíльше подóбається? Купи́ її́.

ОКСÁНА: Дóбре.

дороги́й, дорóжчий (more) expensive (**дешéвий, дешéвший** cheap(er))

The superlative of the adjective

The superlative is formed by prefixing **най-** to the comparative or, where the comparative is formed by means of **більш/менш**, by placing the plain adjective after **найбíльш** 'most'/**наймéнш** 'least'. To render 'of' after a superlative, e.g. 'the best of. . .', one may use the following prepositions: **з** + gen., **сéред** + gen. and **між** 'among' + instr. However, one may also use a comparative adjective followed by **за** + acc. or **від** + gen. (the phrase will include a form of **увéсь**, so it expresses 'better than all'):

Сéред нáших дрýзів Григíр найсимпатичнíший. Hryhir is the most likeable of of our friends.

lit: 'Among our friends Hryhir is the most likeable.'

Між ци́ми книжкáми я вважáю цю найцікавíшою. I find this (to be) the most interesting of these books.

lit: 'Among these books I find this (one) (to be) the most interesting.' (Note the use of the instrumental here.)

Мій бáтько крáщий за всіх íнших батькíв. My father is the best/most handsome father.

lit: 'My father is better/more handsome than all other fathers.'

The analytic superlative (**найбíльш** + plain adjective) is quite widely used, but, unless it *has* to be used, is considered bad Ukrainian. If you know there to be a synthetic superlative (**най-** + comparative) available, use it! For example, since we have the comparative **доро́жчий**, which gives the superlative **найдоро́жчий**, **найбі́льш дороги́й** is to be avoided.

Exercise 13f

Give the comparative and superlative forms for the following adjectives:

(a) вели́кий
(b) га́рний
(c) мали́й
(d) міцни́й

Note: in *8* we met the word **якнайскорі́ше** 'as soon as possible': now you know that this is simply the adverb **як** 'as' + superlative. By following this formula you can say 'as X as possible' based on any adjective or adverb.

Vocabulary and grammar review (2)

Fill in the blanks as you did in Vocabulary and Grammar Review (1), then translate the passages (you may not know all the words, but a little guesswork should do the trick):

Exercise 13g

У готе́лі: Ключ______ вони́ діста́ли від черго́в______ . Вона́ показа́______ їм кімна́т______ й віді́йш______ . Джон відчин______ ______ й оглячу́в сво______ кімна́ту. На ______ бул______ насті́льн______ ла́мпа. Він тако́ж поба́ч______ вели́ке ______, письмо́вий ______, стіле́ць. У ц______ кімна́т______ бу́де почува́тися, як ______до́ма! Але́ од______ ла́мпочка не працю______; він ви́ріш______ ви́кликати черго́в______ .

Exercise 13h

У ва́нн______ Окса́на увімкну́______ сві́тл______: там вона́ поба́чи______ туале́т, ра́ковин______, та ві́шалк______ для рушник______. Але́ там не бу______ ні ми́л______ ні туале́тн______ папе́р______. ______ ща́стя, Окса́на при______ св______ пап______. Із валі́зк______ вона́ ви́йн______ ______ па́сту та щі́тк______. У сво______ кімн______ Джон теж розпак______ св______ валі́______.

Exercise 13i

Ки́їв ______ над Дніпр______. До Ки́______ прибува́ють або́ літак______, або́ ______, або́ маши́н______. У цьо́му мі́ст______ є аеро______ і авто́бус______ вокза́л. Але́ ______ мо́жна зупини́______? У це́нт______ є ______ «Москва́»; зо́всім ______ є й бага́т______ готе́л______, напри́к______ «Ки́їв». Ки́їв став суча́сн______ м______, спра́вжн______ столиц______ вели́кої держа́в______.

Aspect and conjugation review

Exercise 13j

For each of the following verbs, give the missing member of the aspectual pair (not necessarily a true, synonymous pair); then supply the **я** and **вони́** forms (non-past) for each:

(a) прихо́дити:
(b) працюва́ти:
(c) відчини́ти:
(d) розумі́ти:
(e) взя́ти:
(f) да́ти:
(g) ба́чити:
(h) відповісти́:
(i) готува́ти:
(j) накри́ти:

Antonyms

Exercise 13k

For each of the following words there is a corresponding opposite; for verbs and adjectives (as well as adverbs) these are known as 'antonyms', but for nouns they may simply be members of logical pairs, e.g. 'mother–father'. If you cannot think of a word, or have forgotten the meaning of the word given, look it up in the vocabulary.

(a) до́брий; (b) вмика́ти; (c) ба́тько; (d) пита́ти; (e) да́ти; (f) мали́й; (g) сестра́; (h) відхо́дити; (i) син; (j) бабу́ся; (k) писа́ти; (l) жі́нка; (m) кра́ще; (n) батьки́; (o) найбі́льш; (p) вчо́ра

Exercise 13l

Now match each word or phrase in the following list with its most likely partner from among the words given above.

га́рна; з буди́нку; вра́нці; ніж а́вто Іва́на; до́брі; моя́; лист; ціка́вий; кни́жка; сві́тло; день; лю́бить си́на; лю́бить чолові́ка; викладача́; лю́бить ба́тька; йому́ гро́ші.

Numerals

Exercise 13m

Read the following passage and note the use of each numeral; identify the grammatical form of each accompanying noun or noun phrase. The stress markings have been omitted from numerals and accompanying forms on purpose! Mark them in, being especially careful with nouns preceded by 2, 3 and 4.

Дві студентки сидя́ть в кооперати́вному ресторані. Вхо́дить п'ять англійських студентів: до́вго вони́ не мо́жуть сі́сти, тому́ що бага́то наро́ду, мо́же сорок-п'ятдесят голодних чоловік. У студе́нток є ще два вільні місця, але́ для студентів це зана́дто ма́ло; наре́шті знахо́дять стіл. Студе́нтки огляда́ють його́: на ї́хньому столі́ ба́чать три склянки й чотири тарілки, два меню та три серветки. Помічáють (**помічáти**, **-áє-** 'notice, remark'), що усі ціни на меню ще старí. Напрúклад: капýста п'ятдесят три копійки, з сúром чи сметáною сімдесят вісім копійок; м'ясо кóштує бíльше, напр. два карбованці сорок одна копійка (алé йогó у цей день немáє!); мінерáльна водá, двадцять копійок; дві склянки вина, шість карбованців. Тощо. Алé скíльки кóштує все тепéр? Вже не мáємо карбованців, мáємо грúвні!*

*Not yet!

14 До примíських районíв

To the suburbs

In this lesson you will learn about:

- the conditional mood and conditions
- reported statements and questions
- complex and compound sentences
- colours

Нáші дрýзі обговóрюють своï плáни

ОКСÁНА: Ти сúльно вагáєшся, Микóло. Чомý?

МИКÓЛА: Я прóсто не знáю, що ми бýдемо робúти тепéр. Якбú ти сказáла, що бýду такúй стóмлений, я б не повíрив.

ОКСÁНА: Так, ходúти по мíсті, це серйóзна спрáва! А вáрто булó побувáти в Кúєві, чи ні?

МИКÓЛА: Звичáйно, я пóвністю згóден з тобóю. А як тобí здаéться, Джон(е)?

ДЖОН: Дúвно, алé я пóкищо не втомúвся. Колú ти казáв, що бýде багáто врáжень, я прóсто не вíрив, що їх бýде стíльки.

ОКСÁНА: Мáю сýмнів у тóму, що ми бýдемо ще дóвго у Кúєві.

ДЖОН: Це вíрно, і я так дýмаю. А що, як відпочúнемо зáвтра? Якщó ми поїдемо в примíські райóни, зóвсім без цíлі, без яснóго, тóчного плáну, та дóбре відпочúнемо, то післязáвтра змóжемо поїхати дáлі.

ОКСÁНА: Це чудóво, алé дýмаю, що трéба мáти тóчний план. Напрúклад, ми змоглú б провестú ніч під відкрúтим нéбом у намéті, варúти свою вечéрю на багáтті.

Vocabulary

обгово́рювати, -ює-, imperf.	discuss, talk over	**ма́ти, -а́є- су́мнів** or **сумніва́тися, -а́є-**, imperf. **у/в** + loc.	doubt, have doubts about (something)
си́льно	strongly	**ві́рно**	true (it is true)
вага́тися, -а́є-, imperf.	hesitate	**приміськи́й райо́н, -о́го -у**	suburb
якби́ conj. + past tense	if (also **коли́ б**)	**ці́ль, -и**	aim, object(ive)
сто́млений	tired	**ясни́й**	clear
пові́рити, -и-, perf.	believe	**то́чний**	precise, exact
серйо́зний	serious	**да́лі**	further
по́вністю	fully, completely	**під відкри́тим не́бом**	in the open air (lit. 'under an open sky')
ди́вно	strange (it is strange)	**наме́т, -у**	tent
по́кищо	for the time being, until now	**бага́ття, -я,** neut.	fire (open-air)

The conditional mood and conditions

The conditional mood is so called because it is used in response to some underlying condition. It corresponds to English 'I would do (something), if . . .'. But note that 'the cows would come home at five o'clock' is not rendered by the conditional mood if it simply describes a repeated action 'Every day at five o'clock. . . .'.

To form this mood in Ukrainian one simply accompanies the past tense by the particle **би** or, after a vowel, **б**, thus:

Я хоті́в би/хоті́ла б, щоб усі́ до́бре говори́ли украї́нською.	I'd like all [people] to speak Ukrainian well.

Note the position of **би/б**: it must follow some element of the sentence. One might say that normally it will follow the verb, but it may also follow some other word, which it then tends to bring into relief. For example:

Я б хоті́в/хоті́ла, щоб усі́ украї́нці до́бре говори́ли украї́нською.	I would like all [people] to speak Ukrainian well.

There are three conditions in Ukrainian. First, unreal conditions, of the pattern 'If I could, I would', 'If (only) I were . . ., I would . . .', etc.: these are unreal because you can't, so you won't. The conditional mood occurs in both halves of the sentence, 'if' being rendered by **якби́** or **коли́ б** (note that **би/б** is contained in this conjunction, so you again need the past tense form). If the 'if' clause comes first, then the second half may be introduced by **то**. Thus:

Якби́ я була́ бага́та, (то) я купи́ла б вели́ку ха́ту.	If I were rich, I would buy a big house.
Вона́ б приї́хала до Льво́ва, коли́ б він пообіця́в їй кни́жку.	She would come to Lviv, if he promised her this/that book.

The other two types are real conditions ('if' . . . 'then') that refer to the future, and those that are real conditions referring to the present or past. In both cases 'if' is rendered by **якщо́**, those that refer to the present or past are identical in tense to English, but those that refer to the future must have the future tense in both halves of the conditional sentence. Thus:

Якщо́ ми бу́демо в Ки́єві післяза́втра, пошука́ємо Лю́бу.	If we are in Kyiv in two days, we'll have a look for Liuba.
Якщо́ коро́ви вже поверта́ються додо́му, зна́чить, вони́ голо́дні.	If the cows are already coming home, then they are (must be) hungry.
Якщо́ коро́ви вже поверну́лися додо́му, зна́чить, вони́ були́ голо́дні.	If the cows have already come home, then they were (must have been) hungry.

Ябки́ знав, де впа́де, то й соло́мки б підстели́в.
If I'd known where it'd fall, I'd have spread out straw (as a cushion).

Ukrainian proverb

More reported statements and questions

Reported, or indirect, speech was introduced in *5*; as this is a very important part of producing 'correct' Ukrainian, it is worth expanding on what we have said thus far. The essential points to remember are:

(a) The verbs introducing reported speech include any verbs of communication, even if the term 'reported speech' then becomes rather inappropriate, e.g. 'say, think, ask, hope, etc.'.
(b) The reported speech will be in the present if the English has the past and in the future if the English has the conditional.

To this we may add that Ukrainian also retains 'direct questions'. In other words, in English sentences such as 'He asked her if [whether] she had found the exercise book she lost yesterday' and 'She wondered if [whether] he would be there', the conditional clauses 'if/whether she had found the exercise book' and 'whether he would come' are constructed as questions. Ukrainian retains the original tense and word order of the original statement or question, with **чи** for original (or implied) questions and **що** for statements:

Вони́ спита́ли нас, чи ми хо́чемо піти́ на конце́рт (Чи ви хо́чете . . .?)	They asked if/whether we wanted to go to the concert.
Він запита́в її́, чи вона́ знайшла́ той зо́шит, яки́й вона́ згуби́ла вчо́ра (Чи ти знайшла . . .?)	He asked her if she had found the exercise book she had lost/mislaid yesterday.
Їй було́ ціка́во, чи він бу́де там (Чи він бу́де . . .?)	She wondered if he would be there.
Я ж сказа́в, що напишу́ їй листа́ (Я напишу́ . . .)	I said (that) I would write her a letter.
Вона́ сказа́ла, що тре́ба мені́ бу́ти в Москві́ в се́реду (Тре́ба вам . . .)	She said (that) I had to be in Moscow on Wednesday.
Ти сподіва́вся, що вона́ при́йде на мій день наро́дження (Вона́ при́йде . . .)	You were hoping (that) she would come to my birthday.

Exercise 14a

Join the following pairs as (real or unreal) conditional sentences; you may have to adapt some of them somewhat in order to ensure that the results make sense:

(a) Я хо́чу піти́ на конце́рт/Зі́на бу́де ду́же ра́да
(b) Ді́ти вже прийшли́ із шко́ли/Батьки́ вечі́ряють
(c) Вона́ не ме́шкала там/Нам було́ б ду́же прие́мно
(d) Богда́н пита́є мене́, де я живу́/Я не скажу́ йому́

(e) Груше́вський не написа́в свої́х книжо́к/Ми ме́нше зна́ли б про істо́рію Украї́ни.
(f) В ме́не не бу́де вака́цій/не змо́жу поі́хати до Фра́нції
(g) Лі́да ще не поверну́лася додо́му/Вона́ гра́є з і́ншими дітьми́
(h) Ми були́ б в Іспа́нії/Ма́ли час на це
(i) Він не знахо́дить підру́чника/Не змо́же ви́йти сього́дні зі Сла́вою
(j) Ми зо́всім утоми́лися/Ми закінчи́ли впра́ву

Exercise 14b

Transform the following reported speech into a Ukrainian dialogue:

She said that she would be home at nine o'clock. I replied that I wanted to go out to a concert, and asked if she would have time to cook my dinner. At first she said nothing, then she expressed the opinion that I was joking and that I couldn't be the husband she knew so well. I replied that I agreed with her, because I was rather tired.

Vocabulary

вислó́влювати, -ує-, imperf.	to express (perf. **ви́словити, -и-**)
ду́мка, -и	opinion
жартува́ти, -у́є- imperf.	to joke (perf. **пожартува́ти, -у́є-**)

В авто́бусі Окса́на несподі́вано зустріча́ється з Га́лею

ОКСА́НА: О, кого́ ж це я тут ба́чу? Це ти, Га́лю? Приві́т!
ГА́ЛЯ: Приві́т, Окса́но! Що це ти ро́биш тут, в авто́бусі в Ки́єві? Не ві́рю вла́сним оча́м.
ОКСА́НА: Як ба́чиш, ї́ду до примі́ського райо́ну, де є ліс, щоб прогуля́тися з Мико́лою й Джо́ном. Джон приї́хав з А́нглії. Дру́зі, познайо́мтеся, це Га́ля, ми зустрі́лися з не́ю в Оде́сі.

Мико́ла:	Ду́же прие́мно.
Джон:	Мо́же, ра́зом: погуля́емо лі́сом.
Га́ля:	Мені́ ду́же шкода́, але́ сього́дні я не мо́жу, я ї́ду до ті́тки. Сього́дні день її́ наро́дження.
Окса́на:	Це, ма́бу́ть, ті́тка Лю́ба. Скі́льки ж їй ро́ків?
Га́ля:	Так, це ті́тка Лю́ба, та їй вже со́рок ві́сім ро́ків. Як швидко прохо́дить час. Вона́ з чолові́ком ме́шкає в примі́ській зо́ні. Він неда́вно до́сить тя́жко хворі́в, але́ тепе́р уже́ зо́всім ви́дужав. Йому́ п'ятдеся́т оди́н рік.
Окса́на:	Та й нам вже два́дцять три ро́ки. Старі́емося!
Га́ля:	Ах, яку́ нісені́тницю ти гово́риш! Ну, час мені́ вже вихо́дити. Чи зна́єте, як діста́тися до лі́су? Це ще три зупи́нки і вихо́дите, по́тім йді́ть пря́мо оди́н кварта́л, по́тім поверні́ть ліво́руч. І там на ро́зі поба́чите навпро́ти га́рні дере́ва на́шого лі́су.
Окса́на:	Дя́кую, до поба́чення, вве́чері я тобі зателефону́ю, бо, напе́вно, ми поі́demo з Ки́єва вже за́втра.
Га́ля:	Шкода́, але́ все́-таки я сподіва́юся, що ви ще пове́рнетеся до Ки́єва.
Мико́ла:	І ми сподіва́ємося побува́ти в Ки́єві ще пі́сля то́го, як ми вже відві́даємо й і́нші украї́нські міста́. До поба́чення, та й приві́т ва́шій ті́тці!

Vocabulary

несподі́вано	unexpectedly
вла́сний	own (one's own)
походи́ти, -и-, perf.	walk a little, take a walk (note the stress)
прогу́люватися, -ює-, imperf.	take a walk
день, дня наро́дження, masc.	birthday (lit. 'day of birth')
прохо́дити, -и-	pass, slip by (of time)
ме́шкати, -ає-, imperf.	live
примі́ська́ зо́на, -о́ї -и	suburb
ви́дужати, -ає-, perf.	get better, recover (from illness)
тя́жко	seriously
хворі́ти, -і́є-, imperf.	ill, be ill
старі́тися, -і́є-, imperf.	old, age, get old(er)

нісені́тниця, -і	nonsense	**все́-таки**	all the same, none the less
вихо́дити, -и-, imperf.	get down/off, come down/off (perf.: **ви́йти**) (also used is **сходити, -и-,** perf. **зійти́**, -де-)	**сподіва́тися, -а́є-,** imperf.	hope
		наза́д	back
		відві́дати, -ає-, perf. + acc.	visit, call on (imperf.: **відві́дувати,** -**ує**-) (note how here the perfective future has a 'future in the past' sense: 'shall have visited')
зві́дси	from here		
прої́хати, -ї́де-, perf. **до** + gen.	get (somewhere, by transport)		
пря́мо	straight on		
кварта́л, -у	block		
поверну́ти, -не-, perf.	turn (e.g. left and right)		
ріг, ро́гу	corner		
навпро́ти	opposite, facing	**пі́сля то́го, як,** conj.	after
напе́вно	certainly, for sure		

Complex and compound sentences

Earlier in this lesson we looked at conditions and reported speech, and we have already come across the conjunction **пі́сля то́го**, **як** and the relatives **яки́й**, **хто** and **що**. All these represent types of complex sentences. We are already familiar with compound sentences in which clauses are linked by the Ukrainian equivalents of 'and', 'but' and 'or'. Some linkages may be expressed by intonation (in speech), at times ambiguous; however, in the written language one may wish to reduce ambiguity, and the conjunctions are more welcome. For stylistic effect they may also be omitted.

The differences between some of the little words used to join clauses in compound sentences can be subtle; here we just list a few of them (note the commas!) and assure you that spoken usage and reading is the best method of gaining familiarity:

and	*and not*	*but*	*not only . . . but also*	*or*	*either . . . or . . .*
, і/й	**, (а)ні. . .не** + vb.	**, а**	**не ті́льки . . ., а(ле́) (й)**	**, або́**	**або́. . ., або́ . . .**
, а		**, але́**	**не лише́ . . ., а(ле́) (й)**	**, чи**	**чи . . ., чи . . .**
, та		**, та**			**(не) то . . ., (не) то . . .**
, та й		**, зате́**			

Some examples:

Абó ти прúйдеш зі мнóю, абó я пiдý додóму.	Either you'll come with me, or I go home.
Він не тíльки не говóрить украї́нською, алé й прóсто нікóли не говóрить.	He not only doesn't speak Ukrainian, but simply doesn't talk at all.

Most of the others, e.g. **а, і, та** and **алé**, are already familiar to you. Note the comma which will normally precede or be contained in these conjunctions. Complex sentences are those in which one of the clauses is subordinate to or depends on the other in some way. Relative clauses (**якúй**) are complex, and you are familiar with another complex construction using **що**, as in:

Він говóрить, що ми скóро бýдемо вдóма.	He says that we'll be home soon.

We have also encountered **щоб** 'in order that, in order to, that', which may be used before an infinitive when purpose ('in order to') is being conveyed and the subject of the main verb and the infinitive are the same. For example:

Я роблю́ це, щоб прийтú з вáми зáвтра.	I'm doing this in order to come with you tomorrow.

If the subjects are different, then **щоб** is followed by the past tense form (it, too, contains the particle '**б**'):

Я роблю́ це, щоб ти зміг прийтú з нáми зáвтра.	I'm doing this so that you can come with us tomorrow.
Хóчу/прошý/рáджу/накáзую/говорю́/дозволя́ю, щоб ти прийшóв.	I want/ask/advise/order/tell/permit you to come.

The following are all extremely useful. Pay special attention to the sets containing a preposition, which are necessary if a preposition is to be followed by a verb. Thus, in 'before he came', **до** 'before' needs a dummy word (**те** 'that', 'the fact that') to reflect the genitive case required by this preposition.

as if	*when/while*	*after*	*before*
(не)мов	**пóки***	**пíсля тóго, як**	**пéред тим, як**
(не)нáче	**дóки***		**до тóго, як**

***Пóки не** and **дóки не** convey 'until' (literally 'while not'!)

since (time)	*because*	*although*	*so that*
з тóго чáсу, як	**бо**	**хоч(á)**	**так, що**
	томý, що	**незважáючи на**	
	чéрез те, що	**те, що**	
	завдякú тóму, що		
	вналíдок тóго, що		

Note that **те** must be in a case form appropriate to the preposition it follows:

внаслíдок тóго, що	as a result of the fact that . . .
завдякú тóму, що	thanks to the fact that . . .

Exercise 14c

Now translate the following sentences into Ukrainian:

(a) He told me to read the book this evening.
(b) I asked her before he came home.
(c) Do it in such a way that we can have a rest later.
(d) I like Kyiv because it's such a beautiful city.
(e) Although I want to believe you, I just cannot.
(f) Although you are my friend, I simply do not agree with you.
(g) She expresses her opinions as if she really understands the situation.
(h) I know what you want to say.
(i) She was late thanks to ('the fact that') her father wanted to talk to her.
(j) Why you must buy such books I simply do not know.

Exercise 14d

Proverbs (with approximate English renderings):

Де сім няньóк, там дитúна без головú.	Too many cooks spoil the broth.
Поспішúш – людéй насмішúш.	More haste, less speed.
Не кажú гоп, дóки не перескóчиш.	Look before you leap.
Не так склáлося, як бажáлося.	The best-laid plans of mice and men.
За двомá зáйцями не вганя́йся, бо жóдного не (в)піймáєш.	A bird in the hand is worth two in the bush.

Using a dictionary, work out the literal Ukrainian meanings.

Colours

The most commonly used colours (declined as adjectives) include:

чóрний	black	**бíлий**	white
червóний	red	**си́ній**	dark blue
зелéний	green	**жóвтий**	yellow
сíрий	grey	**голуби́й**	light blue
кори́чневий	brown	**oрáнжевий**	orange
рожéвий	rose/pink	**фіолéтовий**	violet
золоти́й	gold(en)	**срíбний**	silver

If you want to find out the colour of something, you can ask:

Яки́й на кóлір X?	*(На кóлір X червóний.)*
Якóго кóльору X?	*(X червóного кóльору.)*

In the first instance, of course, we have to pay attention to the gender of X: the answer could just as easily be **червóна/червóне/червóні**.

Word formation: colours

With these colour words as bases we can express such nuances as 'greenish' or 'green-blue'. In the latter formation, the first element takes on the form of an adverb (in **-о**) and does not change, while the second remains an adjective:

червóно-бíлий	red-white
зóлото-срíбний	gold-silver

Approximation is expressed by the suffix **-увáтий**, which is appended to the stem of the colour:

зеленувáтий	greenish
чорнувáтий	blackish
червонувáтий	reddish

One of the characteristics of Ukrainian, that appears to give it more flexibility than we have in English, is the ability to make compound words from two or more elements that are capable of expressing an idea that requires a phrase or sentence to express in English. Colours enter into such compounds with ease, as we see in a few of the words containing the colour 'black' and 'red', here all to do with physical characteristics:

чорновýсий	a person who has black moustache(s)
чорнозýбий	a person with black/darkened teeth

чорноо́кий	a person with dark ('black') eyes
червонощо́кий	a person with red cheeks
червононі́жка	a type of bird with orange-red legs

The word-forming possibilities of colours are almost endless, but are certainly most common in reference to a person's (animal's, object's) physical characteristics.

Exercise 14e

Translate the following questions into Ukrainian, then answer in Ukrainian; draw from real life! (For vocabulary, refer to the appropriate chapters, e.g. *8* for clothing, or use a dictionary). For 'what colour is . . .' use both constructions given above.

(a) What colour is your car?
(b) Do you like the colour of this shirt?
(c) What colours do you have in your flat/apartment/house? (furniture, for example)
(d) What colour are the eyes of your spouse/boyfriend/girlfriend?
(e) . . . his/her hair?

15 Де що в Україні?

Where is what in Ukraine?

In this lesson you will learn how to:

- ask directions
- find Ukraine and Kyiv (on the map)
- write a letter
- read a Ukrainian advertisement

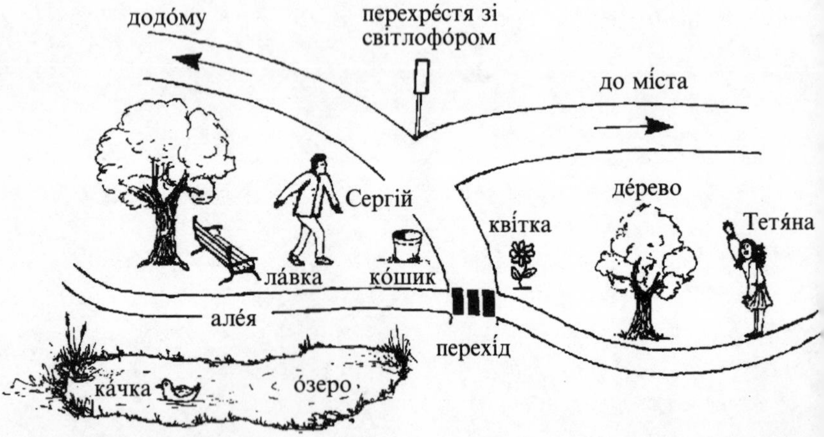

Тетя́на стоїть недалéко від дорóги, у пáрку. Там є дерéва, алéя, óзеро. Навкóло пáрку є дорóги й вýлиці. На перехрéсті є світлофóр. Тетя́на мóже йти́ абó пря́мо абó ліврýч, абó правóруч, абó чéрез парк алéєю; абó нарéшті вонá мóже прóсто перейти́ чéрез парк травóю. Вонá знáє, що на нéї чекáє Сергíй, її нарече́ний. У пáрку є багáто людéй. Вонá мóже запитáти їх, як пройти́ до потрíбного мíсця. Звичáйно, скóро вонá знáйде свогó наречéного. Алé їй трéба йогó дóбре шукáти.

наречéний, наречéна fiancé, fiancée

Що потрíбно сказáти при запитáнні? Можли́во: Скажíть, будь лáска, як менí пройти́ до íншого кінця́ пáрку? – де центр мíста? – де найбли́жчий світлофóр? – де óзеро? – де дерéва? – де той ріг, де лю́ди за зви́чай зустрічáються? – де кав'я́рня? – і т.д.

і т.д. (і так дáлі) 'etc., et cetera'; **за зви́чай** 'habitually'

See this as an exercise, too: replace **Тетя́на** with **Сергíй**, not forgetting to include all other gender changes that will follow ('her' to 'his' etc.). Now read the following section on asking directions: phrases you will certainly need in Ukraine!

Asking directions

The preceding text and picture, as well as the dialogue between Oksana and her friends and Halia in *14*, address the problem of finding your way around an unfamiliar place. When in doubt, it is always possible simply to name one's hoped-for destination and count on gestures to make the answers clear. One might, in such cases, include some of the following phrases:

Ви́бачте!	Excuse me!
Ви не скáжете менí . . .?	Won't you tell me . . .?
Ви не мóжете менí сказáти . . .?	Can't you tell me . . .?
Як (менí) пройти́/проїхати до . . .?	How do I get to . . .?
Будь лáска, повíльно, я не говорю́ дóбре украї́нською.	Slowly, please, I don't speak Ukrainian very well.

The problem, of course, is understanding the answer, the content of which is impossible to predict. You need to be as informed as possible about the general context of your inquiry; then be ready for:

Ідíть . . .!	Go . . . (on foot)!
Ї́дьте . . .,	Go . . . (by transport)!

+ **до** + gen. 'to', **по** + dat./loc. 'along', **від** + gen. 'from' or a straight instrumental

Повернíть	. . . **ліворуч**	turn left
	. . . **правóруч**	turn right
Ідíть	. . . **пря́мо**	Go . . . straight on
	. . . **у нáпрямі/нáпрямку** + gen	in the direction of

Examples:

Іді́ть до університе́ту.
Іді́ть по цій ву́лиці.
Поверні́ть право́руц, коли́ поба́чите книга́рню.
Поверні́ть ліво́руч, по́тім іді́ть пря́мо.
Іді́ть у на́прямі того́ буди́нку, по́тім поверні́ть ліворуц.
Іді́ть у цьо́му на́прямку, по́тім поверні́ть право́руч.
Іді́ть ліво́руч від це́ркви.
Іді́ть то́ю ву́лицею.

The points of the compass

You might also hear someone use the points of the compass, especially with reference to natural formations, such as rivers and mountains:

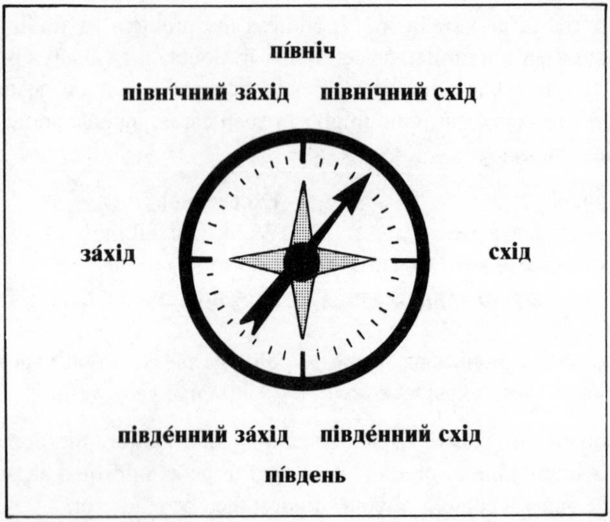

We use **на** + locative or + accusative to form the adverb of direction with the points of the compass; as with other directions, you may also combine the adjective with the word **на́прям/на́прямок** and the preposition **у**. Thus:

на схо́ді, на за́ході, на пі́вдні, на пі́вночі
in the east, west, south, north

на пі́вніч/пі́вдень/схід/за́хід від + gen.
to the north/south/east/west (of)

у схі́дному на́прямі/на́прямку
east(wards)

If you want to say 'in the north of Ukraine', the simplest method is to qualify 'Ukraine' by the adjective referring to the point of the compass. Thus, lit. 'in northern Ukraine':

у півні́чній Украї́ні

In the conversation between Oksana and her friends in *14* we had **на ро́зі** 'on/at the corner', and the expression of distance **кварта́л** all on its own; remember also **кіломе́тр** 'a kilometre' and the inversion of numeral and noun for approximation – **кіломе́трів два** 'about two kilometres'.

Geography: in and around Ukraine

If you are interested in the geography of Ukraine, we provide two schematic maps of Ukraine showing the **о́бласті** 'provinces' and their main cities, the one **автоно́мна респу́бліка** 'autonomous republic' with its main city, the **закордо́нні держа́ви** 'foreign states' that share a **кордо́н** 'frontier' with Ukraine, rivers, reservoirs and two seas, all denoted by a letter or number.

First, match the names of all the various places to the letter or number on the map. Then describe the relative locations of the places, saying in which region, autonomous republic or country they are located and where they are in relation to other places.

Україна

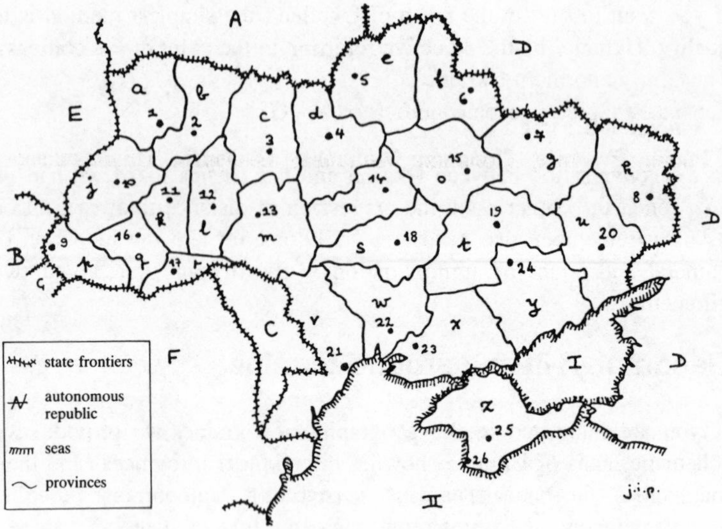
state frontiers
autonomous republic
seas
provinces
j.i.p.

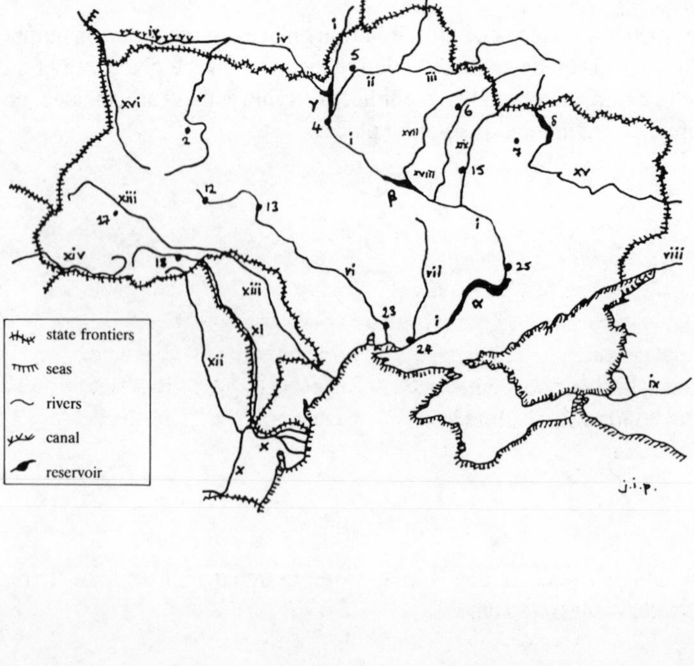
state frontiers
seas
rivers
canal
reservoir
j.i.p.

First look at Map 1.

Exercise 15a

(a)

Match the following seven countries to (A)–(G):

Ро́сі́я; Руму́нія; По́льща; Молдо́ва; Білору́сь; Слова́ччина; Уго́рщина

(b)

There are twenty-six cities on the map. Match them to the number (1)–(26):

Микола́їв	**Ки́їв**	**Запорі́жжя**	**Чернівці́**
Іва́но-Франкі́вськ	**Черка́си**	**Сімферо́поль**	**Терно́піль**
Кіровогра́д	**Луга́нськ**	**Оде́са**	**Полта́ва**
Черні́гів	**Ві́нниця**	**У́жгород**	**Жито́мир**
Дніпропетро́вськ	**Рі́вне**	**Херсо́н**	**Доне́цьк**
Севасто́поль	**Львів**	**Луцьк**	**Су́ми**
Хмельни́цьк	**Ха́рків**		

(c)

In Ukraine there is one autonomous republic; there are twenty-six provinces, of which two are metropolitan areas and have been dealt with in the preceding exercise. Match the republic and provinces to the letters (a)–(z) – (i) has been omitted:

Хмельни́цька	**Су́мська**	**Ха́рківська**	**Черніве́цька**
Іва́но-Франкі́вська	**Черка́ська**	**Крим**	**Запорі́зька**
Кіровогра́дська	**Жито́мирська**	**Терно́пільська**	**Полта́вська**
Черні́гівська	**Ві́нницька**	**Закарпа́тська**	**Оде́ська**
Дніпропетро́вська	**Рі́вненська**	**Херсо́нська**	**Доне́цька**
Микола́ївська	**Льві́вська**	**Лу́цька**	**Луга́нська**
Ки́ївська			

(d)

There are two seas. Is the **Чо́рне мо́ре** designated 'I'? Or is 'I' the **Озі́вське/Азо́вське мо́ре**?

Now for Map 2:

(e)

Rivers are in the sequence (i)–(xix). Match them as usual (you may like to look for other rivers, e.g. the **Збруч**):

Дністéр	**Гори́нь**	**Ти́са**	**Дніпрó**
Дон	**Кубáнь**	**Сірéт**	**Дунáй**
Деснá	**Сейм**	**Вóрскла**	**Сíверний Донéць**
Півдéнний Буг	**При́п'ять**	**Інгулéць**	**Псел**
Сулá	**Зáхідний Буг**	**Прут**	

(f)

There are four reservoirs **водосхóвище (водóймище)** on the map (there are two others, unmarked, on the **Дніпрó**, the **Канíвське** and the **Дніпрóвське;** on the **Оскíл**, a tributary of the **Сíверний Донéць**, there is the **Червонооскíльське**). Allocate the four on the map to the sequence (a)–(d):

Кременчýцьке водосхóвище	**Ки́ївське водосхóвище**
Кахóвське водосхóвище	**Печенíзьке водосхóвище**

Exercise 15b

Join the following pairs of sentences together in ways which seem appropriate (there is not necessarily a single 'answer'):

(a) Я прийшóв до теáтру/Дрýзі вже ввійшли́ ('(had) gone in')
(b) Михáйло сиди́ть удóма/Він хворíє
(c) Óля купи́ла кни́жку/Ніхтó не хóче читáти її́
(d) Він живé в Ки́єві/Він дýже лю́бить це мíсто
(e) Вонá повечéряла/Вонá пішлá до óперного теáтру послýхати óперу
(f) Ми знайшли́ маши́ну/Ми були́ дýже рáді
(g) Булá вóсьма годи́на/Ви́рішили подиви́тися прогрáму
(h) Він пíде в університéт/Він не знайшóв підрýчника вдóма

Reading

Ми всі були́ бі́льше, як три дні в Ки́єві. Андрі́й, мій украї́нський това́риш, вважа́є, що тепе́р ми мо́жемо поду́мати про насту́пний ета́п на́шої поі́здки по Украї́ні, бо вже пі́зно, а ми ще́ не зна́ємо, куди́ поі́демо. Він хо́че, щоб ми провели́ принаймні ти́ждень у Льво́ві, в За́хідній Украї́ні, та по́тім у Ха́ркові, у Схі́дній Украї́ні. Пе́ред тим, як приї́хати до Ки́єва, ми були́ в Оде́сі. Під час перебува́ння в столи́ці ми були́ в багатьо́х місця́х. Усе́ це було́ ду́же ціка́ве, зна́чно цікаві́ше, ніж удо́ма в А́нглії – мо́же тому́, що я не працю́ю тут, у ме́не кані́кули. Я признаю́ся, що рані́ше ма́йже нічо́го не знав про Украї́ну; для ме́не вона́ була́ части́ною Росі́ї, Радя́нського Сою́зу. Так гово́рить і ду́має чима́ло англі́йців про Уельс, Шотла́ндію, та й про Ірла́ндію (півні́чну, мо́же ще й пivде́нну, незале́жну респу́бліку). Можли́во й це по́кищо лише́ мрі́я, але́ я так си́льно хо́чу, щоб наро́ди Євро́пи навчи́лися бу́ти сами́ми собо́ю і шанува́ти себе́.

Vocabulary

това́риш, -а	friend
вважа́ти, -а́є-, imperf.	consider
поду́мати, -ає-, perf.	think
ета́п, -у	stage
поі́здка, -и	journey, trip
щоб	so that, in order that, that
пробу́ти, -де-, perf.	spend (time)
схі́дний	east(ern)
під час, prep. + gen.	during
перебува́ння, -я, neut.	stay, sojourn
кані́кули, кані́кул, pl.	holidays, vacation
признава́тися, -ає́-, imperf.	confess, admit
части́на, -и	part
радя́нський	Soviet
сою́з, -у	union, alliance
півні́чний	north(ern)
півде́нний	south(ern)
респу́бліка, -и	republic
по́кищо	for the time being
лише́	only, just
мрі́я, -ії	dream
Євро́па, -и	Europe
сами́й собо́ю, pron.	oneself
шанува́ти, -у́є- imperf.	respect

Exercise 15c

Respond to the following questions in full, replacing the underlined nouns or phrases with personal pronouns or adverbs (they are all true):

(a) Чи прáвда, що **Одéса** лежи́ть **на висóкому бéрезі**?
(b) Чи далéко **аеропóрт Бори́спіль від цéнтру Ки́єва**?
(c) Чи **рíки Воли́ні та Полíсся** впадáють **до При́п'яті**?
(d) Чи **При́п'ять** притóка Дніпрá?

Впадáти, -áє- до + gen. flow into
притóка, -и tributary

An advertisement

Read the following advertisement, which was published by the British Council in the magazine **Украї́на** (1992) 32. Note how the address at the top left is written, starting with the most general information, namely the town (or the country, if it is mentioned), and ending with the details of the room where the British Council has its office. Remember, if a person were being addressed, their name, in the dative case, would come last of all. For example: **Кравчукові, В.Г.; Хмельницькому, Степанові Михайловичу; Довженко, Мирославі Петрівні**.

БРИТАНСЬКА РАДА

252056 Київ
проспект Перемоги, 37
Київський політехнічний інститут,
корпус 1, кімната 258

БРИТАНСЬКА РАДА СПРИЯЄ КУЛЬТУРНИМ, НАВЧАЛЬНИМ ТА ТЕХНІЧНИМ ЗВ'ЯЗКАМ МІЖ БРИТАНІЄЮ ТА УКРАЇНОЮ

Рада пропонує обмежену кількість стипендій для визначних молодих професіоналів, учених та дослідників з України. Ці стипендії дадуть їм можливість провчитися до одного року з жовтня 1993 в Британському університеті або дослідницькому закладі. Стипендії поділяються на дві категорії:

СТИПЕНДІЇ БРИТАНСЬКОЇ РАДИ

Претенденти повинні обов'язково мати диплом вузу, перевага надається тим, хто викладає або веде дослідницьку роботу в одній з таких галузей:

Англійська мова
Сільськогосподарські науки
Науки про навколишнє середовище
Охорона здоров'я
Управління в бізнесі
Розвиток людських ресурсів
Науки про роль жінок у суспільстві
Різні види мистецтв

СТИПЕНДІЇ МІНІСТЕРСТВА ЗАКОРДОННИХ СПРАВ БРИТАНІЇ

Претенденти повинні мати диплом вузу або досвід в галузі менеджменту. Перевагу будуть мати такі галузі:

Економічна політика та реформи
Державне управління та самоврядування
Комерційне та конституційне право
Міжнародні відносини
Дослідження в сфері засобів масової інформації

Претенденти повинні вільно володіти англійською мовою, мати видатні академічні або професійні здобутки та певний потенціал; їхній вік повинен бути приблизно від 28 до 40 років. Щоб отримати додаткову інформацію та анкети для заповнення, пишіть на вищегадану адресу. Кінцевий термін для повернення заповнених анкет – 31 січня 1993. На жаль, ми не можемо відповідати на окремі телефонні дзвінки.

(A very few changes have been made to the Ukrainian of the last paragraph.)

Vocabulary

сприя́ти, -я́є- + dat., imperf.	favour, support, assist with
навча́льний	educational
зв'язо́к, -зку́	link, connection
пропонува́ти, -у́є-, imperf.	propose, offer
обме́жений	limited, restricted
кі́лькість, -ості	quantity
визначни́й	outstanding, eminent, excellent (person)
учéний, -ого	scholar, scientist (declined as adjective)
дослі́дник, -а	researcher
можли́вість, -ості	possibility, opportunity
за́клад, -у	institution
поділя́тися, -я́є- на + acc., imperf.	be divided into (perf.: **поділи́тися**, -и-)
обов'язко́во	without fail, obligatory
перева́га (надава́тися, -ає́-, imperf)	preference (is given to); **надава́ти п.**: prefer
виклада́ти, -а́є-, imperf.	teach (higher/ further education)
дослі́дницький	research (adj.)
га́лузь, -і, fem.	branch
навколи́шнє середо́вище, -ього -а	environment
охоро́на, -и	defence
управлі́ння, -я, neut.	administration
ро́звиток, -тку	development
суспі́льство, -а	society
мисте́цтво, -а	art
спра́ва, -и	affair
до́свід, -у	experience
самоврядува́ння, -я, neut.	'self-administration'
пра́во, -а	law
міжнаро́дні відно́сини, -их 'zero'	international relations
дослі́дження, -я, neut.	research
за́соби, -ів ма́сової інформа́ції	mass media
ві́льно володі́ти, -і́є- + instr.	to be fluent in (lit. 'to freely master')
найвність, -ості	evidence
ви́датний	excellent
здобу́ток, -тку	gain; here: qualification, achievement
вік, -у	age
прибли́зно	approximately
отри́мати, -ає-, perf.	receive, obtain (imperf.: **отри́мувати**, **-ує-**)
додатко́вий	additional, supplementary
анке́та, -и	application form, questionnaire
запо́внення, -я, neut.	filling in
вищезга́даний	above-mentioned
кінце́вий те́рмін, -ого -у	closing date
пове́рнення, -я, neut.	return
окре́мий	individual, separate
дзвіно́к, -нка́	call

You should be able to guess the other words, if you do not already know them. Do use a dictionary, both in order to get used to the order of the letters in the Ukrainian alphabet and because it is amazing how many new and useful words you will find in a dictionary before you find the one you are looking for! Now attempt one or more of the following assignments:

(a) Ask each other questions about the details of the advertisement.
(b) Try to tell someone about it on the phone.
(c) Write a letter to someone about it, giving the details you feel would be relevant (note the conventions described next).

Майбутні бізнесмени, а також їх батьки!
ліцей бізнесу оголошує набір учнів у 8-й клас.
документи приймаються з 23 по 25 серпня.
☎ 446-48-18, вул. Лагерна, 30/32.

РЕАЛІЗУЄМО *рекламу світлову* фірми PHILIPS

художнє оформлення на замовлення
торговельне обладнання прилавки, стелажі тощо.

Оформлення вітрин
Тел. (044) 272-40-55;
факс. (044) 272-35-40

Юридична фірма
«АТЛАНТ»
РЕЄСТРАЦІЯ

- спільних підприємств,
- приватних підприємств,
- філій підприємств,
- господарських товариств.

Тел. 228-54-95.

Composing a letter

Compose a letter expressing your interest in the preceding advertisement (and give details of your name, address, age, and experience). A formal way of beginning a letter, equivalent to Dear Sir, would be:

Шанóвний добрóдію	Respected sir (antiquated, but not unused)
Вельмишанóвний	Very respected . . .
колéга (masc. and fem.)	Used among colleagues
дорогúй	Dear, may appear in less formal letters + first name or first name and patronymic
лю́бий	Dear only used in familiar letters

Letters might end with:

З пошáною	With respect
Щúро вітáю	Sincerely (lit. 'I sincerely greet') is less formal, and would occur in letters beginning **дорогúй** (appropriate in **Ти** or **Ви** relationships)
Твій	Only used in familiar letters

The upper station of the funicular railway, Kyiv. (**ажіо** is the name of a bank).

16 У примісько́му райо́ні, у лі́сі (1)

In the suburb and the forest (1)

In this lesson you will learn about:

- ‘swimming’,‘flying’ and ‘running’ and travelling by air and sea
- indefinite pronouns
- directional adverbs
- some more words for flora and birds
- and some new words for travelling and public transport

Дру́зі гуля́ють лі́сом

Oksana and Mykola are walking in a forest outside Kyiv

ОКСА́НА: Слу́хай, Мико́ло, чи ліси́ скрізь такі́ га́рні в Украї́ні?

МИКО́ЛА: Так, в нас є бага́то вели́ких, краси́вих лісі́в. А у вас в Англії?

ОКСА́НА: На жаль, у нас ма́ло лісі́в тепе́р. На пі́вночі, напри́клад, ма́ємо перева́жно го́ри і вели́кі поля́, де росте́ лише́ ве́рес.

МИКО́ЛА: І в нас є ве́рес. Ми залюбки́ п'ємо́ ве́ресовий мед.

ОКСА́НА: Я ду́же люблю́ ве́ресовий мед. Ве́рес – росли́на з пурпуро́вими квітка́ми. І там у нас живу́ть ті́льки вівці́; люди́ну поба́чиш зрі́дка. І́нколи тури́стів бува́є бі́льше, ніж туте́шніх ме́шканців.

МИКО́ЛА: Ціка́во. Як ти ба́чиш, тут є со́сни, ли́пи, бере́зи то́що.

ОКСА́НА: А як зве́ться та росли́на там, бі́ля мале́нького де́рева?

МИКО́ЛА: Украї́нською це гриб. Коли́ ми гуля́ємо лі́сом, лю́бимо збира́ти гриби́. Вони́ ду́же смачні́!

Vocabulary

скрізь	everywhere
краси́вий	beautiful
перева́жно	primarily
рости́, -сте́-, imperf.	grow
ве́рес or **ве́ріс, -у**	heather
ве́ресовий мед, -ого -у	heather ale/mead
Що таке́?	'what is . . .', asking for a definition or description
росли́на, -и	plant
пурпуро́вий	purple
вівця́, -і́	sheep
люди́на, -и (fem.)	person
зрі́дка	seldom (adv.)
тури́ст, -а	tourist
ме́шканець, -нця	inhabitant
туте́шний	local
сосна́, -и́	pine tree
ли́па, -и	lime or linden tree
бере́за, -и	birch tree
зва́тися, -ве́-, imperf.	to be called (synonym of **називა́тися**)
гриб, -а́	mushroom
збира́ти, -а́є-, imperf.	collect, gather (perf. **зібра́ти, збере́-**)

Notes on the dialogue

Ukrainians love to go for walks in the countryside, especially to pick mushrooms! Children grow up learning the names of various kinds of mushrooms, as well as how to tell edible and inedible ones apart. This love of nature cannot be overemphasized and extends to the knowledge and use of all manner of herbs; the following list of items is not meant to be learned by heart at this stage, but rather for future reference (if you spend any time at all with a Ukrainian family, you will certainly be exposed to some of them!). Of course, Ukrainians will also be interested in you, so it would be helpful to know the names of some plants and trees native to your country; we have included some here.

дуб, -а	oak
я́сен, -а	ash
кашта́н, -а	chestnut (tree and fruit)
клен, -а	maple
троя́нда, -и	rose
тюльпа́н, -а	tulip
рома́шка, -и, маргари́тка, -и	daisy
черво́на гвозди́ка, -ої -и	carnation
кульба́ба, -и	dandelion
польова́ кві́тка, -о́ї -и	wild flower
трава́, -и́	grass

Exercise 16a

Пра́вда або́ непра́вда? Check these statements, which refer to **Дру́зі гуля́ють лі́сом**. Say aloud and write out your answers:

(a) Микола вважа́є, що ліси́ скрізь га́рні.
(b) Є бага́то лісі́в в А́нглії.
(c) Ве́рес – це росли́на з чо́рними квітка́ми.
(d) На вели́ких поля́х поба́чиш ті́льки тури́стів.
(e) Украї́нці лю́блять збира́ти у лі́сі гриби́.

Exercise 16b

Write to your Ukrainian friend, describing as many of the flowers, plants or trees listed here as you can; use the colour terminology given to you in *14*, as well as any other descriptive adjectives you might need.

Пта́хи́ літа́ють

As they walk, Mykola and Oksana come to a small lake, where they observe some of the wildlife indigenous to the region

ОКСА́НА: Мико́ло, куди́ летя́ть ці пта́хи́?
МИКО́ЛА: Не зна́ю, але́ здає́ться, що на пі́вніч: тепе́р те́пло.
ОКСА́НА: Так. Чи де́які пта́хи́ залиша́ються у цьо́му райо́ні під ча́с зими́?
МИКО́ЛА: Мммм, так; напри́клад, сова́ не відліта́є. Вона́ ма́є звича́йно своє́ гніздо́, і літа́є лише́ з де́рева на де́рево.
ОКСА́НА: Диви́ся! Там лети́ть яки́сь птах; ціка́во, куди́ це він лети́ть.
МИКО́ЛА: Мо́же до гнізда́; а зві́дки мені́ зна́ти?

Vocabulary

птах, -á	bird
кудú	to where, whither, which way
летíти, -ú, imperf., det.	fly
літáти, -áє-, imperf. indet.	fly
дéякий	some (kind of), a certain
залишáтися, -áє-, imperf.	to stay (lit: 'leave oneself'; perf.: **залúшитися, -и-**)
совá, -ú	owl
гніздó, -á	nest
якийсь	some, certain
звíдки	from where (whence); coll.: 'how should (I know)?'

Supplementary vocabulary: birds

гýска, -и	goose	**журавéль, -ля́**	crane
кáчка, -и	duck	**зозýля, -і**	cuckoo
горобéць, -бця́	sparrow	**лéбідь, -едя**	swan
вóрон, -а	raven	**синúця, -і**	titmouse
ворóна, -и	crow	**сóкіл, -ола**	hawk, falcon
гóлуб, -а	pigeon	**чáйка, -и**	(sea)gull

'Flying', 'swimming' and 'running'

These activities are expressed in Ukrainian using verbs of motion that work just like those you have already learned. In the preceding dialogue, for example, we see two verbs for 'flying': **літáти** and **летíти**. The former indicates habitual or aimless flying, while the latter (the 'determinate') indicates motion in progress toward a particular goal. Compare the following examples with 'swimming' and 'running' verbs:

'Swimming'

рúби плáвають у цьóму óзері	fish swim (around) in this lake
чóвен пливé рíчкою	the boat is 'swimming' along the river
рúба пливé до бéрега	the fish is swimming toward the bank

пла́вати	**плисти́**
пла́ваю	**пливу́**
пла́ваєш . . .	**пливе́ш . . .**
пла́вають	**пливу́ть**
пла́вав	**плив**
пла́вала . . .	**плила́ . . .**

'Running'

ді́ти бі́гають по кімна́ті	the children are running about the room
куди́ ти біжи́ш?	(to) where are you running?
він бі́гає ко́жного ра́нку	he runs/goes running every morning

бі́гати	**бі́гти**
бі́гаю	**біжу́**
бі́гаєш . . .	**біжи́ш . . .**
бі́гають	**біжа́ть**
бі́гав	**біг**
бі́гала . . .	**бі́гла**

Indefinite pronouns

In *4* you were given the pronominal form **щось** 'something'; this is referred to as an 'indefinite' pronoun. Other indefinites can be formed in the same way, that is simply by adding the particle **сь** to an interrogative adverb or pronoun:

де? : десь	'where' + 'some' becomes somewhere
хто? : хтось	someone
яки́й? : яки́йсь	some kind (of . . .)
чому́? : чому́сь	for some reason

These indefinites are declined as one expects, except that the particle is always appended to the declined form (**хтось: кому́сь**). In the dialogue above we also use the form **де́який** 'a certain', which is not quite the same as **яки́йсь** 'some kind (of . . .)'; as you can see, however, in a given situation both can be used. Also, with a prefixal formant **де-** we can produce **де́хто** and **де́що**, which are in practice synonyms of **хтось** and **щось**. Note that all of these indefinites express the thought 'some' in English equivalents. When we wish to be more indefinite, in the sense of 'any' (no particular thing or person in mind), then there are two possibilities:

Х-нéбудь:	**хто-нéбудь**	anyone
	що-нéбудь	anything

and, more indefinite:

бýдь-Х:	**бýдь-хто**	anyone, whoever
	бýдь-що	anything, whatever
	бýдь-коли	(when)ever

For example:

Чи хтось прийшóв?	Has anyone come?
Чи він бýдь-що читáв учóра?	Did (he) read anything (at all) yesterday?
Чи він ходи́в учóра куди-нéбудь?	Did (he) go anywhere (at all) yesterday)

The **бýдь-Х** form is the most general indefinite. The key element in the English equivalent may be 'ever': **бíльше, ніж бýдь-коли** 'bigger than ever'. Indefinites can also be made with other prefixal formants, but for the time being these should be left for passive knowledge: **аби́-** (any-), **хтóзна-** (some), **кáзна-** (some-; on its own **кáзна!** means 'Who knows! The devil only knows!').

It is not easy becoming really proficient in using these pronouns: just try to note the most obvious patterns. Thus, there is a tendency for the more indefinite ones to be used in questions and in the future tense and conditional ('did anyone call/ring this morning?', 'if I see anyone I know I'll tell you') and the more definite ones with the past tense ('someone said "hello", but I don't remember who'). Follow these principles in the next exercise.

Exercise 16b

Choose the indefinite form that 'feels' best in the following sentences. Make sure and decline them where appropriate.

1 Я хóчу піти́ (куди́сь, куди-нéбудь), алé не знáю куди́.
2 Де ти був? (Хтось, Хто-нéбудь) телефонувáв, щоб говори́ти з тобóю.
3 Чи ви читáли (щось, що-нéбудь) учóра ввéчері?

4 Якщó (хтось, хто-нéбудь) потелефонýє, скажíть, прóшу, що мене́ немáє.
5 Я побáчив (хтось, хто-нéбудь) на вýлиці, алé на жаль не знáю, чи то був Івáн.

Directional adverbs

Alongside the adverbs of place you already know we have adverbs used with motion verbs:

де?	where	**куди́?**	to where	**звíдки?**	from where
тут	here	**сюди́**	to here	**звíдси**	from here
там	there	**туди́**	to there	**звíдти**	from there

Examples:

Куди́ йдéш, Марíю?
Звíдки ви приї́хали сьогóдні? З Одéси?
Йди́ сюди́, дрýже.

Travelling by air, train, boat and car

Подорожувáти, **-ýє-** is the general word for 'to travel' in Ukrainian. It is imperfective, and if one needs a perfective, as in 'to make a journey', then the expression **відбýти**, **-де- пóдорож** is available (**пóдорож**, **-і** 'journey'). To convey 'by . . .' we may simply use the instrumental singular of **літáк**, **-á** 'aeroplane', **пóїзд**, **-у** 'train', **пароплáв -а** 'steamer' (or **теплохíд**, **-хóду** 'diesel-engined ship') and **маши́на**, **-и** 'car': **ї́хати літакóм**, **пóїздом**, **пароплáвом**, **маши́ною**. For 'flying' and 'sailing' one can also use **літáти/летíти** and **плáвати/плисти́**, which we met earlier in this lesson.

In *9* we learned about prefixed verbs of motion; this applies equally to **літáти/лети́ти** and **плáвати/плисти́**, with the qualification that **плáвати** when prefixed and imperfective becomes **-пливáти**. Thus:

	to depart	*to reach*	*to arrive*
car/train	**від'їжджáти**	**доїжджáти**	**приїжджáти**
	від'ї́хати	**дої́хати**	**приї́хати**
plane	**відлітáти**	**долітáти**	**прилітáти**
	відлетíти	**долетíти**	**прилетíти**
boat	**відпливáти**	**допливáти**	**припливáти**
	відплисти́	**доплисти́**	**приплисти́**

Compare the following examples and note **з** 'from' and **до** 'at', followed by the genitive case:

> **Ми лю́бимо подорожува́ти.**
> **Учо́ра Ва́ня дої́хав до Ки́єва з Оде́си.**
> **Сього́дні О́льга прилети́ть до Ха́ркова з Ки́єва?**
> **Ма́ма від'ї́хала з Москви́ о п'я́тій годи́ні.**

A few useful words for travellers

довідко́ве бюро́, -ого -ó	information (office) (**бюро́** is indeclinable)
інформа́ція, -ї	information
світлове́ табло́, -óго -ó	video display with information
ро́зклад, -у поїздí́в	train timetable (as displayed on a board; **табло́** is indeclinable)
повідомля́ти, -я́є-, imperf.	to notify, inform (+ acc. **про** + acc. 'someone about something') (perf. **повідо́мити, -и-**)
затри́мка, -и	delay (+ genitive: **затри́мка ре́йсу** 'delay of the trip/journey', from **рейс, -у**)
зал, -у чека́ння	waiting room
ка́мера, -и схо́ву	left luggage office
кімна́та, -и відпочи́нку	room for resting, not Amer. 'restroom' (toilet)!
кімна́та, -и ма́тері й дити́ни	nursery
меди́чний пункт, -ого -у	first-aid station
гучномо́вець, -вця	loudspeaker
реєстра́ція, -ї	registration
відправля́тися, -я́є-	to depart, set off (**відпра́влення, -я** 'departure')
прибува́ти, -а́є-	to arrive (**прибуття́, -я́** 'arrival')
підво́зити, -и-	to give a lift, to take (someone somewhere) (**підвезти́, -зе́-**, with **до** + gen.)
вча́сно	in time
кіо́ск, -а	kiosk (**книжко́вий, газе́тний** 'for books, newspapers'
перехі́д, -хо́ду	passageway, corridor (with **підзе́мний**: 'underground passageway')

Read the following sample situation(s):

Чи ви не ска́жете мені́, де мо́жна діста́ти квито́к?
Звича́йно. Ка́си розташо́вані в центра́льному за́лі. Іді́ть пря́мо.
Дя́кую.

Да́йте, будь ла́ска, зворо́тний квито́к Ки́їв-Ха́рків.
Про́шу. З вас . . .
Та скажі́ть, будь ла́ска, на яку́ платфо́рму мені́ пройти́.
Про це мо́жете дізна́тися із ро́зкладу відпра́влення поїзді́в, що ви́сить он там у за́лі.
Коли́ відправля́ється по́їзд?
Че́рез де́сять хвили́н. Вам тре́ба поспіша́ти, а то не встигнете на ньо́го.
Чи не ска́жете, де ка́мера схо́ву?
Вона́ там, неподалі́к від кав'я́рні. Тепе́р ви́бачте, добро́дію, за ва́ми вже стоїть до́вга че́рга́, я не мо́жу бі́льше відповіда́ти на ва́ші запита́ння.
Ви́бачте. Щи́ро дя́кую вам за ва́шу допомо́гу.

Vocabulary

розташо́ваний	located, situated	**а то**	or else, because (in the sense: 'if you don't, you'll . . .)
зворо́тний	return, round trip (adjective)	**неподалі́к від** + gen.	near, not far from
пройти́, -де-, perf.	to get to, to make one's way to (imperf. **прохо́дити**, -и-)	**допомо́га, -и**	help
поспіши́ти, -и́-, perf.	to hurry, rush (imperf. **поспіша́ти**, -а́є-)		

If you travel to Ukraine on **Міжнаро́дні Авіалі́нії Украї́ни** 'Air Ukraine International', everything in the aeroplane will be in both English and Ukrainian. For the sake of the stresses, however, and for those of you who are just interested, let us note the following. First, on the back of the seat in front:

Застебні́ть прив'язні́ ре́мені
Fasten seat belt[s] (*Given as 'belt' in plane*)
Рятува́льний жиле́т під сиді́нням
Life vest under seat

Secondly, by the emergency exit:

Користу́йтеся тільки під час ава́рії	
Emergency use only	
Зня́ти	Remove
кри́шку	cover
Потягну́ти	Pull

In the lavatory, the flush is designated by:

Вмив уніта́зу

and there is, of course, no smoking there:

Не пали́ти в туале́ті

Exercise 16c

Imagine you are about to travel by air or train. Describe how you get to the station or airport, obtain your ticket, do everything else you need to do, then get your plane or train. At registration, or when you are looking for a place on the train, you may need to find a seat where you can either smoke or not. 'To smoke' is **кури́ти**, **-и-** as well as **пали́ти, -и-: Чи ви ку́рите?** 'Do you smoke?', and you will be a smoker **курéць, -рця́** or a non-smoker **некурéць**, **-рця́**. On the train look for a **ваго́н, (-а) для курці́в** or a **ваго́н для некурці́в**. Was the compartment **купé** (indecl.) **по́вний** 'full' or **поро́жній** 'empty', and were it and the seat (**сиді́ння**, **-я** or **мі́сце**, **-я**) **зру́чни́й** 'comfortable'? You might need to look for a vacant seat: **Чи тут ві́льно? Чи тут є ві́льне мі́сце?** 'Is it vacant here?' 'Is there a free seat here?' ('not free, occupied' **за́йнятий**, which also means 'busy').

Another advertisement

Read the following promotional passage from the Ukrainian magazine **Украї́на** (1992) 36. You should be able to understand much of it without any trouble. After you have worked through it the first time, read it again immediately; if you can, read it a third time after you have set it aside for some time. Try to give answers in Ukrainian to the following questions in English. The questions follow the order of the content of the passage.

УВАГА! УВАГА! УВАГА!

Звертаємось до наших давніх шанува́льників!
Звертаємось до всіх, хто ще роздумує над проблемою: на якому виданні зупинити свій вибір; хто не встиг цього зробити до 10 листопада.
Якщо ви хочете знати про все суттєве, що відбувається в нашій державі, вам аж ніяк не потрібно передплачувати кілька видань. Їх замінить національний тижневий часопис «Україна».

Тижневик «Україна» в 1993 році – це:

- наша держава вчора, сьогодні, завтра;
- наша економіка і політика в інформації, аналізах, прогнозах;
- людина крізь призму сьогодення;
- а ще гумор, спорт, пригоди, фантастика, корисні поради і кросворди.

Модель «Україна»-93 – це краще від знаного вами часопису. Працюємо під девізом: «Замість старої «України» – чотири нові журнали». Під спільною назвою протягом року ви одержуватимете щомісяця чотири нові «журнали в журналі»: «Україна і світ», «Життя держави», «Історія, література, мистецтво», «Українська душа». А до цього – протягом року чотири спецвипуски, два з яких уже в роботі: в кінці січня одержите обіцяний випуск з узорами та рекомендаціями для вишивання, в кінці травня – довідник з рецептами народних цілителів.
Разом – традиційні 52 зустрічі за рік.
І все це на теперішні часи за найнижчою передплатною ціною: на рік – 390 купонів, на півроку – 195 купонів, на квартал – 97,5 купона, на місяць – 32,5 купона.
Порівняйте з вартістю передплати інших видань, і ви зрозумієте, що засновник «Україна» концерн «Крим-Континенталь» та його президент Юрій Колесников дбають не тільки про інформаційну та духовну насиченість вашого життя, а й щоб ваш гаманець не схуднув.
Ми коротко втаємничили вас у наші плани. З першими випусками «журналів у журналі» ви маєте нагоду познайомитись вже в листопаді та грудні нинішнього року. Поділіться своїми думками і щодо наших планів, і щодо перших випусків оновлюваної «України». Що вам до душі, що ні, а головне – чому? Запропонуйте свою концепцію «України» – найсуттєвіше ми візьмемо на озброєння, а це буде корисним і часописові, і його читачам.
Хотілося б знати вашу думку: яким повинен бути національний часопис? З радістю прислухаємось до ваших порад.
Передплачуйте «Україну» і радьте це зробити друзям і знайомим на рідній землі і в діаспорі!
Тижневик «Україна» – в кожну українську родину! В кожну школу! В кожну бібліотеку! В кожну військову частину!

Here are some words to help you understand the article:

Vocabulary

звертáтися, -áє-, imperf. **до** + gen.	address, turn to (perf. **звернýтися, -не-**; note the very common phrase **звертáти/звернýти ввáгу на** + acc. 'to pay attention to, take into account')
шанувáльник, -а	adherent, supporter
роздýмувати, -ує- над + instr.	ponder, think over
зупини́ти, -и- ви́бір на + loc.	choose (lit. 'to halt one's choice on ...')
вcти́гнути, -не-, past **вcти́г(ла ...)**	manage to, have time to (imperf. **встигáти, -áє-**)
сýттєвий	essential
нія́к не	not at all
передплáчувати, -ує-, imperf.	subscribe to, lit. 'pre-pay' (**передплáта** 'subscription, prepayment')
заміни́ти, -и-, perf.	replace (imperf. **замі́нювати, -ює-**)
пригóда, -и	adventure, event, accident
зáмість + gen.	instead of
мистéцтво, -а	art
спецви́пуск, -у	special issue
обі́цяний	promised
узі́р, узóру	pattern, model
вишивáння, -я, neut.	embroidery
дові́дник, -а	information booklet, reference handbook
цілúтель, -я	healer
порівня́ти, -я́є-, perf.	compare (imperf. **порі́внювати, -ює-**) + **з** + instr. 'with'
вáртість, -ості	value, cost
заснóвник, -а	founder
дбáти, -áє-, imperf. **про** + acc.	care about, look after
наси́ченість, -ості	fullness
гаманéць, -нця́	purse
схýднути -не- perf.	grow thin
втаéмничати, -ає-, imperf.	bring someone into, involve, confide (followed by the accusative of the person(s) to whom something is being confided, and **у/в** + acc. of what is being confided)
онóвлюваний	renewed, revived
що вам до душі́?	what pleases you?
головнé	the main thing, most of all
запропонувáти, -ує-, perf.	propose, suggest (imperf. **пропонувáти, -ýє-**)

узя́ти, візьме-, perf. **на озбро́єння**	to take on
кори́сний + dat.	useful to/for
чита́ч, -а́	reader
з ра́дістю	gladly, with pleasure
прислу́хатися, -ає-, perf. **до** + gen.	listen to (imperf. **прислуха́тися, -а́є-**)
пора́да, -и	advice (a piece of). Plural often used for 'advice' in general
ра́дити, -и-, imperf.	advise (perf. **пора́дити**, **-и-**; plus the accusative of what you advise, or plus an infinitive (or both), and the dative of the person(s) being advised)
військова́ части́на, -о́ї -и	military/army unit

And now some questions – when you know (or have found) the answers try to express them in Ukrainian:

(a) Is *Ukrayina* a daily, monthly or weekly magazine?
(b) What do you think **щоде́нник**, **щомі́сячник**, **щоти́жня** and **щотижне́вик** mean?
(c) Does the magazine concentrate on Ukraine's present?
(d) Does it only contain articles on famous writers?
(e) Who does it examine 'through the prism of today's events'?
(f) What does it aim to provide in addition to current events and useful advice?
(g) What is the new magazine's motto?
(h) The name *Ukrayina* brings together four new magazines under a common name. Taking them in order, in which one is art discussed, and in which the Ukrainian 'soul'?
(i) How many special issues will there be each year?
(j) When is the special issue on embroidery and needlework scheduled to appear?
(k) When will the special reference section on medical matters appear?
(l) How much is the subscription for the various periods of the year? (Note that the reference here is to **купо́ни**.)

The Kyiv metro is very efficient, clean, and with frequent trains. Prices are changing; in December 1993 a single journey cost 30 karbovantsi (abbr.: krb.) (the bus cost 30 krb.; the tram and trolleybus cost 20 krb.). One may buy a paper ticket at the ticket office in the station (the metal jetons/tokens for the machines are for the moment more or less collectors' items). But it's better to buy a monthly pass. There is the usual crush to get into the carriages, where you will see advertisements and various official notices, e.g.

не притуля́тися	'Don't lean' (on the doors)

and

місця́
для інвалі́дів
осі́б лі́тнього ві́ку
та пасажи́рів з дітьми́
'Seats for invalids, elderly people, and passengers with children'

When the train nears a station, the tape announces:

Ста́нція [*NAME*]

(Just before the **Дніпро́** (station) we hear that the exit is not on the usual side: **Ви́хід на пра́ву платфо́рму**; at six stations we will be told that there is a connection to another metro station: **Перехі́д на ста́нцію** [*NAME*]; and at certain stations there is access to suburban trains (**приміські́ електропоїзди́**).)

If the station is the terminus, we then hear:

Кінце́ва. По́їзд да́лі не йде́
(One may hear **не ї́де**, but that is considered a mistake.)

Just before the train sets off again we are warned to be careful, that the doors are closing (they close quite violently), and the next station is . . .:

Обере́жно. Две́рі зачиня́ються. Насту́пна ста́нція [*NAME*]

Public transport

There follows a plan of Kyiv and of the Kyiv metro, the **метро́** or **метрополіте́н** (underground, Amer. subway). The following selection of verbs and patterns, some of which you may already know (see *5*), are used when travelling by public transport. Note also the names of some points of interest in Kyiv:

Vocabulary

зайня́ти мі́сце у/в + loc. — to get on
зійти́, схо́дити; злі́зти, зла́зити: з + gen. — to get off
пересі́сти, пересіда́ти на + acc. — to change
(за)плати́ти — to pay
опусти́ти моне́ту в ка́су-автома́т — to put a coin in the 'gate'
проби́ти компо́стером тало́н, яки́й мо́жна придба́ти в водія́ — to cancel a ticket (got from the driver)
прохо́дити че́рез товчію́/да́вку (you usually ask the people between you and the exit if they are getting off at the next stop, thus: **Чи схо́дите на насту́пній ста́нції/зупи́нці? Чи схо́дите? Чи зара́з схо́дите?** (or **вихо́дите**) — to get through the crowd
пропонува́ти кому́сь мі́сто — to offer someone a seat
проїзни́й (квито́к, -тка́) — ticket
прої́зд, -у у метро́ — a journey on the metro
дрібні́ гро́ші, -и́х -ей — small change
зда́ча, -і — change (what's given back to you)
автома́т, -а для розмі́ну гро́шей — machine giving change
маршру́т, -у — one's route
ва́ртість, -ості квитка́ — cost of a ticket
за́соби, -ів тра́нспорту — means of transport
велосипе́д, -а — bicycle
мотоци́кл, -а — motorcycle
фунікуле́р, -а — funicular railway
таксі́ (indecl.) — taxi
шофе́р таксі́ — taxi driver
зупи́нка, -и авто́буса/ троле́йбуса/ трамва́я — bus/tram/trolley stop
ста́нція, -ї метро́ — metro station
найбли́жча ста́нція метро́ — the nearest metro station
річкови́й вокза́л, -о́го -у — river station
вокза́л, -у — railway station
залізни́ця, -і — railway
ка́са, -и — ticket office, tickets
ке́мпінґ, -у — camp site
рестора́н, -у («Млин», «Ната́лка») — restaurant
кав'я́рня, -і, кафе́ (indecl.) — café
готе́ль, -лю «Ли́бідь», «Дніпро́», «Ки́їв» — hotels

Ки́ївський Університе́т, -ого -у	Kyiv University
Ки́єво-Пече́рська Ла́вра, -ої -и	The Kyiv Caves Monastery
Софі́йська це́рква, -ої -и; Собо́р, -у св'ято́ї Софі́ї; Софі́йський собо́р, -ого -у	St. Sophia
(драмати́чний) теа́тр, (-ого) -у і́мені Іва́на Франка́	The Ivan Franko Theatre
па́м'ятник, -а князя́ Володи́мира Вели́кого	The Volodymyr the Great monument
міліціоне́р, -а; поліце́йський, -ого	policeman

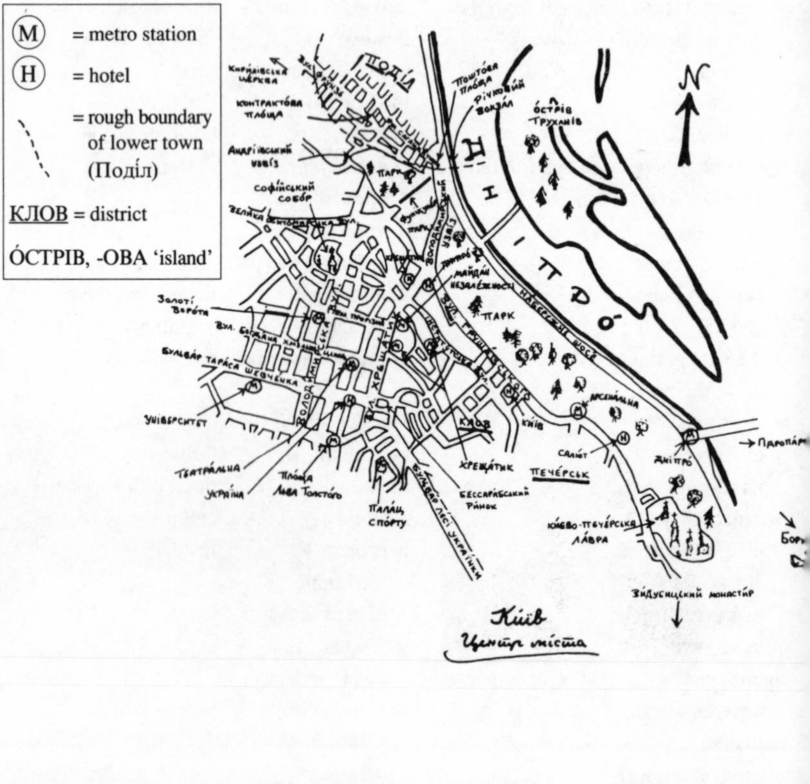

Ки́їв і метро́

Single tickets

Monthly tickets

Sample dialogues

Ви́бачте, де мо́жна купи́ти квито́к?
У водія́.
Дя́кую.

Скажі́ть, будь ла́ска, де мені́ зійти́: я ї́ду в готе́ль «Украї́на».
Вам тре́ба пересі́сти на авто́бус № 35 бі́ля річково́го вокза́лу.
А по́тім?
По́тім тре́ба запита́ти водія́ авто́буса.

Чи вихо́дите на насту́пній (зупи́нці)?
Вихо́джу.

Ви́бачте, де мо́жна заплати́ти?
Опусті́ть гро́ші в ка́су-автома́т.
Ой! Але́ нема́є дрібни́х гро́шей.
Там є автома́т, там на зупи́нці; іді́ть, бу́демо чека́ти на вас.
Дя́кую!

The number of different situations we could come up with here is, of course, endless. Read these over several times until you can play the role of the traveller without looking at all the words.

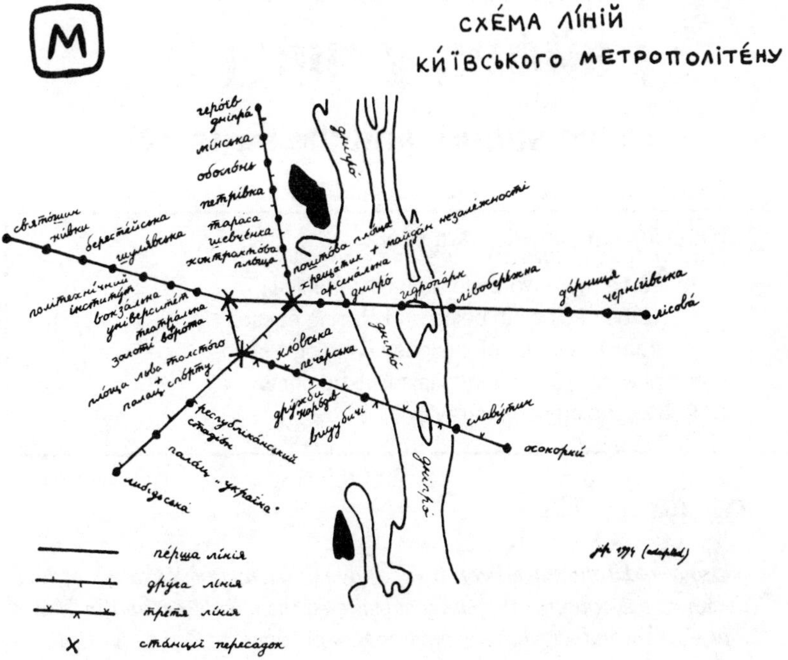

Notes

(1) Stretches of line are under construction beyond **Золоті́ воро́та** and **Осокоркú (Діля́нка спору́джується).** Due to open in 1995–1996. Others are planned (**діля́нка проєкту́ється**).

(2) The two stations **Пече́рська** and **Дру́жби наро́дів** are in fact one, **Пече́рська**. However, the latter, older, name was still in the station and on the train announcements tape in December 1993.

17 У приміськóму райóні, у лíсі (2)

In the suburb and the forest (2)

In this lesson you will learn about:

- some more words for animals and fish
- verbs of placing, being and placing oneself
- transitive verbs of motions ('carrying', 'taking')
- playing games and musical instruments
- describing people (review)

На дáчі

Oksana and John have been invited to visit friends of Mykola's at their dacha in the country; they have completed their walk around the forest and are now gathered at the dacha. Also present are Petro and Halia

ПЕТРÓ: Микóло, звíдки ви з Оксáною приї́хали сьогóдні?

МИКÓЛА: З міста; спочáтку ми ї́хали пóїздом, пóтім автóбусом, і нарéшті прийшли́ сюди́ пíшки.

ПЕТРÓ: Трéба ходи́ти пíшки, бо тут на селí не мáємо дуже надíйного трáнспорту. А тобí, Оксáно, подóбається тут у нас?

ОКСÁНА: Звичáйно! І вáша дáча дýже гáрна. В нас немáє можли́вості ї́здити на дáчу напри́кінці кóжного ти́жня.

ПЕТРÓ: Як . . . алé у вас є дáча, прáвда?

ОКСÁНА: Ні, не так, як у вас. Íноді багáті лю́ди мáють лíтній буди́нок, алé це не такí звичáйні лю́ди, як ми.

ГÁЛЯ: Знáєш, Оксáно, тут не кóжна «дáча» мáє буди́нок; то мóже бýти лишé ділянка.

ОКСÁНА: Що то такé?

ГÁЛЯ: Ну, то є мíсце без хáти; тíльки землЯ́, де мóжна вирóщувати горóдину та садовинý.

ПЕТРÓ: Дрýзі, вибачáйте. . . алé тепéр час підняти кéлехи! (Усі берýть кéлехи в рýки.) За вáше здорóв'я!

(a) As Petro and Halya have indicated, a dacha is not always a sumptuous summer residence (although it can be!), nor does it even have to refer to a building. Many families have a place they can go to for relaxation, whether it is for recreational activities (walking, mushroom picking) or growing vegetables. These dachas are usually found in clusters, one next to another; we are not talking of summer houses with lots of land!

(b) **За ва́ше здоро́в'я!** Friends toasting each other may also say **Бу́дьмо!**, or **Бу́дьмо здоро́ві!** The friends may toast each with **горі́лка, -и** '(Ukrainian) vodka'. The choicest is **з пе́рцем** 'pepper'.

Vocabulary

на селі́	in the country
наді́йний	reliable
можли́вість, -ості	possibility
да́ча, -и	dacha
напри́кінці́	finally (adv.); at the end of (prep. + gen.)
і́ноді	sometimes
бага́тий	rich
лі́тній	summer (adj.)
звича́йний	ordinary
лише́	only
діля́нка, -и	plot of land
земля́, -і́	land, earth, ground
виро́щувати, -ує-, imperf.	grow (something), trans.
вибача́йте	excuse me
ке́лех, -а	glass, chalice
підня́ти, підійму́, підійме-, perf.	to raise (imperf.: **підніма́ти** or **підійма́ти**, **-а́є-**)
лови́ти ри́бу	to fish
ри́бна ло́вля	fishing
полюва́ти, -ю́є	to hunt
полюва́ння, -я	hunting

The following is a partial list of some of the animals one might see in a country setting; some are hunted, others are not. Ukrainians also like to eat fish, so the list includes the names of some common fish (caviar is of course a fish product!):

осете́р, -тра́	sturgeon
ікра́, -и́	caviar
лосо́сь, -я	salmon
оселе́дець, -дця	herring (salt)
щу́ка, -и	pike
ко́роп, -а	carp
ка́мбала, -и	flounder/sole
бі́лка, -и, виві́рка, -и	squirrel
за́єць, за́йця	hare
їжа́к, -а́	hedgehog
борсу́к, -а́	badger
лиси́ця, -і	fox
вовк, -а	wolf
ведмі́дь, -ме́дя	bear
о́лень, -я	deer
бобе́р, -бра́	beaver

Word-formation: meat

We have special English names for the foods that animals provide, and so does Ukrainian: usually the connection between animal and food is much closer than it is in English (cf. cow/beef, deer/venison, pig/pork), as it often involves the simple presence of a suffix which (in effect) expresses 'meat of X':

осете́р, -тра́	sturgeon	**осетри́на, -и**	sturgeon
лосо́сь, -я	salmon	**лососи́на, -и**	salmon
гу́ска, -и	goose	**гуся́тина, -и**	goose
теля́, теля́ти	calf	**теля́тина, -и**	veal
свиня́, -і́	pig	**свини́на, -и**	pork
бара́н, -а́	ram	**бара́нина, -и**	lamb/mutton

(The general word for 'sheep' is **вівця́**, -і́)

Other names for meats are either unrelated to the animal name, as in English, or are the same word as that for the animal itself:

ку́рка, -и	chicken
ка́чка, -и	duck

But

коро́ва, -n	cow
я́ловичина, -и	beef

Verbs of position

In Ukrainian, verbs of 'putting something somewhere', 'being (put) somewhere' and 'putting oneself somewhere' are closely linked and correspond to 'lying', 'standing', and 'hanging'. If we characterize them as 'placing', 'being' and 'placing oneself', they are as follows:

Placing	*Being*	*Placing oneself*
(по)кла́сти	**лежа́ти**	**ляга́ти/лягти́**
(по)ста́вити	**стоя́ти**	**устава́ти/уста́ти**
		става́ти/ста́ти
(по-)сади́ти	**сиді́ти**	**сіда́ти/сі́сти**
ві́шати/пові́сити	**ви́сіти**	**ві́шатися/пові́ситися**

Note that the verbs in the second column do not have a perfective. You can put **по**- before them, which does make them perfective, but also gives the added sense of 'a little, a bit'.

Looking into the meanings of the verbs, then, in the three columns, we have:

- to put something in a lying/standing/sitting/hanging position
- to be in a lying/standing/sitting/hanging position
- to put oneself in a lying/standing/sitting/hanging position

Remember that any expression of place associated with a verb in the first or third column will normally convey motion, i.e. a preposition that can take the accusative will normally do so, while a verb in the second column will not convey motion. Compare the two examples for **сиді́ти** and **сі́сти** in the list below.

Examples:

О́льга покла́ла кни́жку на стіл; тепе́р кни́жка лежи́ть на столі́.
Оле́кса сів на стіле́ць; тепе́р він сиди́ть на стільці́.

Set phrases are more difficult to acquire (and also to find in a dictionary) when learning a new language; here are a few connected with these verbs:

(по)кла́сти край + dat.	put an end to
(по)кла́сти гро́ші до оща́дної ка́си	deposit money in the savings bank
(в)кла́сти гро́ші до оща́дної ка́си	deposit money in the savings bank
мені́ це лежи́ть на се́рці	this weighs heavily on me
ця су́кня не лежи́ть до́бре на ній	this dress does not suit her
со́нце ляга́є (or **сіда́є**)	the sun is setting
(по)ста́вити пе́ред собо́ю завда́ння	set oneself a task
(по)ста́вити запита́ння	ask a question (also **задава́ти комусь запита́ння**)
стоя́ти на па́льцях	stand on tiptoe
стоя́ти в че́рзі́	queue (+ **за** instrumental 'for')
стоя́ти за + acc.	defend, stand up for
воло́сся ста́ло мені́ ду́ба	my hair stood on end
вона́ сиді́ла за столо́м	she was sitting at the table
йому́ не сиди́ться	he's fidgety, can't sit still
він сів до сто́лу	he sat down at the table
ві́шати го́лову	be downcast
майбу́тнє ви́сить на волоску́/ни́тці	the future hangs by a thread
вона́ йому́ ві́шається на ши́ю	she clings to him (metaphorically; usually of women to men, in current usage)

Remember that the verb **ставáти/стáти** can also mean 'to become', followed by the instrumental (unless used impersonally); a synonym is **(з)роби́тися** lit. 'to make oneself':

він зроби́вся дирéктором	he's become director (**став** would be more neutral; **зроби́вся** suggests he achieved something in order to be made director)
їй рáптом стáло знáчно холоднíше	she suddenly became much colder (lit. 'to her it became . . .')

These verbs are a very rich source of new verbs in Ukrainian, and sometimes English can point the way. For instance, in English we say 'to put off' in the sense of 'to postpone'. Can we do this in Ukrainian? The answer is that we can:

відкладáти, -áє-, відклáсти, -дé- to postpone

It also means 'to put aside', as when one puts **грóші** 'money' aside in case one might need it in the future.

Хто йдé, несé; хто ї́де, везé!

ДЖОН:	Микóло, коли́ ми йшли сюди́, ми везли́ зі собóю тéплі піджаки́ . . .
МИКÓЛА:	Ні; якщó йдéш пíшки, то знáчить, що несéш щось.
ДЖОН:	Чому́? А, так; везу́ щось, тíльки якщó ї́ду! Дя́кую.
МИКÓЛА:	Так. Ну, а що: ви ду́мали, що бу́де хóлодно?
ДЖОН:	Сáме так. Алé тут зóвсім не хóлодно!

Vocabulary

везти́, -зé-	to take by vehicle (det.)	**нести́, -сé-**	to take by foot, to carry (det.)
зі собóю	along, lit. 'with oneself'	**сáме так**	exactly! ('just so')
піджáк, -á	jacket (man's)		

Transitive verbs of motion

Next to the intransitive verbs of motion that express movement under one's own steam (be it a person or a vehicle), there are also verbs for transporting things or people, that is, 'carrying' by foot or by vehicle. As verbs of motion, these also work according to the structure already learned, incorporating indeterminate and determinate imperfectives and perfectives. Study the use of transitives together with the intransitives in the following sentences, and note that they will almost always be of the same type: in other words, an indeterminate will be used with another indeterminate and so on:

носи́ти, нести́ carrying, moving an object when on foot

ношу́	**несу́**
но́сиш . . .	**несе́ш . . .**
но́сять	**несу́ть**
носи́в	**ніс**
носи́ла . . .	**несла́ . . .**

Ми ходи́ли по мі́сту ввесь день, і тре́ба було́ носи́ти на́ші портфе́лі зі собо́ю.

Коли́ листоно́ша йшо́в до на́шого до́му, він ніс вели́кий паке́т до нас.

Га́ля за́вжди́ но́сить таки́й га́рний о́дяг.

вози́ти, везти́ transporting, taking an object (or person) when using a vehicle

вожу́	**везу́**
во́зиш . . .	**везе́ш . . .**
во́зять	**везу́ть**
вози́в	**віз**
вози́ла . . .	**везла́ . . .**

Щодня́ грузовики́ ї́здять з Ки́єва до Москви́; во́зять туди́ о́вочі.
Ба́чиш там маши́ну? Вона́ ї́де до парла́менту; мо́же везу́ть туди́ яку́сь важли́ву люди́ну.

Vocabulary

портфе́ль, -ю	briefcase	**о́дяг**	clothes (note: singular in Ukrainian!)
листоно́ша, -и, masc.	postman, mailman	**парла́мент, -у**	parliament
		важли́вий	important

As is the case with all other verbs of motion that you have encountered before this lesson, these transitives, as well as 'swim/fly/run', may be prefixed to form new imperfective/perfective verbs that are more specific with regard to the direction of motion. Sometimes the meaning may be altered to the extent that a different English equivalent is required. Note the change in place of stress in new imperfectives.

Він вино́сив дити́ну з кімна́ти, коли́ поба́чив О́льгу.	He was carrying the child out of the room when he saw Ol'ha.
Давні́ше Росі́я виво́зила на́фту у схі́дну Євро́пу.	Before (earlier) Russia used to export oil to East Europe. (cf. **Уво́зити** 'import')
Пта́хи́ відліта́ють на пі́вдень.	Birds fly (away) to the South.
Літаки́ приліта́ють в Ки́їв з А́нглії ко́жного ти́жня.	Planes fly to (arrive by flying) Kyiv from England every week.
Пароплáв відплива́є в Чо́рне мо́ре.	The (steam)ship is going out/away into the Black Sea.

We might mention here a third verb of motion that involves 'taking', though here the sense is not of carrying, on foot or by some means of transport, but rather of leading someone, who remains on foot. The verb is **води́ти/вести́/повести́**. It conjugates as follows:

вожу́	**веду́**
во́диш . . .	**веде́ш . . .**
во́дять	**веду́ть**
води́в	**вів**
води́ла . . .	**вела́ . . .**

Ма́ма вела́ дити́ну по ву́лиці, коли́ поба́чила свою́ по́другу.
Ко́жний день я вожу́ дити́ну в шко́лу.

Playing games and musical instruments

The verb **гра́ти**, **-а́є-** 'to play' tends to be reflexive when used on its own in the sense of 'playing, amusing oneself'. As a verb of action, like 'to work', **гра́ти** does not have a ready-made perfective companion, though the verb **зігра́ти** may convey 'to have/finish a game (of)'. Related verbs include **програва́ти**, **-ає́-**, perf. **програ́ти**, **-а́є-** 'to lose' and **вигрaва́ти**, **-ає́-**, perf. **ви́грати**, **-ає-** 'to win'. When **гра́ти** is used in the sense of 'playing a game' ('game' **гра**, **-и**), it is constructed with the preposition **у/в** + acc. Thus:

Коли́ Мико́ла грав у те́ніс, його́ брат і сестра́ гра́ли з батька́ми в ка́рти.	When Mykola was playing tennis, his brother and sister were playing cards with their parents.
На́ша кома́нда ви́грала сього́дні; на жаль, вона́ програ́ла вчо́ра.	Our team won today; unfortunately, it lost yesterday.

The construction required for 'playing an instrument' is **гра́ти на** + loc. (sometimes one encounters the accusative). Thus:

Усі́ мої́ ро́дичі залюбки́ гра́ють на музика́льних інструме́нтах: двою́рідна сестра́ Окса́на гра́є на скри́пці, ті́тка Тетя́на гра́є на роя́лі, дя́дько Андрі́й гра́є на гіта́рі, та батьки́ гра́ють на бараба́нах.
All my relatives enjoy playing musical instruments: my cousin Oksana plays the violin, my aunt Tetiana plays the piano, my uncle Andrii plays the guitar and my parents play the drums.

Another useful set phrase is **гра́ти ро́лю** 'to play a role/part' (followed by the genitive when it means 'to play the role of . . .' (**ро́ля**, **-і** 'role, part'):

Га́нна Анато́ліївна Коцюби́нська гра́ла ро́лю Софі́ї в п'є́сі Іва́на Тобіле́вича «Безтала́нна».
Hanna Anatoliyivna Kotsiubyns'ka played the role of Sofiya in Ivan Tobilevych's (Ivan Karpenko-Karyi's) play *Beztalanna*.

Exercise 17a

Here are a few names of games and instruments. See if you can identify them, (except where the answer or a clue is given) and answer the question.

На яко́му інструме́нті ви гра́єте?

(a) контраба́с
(b) фле́йта

(c) саксофо́н
(d) тарілки́
(e) труба́
(f) віо́ля
(g) віолонче́ля
(h) банду́ра bandura (Ukrainian national instrument)
(i) сопі́лка sopilka, fife (Ukrainian flute)
(j) акордео́н
(k) губна́ гармо́ніка

У яку́ гру ви хоті́ли б гра́ти?

(l) хоке́й
(m) ша́хи
(n) волейбо́л
(o) квач (у квача́) tag
(p) кре́м'яхи jacks
(q) футбо́л
(r) ку́льки marbles
(s) бейсбо́л
(t) схо́ванки схова́ти, -а́є- 'to hide' (perf.); (imperf. **хова́ти**)
(u) ша́шки Hint: not quite chess!

Reading

Топогра́фія-геогра́фія Украї́ни

Украї́на – це ду́же вели́ка краї́на; вона́ така́ ж вели́ка, як Фра́нція, але́ набага́то менша, ніж Росі́я. На терито́рії Украї́ни є вели́кі го́ри (на за́ході, у Закарпа́тті та у Прикарпа́тті), ме́нші го́ри (у сере́дині, поді́льска височина́; до схо́ду, придніпро́вська височина́), та широ́кі рівни́ни (на пі́вдні й схо́ді). Істо́рія ціє́ї краї́ни ті́сно пов'язана з трьома́ могу́тніми рі́ками: Дністро́м, Бу́гом, та Дніпро́м. Дністе́р ма́є своє́ джерело́ на кра́йньому за́ході, поблизу́ по́льського кордо́ну; він тече́ на пivде́нний схід, уздо́вж молда́вського кордо́ну, а наре́шті че́рез Молдо́ву в Чо́рне мо́ре (звича́йно, усі́ ці річки́ течу́ть туди́). Буг протіка́є східні́ше, тече́ на пі́вдень че́рез Хмельни́цьк та Микола́їв; його́ джерело́ мі́ститься в Поді́льській височині́. Оста́ння ріка́ – Дніпро́ – почина́ється побіля́ білору́сько-украї́нського кордо́ну; він протіка́є повз Ки́їв, Запорі́жжя, та Херсо́н. Хоча́ в Украї́ні нема́є вели́ких озе́р, є три о́зера-водо́ймища, які́ зв'я́зує Дніпро́: Ки́ївське, Кременчу́цьке, та Кахо́вське. Всі три рі́чки використо́вуються як тра́нспортні шляхи́ для переве́зення різномані́тних това́рів і сировини́ з півночі на пі́вдень, з пі́вдня на пі́вніч; ти́ми сами́ми во́дними шляха́ми Украї́на ввóзить всіля́кі това́ри з-за кордо́ну.

Vocabulary

таки́й же . . ., як	just as . . . as
набага́то	much (used with comparatives)
терито́рія, -ї	territory
гора́, -и́	mountain
Закарпа́ття, -я, neut.	Transcarpathia
Прикарпа́ття, -я, neut.	part of Subcarpathian Ukraine
поді́льський	of Podolia
височина́, -и́	high ground
придніпро́вський	pertaining to the Dnieper region
широ́кий	broad, wide
рівни́на, -и	plain(s)
ті́сно	closely
пов'я́заний	tied, connected
могу́тній	great, powerful
Дністе́р, -тра́	Dniester
Буг, -а	Buh, Bug river
Дніпро́, -а́	Dnieper
джерело́, -а́	source
кра́йній	extreme
поблизу́	near
по́льський	Polish
текти́, -че́-, imperf.	to flow, flows
уздо́вж + gen.	along
молда́вський	Moldavian, Moldovan
Молдо́ва, -и (former **Молда́вія**)	Moldova
Чо́рне море, -ого -я	the Black Sea
рі́чка, -и	river
оста́нній	last, final
побіля́, prep. + gen.	near
білору́ський	Belarussian
протіка́ти, -а́є-, imperf.	to flow by, through
повз, prep. + gen.	past
о́зеро, -а	lake
водо́ймище, -а	reservoir
зв'я́зувати, -ує-, imperf.	connect
використо́вуватися, -ує-	be used
різномані́тний	varied
проду́кти, -ів (проду́кт, -у)	produce
во́дний	water (adjective)
шлях, -у́	way, path
всіля́кий	every kind of . . .
това́р, -у	product, (pl.) wares
з-за кордо́ну	from abroad
переве́зення, -я	conveying
різномані́тний	varied
сировина́, -и́	raw materials

Exercise 17b

Translate into Ukrainian:

(a) Every day I take Halya to the library; we go by car.
(b) He arrived (by plane) yesterday; he brought me a new Ukrainian dictionary!
(c) Do you carry your child when you walk in the park?
(d) No, she can already walk ('already walks').
(e) The lorry/truck entered the city in the evening; it was bringing bread for the people.
(f) Does England import gas?
(g) No, in fact we export gas!

Exercise 17c

Prepare a short description of your home region so that you can discuss it when a Ukrainian asks you to do so; include topography and animal life (you have already covered trees and flowers!). Go back and review weather terminology if you have to; you are sure to have to discuss weather when you talk about your home.

As reinforcement and expansion of what you learned in *7* and *8*, describe someone, or ask a fellow learner questions about what someone is wearing or looks like. The following words, some repeated from *7* and *8*, might come in useful.

Vocabulary

носи́ти	wear (habitually)
до́бре (не) лежа́ти (item of clothing in nominative, with person affected in loc. after **на**)	to suit (or not)
just **бу́ти у/в** + loc.; or putting the item of clothing in the nominative, **на** + person affected (loc.) + **бу́ти** + item of clothing (nom).	be wearing
біля́вий; блонди́н(ка)	blonde
кашта́нового ко́льору;	chestnut

гніди́й (horse)	
ко́лір (ко́льору) обли́ччя	complexion
те́мний (in compounds: **те́мно-)**	dark
о́чі, -е́й (о́ко, -а)	eyes
воло́сся, -я, neut.	hair
сві́тлий (in compounds: **я́сно-)**	light
до́вгий	long
руда́вий, руди́й	red (hair)
коро́ткий	short
низьки́й	short, low
висо́кий	tall
торби́нка, -и	bag
по́яс, -а	belt
блу́з(к)а, -и, ко́фта, -и	blouse
чобітки́, чобітκі́в (чобіто́к, -тка́); чо́боти, чобі́т (чо́біт, чо́бота)	boots
ке́пка, -и	cap
су́кня, -і; суко́нка, -и	dress
рукави́ці, -ць (рукави́ця, -і)	gloves
ху́сточка, -и	handkerchief
капелю́х, -ха; ша́пка, -и	hat
жаке́т, -у (woman's), **ку́ртка, -и** or **піджа́к, -а́** (man's)	jacket

нічна́ соро́чка, -о́ї -и	nightdress
комбінезо́н, -у	overalls
плащ, -а́; пальто́, -а́	overcoat
штанці́, -і́в	panties
све́тер, -тра	pullover
гамане́ць, -нця́	purse
піжа́ма, -и	pyjama(s)
дощови́к, -а́	raincoat
кашне́, indecl.; **ша́лик, -а; шарф, -а**	scarf
соро́чка, -и	shirt
ме́шти, -мешт, (ме́шта, -и); черевики, -ів (череви́к, -а); ту́флі, -фель (ту́фля, -і)	shoes
спідни́ця, -і	skirt
ка́пці, -ів (ка́пець, -пця)	slippers
тенісі́вки, кросі́вки	sneakers, trainers
шкарпе́тки, -ток (шкарпе́тка, -и)	socks
панчо́хи, -чі́х (панчо́ха, -и)	stockings
костю́м -а	suit
те́ніска, -и	T-shirt
крава́тка	tie
колго́тки, -ток	tights
штани́, -і́в	trousers, pants
парасо́лька, -и	umbrella
спі́дня білизна, -ьої -и	underclothes

18 Що бу́де пі́сля Ки́єва?

What after Kyiv?

In this lesson you will learn more about:

- the numerals 1–4 and collective numerals
- first names, patronymics and family names
- members of the family

and be introduced to:

- passive participles
- the verb **удава́тися**
- neuter nouns in **-я**
- adverbial participles

На да́чі

На да́чі Окса́на, Джон і Петро́ розмовля́ють з Бондарчука́ми, Олекса́ндром та Есфі́р, про життя́ на селі́ й про рі́зні міста́ Украї́ни.

ОКСА́НА: Я така́ ра́да, що я в Украї́ні. Я тут упе́рше. Та й тут на селі́ все таке́ га́рне.

ПЕТРО́: І хоча́ як студе́нт я пови́нен серйо́зно вчи́тися, я ча́сто приї́жджаю до лі́су прогу́лятися. Тут ду́мати мо́жна, диви́тися на приро́ду, на твари́н.

ОКСА́НА: Як до́бре бу́ти на ці́й да́чі, про́сто сиді́ти на вера́нді та пи́ти ка́ву. Чи не зна́єте, коли́ її збудо́вано?

ОЛЕКСА́НДР: То́чно не зна́ю. Діду́сь давно́ каза́в мені́, що та́то його́ (це було́ на поча́тку столі́ття), купи́в зе́млю в збідні́лого росі́йського аристокра́та.

ЕСФІР: Так, ха́ти тут були́, але́ ціє́ї не було́. Коли́ він купи́в зе́млю, він з дру́зями ви́рішили, де собі

	збудува́ти да́чу.
Олександр:	Завдяки́ то́му, що да́ча не ду́же вели́ка, нам вдало́ся зберегти́ її́ як на́шу за часі́в Радя́нського Сою́зу. Оста́ннім ча́сом лю́ди отри́мують наза́д свою́ зе́млю.

Vocabulary

твари́на, -и	animal	**удава́тися, -ає́-**	be successful, manage (impers.)
вера́нда, -и	veranda, porch	**зберегти́, -же́-** perf.	keep, hold
збудо́вано p. pass. pcple impers.	built (impers.)	**за часі́в** + gen.	during [the time of]
будува́ти, -у́є-, imperf.	build (perf. **збудува́ти**, -у́є-)	**якра́з**	just, precisely
давно́	long ago	**оста́ннім ча́сом**	recently
поча́ток, -тку	beginning	**отри́мувати, -ує-**	recover, get (perf. **отри́мати, -ає-**)
столі́ття, -я, neut.	century	**наза́д**	back
збідні́лий	impoverished		
аристокра́т, -а	aristocrat		

Exercise 18a

Answer the following questions:

(a) З ким розмовля́є Окса́на?
(b) Скі́льки їх там на да́чі?
(c) Де лю́бить Петро́ прогу́люватися?
(d) Що ро́бить Джон у лі́сі?
(e) Коли́ збудува́ли да́чу?
(f) У ко́го купи́в ді́дів та́то зе́млю?
(g) Про що вони́ розмовля́ють?
(h) Чи ви б хоті́ли ме́шкати на селі́ у такі́й ха́ті?

ді́дів grandfather's (poss. adj.)

The numerals 1–4 (review)

We first considered these numerals in *8*. Here we extend what we know of them to the cases other than the nominative and inanimate accusative, in other words, to the genitive-like animate accusative (used in the main only in reference to humans), the genitive proper and the dative, instrumental and locative. If you look up these numerals in the reference section you will see that they have a full declension, with endings approximating to those we find in adjectives. The basic rule is that the numeral will be in the case required by the construction:

О́гляд чотирьо́х міст.	A look round four cities. (genitive after the noun **о́гляд**)
Я ніко́ли не чита́ла тих трьо́х книжо́к.	I've never read those three books. (genitive after negative verb)
У цих двох кімна́тах ме́шкає роди́на з двома́ дітьми́.	In these two rooms there lives a family with two children. (locative after **у** and instrumental after **з**)

Where groups are concerned, 2 and 3 have special nominative and accusative forms: **дво́є** and **тро́є** (groups are 'less animate', but it is possible to use **двох** etc. as their animate accusative). These forms are used as a rule with male groups, pronouns, nouns without singular forms (e.g. **но́жиці**, **-ць** 'scissors', **окуля́ри**, **-ів** 'spectacles', **ме́блі**, **-ів** 'furniture', **две́рі**, **-е́й** 'door'), animals (masc. and neut.) and nouns such as **ді́ти**, where the plural differs markedly from the singular (**дити́на**). Thus:

дво́є двере́й	two doors
тро́є хло́пців	three boys
нас бу́ло тро́є	there were three of us
дво́є діте́й	two children
дво́є бобрі́в	two beaver(s)

As you can see, these forms are followed by the genitive plural of the counted noun when the phrase as a whole is in the nominative/accusative.

Зага́дка

Хто ма́є шість ніг, а хо́дить ті́льки на чотирьо́х?
[The solution will be found after the next section.]

The past passive participle

Ukrainian possesses the following participles: present active, present passive, past active and past passive, of which the last-named is most common and useful. First, a participle is essentially an adjective that relates to a verb. A 'mooing cow' or 'a cow mooing in the meadow' are really 'a cow *which is mooing*'; 'a symphony composed last year' is 'a symphony *that was composed* last year'. In the first of these examples, the cow is carrying out the action and thus is 'active'; in the second, the symphony was not doing the composing, but 'was composed' and thus is passive. Verbs such as 'come' or 'moo' cannot form passive participles, since only verbs that have direct objects can do so. 'I read the book' can be transformed into the passive 'the book is/was read by me' thus, in a passive sentence the original object becomes the subject.

The past passive participle has one form, which looks clearly adjectival:

-ний, **-на**, **-не**, etc.
or
-тий, **-та**, **-те**, etc.

and another, impersonal form:

-но, **-то**

As examples of the first forms, we have:

збудо́вана ха́та	a built house (a house that was built)
ви́питий чай	the drunk tea (the tea that was drunk)
прочи́тані ві́рші	the read poetry (the poetry that was read)
ві́рші прочи́тані	the poetry has been read

Note that reversing the order (as in the last example), with the participle placed second, results in a complete sentence with the predicate (here: the verb 'to be') implied. Particularly common in Ukrainian is a variant on the last example, where the subject (e.g. **ві́рші**) appears in the accusative case and accompanies the participle in its impersonal form in **-но**, **-то**. Thus:

Ві́рші прочи́тано мно́ю.	The poetry has been read by me.
Хло́пця при́слано.	The boy has been sent.
Ді́вчинку вми́то.	The little girl has been washed.

The instrumental is used to denote the person or thing by which something is done. This is the general rule for the passive, i.e. it is not restricted to the impersonal passive. Thus:

Ві́рші прочи́тані мно́ю. The poetry has been read by me.

In general, this participle is formed almost exclusively from perfective verbs, since the actions described have all been completed.

The choice of **-ний** or **-тий** depends entirely on the conjugation type of the verb in question. The **-т-** form is found in a narrower range of verbs than the **-н-** form; it is nevertheless frequently encountered because some very common verbs are involved. These belong to:

(a) verbs with an infinitive in **-ути**, **-ерти**, **-оти**
(b) verbs with monosyllabic roots + **-ити**, **-іти**
(c) verbs in **-ати/-яти** where an **н** or **м** appears instead of **а/я** in the present, that is, the perfective future tense, e.g. **поча́ти, узя́ти**

For example

забу́тий	forgotten	**забу́ти**	to forget
за́пертий	locked	**запе́рти**	to lock up
мо́лотий	ground	**моло́ти**	to grind
ви́питий	drunk	**ви́пити**	to drink
нагрі́тий	heated	**нагрі́ти**	to heat
по́чатий	begun	**поча́ти**	to begin
взя́тий	taken	**взя́ти**	to take

There are sometimes optional forms: thus **замкну́ти**, **-не́-**, the perfective of **замика́ти**, **-а́є-** 'lock up, close', has the very common **за́мкнений** in addition to the 'regular' **за́мкнутий**.

All other verbs have the **-н-** form, replacing in a straightforward fashion the **-ти** of the infinitive (note the position of the stress!):

напи́саний, прочи́таний read, written

- Verbs in **-увати** take the ending **-ований**: **збудува́ти** 'to build', **збудо́ваний** 'built'.
- Second conjugation verbs replace **-и-** with **-е-** (preceded by the consonant as changed in the first person singular): **зроблю́** 'I shall do', **зро́блений** 'done'.
- Verbs in which a consonant precedes the ending **-ти**, where the final consonant of the stem has **-ений** added to it: **привести́** 'to bring', **приведе́** 'will bring' **приве́дений** 'brought'.

The most important thing to remember is that these forms are rarely encountered in spoken Ukrainian, except when particular common forms have been generalized as adjectives (that is, are no longer thought of as pure 'participles'): **зачи́нений** 'closed (as in doors, windows)',

відчи́нений 'open (windows etc.)', **відкри́тий** 'open (session, meeting)', etc. It is crucial to be able to recognize and translate such forms, but not so crucial to be able to form them; those that are commonly used as adjectives you will learn, when you come across them, as adjectives.

Відга́дка: Ве́ршник 'a horseman'

Удава́тися

In the meaning 'to succeed in doing something, to manage to do something', this verb occurs only in the third person singular (neuter when in the past tense), with the person who succeeds expressed in the dative case. Thus:

Чи тобі́ вдало́ся купи́ти той підру́чник?	Did you manage to buy that textbook?

Here we can see **купи́ти той підру́чник** as the subject, giving us 'Was buying that textbook a success for you?' From here we can extend the use of the verb to clearly personal uses, e.g. **Ця по́вість удала́ся** 'This story was successful'. From these examples we see that the perfective form is **уда́тися**, conjugated like **дава́ти, да́ти** 'to give'.

Neuter nouns in -я

There are several types of neuter nouns in **-я**, which broadly fall into three classes: those with an **-ен-** extension, e.g. **ім'я́** 'first name'; those denoting young animals, e.g. **порося́**, with a **-ят-** extension; and those ending in **-р'я**, e.g. **подві́р'я** 'yard', or in a doubled consonant + **-я**, e.g. **життя́, пита́ння, заняття́**. The last model, which is extremely common in Ukrainian, essentially has a single declension pattern where **-я** is the ending for five cases:

-я	singular: nominative, accusative, genitive plural: nominative, accusative
-ю	dative singular
-ям	instrumental singular (very exceptional!!!)
-і	locative singular, -**ї** after ', e.g. **подві́р'ї** (expected ending)
-їв	genitive plural: -**їв** after ', e.g. **подві́р'їв**. Compare nouns in **-ння**, where we have **-нь**, e.g. **пита́нь**. Some nouns have this as an option, e.g.

	весíлля 'wedding (feast)', with **весíль**, **весíллíв**.
-ям, **-ями**, **-ях**	dative, instrumental, locative plural (expected)

See the reference section for the tables. For example:

Це пéрше заняттý.
Ми читáємо вісімнáдцяте заняттý.
Вонú займáються питáннями украї́нського життý.
Студéнти! Чи сьогóдні немáє íнших запитáнь?

Exercise 18b

Form the past passive participles, where possible, from the following verbs, then make up sentences with the **-но/-то** forms of at least five of them:

зробúти
пúти
дістáти
знайтú
пошукáти
збудувáти
пітú
купúти
прочитáти
розмовлýти
узяти
вúсловити

Exercise 18c

The article which follows is taken from the issue of 4 July 1991 of the newspaper **За Вільну Україну**. It reports the recognition of 16 July as Ukrainian Independence Day and the consequent desirability, since that day was a Tuesday in 1991, of making the preceding Monday a holiday as well, the population working instead on the previous Saturday or Sunday. Try to answer the questions in Ukrainian. The language is rather official, so look first at the notes on words, phrases and word relationships immediately following the text.

День відпочинку перенесено

У зв'язку з визнанням 16 липня – День незалежності України неробочим днем та щоб створити сприятливі умови для відпочинку трудящих і раціонального використання робочого часу в липні 1991 р. Кабінет міністрів Української РСР постановив перенести день відпочинку з суботи 13 липня на понеділок 15 липня, а на підприємствах, в установах, організаціях, де встановлено шестиденний робочий тиждень з вихідним днем у неділю, – з неділі 14 липня на понеділок 15 липня.

Підприємствам і організаціям з п'ятиденним робочим тижнем надано право проводити за погодженням з профспілковими комітетами роботу 14 липня 1991 року. Робота у названий день може компенсуватися, за погодженням сторін, наданням іншого дня відпочинку або в грошовій формі в подвійному розмірі. За бажанням працівника цей день може бути приєднаний до щорічної відпустки з оплатою у тому ж порядку, в якому оплачуються дні відпустки.

(a) Note the closeness of the nouns derived from verbs to the past passive participle, except for the presence of the double or geminate consonant before the ending and the derivation from imperfective as well as from perfective verbs. Thus:

Noun	*Participle*	*Perfective infinitive*	*Imperfective infinitive*
ви́знання	**ви́знаний**	**ви́знати**	**визнава́ти**
ство́рення	**ство́рений**	**створи́ти**	**ство́рювати**
нада́ння	**на́даний**	**нада́ти**	**надава́ти**
пого́дження	**пого́джений**	**пого́дитися**	**пого́джуватися**
бажа́ння	**ба́жаний**	**побажа́ти**	**бажа́ти**
ви́користання	**ви́користаний**	**ви́користати**	**використо́вувати**

The meanings of the verbs, respectively are 'to acknowledge, recognize', 'to create', 'to grant', 'to agree', 'to desire' and 'to utilize, take advantage of'.

(b) Note the adjectives derived from nouns, numerals, verbs and compounds:

(не)робо́чий день '(non'-)working day'	**робо́та** 'work'
профспілко́вий 'trades union'	**спі́лка** 'union, association'
п'яти/шестиде́нний 'five/six-day'	**п'ять/шість день** 'five/six days'
подві́йний 'double'	**два, дві (двоє́)** 'two'
сприя́тливий 'favourable'	**сприя́ти** 'to favour, help'

щорі́чний 'annual' — **рік** 'year'

(c) We also have nouns related closely to verbs:

працівни́к 'worker' — **працюва́ти** 'to work'
відпу́стка 'holiday/leave' — **відпусти́ти, відпуска́ти** 'to release'
опла́та 'payment' — **оплати́ти(ся), опла́чувати(ся)** 'to pay (a wage)'

(d) The odd equation of:

приє́днаний до (приєдна́ти, приє́днувати) — 'won over, connected to' from **один** 'one'

Note also the constructions: **перенести́ з . . . на . . .** 'to transfer from . . . to . . .', **у зв'язку́ з . . .** 'in connection with . . .', **у то́му поря́дку, у яко́му** 'in the same way as . . .'.

Now answer the following questions in Ukrainian:

(a) Яки́м днем ви́знано 16 ли́пня?
(b) Які́ умо́ви уря́д хо́че ство́рити для громадя́н?
(c) Де встано́влено шестиде́нний робо́чий ти́ждень?
(d) Як назива́ється украї́нською день, коли́ не працю́ють?
(e) У яки́х умо́вах мо́жуть працюва́ти 16 ли́пня?
(f) Якщо́ лю́ди бу́дуть працюва́ти того́ дня, яку́ опла́ту вони́ оде́ржать?

у́ря́д, -у 'office, post, government'

Есфі́р прига́дуються колишні часи́

ДЖОН: На́віть в А́нглії, у свої́х підру́чниках, я чита́в про ці місця́, про Пу́щу-Води́цю, що зо́всім недале́ко від столи́ці. Так, око́лиці Ки́єва спра́вді ду́же га́рні. Але́ все ж таки́ обов'язко́во тре́ба поїхати да́лі подиви́тися на і́нші міста́, на нові́ ландша́фти.

ЕСФІ́Р: Я цілко́м зго́дна з тобо́ю. А тепе́р уже́ час обі́дати. Пі́сля обі́ду я покажу́ тобі́ одну́ англі́йську кни́жку, що її́ дала́ ті́тка ма́мі, коли́ вона́ приї́жджа́ла до Ки́єва з А́нглії бага́то ро́ків тому́.

ОКСА́НА: Зна́чить, і в те́бе є англі́йська роди́на. Про́сто неймові́рно!

ОЛЕКСА́НДР: Так, роди́на Есфі́р це вели́ка євре́йська роди́на з Черніве́ць, у півде́нно-за́хідній Украї́ні, недале́ко від Руму́нії.

ЕСФІ́Р: Це одне́ з забу́тих, але́ вели́ких, міст ціє́ї части́ни Євро́пи, коли́сь живи́й культу́рний центр; там народи́вся славе́тний пое́т Цела́н.

ОЛЕКСА́НДР: Іноді ї́здимо провести́ там днів п'ятна́дцять, то́бто ти́жнів два, там іще́ ме́шкають ро́дичі Есфі́р.

ЕСФІ́Р: Зате́ сті́льки зміни́лося; мо́же, бу́де відро́дження тих днів, того́ бага́того життя́. Ой, як я засмути́лася, воскреша́ючи в па́м'яті часи́, що їх сама́ не зна́ла. Геть такі́ ду́мки! Тепе́р бу́демо обі́дати, дру́зі!

Vocabulary

прига́дуватися, -ує-, imperf.	come to someone's (dat.) mind (note that **Есфі́р** is indeclinable)
коли́шній	former
час, -у́	time
підру́чник, -а, loc. **-у**	textbook, manual
ландша́фт, -у	landscape
цілко́м	quite, entirely
неймові́рний	incredible
євре́йський	Jewish
Чернівці́, -вці́в or **-ве́ць** (pl.)	Chernivtsi
Руму́нія, -ї	Rumania/ Romania
забу́тий	forgotten
культу́рний	cultural
народи́тися, -и-, perf.	be born (imperf. **наро́джуватися, -ує-**)
славе́тний	famous, renowned
провести́, -де́-, perf.	spend (time)
то́бто	that is, in other words
ро́дич, -а	relative
зате́	however, but
відро́дження, -я, neut.	rebirth, renaissance
засмути́тися, -и-, perf.	become sad, be saddened
воскреша́ти в па́м'яті, -а́є-, imperf.	recollect, remember, recall
геть	away (interjection)

(Note that Esfir's nostalgia for those old days will not be shared by all Ukrainians.)

First names, patronymics and family names

In addressing someone with whom you use **ти**, the first name is used on its own and in the vocative. You are already familiar with this, but might note that where the first name does not clearly belong to a particular or appropriate declension, for example, **Есфі́р** 'Esther', which refers to a woman but looks masculine, the name is indeclinable.

Where **ви** is used between people, the Western Ukrainian tradition is to use either the first name on its own or **па́не** or **па́ні** (vocatives of **пан** and **па́ні**) followed by the vocative of the first name. More formally, one uses **па́не** and **па́ні** followed by the family name or, in the Western Ukraine, the first name and patronymic in the vocative. Setting aside tradition, the use of the first name and patronymic without **па́не/па́ні** is now widespread in Western Ukraine, too.

Remember also **громадя́нине** and **громадя́нко**, the vocatives of **громадя́нин** and **громадя́нка** 'citizen', and **това́ришу** and **това́ришко**, the vocatives of **това́риш** and **това́ришка** 'comrade': these will probably not be used in reference to you, but will certainly be heard (other forms of address are listed in *4*).

The patronymic

The patronymic is one's 'second name', and is formed from one's father's name with the suffixes **-ич**, **-ович** or **-йович** in the masculine and **-івна** or **-ївна** in the feminine. Some examples:

Лука́	**Мико́ла**	**Сергі́й**	**Петро́**	**Іва́н**
Луки́ч	**Микола́йович**	**Сергі́йович**	**Петро́вич**	**Іва́нович**
Луківна	**Микола́ївна**	**Сергі́ївна**	**Петрі́вна**	**Іва́нівна**

It declines like a noun, with the masculine vocative singular in **-чу** and the feminine vocative singular in **-но**. Thus:

Іва́не Микола́йовичу, де ва́ша маши́на? Та куди́ ж ви ї́дете за́втра, А́нно Сергі́ївно?
Ivan Mykolayovych, where's your car? And where are you going tomorrow, Anna Serhiyivna?

Bear in mind that one uses the full first name together with the patronymic. In other words, **Яросла́ва Миха́йлівна** is preferable to **Сла́ва Миха́йлівна**.

Surnames (family names)

To a large extent these decline as expected: if they look like adjectives, then they decline like adjectives, if they look like nouns, then they decline like nouns. If the surname looks like a feminine noun, then it declines as such, whether referring to a man or to a woman. Exceptions include women's surnames ending in **-ко** and in a consonant, which do not decline, and surnames in **-ин**, **-ов**, **-їв** and **-ив**: in the latter the feminine forms, if they are declined, take an adjectival declension, while the masculine forms decline like nouns except for the instrumental singular, which has adjectival **-им**. In the plural such surnames decline like adjectives except for the nominative, which is in **-и** rather than the expected adjectival **-і**. Here are some examples:

Surname	*Masculine*	*Feminine*	*Plural*
Бондаре́нко	**Бондаре́нко** (noun decl.)	**Бондаре́нко** (indecl)	**Бондаре́нки** (fem. no change)
Груше́вський	**Груше́вський** (adj. decl.)	**Груше́вська** (adj. decl.)	**Груше́вські** (adj. decl.)
Кравчу́к	**Кравчу́к** (noun decl.)	**Кравчу́к** (indecl.)	**Кравчукú** (fem. no change)
Прокопо́вич	**Прокопо́вич** (noun decl.)	**Прокопо́вич** (indecl.)	**Прокопо́вичі** (fem. no change)
Микола́їв	**Микола́їв** (instr. **-им**)	**Микола́єва** (adj. decl.)	**Микола́єви** (adj. decl. exc. nom.)
Га́ршин	**Га́ршин** (instr. **-им**)	**Га́ршина** (adj. decl.)	**Га́ршини** (adj. decl. exc. nom.)
Хма́ра	**Хма́ра** (noun decl.)	**Хма́ра** (noun decl.)	**Хма́ри** (noun decl.)

The formulae for asking someone's name are repeated here in summary form:

(a) In general:	**Як тебе́/вас зва́ти/звуть?**	**Мене́ звуть Петро́**
(b) First name:	**Як твоє́ ім'я́?**	**Мене́ звуть Окса́на**
		Моє́ ім'я́ Іва́н
(c) Patronymic:	**Як вас/тебе́ по ба́тькові?**	**Петрі́вна**
	Як ва́ше патроні́мі́чне ім'я́?	
(d) Surname:	**Як твоє́/ва́ше прі́звище?**	**Моє́ прі́звище Савчу́к**

For inanimates one may use:

звáтися
Як . . . звéться/звýться? (also with animates)
називáтися
Як назива́ється/назива́ються . . .? (inanimates only)

The thing for which you are seeking a name is the subject of the verb (note that it is reflexive in both instances) and appears in the nominative.

The members of the family

Here are the terms for a few members of the family: **роди́на** (extended family), **сім'я́** (immediate family). The list is far from exhaustive, but to be exhaustive would create confusion. This is enough for the moment!

Vocabulary

дідýсь, -я́	grandfather
бабýся, -і	grandmother
бáтько, -а/ тáто, -а	father
мáти, мáтері/ мáма, -и	mother
сестрá, -и́	sister
брат, -а	brother
дружи́на, -и (masculine or feminine)	spouse
чоловíк, -а	husband
жíнка, -и	wife
син, -а	son
дóня, -і; дóнька, -и; дочкá, -и́	daughter
двою́рідний брат, -ого -а	cousin (male)
двою́рідна сестрá, -ої -и́	cousin(female)
онýк, -а (внук, -а)	grandson
онýка, -и (внýка, -и)	granddaughter

тíтка, -и	aunt
дя́дько, -а	uncle
тéща, -і (wife's mother); **свекрýха, -и** (husband's mother)	mother-in-law
тесть, -я (wife's father); **свéкор, -кра** (husband's father)	father-in-law
брат жíнки, чоловíк сестри́	brother-in-law
сестрá чоловíка, жíнка брáта	sister-in-law
чоловíк дочки́ (зять, -я)	son-in-law
жíнка си́на (невíстка, -и)	daughter-in-law

Exercise 18d

Translate the following sentences into Ukrainian:

(a) I was talking with Ivan Serhiyovych.
(b) Oksana introduced me to her teacher, Hanna Petrivna.
(c) I don't know Mrs Prokopovych at all.
(d) I'm so glad that Mykola Savchuk is not here.
(e) A person with a surname like Holubenko is often from Eastern Ukraine.
(f) Slavko and Esfir Bondarchuk, like Nina Prokopovych, are from Western Ukraine.
(g) Natalka Mykolayeva is from Western Ukraine too.
(h) Ihor Svyshchuk lives near Odessa, in Southern Ukraine.

(As well as just using **з** + gen., one may use the verb **похóдити, -и- з** + gen. in the sense 'be from, originate from'; used with the preposition **на** + acc., it has the meaning 'be like, similar to').

The adverbial participles

Earlier in this lesson we made our first acquaintance with the adjectival participles, often also referred to as verbal adjectives. Related to the participles are the gerunds, alternatively referred to as verbal adverbs. There are two categories of these in Ukrainian, one formed from imperfective verbs and the other from perfective verbs. Examples in English would be, respectively, 'walking along the street' and 'having read the book'. They may be synonymous with 'when I was walking along the street' and 'when I had/since I have read the book'. Just as, 'walking along the street minding my own business, this oaf came and bumped into me' the gerund is unacceptable in English, it is not possible in Ukrainian either, since while 'I' am doing the walking, 'this oaf' is doing the bumping. However, in saying 'walking along the street minding my own business, I suddenly became involved in an argument' the gerund is possible. As is the case with participles, these forms are not used in speech; spoken Ukrainian will make use of a more explicit (and natural) statement, for example 'while I was walking . . .'. You need only to be able to recognize the forms, since they belong very much to literary Ukrainian. The following are imperfective gerunds ('while doing X, I . . .'):

шукáти	**шукáють**	**шукáю-**	**шукáючи**
ітú	**ідýть**	**ідý-**	**ідучú**
робúти	**рóблять**	**рóбля-**	**рóблячи**
везтú	**везýть**	**везý-**	**везучú**
одягáтися	**одягáються**	**одягáю-**	**одягáючись**

The perfective gerund is used when the action it describes entirely precedes the action of the main verb ('having X-ed, I . . .; when I had X-ed, I . . .'):

пошукáти	**пошукáв**	**пошукáвши**
пітú	**пішóв**	**пішóвши**
зробúти	**зробúв**	**зробúвши**
повезтú	**повíз**	**повíзши**
одягнýтися	**одягнýвся**	**одягнýвшись**

Compare:

Ідучú по вýлиці, я побáчив сестрý.
Побáчивши сестрý, я побíг до нéї.
Він був вдóма цíлий день, шукáючи свій новúй словнúк.
Знайшóвши свій новúй словнúк, він пошукáв дéкілька новúх слів.

Note the following frozen formula:

Незважáючи на те, що . . .	In spite of the fact, that . . .;
(**не + зважáти** 'to consider')	X notwithstanding, . . .

Exercise 18e

Join the following pairs of sentences together in ways which seem appropriate (there is not necessarily a single 'answer'):

(a) Він знайшóв брáта/Він повернýвся з ним додóму
(b) Ми поїхали за мíсто до селá/Ми провелú там тúждень
(c) Сестрá бажáє попрацювáти за кордóном/Вонá повúнна поговорúти з батькáми про робóту за кордóном
(d) Ми пообíдали/Вонá показáла менí свою кнúжку
(e) Ви прочитáли про окóлиці Кúєва/Ви дізнáлися, що Пýща-Водúця недалéко
(f) Я згáдую часú вíльної Украї́ни/Роблю́ся такóю сумнóю
(g) Петрó прокúнувся о сьóмій/Він швúдко помúвся та поголúвся

Vocabulary

оскі́льки	since, because, in so far as	**ми́тися, -и́є-**, imperf.	wash, have a wash, wash up (perf. **поми́тися**, **-и́є-**)
прокинутися, -не-, perf.	wake up (imperf. **прокида́тися**, **-а́є-**)	**голи́тися, -и-**, imperf.	shave (perf. **поголи́тися**, **-и-**)
засну́ти, -не́-, perf.	fall asleep (imperf. **засипа́ти**, **-а́є-**)		

There follows an election statement-cum-pamphlet, unstressed, by Iurii Shcherbak (now Ukrainian Ambassador to Israel and noted as one of the first people to describe and investigate the Chernobyl (**Чорно́биль**) catastrophe). A short vocabulary is given, but try first of all to see how much you can understand.

Vocabulary

ви́бори, -ів	elections	**необхі́дний**	indispensable
світ, -у	world	**нега́йний**	urgent
зму́чений	exhausted (by), weary (of)	**стано́вище, -а**	situation
		за́хист, -у	refuge, defence
неста́ток, -тку	shortage	**трудівни́к, -а́**	worker
зли́дні, -ів	toil	**перехі́д, -хо́ду до**	transition to
стоми́тися, -и-	be tired		
балакани́на, -и	idle talk	**ство́рення, -я**	creation
безси́лля, -я	impotence, powerlessness	**процвіта́ючий**	thriving, prosperous
законода́вча вла́да, -ої -и-	executive power	**ма́ючи**	having
		до́свід, -у	experience
небезпе́ка, -и	danger	**Да́рниця, -і**	Darnytsia (a suburb of left-bank, i.e. eastern Kyiv)
відверну́тися, -не- від	turn away from		
зневі́ритися, -и- у/в	lose confidence in		
		колки́й	sharp
зда́тність, -ості до	fitness for	**триво́жний**	anxious
		раді́ти, -і́є- + dat. or **з** + gen.	rejoice at
ви́гідно	of advantage, advantageous		
		ось-ось	very soon, imminently
вкрай	extremely		

14 ЖОВТНЯ – ВСІ НА ВИБОРИ!

КАНДИДАТ У НАРОДНІ ДЕПУТАТИ УКРАЇНИ

українець, безпартійний. Письменник, доктор медичних наук Голова української екологічної асоціації «Зелений світ»

ЮРІЙ ЩЕРБАК

Змучений нестатками і злиднями народ стомився від балаканини, від безсилля законодавчої влади. Є небезпека, що люди можуть відвернутися від молодої демократії, зневіритися в її здатності до прийняття радикальних рішень. Кому це вигідно – хіба важко зрозуміти?

А рішення ці вкрай необхідні. Це – негайна стабілізація економічно-фінансового становища України, соціальний захист трудівника в період переходу до ринкової економіки, створення суверенної процвітаючої республіки Україна.

Сьогодні, в критичну хвилину нашої історії, маючи певний політичний і державний досвід, гадаю, що зможу бути корисним українському парламенту і виборцям Києва.

Ходжу по Дарниці, зустрічаюся з людьми, відповідаю на їхні запитання – часто колькі, тривожні. Радію з того, що на радіозаводі в Дарниці ось-ось відкриється виробництво одноразових шприців. Бачив складні технологічні лінії, що ось-ось вступлять в дію. Серце переповнюється сумом, коли бачу старі дарницькі «хрущоби» у районі Ленінградської площі, де жити, особливо на перших поверхах, неможливо. Як вирішити цю проблему? Як зберегти громадський мир і спокій, як нагодувати і вдягти людей, як забезпечити їх повноцінною медичною допомогою, ліками? Тільки діяти. Активно і наполегливо. Рішуче й водночас, обережно, розважливо. Розробляти не тільки справедливі закони, а й дбати про механізм їхнього впровадження в життя, думаючи про соціальні й політичні наслідки прийняття тих чи інших рішень.

ВІН ПОТРІБЕН УКРАЇНІ!

Українська екологічна асоціація «ЗЕЛЕНИЙ СВІТ»

одноразо́вий шприц, -ого, -а	disposable syringe (to be used once)	**наполегли́во**	urgently
ді́я, -ї	action	**розробля́ти, -я́є-**	elaborate, devise
хрущо́ба, -и*	slum	**справедли́вий**	just, fair
зберегти́, -же́-	save, maintain	**зако́н, -у**	law
грома́дський	public, community	**впрова́дження, -я в життя́**	realization (bringing them to life)
мир, -у	peace	**на́слідок, -дку**	consequence, effect
спо́кі́й, -о́ю	calm, tranquillity		
нагодува́ти, -у́є-	feed		
забезпе́чити, -и-	provide, protect		
повноці́нний	standard, full-fledged		

* A coinage from the usual word, **трущо́ба**, **-и** and **Хрущо́в** 'Khrushchev'.

Exercise 18f

On the basis of this pamphlet, try to imagine what an even briefer, punchier pamphlet might be, for distribution nearer the day of the elections.

19 Розмо́ва пі́сля обі́ду

A conversation after dinner

In this lesson you will learn more about:

- verbs of liking and disliking
- verbs of applying for, joining and making appointments

Розмо́ва в віта́льні

Дру́зі пообі́дали. Тепе́р вони́ сидя́ть у віта́льні, п'ють ка́ву та ї́дять шокола́дні цуке́рки. Есфі́р ра́птом згада́ла, що хоті́ла показа́ти Окса́ні, та не лише́ Окса́ні, ту англі́йську кни́жку, про яку́ вона́ зга́дувала. Есфі́р вста́ла та підійшла́ до книжко́вої ша́фи, що стої́ть бі́ля двере́й; вона знайшла́ там кни́жку, взяла́ її́ та поверну́лася з не́ю в рука́х. Розкрива́ючи кни́жку, вона́ всміхну́лася та й сказа́ла: «Оця́ мале́нька кни́жка, що її́ написа́в Маркія́н Терле́цький, назива́ється «Мандрі́вка по Украї́ні»; її́ ви́дано ти́сяча дев'ятсо́т сімдеся́т пе́ршого ро́ку в Ло́ндоні. Послу́хайте де́кілька ре́чень: «Львів – це найбі́льше мі́сто не лише́ Галичини́, але́ і всіє́ї За́хідної Украї́ни, воно́ нарахо́вує 553 (тепе́р 883) ти́сячі ме́шканців. Зра́зу ж ї́демо на так зва́ний Висо́кий За́мок; – це па́ркова гора́, що на ні́й стоя́в коли́сь княжи́й за́мок. Заснува́в мі́сто коро́ль Дани́ло і в честь свого́ си́на Льва назва́в його́ Льво́вом. У підні́жжя За́мкової гори́ лежи́ть найдавні́ша части́на мі́ста. З тих часі́в збереглися ще де́які церкви́. [. . .] В сере́дині мі́ста, се́ред ри́нку, стої́ть ра́туша з висо́кою ве́жею. У старі́й части́ні мі́ста бага́то га́рних буді́вель.» Львів тепе́р вели́кий промисло́вий центр. Це пра́вда, хоча́ незале́жна Украї́на з її́ міста́ми ма́є бу́ти гото́вою зустрі́ти чима́ло пробле́м. Але́ ми поду́жаємо перешко́ди, гада́ю.»

Vocabulary

шоколáдні цукéрки, -их -рок/ків	chocolates (from **цукéрка**, -**и** or **цукéрок**, -**рка**)
рáптом	suddenly
згадáти, -áє-, perf.	recall (imperf. **згáдувати**, -**ує**-)
книжкóва шáфа, -ої -и	bookcase
розкривáти, -áє-, imperf.	open (wide; perf. **розкри́ти**, -**и́є**-)
всміхнýтися, -нé-, perf.	to smile (imperf. **всміхáтися**, -**áє**-)
мандрíвка, -и	ramble, journey
ви́дано, impers. p. pass. pcple	published
дéкілька (gen. pl.)	several, a few
найбíльший	biggest
нарахóвувати, -ує-, imperf.	to reckon, count (+ quantitative expression)
зрáзу	first of all, at once, right away
висóкий	high, tall
зáмок, -мка	castle
пáрковий	park (adj.)
горá, -и́	hill, mountain
кня́жий	prince's
заснувáти, -ýє-, perf.	found
гóрод, -у	town, fort, stronghold
корóль, -ля́	king
в чéсть + gen.	in honour of . . .
підні́жжя, -я, neut.	foot (of a hill, etc.)
дáвній	ancient
зáмковий	castle (adj.)
зберегти́ся, -жé, perf.	be preserved (imperf. **зберігáтися**, -**áє**-)
цéрква, -и	church
серéдина, -и	middle
сéред + gen., prep.	in the middle of
рáтуша, -і	town hall
вéжа, -і	tower
будíвля, -і	building
промислóвий	industrial
бýти готóвим зустрі́ти	face (lit. 'be ready to meet')
зустрі́ти, -не-, perf.	meet
подýжати, -ає-, perf.	overcome
перешкóда, -и	obstacle
гадáти, -áє-, imperf.	think, imagine (another word for imagine, more intensive in meaning, is **уявля́ти**, -**я́є**- **собі́**, perf. **уяви́ти**, -**и**- **собі́**, as in **Уяві́ть собі́**, 'Just imagine!')

Lexical topics

Do note that what follows is approximate. It really is impossible to give exact equivalents all the time, and one should not think in terms of 'translation' or 'synonyms'.

Verbs of liking, disliking and the other emotions!

We have already encountered the verbs **люби́ти** and **подо́батися**, the first conveying a relatively deeply felt and permanent liking, and the second conveying something more temporary, more immediate, smacking more of a reaction, making its perfective form **сподо́батися** very frequent in occurrence. These two verbs are used in different constructions, as illustrated by the following examples:

Люблю́ Ки́їв, це таке́ га́рне мі́сто, та й, до то́го ж, мі́сто, де я народи́вся.	I love Kyiv, it's such a beautiful city, and moreover the city where I was born.
Мені́ ду́же сподо́балася п'є́са, що на ній ми булú позавчо́ра.	I really like the play we were at at two days ago.

We can convey the opposite simply by negating both verbs, and nuance the negation by negating elements other than the verbs themselves. For example:

Мені́ не ду́же сподо́балася та п'є́са.	I didn't like that play very much.

Let us go through a few other very useful verbs. At this point, learn actively only those that you feel you would/might need; others ought to be learned for recognition only.

admire	**милува́тися**, **-у́е-** (+ instr.) (person or thing); be careful that this may also mean 'to caress each other' when used without the instrumental: the non-reflexive form means 'to caress someone'. You might of course, use **ду́же люби́ти** instead. The verb **захопи́тися**, **-и-**, imperf. **захо́плюватися**, **-юе-** (+ instr.) means 'to be enraptured by, transported'; its non-reflexive form means 'to enrapture, enchant'. Use it with the appropriate tone of voice, as it can be used ironically!

be enthusiastic about	Here **захопи́тися**, just mentioned, is most appropriate. 'Enthusiastic' might be **захо́плений** or **спо́внений ентузіа́зму** lit. 'full [filled] of enthusiasm'.
adore	Most general, though a bit bookish, is **покловя́тися**, **-я́є-**, **поклони́тися**, **-и-** (+ dat.). It may be used, too, if you wish someone to convey your regards to someone else for you, e.g. **Поклони́ся йому́ від ме́не!** 'Give him my regards!' It is always safe just to qualify **люби́ти** by an appropriate adverb, e.g. **ду́же** 'very (much)', or **над усе́** 'above all'.
envy	**за́здрити**, **-и-** (+ acc.) or **за́здритися на** + acc., in the sense 'to be covetous, greedy for'. The noun may be **за́здрість, -ості** with **до** + gen. conveying 'of', or **за́здрощі**, **-ів** (pl. only). 'Envious' is **за́здрісний.**
be jealous of	**ревнува́ти**, **-у́є-** (+ acc.). 'Jealousy' is usually **ре́внощі**, **-ів** (pl. only). And 'jealous' may be **за́здрісний, завидю́щий** or **ревни́вий до** + gen. ('of').
hate	**нена́видіти**, **-и-** (+ acc.). The noun is **нена́вість**, **-ості**. In the sense of 'to feel awkward about', e.g. 'I hate to disappoint you', one may have **Мені́ незру́чно розчарува́ти вас**, lit. 'it is awkward for me to disappoint you' (**розчаро́вувати**, -ує- (imperf.)) and **не спра́вджувати**, -ує- (**сподіва́нь/наді́й**) 'not to justify' (expectations/hopes)'. Alternatively, just **не хоті́ти** or **почува́ти**, **-а́є- ні́яковість** 'to feel embarrassment'.
suspect	Simplest here is to use **ду́мати**, **припуска́ти** or **вважа́ти**, with all of which we are familiar. If it is a matter of doubt or hestitation, then it is appropriate to use **сумніва́тися**, **-а́є- в/у** + loc. or **ма́ти, -а́є- су́мнів в/у** + loc. 'to doubt something'. Where it really is a question of suspicion, then the verb is **підозріва́ти**, **-а́є-** + acc. + **в/у** + loc. 'to

	suspect someone of something'. 'Suspicious, suspect' is **підозрі́лий**, and suspicion **підозрі́ння**, **-я** neut. or **підо́зра**, **-и**. When you accuse someone of something, the verb is **обвинува́чувати**, **-ує-** (+ acc. of person + **в/у** + loc.)
insist	Quite close would be **насті́йно вимага́ти**, **-а́є-** lit. 'to demand insistently'.

Verbs of applying for, joining and making appointments

Such expressions are extremely useful these days.

apply for	Probably the most appropriate verb is **зверта́тися**, **-а́є- за** + instr., though **пода́ти зая́ву** 'to put in an application' is also useful. An 'application' and an 'applicant' would be respectively **зая́ва**, **-и** and **претенде́нт**, **-а** or **кандида́т**, **-а**. An 'application form' is **анке́та**.
enrol	'To enrol for/in' can be rendered by **записа́тися**, **-ше- на** + acc. Non-reflexively it would convey 'to enrol someone', also covered by **вно́сити**, **-и- кого́ до спи́ску/спи́ска**, lit. 'to enter someone on the list'. Alternatively, there is **реєструва́ти**, **-у́є-**.
join	**вступа́ти**, **-а́є-**, perf. **вступи́ти**, **-и- + у/в +** acc. are appropriate here. A 'member' is **член**, **-а**, and new members are 'received': **прийма́ти**, **-а́є-**, perf. **прийня́ти**, **прийму́**, **при́ймеш**, with the derived neuter noun **прийня́ття** 'reception, acceptance'. You might use **член** to convey most simply that you 'belong' to some **спі́лка**, **-и** 'association'. In the 'possessions' sense, 'to belong to' is **нале́жати**, **-и- до** + gen. (as in 'X belongs to the government').
make an appointment	An 'appointment' is **зу́стріч**, **-і**, fem. If you simply arrange to meet someone, especially a friend, then you may simply **домо́витися зустрі́тися** (**з** + instr.) If you need to see the doctor, then **проси́ти зу́стріч у (лі́каря)**

would be appropriate, or, if the appointment is definitely made, then **записа́тися на зу́стріч у (лі́каря)**.

Exercise 19a

Translate the following passage into Ukrainian:

When I arrived at their dacha, Oleksandr was sitting on the veranda, reading. He looked at me and smiled. I knew he was very glad I had decided to discuss the question of my life abroad. 'Sit down,' he said. 'Esther is with her brother in the village. We'll talk when she gets back.' There were two chairs on the veranda. I sat down and began to tell Oleksandr of the three men who suddenly left the village yesterday.

Exercise 19b

One short article and one short extract from an interview follow. They have been taken from «**Україна**« (1992) 35: 5, 20 and have been somewhat edited. The first is a sort of court circular, and reports, in extreme 'officialese', on recent travels undertaken by members of the Ukrainian government, notably the President. In the second the political pundit **Дмитро Гнатович Видрін** responds to questions from journalist **Петро Коломієць**. Read them carefully, then try to answer the questions.

A. З далеких країн повернувся Президент України Леонід Кравчук. З 29 жовтня по 3 листопада він перебував на запрошення Голови Китайської Народної Республіки Ян Шанкуня з офіційним візитом в КНР. Переговори і зустрічі Президента Кравчука з Головою КНР (. . .) пройшли, як зазначається в спільному українсько-китайському Комюніке, «в дружній, відвертій і діловій атмосфері». У цьому ж документі підкреслено, що Україна визнає Уряд КНР єдиним і законним Урядом Китаю, а Тайвань – невід'ємною частиною його території. Підтверджено, що Україна не буде встановлювати з Тайванем офіційних відносин. Китай, у свою чергу, визнає незалежність, суверенітет і територіальну цілісність України.

Із 3 по 5 листопада Президент Кравчук на запрошення Президента Монголії П. Очирбата відвідав з офіційним візитом Монголію, зустрічався з президентом П. Очирбатом, іншими монгольськими керівниками. В центрі уваги переговорів були нинішній стан та перспективи розвитку двостороннього співробітництва.

Мости на Схід наводяться.

Наводяться мости й через екватор – Голова Верховної Ради України Іван Плющ з делегацією побував у Австралії.

Vocabulary

з + gen. **по** + acc.	from . . . to . . . (inclusive); without emphasizing the inclusiveness of the period (i.e., ‘up to date X’), one may use **з** + gen. **до** + gen.; this may also be used for movement from one place to another.
перебува́ти, -а́є- з офіці́йним візи́том	be on an official visit somewhere (perf. **перебу́ти**)
відві́дувати з офіці́йним візи́том	make an official visit (the person or place visited goes into accusative; perf. **відві́дати**, -ає-)
перегово́ри, -ів	negotiations (‘to negotiate’ **вести**, -де́- **перегово́ри**)
пройти́, де́-, perf.	lit. ‘pass’, here: ‘take place’
невід’ємний	inseparable, inalienable, integral
підтве́рджено	it was declared, affirmed, asserted
встано́влювати, відно́сини з + instr.	establish relations with (imperf. **-ує-**; perf. **встанови́ти, -и-**)
у свою́ че́ргу́	in (its) turn
ці́лісність, -ості	integrity
керівни́к, -а́	leader
ни́нішній стан, -ього -у	the present situation
перспекти́ви, перспекти́в	prospects (‘for’ gen.)
двосторо́нній	bilateral, mutual
співробі́тництво, -а	collaboration; ‘to collaborate’ **співробі́тничати, -ає-** (**з** + instr.); note another common compound: **безробі́тний** ‘unemployed’,

безробі́тник/-ниця ‘unemployed person (masc./fem.), **безробі́ття, -я** ‘unemployment’

мости́ наво́дяться	bridges are being built/erected
побува́ти, -а́є-/ побу́ти, -де- з делега́цією	to be (spend some time) with a delegation somewhere

Now attempt to answer, orally and in written Ukrainian, the following questions:

(a) З я́ких краї́н що́йно поверну́вся Леонід Кравчу́к?
(b) Що підкре́слено в Комюніке́?
(c) Скі́льки днів був Президе́нт у Монго́лії?
(d) Що було́ в це́нтрі ува́ги перегово́рів?
(e) Де був Іва́н Плющ?

B. Я прочитав прогноз, який склав відомий політолог, один із керівників політологічного «Інно-центру» Дмитро Гнатович Видрін. На початку літа він спрогнозував розвиток політичної та економічної обстановки в Україні на початок осені. Прогноз збігся на 95 відсотків. Поцікавимось у політолога, кандидата філософських наук Дмитра Видріна, що ж нас чекає в наступному році.

Дмитре Гнатовичу, які, на вашу думку, шанси у СНД? Чи не вийде з нього Україна?
СНД найближчим часом збережеться. Хоча досить впливові сили прагнуть, щоб Україна вийшла із співдружності. Річ у тім, що СНД – дуже складний комплекс, де взаємодіють сили притягування та відштовхування. І залежно від того, яка сила переважатиме, відбудеться або ж віддалення України від СНД, або ж тимчасове, підкреслюю, перебування в ньому. Те, що СНД з часом зникне як політичне утворення, у мене не викликає сумнівів.
Значить, якщо певні частини колишнього Союзу створять конфедеративне об’єднання, то Україна до нього не приєдна́ється?
Впевнений, що ні. Нині визначальним є курс на здобуття повноцінної державності.
Але ж Київ може мати серйозні суперечності з такими регіонами, як Крим та Донбас, де переважає російськомов-

не населення й де є щільніші контакти із північно-східним сусідом.

Проблему СНД не варто пов'язувати з проблемою сепаратизму в Криму та на Донбасі. Суть справи в тому, що вчасно не було вжито політичних заходів, щоб ця проблема не виникла навіть у зародку. Для цього просто треба було використати світовий досвід. У Криму та на Донбасі є свої економічні, в тім числі й зовнішньоторговельні, мовні та культурні інтереси. Значить, цим регіонам треба було б надати права, котрі б гарантували задоволення їх інтересів. Та, повторюю, час було згаяно.

Vocabulary

СНД (indecl.; gender unclear)	**Співдру́жність Незале́жних Держа́в** Commonwealth of Independent States (CIS)
скла́сти, -де́-, perf.	compose (imperf. **склада́ти, -а́є-**)
відо́мий	famous
прогнозува́ти, -у́є-, imperf.	forecast (perf. **спрогнозува́ти, -у́є-**)
обстано́в(к)а, -и	situation, setting
збі́гтися, like **бі́гти**	to shrink (lit. 'run together, gather'; imperf. **збіга́тися**) (note **збі́льшувати(ся)**, -ує-, perf. **збільши́ти(ся)**, **-и-** 'increase')
на 95 відсо́тків	by 95 percent ('had shrunk by 95 percent'); from **відсо́ток, -тка** 'per cent'
поціка́витися, perf. **у/в** + gen.	ask (i.e. to show enough interest to ask someone something) (imperf. **ціка́витися**, **-и-**)
найбли́жчим ча́сом	in the immediate future
впливо́вий	influential (**вплив, -у** 'influence', **вплива́ти**, **-ає-**, perf. **впли́нути, -не- на** + acc. 'influence', have an influence on')
пра́гнути, -не- imperf.	aim, long, tend
річ у тім, що	the fact is that . . . (also **спра́ва в то́му, що**)
складни́й	complex, complicated
взаємоді́яти, -і́є-, imperf.	to interact (**взає́мний** 'mutual')

притягува́ння, -я	(force of) attraction (**притяга́ння** is more common; **притяга́ти**, -**а́є**-, perf. **притягну́ти**, -**не**- 'attract'; **(по)тяга́ти/тягну́ти**, -**а́є**-/-**не**-, perf. **потягну́ти**, -**не**- 'pull, drag')
відшто́вхування, -я, neut.	repulsion, pushing away (**відшто́вхувати** -**ує**-, perf. **відштовхну́ти**, -**не́**- 'push away, jostle'; **штовха́ти**, -**а́є**-, perf. **штовхну́ти** 'push (refl. 'to jostle')
зале́жно від + gen.	depending on
переважа́ти, -а́є-, imperf.	prevail (perf. **перева́жити**, -**и**-)
відбу́тися, -де-	happen, take place (imperf. **відбува́тися**, -**а́є**-)
або́ ж . . . або́ ж . . .	either . . . or . . .
відда́лення . . . від + gen.	the departure/removal (of . . .) from . . .
тимчасо́вий	temporary, provisional
зни́кнути, -не-, perf.	disappear, vanish (imperf. **зника́ти**, -**а́є**-)
утво́рення, -я, neut.	creation
створи́ти, -и-, perf.	create (imperf. **ство́рювати**, -**ює**-)
об'єдна́ння, -я, neut.	union, association
приєдна́тися, -а́є-, perf.	join (imperf. **приє́днуватися**, -**ує**-)
виклика́ти, -а́є-, imperf.	evoke, arouse (perf. **ви́кликати**, -**че**-)
впе́внений	sure, certain
ни́ні	now, today
визнача́льний	set, assigned, pre-eminent
здобу́ття, -я, neut.	acquisition, realization, achievement
повноці́нний	complete, standard
ви́никнути, -не-, perf.	emerge, crop up (imperf. **виника́ти**, -**а́є**-)
супере́чність, -ості	dissention, quarrel, variance ('quarrel' **супере́чка**, -**и** 'to quarrel (with)' **супереча́тися**, -**а́є**- (**з** + instr.))
російськомо́вний	Russian-speaking
насе́лення, -я, neut.	population
щі́льний	tight, close
пов'я́зувати, -ує-, imperf.	tie, link (also **в'яза́ти**, -**же**-; perf. **пов'яза́ти**, -**же**-)

суть, -і	the essence, core
вча́сно	just at the right time, timely (here, because of the negative, 'at the wrong time')
вжи́ти, -ве́- imperf.	use, make use of (imperf. **ужива́ти**, -а́є-; reflexive very common, in the sense 'be used')
за́хід, за́ходу	measure, used with **ужи́ти** and appropriate adjectives, e.g. **рішу́чий** 'decisive', in the sense of 'to take decisive measures'
у за́родку	in the bud, in the embryo (here 'to be nipped (vanish) in the bud')
світови́й до́свід, -ого -у	worldly/everyday experience
в тім числі́	including, among them (adverb)
зо́внішній	external ('internal' **уну́трішній**)
нада́ти, like **да́ти,** perf.	grant, confer (imperf. **надава́ти**, -ає́-)
гарантува́ти, -у́є-, imperf.	guarantee
задово́лення, -я, neut.	satisfaction
зга́яти, зга́ю, зга́єш, perf.	waste, lose

Now attempt to answer, orally and in written Ukrainian, the following questions (we leave this to you; answers are not suggested in the key):

(a) Заголо́вок ціє́ї статті́ – «Не́бо на зе́млю не впаде́, Дніпро́ наза́д не потече́». Що розумі́єте під таки́м заголо́вком?
(b) Хто хо́че, щоб Украї́на ви́йшла із СНД?
(c) Яке́ є майбу́тнє, на ду́мку політо́лога, у СНД?
(d) Які́ регіо́ни в Украї́ні мо́жуть ви́йти з не́ї?
(e) Як характеризу́ються ці регіо́ни? Які́ в них спеціа́льні інтере́си?

20 Вируша́ємо по Украї́ні

We set off around Ukraine

In this lesson we shall discuss:

- active participles
- negation
- comparison of adverbs
- passive constructions

Дру́зі поверта́ються з да́чі до Ки́єва

Тепе́р уже́ час поверта́тися до Ки́єва. Усі́ пообі́дали та пі́сля обі́ду до́бре відпочи́ли, ле́жачи на траві́ за буди́нком. Там Окса́на й Петро́ пово́лі веду́ть розмо́ву про свої́ вра́ження від поба́ченого в столи́ці. Але́ прохо́дить час, со́нце пово́лі схиля́ється до о́брію, почорні́лі дере́ва та о́зеро нага́дують дво́м дру́зям, що тре́ба поду́мати про насту́пний ета́п ї́хньої мандрі́вки по Украї́ні.

Підня́вшись, вони́ йду́ть шука́ти Джо́на, яко́го наре́шті знахо́дять у ку́хні. Там Бондарчуки́ пока́зують йому́ кольоро́ву кни́жку із традиці́йними украї́нськими стра́вами. Петро́ ка́же Джо́нові, що їм, на жаль, тре́ба попроща́тися з Есфі́р та Олекса́ндром і ї́хати у зворо́тному на́прямі. Есфі́р та Олекса́ндр пови́нні навести́ поря́док у се́бе, поспа́ти, та по́тім поду́мати про насту́пний ти́ждень. Джо́н ду́же ра́дий, що зустрі́в нови́х дру́зів і що вони́ відкри́ли йому́ чима́ло про культу́рну багатогра́нність Украї́ни. На проща́ння госпо́дарі дару́ють їм кві́ти з са́ду.

Vocabulary

вся́кий	all sorts of
захо́дити, -и-, imperf.	set (of the sun)
пово́лі	slowly
схиля́тися, -я́є-, imperf.	incline
о́брій, -ю	horizon
почорні́лий	black(ened)
нага́дувати, -ує-, imperf.	remind (+ dat. + acc.)
традиці́йний	traditional
блю́до, -а	dish
попроща́тися, -а́є-, perf.	say good-bye to (**з** + instr.; imperf. **проща́тися**, -**а́є**-)
у зворо́тному на́прямі	back (**наза́д**); lit. 'in the reverse direction'
навести́, -де́-, perf. **поря́док**	tidy up (imperf. **наво́дити**, -**и**-)
відкри́ти, -и́є-, perf.	reveal (imperf. **відкрива́ти**, -**а́є**-)
багатогра́нність, -ості	variety
госпо́дар, -я/я́	host
на проща́ння	as a farewell present (lit. 'for the farewell')
дарува́ти, -у́є-, imperf.	give (as a present) (perf. **одарува́ти**, -**у́є**-)
кві́тка, -и (pl. often **кві́ти, -ів**)	flower
са́д, -у	garden

Exercise 20a

Answer the following questions on the text:

(a) Куди́ поверта́ються на́ші дру́зі?
(b) Що ро́блять пі́сля обі́ду?
(c) Про що їм тре́ба поду́мати?
(d) Що ро́блять Есфі́р та Олекса́ндр у ку́хні?
(e) Що дару́ють їм на проща́ння?

Active Participles

The active participles, which, in their 'present' form, occur mainly from imperfective verbs, and in their 'past' form from perfective verbs, are only used as literary (bookish) forms. You need to be able to recognize them, not to form them; in practice, you will find that many 'adjectival' forms were originally participles. This was also the case with passive participles, which we discussed earlier; here, of course, the active participle expresses 'who is X-ing' or 'who was X-ing/who has X-ed', as in 'I know the man who is reading the newspaper'/'I know the man reading [participle] the newspaper'. Compare the passive: 'the newspaper that was read by the man'.

The present active participle looks like the imperfective gerund with an adjectival ending. It is formed on the basis of the third person plural of the present tense; remove the final **-ть**, and replace it with **-чий**. (In a very few instances one may find 'participles' in **-щий**; these are direct, if not always identical, transplantations from Russian, e.g. **трудя́щий** 'hard-working'.) The participle agrees with the noun to which it refers; although it is similar in form, do not confuse it with the gerund. Some examples:

шука́ти	**шука́ють**	**шука́ючий**
говори́ти	**гово́рять**	**гово́рячий**
дарува́ти	**дару́ють**	**дару́ючий**

These would be translated, respectively, as 'one who is searching', 'one who is speaking' and 'one who is giving'; making true participial sentences with these forms would be artificial, as the more common use of such words, when they occur in classical or scientific literature, is adjectival.

The past active participle has two forms. They are both more or less adjectives, and one is practically obsolete. The more common one consists of the feminine form of the past tense of a perfective verb, with the **-ла** ending replaced by **-лий**, as in our example **почорні́лий** 'black(ened)' in the text. Note also the following example (taken from an older Ukrainian grammar), which is used here purely as an adjective:

> **'з лексики випадають застарілі слова'** 'from the lexicon "fall out" obsolete (lit.: 'which have become old') words'

As with the present active participle, these examples should merely be noted as you come across them. The second, obsolete, past participle, consists of the masculine form of the past tense of a perfective verb with **-ший** appended. One that is quite common is **бу́вший** 'former', from the past tense, **був**, of **бу́ти** 'to be', although it is frequently replaced by **коли́шній**. However, setting aside such exceptions, you do not use active participles in speech.

The following phrase, containing a present active participle, comes from a grammar of Ukrainian:

> **У мовленні збігається процес використання мови, як об'єктивно існуючого фактора . . .**
> lit.: In speech the process of the use of language, as an objectively existing factor, coincides with . . .

Examples such as these must be taken with a grain of salt: as people do not really use them in speech, they come across as awkward and artificial.

Review of numeral declensions

Exercise 20b

Write out in full the following phrases containing numerals (the dots should help!); refer back to previous lessons if you need to:

(a) У 20 дом . .
(b) 18 підру́чник . .
(c) Да́йте 23 олівц .
(d) Вона́ ба́чить 37 студе́нт . .
(e) У тих 8 магази́н . .
(f) Усі́м 49 украї́нц . .
(g) 1993 рік .
(h) До це́нтру пі́деш 2 ву́лиц . . .
(i) Там живе́ 69 інжене́р . .
(j) Ци́ми дня́ми я вчу́ся ті́льки 1 мов .

День від'ї́зду

ОКСА́НА: До́брий день, Джо́не. Як ти спа́в?
ДЖОН: До́сить до́бре, дя́кую, а ти?
ОКСА́НА: І я до́бре. Сього́дні вируша́ємо, чи не так?
МИКО́ЛА: До́брого ра́нку, дру́зі! Так, за́втра бу́демо у Льво́ві.
ДЖОН: Чи зна́єте, як дале́ко Львів від Ки́єва, та як до́вго бу́демо ї́хати маши́ною?
МИКО́ЛА: Я про́сто не зна́ю. Усе зале́жить від на́ших дорі́г.
ОКСА́НА: Гада́ю, що ві́дстань від Ки́єва до Льво́ва бу́де принаймні 500 кіломе́трів.
ДЖОН: Зна́чить, спа́тимемо в готе́лі, але́ в яко́му мі́сті?
МИКО́ЛА: Я ду́маю, що до́бре бу́де зроби́ти дві зупи́нки, спочა́тку, сього́дні, у Жито́мирі, по́тім, за́втра, в Рі́вному чи в Терно́полі.
ДЖОН: Це напра́вді фантасти́чно! Бу́демо ма́йже ти́ждень у Льво́ві.
ОКСА́НА: Та бу́демо поверта́тися до Оде́си че́рез рі́зні ду́же ціка́ві міста́, як, напри́клад, Чернівці́.

Мико́ла:	Так, про це мі́сто розповіда́ла Есфі́р. Ча́сом мені́ зда́ється, що все було́ зна́чно кра́ще в ті мину́лі дні́.
Окса́на:	О, не зна́ю, наві́що згадува́ти про ті старі́ часи́. Життя́ було́ пе́вно ду́же важке́. Та й тре́ба ду́мати про на́ші дні.
Джон:	Так. Коли́ я поверну́ся до А́нглії, я із таки́м задово́ленням всі́м розповіда́тиму про те, що ба́чив в Украї́ні. В ме́не відчуття́, що це поча́ток відно́влення. Я ніко́ли не мав тако́го вра́ження в і́ншій краї́ні.

Vocabulary

зале́жати, -и-	depend (**від** + gen. 'on')
ві́дстань, -і	distance
кіломе́тр, -а	kilometre
Жито́мир, -а	Zhytomyr
Рі́вне, -ого (adj. decl.)	Rovno
Терно́піль, -поля	Ternopil'
фантасти́чний	fantastic
Чернівці́, -вці́в or **-ве́ць,** masc.	Chernivtsi, Czernowetz
задово́лення, -я. neut.	satisfaction, pleasure
розповіда́ти, -а́є-, imperf.	relate, recount
відчуття́, -я́	feeling
відно́влення, -я	renewal, revival

Note: If you are saying you are going from one place to another, then you use **з . . . до . . .** However, if you're talking of the distance from one place to another, or of the beautiful scenery, you use **від . . . до . . .**

More negation

As you know, the general word of negation is **ні** 'no', though very often Ukrainians will repeat a part of a question when they respond, e.g.

Хо́чеш прийти́?	Do you want to come?
(Ні), не хо́чу.	No, I don't [want].

It is useful to bear in mind that Ukrainians may also respond to negative questions in ways we find unusual. For example:

Чи ти не хо́чеш прийти́?	Don't you want to come?

Да, не хóчу.	No, I don't want [to come] (agreeing with the questioner, who anticipates the negative)

The basic negative particle in Ukrainian is **не** and its normal position is immediately before the verb; indeed in the case of **немá**, **немáє** 'there is/are not' it is fused to a verb form. If we wish to say 'nothing, not anything', etc., then the cardinal rule is that **не** must remain with the verb alongside **ніхтó**, **нщó**, **нідé**, **нікýди**, **нізвíдки**, **нікóли**, and **ні**. All these have the straightforward negative meanings 'no-one, nothing, nowhere, (to) nowhere, (from) nowhere, never, neither/nor/not even'. Thus Ukrainian, like many other European languages, has 'double negatives'; you can use more than one of these negative words in the same sentence, in addition to the obligatory **не**. Note also how a preposition splits the negative:

Вонá ні з ким не розмовля́ла.	She wasn't talking to anyone.
Я ні про щó не розповідáв.	I wasn't relating anything.
Я нікóго не бáчу.	I see no-one/I don't see anyone.
Ми нікóли не булú там.	We were never there/have never been . . .
Він нідé не був.	He hasn't been anywhere/ was nowhere.
Мáма нікóли нідé не булá.	Mother has never been anywhere.

There is also a set of 'negative impersonals', which are usually differentiated from the others simply by their place of stress: **ні́де** 'there is nowhere/no place [for me to . . .]', **ні́коли** 'there is no time [for me to . . .]', **ні́куди** 'there is nowhere [for me to go] to', **ні́чого** 'there is nothing, it is useless, there is no point [to do, in doing . . .]', **ні́як** 'there is no possibility [of doing . . .]' and **ні́кому** 'there is no-one [to tell something to]'. Because they are impersonal, these have a dative subject and are followed by an infinitive. Thus:

Тобí ні́куди йтú.	You've nowhere to go (to).
Їм ні́де сíсти.	They've nowhere to sit.
Менí ні́де дíтися.	I've nowhere to hide (put myself).
Ні́кому сказáти про те, що трáпилося.	There's no-one to tell what happened.
Ні́чого робúти.	There's no option.

More on comparison of adverbs

The basis for the formation of comparative and superlative adverbs is as given for the comparison of adjectives in *13*, the only difference being that the ending is **-ше** or **-ш** (**-ше** is preferred). It is also possible to form these adverbs by placing the basic adverbial form after **більш** 'more' or **найбíльш** 'most'. The comparatives may be qualified by such words as **знáчно**, **багáто**, **далéко** 'much', **трóхи** 'a little' or **ще** 'even'. The superlatives may be intensified by prefixing such forms as **що-**, **як-**, **щояк-**, Thus:

рáно	**ранíше**	**найранíше**
дóбре	**крáще**	**найкрáще**
погáно	**гíрше**	**найгíрше**
дóрого	**дорóжче**	**найдорóжче**

Ідíть якнайскорíше!
Читáй трóхи бíльше!
Вонá пúше знáчно крáще українською ніж англíйською.
Я, на жаль, говорю́ далéко гíрше українською від ньóго.

Exercise 20c

Translate the following sentences into Ukrainian:

(a) Why does he know nothing about Ukrainian history?
(b) If I could, I would go there as soon as possible.
(c) There is no point reading much more about Kyiv.
(d) Talking with my friend, I learned that no-one wanted to go home.
(e) He feels a little better today.
(f) Do call, please, you always say you have no time.
(g) I have never been to Chernivtsi.
(h) How far is it from L'viv to Ivano-Frankivs'k?
(i) Read that book as slowly as possible; it is so interesting.
(j) Everyone wants to spend summer by a lake or the sea.

More on the passive

We have seen some passive constructions: now let us summarize what we have covered. Essentially, passive forms may be conveyed using imperfective reflexive verbs, by perfective passive participles, and by the indefinite general form. Thus:

Тепе́р чита́ється нова́ кни́жка.	A new book is now being read.
Він уважа́ється чудо́вим студе́нтом.	He is considered a wonderful student. (Note the instrumental.)
Усе́ це вже забу́то.	All this has already been forgotten.
Його́ знайшли́ вчо́ра на да́чі дру́га.	He was found yesterday at a friend's dacha.
Ї́ї ду́же не лю́блять.	She is really not liked (loved).

Exercise 20d

You are at the airport in Kyiv, about to return home. Using the vocabulary items provided thus far (especially for travellers, with airport terminology!), narrate each step of your progress through the airport.

Exercise 20e

You have now arrived back home and are having a meal with a Ukrainian. Tell her or him about your impressions of Ukraine, and make up questions that she or he might ask about your stay there.

Now that you have reached the end of the course, we feel there is no better way to finish this book that to provide you with a sample of the poetry of Taras Shevchenko. Read it without a dictionary first, then use the dictionary to get an idea of its meaning. The stresses are given in such a way as to help you read the poem – particularly out loud!

Запові́т

Як умру́, то похова́йте
Мене́ на моги́лі,
Серед сте́пу широ́кого,
На Вкраї́ні ми́лій,
Щоб лани́ широкопо́лі,
І Дніпро́, і кру́чі
Було́ ви́дно, було́ чу́ти,
Як реве́ реву́чий.
Як понесе́ з Украї́ни
У си́нєє мо́ре
Кро́в воро́жу . . . отоді́ я́
І лани́, і го́ри –
Все́ поки́ну і поли́ну
До са́мого бо́га
Моли́тися . . . а до то́го
Я́ не зна́ю бо́га.
Похова́йте та встава́йте,
Кайда́ни порві́те
І вра́жою зло́ю кро́в'ю
Во́лю окропі́те.
І мене́ в сім'ї́ вели́кій,
В сім'ї́ во́льній, нові́й,
Не забу́дьте пом'яну́ти
Незли́м ти́хим сло́вом.

Reference section

What follows is a sketch of Ukrainian grammar. Some information here is not in the lessons, and there is, on occasion, information in the lessons which is not to be found here.

Grammatical terms used in this book

accusative	case of the *direct object* (see below): **Він читáє книжку**
adjective	modifies a noun, answers the question 'what is X like?' 'the *long* book', 'an *interesting* story'
adjectival participle	an *-ing* form of a verb which means the same as 'who/which . . .', e.g. 'He phoned the man selling a canoe' (= 'who was selling')
adverb	modifies action, answers the question 'how': 'he reads *slowly*', 'John does this *well*'
adverbial participle	an *-ing* form of a verb which means the same as 'when, if, because . . .', e.g. 'Looking through the window, Joan saw just what she had been looking for' (= 'when she was looking . . .'), 'They were so tired they went to bed *without undressing*' (= a negative adverbial participle).
article	'*the* book' (definite); '*a* library' (indefinite).
aspiration	the puff of air that accompanies the pronunciation of sounds to varying extents. For example, in standard English *p* at the beginning of a word is accompanied by a quite noticeable aspiration; people from northern England have much less aspiration in their *p*, *t*, *k*, something that is close to the situation in Ukrainian.
cardinal	numeral indicating how many (one, two . . .).
case	form of a word (noun, adjective, pronoun) showing the function of that word in a sentence; expressed by an ending
conjugation	set of verb endings indicating who or what is

	carrying out the action: 'John read*s*', **Микóла читáє**
dative	case of the *indirect object* (see below)
declension	set of case endings (see 'case' above)
definite	see 'article' above
direct object	thing/person at which a verbal action is directed: 'she bought *the book*', 'we saw *John*'
ending	element(s) added to the stem of a word: book+*s*; an ending in Ukrainian can be 'zero': **брат** + zero, **кни́жк + а**; **пóл + е**
gender	'natural' gender: distinction of sex (male-female); 'grammatical' gender: distinction of declensional types according to the ending in the nominative singular.
genitive	case of possession, often in English 'of': 'the capital *of England*', '*England's* capital'
gerund	see 'adverbial participle'
imperative	the verb form used to convey commands: '*Write* this down immediately!'
indefinite	see 'article' above
indirect object	recipient of the *direct* object (see above): 'the teacher gave the book *to the student*'
instrumental	case expressing 'by means of', 'together with'
interjection	a word or phrase expressing emotion: 'Oh!'
lexicon	the set of words ('lexical items') that make up the vocabulary of a language; sometimes = 'vocabulary'
locative	case of location (*in* the city); in Ukrainian this case is used only with a preposition; in grammars it may be referred to as the 'prepositional'
mood	a verb form conveying the attitude of the speaker to what is being said: e.g. the 'indicative' mood conveys plain statements, as in 'I am reading a book, and the 'conditional' mood hints at an underlying condition or 'if': 'I would like to go to Kyiv'
nominative	case of the subject (see below)
noun	object (pencil), person (John, woman) or concept (freedom)
ordinal	numeral indicating relative order (first, second . . .).
palatalization	the modification of the pronunciation of a conso-

	nant when it is almost simultaneously accompanied by a 'y'-sound; thus the variations of the *ss*, *t*, *d* and *n* in *issue*, *tune*, *dew*, *new*. Such 'palatalized', or 'soft', consonants are a feature of Ukrainian pronunciation.
paradigm	a set of declined or conjugated forms (e.g., the present paradigm of **іти́** 'go', is **іду́, іде́ш, іде́, ідемо́, ідете́, іду́ть**)
participle	see 'adjectival participle' and compare 'adverbial participle'
plural	when reference is to more than one item or person.
prefix	element added to the beginning of a verb to denote an action different from that of the unprefixed verb: 'Jack *pre*paid the bill'. 'I *under*estimated him'
preposition	grammatical word relating two things/people: 'a book in a library', 'the letter from mother'. Use of a preposition in Ukrainian requires that the following word occurs with a particular case ending.
pronoun	personal 'I, you', possessive 'my, your' or interrogative 'who? what?'
root	the core of a word, to which can be added prefixes, derivational suffixes, stem-marking suffixes, endings
singular	when reference is to a single person or item, e.g. 'a pencil', or something collective or uncountable, e.g. 'foliage', 'honey'
stem	the form of a word minus the ending, e.g. **книжк-**, **добр-**, **прочитай-**, **говори-**, **передай-**. In verbs, that portion between the root and the ending may be referred to as the 'theme', namely **-е-** and **-и-**. In this course we give **-ає-** and **-яє-** for first-conjugation verbs where the **а/я** of the infinitive, i.e. **-ати/-яти**, is retained in the present tense.
stress	greater emphasis on one vowel/syllable within a word: compare the two different places of stress in '*cóntent*' and '*contént*'
subject	actor; thing/person carrying out the main action of a sentence: '*John* read the article'
suffix	a word-formational element: e.g. Eng. *-tion*, *-ment*, *-ness*, *-er* (the speaker); Ukr. **-ник** (see *1*)

tense	time as expressed by the verb (past, present, future)
verb	word expressing action: 'Louise *writes* letters'
vocative	case of address: 'John!' Nouns in Ukrainian may have a distinct vocative form in the singular: **Івáне!**
voice	in pronunciation, a sound articulated with accompanying vibration in the throat (the vocal chords or folds), e.g. voiced *z* as against voiceless *s*; in the verb, the contrast between, for example, the 'active' voice in 'John sees Mary' and the 'passive' voice in 'John is seen by Mary'
word-formation	the process of building words from a given word or base form: 'transform' to 'transformation'

Abbreviations

acc.	accusative
act.	active
adj.	adjective/adjectival
adv.	adverb/adverbial
coll.	colloquial
comp.	comparative
cond.	conditional
conj.	conjugation
dat.	dative
decl.	declension
dem.	demonstrative
det.	determinate
fem.	feminine
fut.	future
gen.	genitive
imp.	imperative
imperf.	imperfective
impers.	impersonal
indef.	indefinite
indecl.	indeclinable
indet.	indeterminate
inf.	infinitive
instr.	instrumental

intrans.	intransitive
lit.	literally
loc.	locative
masc.	masculine
n.	noun
neut.	neuter
nom.	nominative
num.	numeral
p.	past
pass.	passive
pcple.	participle
perf.	perfective
pl.	plural
poss.	possessive
prep.	preposition
pres.	present
rel.	relative
pron.	pronoun
sing., sg.	singular
sup.	superlative
t.	tense
trans.	transitive
v.	verb
voc.	vocative

Declension

Nouns

Below are representative noun paradigms. Note instances when two cases have the same form, and pay especially close attention to stress patterns: shifting stress is extremely common (within the singular, see the feminine; we also find singular versus plural). Certain vocatives will hardly every occur. One might prefer always to list the vocative separataely, but we have here followed the convention of listing it together with the nominative in the plural.

Feminine hard stems in **-а** (*first declension*)

Nom.	**дружи́на**	**кни́жка**	**рука́**	**голова́**
Gen.	**дружи́ни**	**кни́жки**	**руки́**	**голови́**
Dat.	**дружи́ні**	**кни́жці**	**руці́**	**голові́**
Acc.	**дружи́ну**	**кни́жку**	**ру́ку**	**го́лову**
Instr.	**дружи́ною**	**кни́жкою**	**руко́ю**	**голово́ю**
Loc.	**дружи́ні**	**кни́жці**	**руці́**	**голові́**
Voc.	**дружи́но**	**кни́жко**	**ру́ко**	**го́лово**

Nom.Voc.	**дружи́ни**	**книжки́**	**ру́ки**	**го́лови**
Gen.	**дружи́н**	**книжо́к**	**рук**	**голі́в**
Dat.	**дружи́нам**	**книжка́м**	**рука́м**	**голова́м**
Acc.	**дружи́ни**	**книжки́**	**ру́ки**	**го́лови**
Instr.	**дружи́нами**	**книжка́ми**	**рука́ми**	**голова́ми**
Loc.	**дружи́нах**	**книжка́х**	**рука́х**	**голова́х**

Feminine soft stems in **-я** *and mixed stems (first declension)*

Nom.	**ста́нція**	**ку́хня**	**душа́**
Gen.	**ста́нції**	**ку́хні**	**душі́**
Dat.	**ста́нції**	**ку́хні**	**душі́**
Acc.	**ста́нцію**	**ку́хню**	**ду́шу**
Instr.	**ста́нцією**	**ку́хнею**	**душе́ю**
Loc.	**ста́нції**	**ку́хні**	**душі́**
Voc.	**ста́нціє**	**ку́хне**	**ду́ше**

Nom./Voc.	**ста́нції**	**ку́хні**	**ду́ші**
Gen.	**ста́нцій**	**ку́хонь**	**ду́ш**
Dat.	**ста́нціям**	**ку́хням**	**душа́м**
Acc.	**ста́нції**	**ку́хні**	**ду́ші**
Instr.	**ста́нціями**	**ку́хнями**	**душа́ми**
Loc.	**ста́нціях**	**ку́хнях**	**душа́х**

Masculine hard stems (second declension)

Nom.	**стіл**	**буди́нок**	**ве́чір**	**син**
Gen.	**стола́/сто́лу**	**буди́нку**	**ве́чора**	**си́на**
Dat.	**столу́**	**буди́нку**	**ве́чору**	**си́нові, -у**
Acc.	**стіл**	**буди́нок**	**ве́чір**	**си́на**
Instr.	**столо́м**	**буди́нком**	**ве́чором**	**си́ном**
Loc.	**столі́**	**буди́нку**	**ве́чорі**	**си́ні**
Voc.	**сто́ле**	**буди́нку**	**ве́чоре**	**си́ну!**

Nom./Voc.	**столи́**	**буди́нки**	**вечори́**	**сини́**
Gen.	**столі́в**	**буди́нків**	**вечорі́в**	**сині́в**
Dat.	**стола́м**	**буди́нкам**	**вечора́м**	**сина́м**
Acc.	**столи́**	**буди́нки**	**вечори́**	**сині́в**
Instr.	**стола́ми**	**буди́нками**	**вечора́ми**	**сина́ми**
Loc.	**стола́х**	**буди́нках**	**вечора́х**	**сина́х**

Masculine soft stems and mixed stems (second declension)

Nom.	**хло́пець**	**день**	**учи́тель**	**това́риш**	**школя́р**
Gen.	**хло́пця**	**дня**	**учи́теля**	**това́риша**	**школяра́**
Dat.	**хло́пцеві, -ю**	**дню**	**учи́телеві, -ю**	**това́ришеві, -у**	**школяре́ві, -у́**
Acc.	**хло́пця**	**день**	**учи́теля**	**това́риша**	**школяра́**
Instr.	**хло́пцем**	**днем**	**учи́телем**	**това́ришем**	**школяре́м**
Loc.	**хло́пцеві**	**дні**	**учи́телі, -ю**	**това́ришеві, -і**	**школяре́ві, -у́**
Voc.	**хло́пче**	**день**	**учи́телю**	**това́ришу**	**школя́ре**
Nom./Voc.	**хло́пці**	**дні**	**учителі́**	**товариші́**	**школярі́**
Gen.	**хло́пців**	**дней**	**учителі́в**	**товариші́в**	**школярі́в**
Dat.	**хло́пцям**	**дням**	**учителя́м**	**товариша́м**	**школяра́м**
Acc.	**хло́пців**	**дні**	**учителі́в**	**товариші́в**	**школярі́в**
Instr.	**хло́пцями**	**дня́ми**	**учителя́ми**	**товариша́ми**	**школяра́ми**
Loc.	**хло́пцях**	**днях**	**учителя́х**	**товариша́х**	**школяра́х**

Neuter hard stems (second declension)

Nom./Voc.	**мі́сто**	**вікно́**	**по́ле**
Gen.	**мі́ста**	**вікна́**	**по́л**
Dat.	**мі́сту**	**вікну́**	**по́лю**
Acc.	**мі́сто**	**вікно́**	**по́ле**
Instr.	**мі́стом**	**вікно́м**	**по́лем**
Loc.	**мі́сті**	**вікні́**	**по́лі, по́лю**
Nom./Voc.	**міста́**	**ві́кна**	**поля́**
Gen.	**міст**	**ві́кон**	**полі́в (піль)**
Dat.	**міста́м**	**ві́кнам**	**поля́м**
Acc.	**міста́**	**ві́кна**	**поля́**
Instr.	**міста́ми**	**ві́кнами**	**поля́ми**
Loc.	**міста́х**	**ві́кнах**	**поля́х**

Neuter soft stems and mixed stems (second declension)

Nom./Voc.	**мі́сце**	**кільце́**	**прі́звище**
Gen.	**мі́сця**	**кільця́**	**прі́звища**
Dat.	**мі́сцю**	**кільцю́**	**прі́звищу**
Acc.	**мі́сце**	**кільце́**	**прі́звище**
Instr.	**мі́сцем**	**кільце́м**	**прі́звищем**
Loc.	**мі́сці**	**кільці́**	**прі́звищу**
Nom./Voc.	**місця́**	**кі́льця**	**прі́звища**
Gen.	**місць**	**кі́лець**	**прі́звищ**
Dat.	**місця́м**	**кі́льцям**	**прі́звищам**
Acc.	**місця́**	**кі́льця**	**прі́звища**
Instr.	**місця́ми**	**кі́льцями**	**прі́звищами**
Loc.	**місця́х**	**кі́льцях**	**прі́звищах**

Neuter nouns with stem-final geminate consonants
(second declension)

Nom./Voc.	**пита́ння**	**почуття́**
Gen.	**пита́ння**	**почуття́**
Dat.	**пита́нню**	**почуттю́**
Acc.	**пита́ння**	**почуття́**
Instr.	**пита́нням**	**почуття́м**
Loc.	**пита́нні**	**почутті́**
Nom./Voc.	**пита́ння**	**почуття́**
Gen.	**пита́нь**	**почутті́в**
Dat.	**пита́нням**	**почуття́м**
Acc.	**пита́ння**	**почуття́**
Instr.	**пита́ннями**	**почуття́ми**
Loc.	**пита́ннях**	**почуття́х**

Feminine consonant stems (including those ending in **-ь***)*
(third declension)

Nom.	**ніч**	**тінь**	**кість** (+ all forms in **ність**)
Gen.	**но́чі**	**ті́ні**	**ко́сті**
Dat.	**но́чі**	**ті́ні**	**ко́сті**
Acc.	**ніч**	**ті́нь**	**кість**
Instr.	**ні́ччю**	**ті́нню**	**кі́стю**
Loc.	**но́чі**	**ті́ні**	**ко́сті**
Voc.	**но́че**	**ті́не**	**ко́сте**

Nom./Voc.	**но́чі**	**ті́ні**	**ко́сті**
Gen.	**ноче́й**	**ті́ней**	**косте́й**
Dat.	**ноча́м**	**ті́ням**	**костя́м**
Acc.	**но́чі**	**ті́ні**	**ко́сті**
Instr.	**ноча́ми**	**ті́нямн**	**костя́ми**
Loc.	**ноча́х**	**ті́нях**	**костя́х**
		(**тінь** 'shadow, shade')	

Neuter consonant stems (fourth declension)

Nom./Voc.	**ім'я́**	**теля́**
Gen.	**і́мені**	**теля́ти**
Dat.	**і́мені**	**теля́ті**
Acc.	**ім'я́**	**теля́**
Instr.	**і́менем/ім'я́м**	**теля́м**
Loc.	**і́мені**	**теля́ті́**
Nom./Voc.	**імена́**	**теля́та**
Gen.	**іме́н**	**теля́т**
Dat.	**імена́м**	**теля́там**
Acc.	**імена́**	**теля́та**
Instr.	**імена́ми**	**теля́тами**
Loc.	**імена́х**	**теля́тах**

'Irregular' forms
*(**ма́ти** comes strictly speaking under the third declension)*

Nom.	**дити́на**	**люди́на**	**росія́нин**	**друг**	**ма́ти**
Gen.	**дити́ни**	**люди́ни**	**росія́нина**	**дру́га**	**ма́тері**
Dat.	**дити́ні**	**люди́ні**	**росія́нинові, -у**	**дру́гові, -у**	**ма́тері**
Acc.	**дити́ну**	**люди́ну**	**росія́нина**	**дру́га**	**ма́тір**
Instr.	**дити́ною**	**люди́ною**	**росія́нином**	**дру́гом**	**ма́тір'ю**
Loc.	**дити́ні**	**люди́ні**	**росія́нинові**	**дру́гові**	**ма́тері**
Voc.	**дити́но**	**люди́но**	**росія́нине**	**дру́же**	**ма́ти**
Nom./Voc.	**ді́ти**	**лю́ди**	**росія́ни**	**дру́зі**	**матері́**
Gen.	**діте́й**	**люде́й**	**росія́н**	**дру́зів**	**матері́в**
Dat.	**ді́тям**	**лю́дям**	**росія́нам**	**дру́зям**	**матеря́м**
Acc.	**діте́й**	**люде́й**	**росія́н**	**дру́зів**	**матері́в**
Instr.	**дітьми́**	**людьми́**	**росія́нами**	**дру́зями**	**матеря́ми**
Loc.	**ді́тях**	**лю́дях**	**росія́нах**	**дру́зях**	**матеря́х**

Adjectives

Hard stems

	Masculine	*Neuter*	*Feminine*	*Plural*
Nom.	**вели́кий**	**вели́ке**	**вели́ка**	**вели́кі**
Gen.	**вели́кого**		**вели́кої**	**вели́ких**
Dat.	**вели́кому**		**вели́кій**	**вели́ким**
Acc.	as Nom. or Gen.	as Nom.	**вели́ку**	as Nom. or Gen.
Instr.	**вели́ким**		**вели́кою**	**вели́кими**
Loc.	**вели́кому/ім**		**вели́кій**	**вели́ких**

Soft stems

Nom.	**коли́шній**	**коли́шнє**	**коли́шня**	**коли́шні**
Gen.	**коли́шнього**		**коли́шньої**	**коли́шніх**
Dat.	**коли́шньому**		**коли́шній**	**коли́шнім**
Acc.	as Nom. or Gen.	as Nom.	**коли́шню**	as Nom. or Gen.
Instr.	**коли́шнім**		**коли́шньою**	**коли́шніми**
Loc.	**коли́шньому/ім**		**коли́шній**	**коли́шніх**

Comparison

Regular comparatives:

adjective (minus **-ий** ending)	adverb (minus **-о/е** ending)
+ і́ший	**+ -і́ше**
холодні́ший	**холодні́ше**
теплі́ший	**теплі́ше**

For more information, see *13* and *20*.

Pronouns

Personal

	I (1sg)	you (2sg)	he/it	it	she/it (3sg)
Nom.	**я**	**ти**	**він**	**воно́**	**вона́**
Gen.	**ме́не́***	**те́бе́***	**його́/ньо́го***		**ї́ї/не́ї***
Dat.	**мені́**	**тобі́**	**йому́**		**їй**
Acc.	**ме́не́***	**те́бе́***	**його́/ньо́го***		**ї́ї/не́ї***
Instr.	**мно́ю**	**тобо́ю**	**ним**		**не́ю**
Loc.	**мені́**	**тобі́**	**ньо́му/нім**		**ній**

	we (1pl)	you (2pl)	they (3pl)
Nom.	**ми**	**ви**	**вони́**
Gen.	**нас**	**вас**	**їх/них***
Dat.	**нам**	**вам**	**їм**
Acc.	**нас**	**вас**	**їх/них***
Instr.	**на́ми**	**ва́ми**	**ни́ми**
Loc.	**нас**	**вас**	**них**

*Stress shifts left (1st-2nd persons: **мене́/до ме́не**) and initial **н-** appears (3rd persons) after a preposition (**його́/до нього**)!

Себе́ 'self' (reflexive) declines like **ти**, but has no nominative form.

Possessive

my/mine

	Masc.	*Neut.*	*Fem.*	*Pl.*
Nom.	**мій**	**моє́**	**моя́**	**мої́**
Gen.	**мого́**		**моє́ї**	**мої́х**
Dat.	**моєму́**		**мої́й**	**мої́м**
Acc.	Nom./Gen.	**моє́**	**мою́**	**мої́/мої́х**
Instr.	**мої́м**		**моє́ю**	**мої́ми**
Loc.	**моє́му/мої́м**		**мої́й**	**мої́х**

our(s)

	Masc.	*Neut.*	*Fem.*	*Pl.*
Nom.	**наш**	**на́ше**	**на́ша**	**на́ші**
Gen.	**на́шого**		**на́шої**	**на́ших**
Dat.	**на́шому**		**на́шій**	**на́шим**
Acc.	Nom./Gen.	**на́ше**	**на́шу**	**на́ші/на́ших**
Instr.	**на́шим**		**на́шою**	**на́шими**
Loc.	**на́шому/на́шім**		**на́шій**	**на́ших**

NB: **твій**, **ваш** and **свій** are declined just like **мій** and **наш**. The 3rd person possessives **його́** and **її́** are indeclinable, while **ї́хній** is declined like a soft stem adjective.

Interrogative

хто? 'who?'	**що?** 'what?'		**чий** 'whose?'			
			Masc.	*Neut.*	*Fem.*	*Pl.*
Nom.	**хто**	**що**	**чий**	**чиє́**	**чия́**	**чиї́**
Gen.	**ко́го́***	**чо́го́**	**чийо́го**		**чиє́ї**	**чиї́х**
Dat.	**кому́**	**чому́**	**чийо́му**		**чиї́й**	**чиї́м**
Acc.	**ко́го́***	**що**	Nom./Gen.	**чиє́**	**чию́**	Nom./Gen.
Instr.	**ким**	**чим**	**чиї́м**		**чиє́ю**	**чиї́ми**
Loc.	**ко́му/кім**	**чо́му/чім**	**чийо́му/чиє́му/ чиї́м**		**чиї́й**	**чиї́х**

NB: Other interrogative pronouns (e.g. **котри́й** 'which', **яки́й** 'what kind of') are declined as adjectives; the negative pronouns **ніхто́** and **нішо́** decline like **хто** and **що**, but prepositions occur between the prefix **ні-** and the declined form of **хто, що, (ні з ким, ні до чо́го)**.

*Stress moved left when governed by a preposition.

Demonstrative

цей 'this'

	Masc.	*Neut.*	*Fem.*	*Pl.*
Nom.	**цей**	**це**	**ця**	**ці**
Gen.	**цьо́го́***		**ціє́ї**	**цих**
Dat.	**цьому́**		**цій**	**цим**
Acc.	Nom./Gen.	**це**	**цю**	Nom./Gen.
Instr.	**цим**		**ціє́ю**	**ци́ми**
Loc.	**цьо́му/цім**		**цій**	**цих**

той 'that'

	Masc.	*Neut.*	*Fem.*	*Pl.*
Nom.	**той**	**те**	**та**	**ті**
Gen.	**то́го́***		**тіє́ї/то́ї**	**тих**
Dat.	**тому́**		**тій**	**тим**
Acc.	Nom./Gen.	**те**	**ту**	Nom./Gen.
Instr.	**тим**		**тіє́ю**	**ти́ми**
Loc.	**то́му/тім**		**тій**	**тих**

Quantitative

весь 'all'

	Masc.	*Neut.*	*Fem.*	*Pl.*
Nom.	**весь/увéсь/ввесь**	**все/усé**	**вся/уся́**	**всі/усí**
Gen.	**всьóгó***		**всієї**	**всіх**
Dat.	**всьомý**		**всій**	**всім**
Acc.	Nom./Gen.	**все/усé**	**всю**	Nom./Gen.
Instr.	**всім**		**всією**	**всімá**
Loc.	**всьóму/всім**		**всій**	**всіх**

*Retraction of stress to left when used with a preposition.

Numerals

Cardinal		*Ordinal*
1	**оди́н, однá, однé**	**пéрший**
2	**два** (masc., neut.), **дві** (fem.)	**дрýгий**
3	**три**	**трéтій**
4	**чоти́ри**	**четвéртий**
5	**п'ять**	**п'я́тий**
6	**шість**	**шóстий**
7	**сім**	**сьóмий**
8	**ві́сім**	**вóсьмий**
9	**дéв'ять**	**дев'я́тий**
10	**дéсять**	**деся́тий**
11	**одинáдцять**	**одинáдцятий**
12	**дванáдцять**	**дванáдцятий**
13	**тринáдцять**	**тринáдцятий**
14	**чотирнáдцять**	**чотирнáдцятий**
15	**п'ятнáдцять**	**п'ятнáдцятий**
16	**шістнáдцять**	**шістнáдцятий**
17	**сімнáдцять**	**сімнáдцятий**
18	**вісімнáдцять**	**вісімнáдцятий**
19	**дев'ятнáдцять**	**дев'ятнáдцятий**
20	**двáдцять**	**двадця́тий**
30	**три́дцять**	**тридця́тий**
40	**сóрок**	**сорокóвий**
50	**п'ятдеся́т**	**п'ятдеся́тий**
60	**шістдеся́т**	**шістдеся́тий**

70	**сімдеся́т**	**сімдеся́тий**
80	**вісімдеся́т**	**вісімдеся́тий**
90	**дев'яно́сто**	**дев'яно́стий**
100	**сто**	**со́тий**

NB: Cardinal '1' is declined as an end-stressed pronoun (e.g. **той**, **та**, **те**); ordinals are declined like adjectives.
*Note the stress difference between certain ordinals and cardinals.

Selected cardinal paradigms

оди́н

	Masc.	*Neut.*	*Fem.*	*Pl.*
Nom.	**оди́н**	**одно́/одне́**	**одна́**	**одні́**
Gen.	**одного́**		**одніє́ї/одно́ї**	**одни́х**
Dat.	**одному́**		**одні́й**	**одни́м**
Acc.	Nom./Gen.	**одно́/одне́**	**одну́**	Nom./Gen.
Instr.	**одни́м**		**одніє́ю/одно́ю**	**одни́ми**
Loc.	**одно́му/одні́м**		**одні́й**	**одни́х**

In the cases other than nom. the stress may under certain circumstances move to the first syllable.

	два	**дві**	**три**	**чоти́ри**
	Masc./Neut.	*Fem.*		
Nom.	**два**	**дві**	**три**	**чоти́ри**
Gen.	**двох**		**трьох**	**чотирьо́х**
Dat.	**двом**		**трьом**	**чотирьо́м**
Acc.	Nom./Gen.		Nom./Gen.	Nom./Gen.
Instr.	**двома́**		**трьома́**	**чотирма́**
Loc.	**двох**		**трьох**	**чотирьо́х**

	п'ять	**шість**	**сім**
Nom.	**п'ять**	**шість**	**сім**
Gen.	**п'яти́, п'ятьо́х**	**шести́, шістьо́х**	**семи́, сімо́х**
Dat.	**п'яти́, п'ятьо́м**	**шести́, шістьо́м**	**семи́, сімо́м**
Acc.	Nom./Gen.	Nom./Gen.	Nom./Gen.
Instr.	**п'ятьма́, п'ятьома́**	**шістьма́, шістьома́**	**сьома́, сімома́**
Loc.	**п'яти́, п'ятьо́х**	**шести́, шістьо́х**	**семи́, сімо́х**

	ві́сім	де́в'ять	де́сять
Nom.	**ві́сім**	**де́в'ять**	**де́сять**
Gen.	**восьми́, вісьмо́х**	**дев'яти́, дев'ятьо́х**	**десяти́, десятьо́х**
Dat.	**восьми́, вісьмо́м**	**дев'яти́, дев'ятьо́м**	**десяти́, десятьо́м**
Acc.	Nom./Gen.	Nom./Gen.	Nom./Gen.
Instr.	**вісьма́, вісьмома́**	**дев'ятьма́, дев'ятьо́ма**	**десятьма́, десятьома́**
Loc.	**восьми́, вісьмо́х**	**дев'яти́, дев'ятьо́х**	**десяти́, десятьо́х**

(11–19 decline like 5)

	шістдеся́т	сто
Nom.	**шістдеся́т**	**сто**
Gen.	**шістдесяти́, шістдесятьо́х**	**ста**
Dat.	**шістдесяти́, шістдесятьо́м**	**ста**
Acc.	Nom./Gen.	**сто**
Instr.	**шістдесятьма́, шістдесятьо́ма**	**ста**
Loc.	**шістдесяти́, шістдесятьо́х**	**ста**

	дві́сті	п'ятьсо́т
Nom.	**дві́сті**	**п'ятсо́т**
Gen.	**двохсо́т**	**п'ятисо́т**
Dat.	**двомста́м**	**п'ятиста́м**
Acc.	**дві́сті**	**п'ятсо́т**
Instr.	**двомаста́ми**	**п'ятьмаста́ми, п'ятьомаста́ми**
Loc.	**двохста́х**	**п'ятиста́х**

(50, 70, 80 decline like 60; 300, 400 follow the pattern of 200 and 600–900 that of 500)

*Note the variant forms; the latter can only be used with animates.

Со́рок, **дев'яно́сто** and **сто** have the ending **-а** in all cases except the nom./acc. (stressed in the case of **со́рок**). The three variants of 'both' (**оби́два** (masc./neut.) **оби́дві** (fem.) and **обо́є** (masc+fem)) all decline like **два**: Gen. **обо́х** etc. There are numerous 'collective' numerals, e.g. **двоє́**, **тро́є**, etc. These decline like the cardinals in the genitive, dative, instrumental, locative and, optionally, the animate accusative.

A few prepositions and case government

Preposition	*Case*	*Meaning and/or use*
бі́ля	genitive	next to; near
бли́зько	genitive	near
для	genitive	for
до	genitive	motion to; until; before (time)
з (із, зі, зо)	genitive	from (various meanings)
	instrumental	with
за	accusative	for; within period of time
	instrumental	behind, beyond, in the presence of, thanks to, with, after, to fetch ('for')
	genitive	during
на	locative	place where (on, at)
	accusative	motion (on) to
над	instrumental	over, above
о (об)	locative	time expressions
пе́ред	instrumental	before (time, place)
під	instrumental	under (place)
	accusative	motion to: 'underwards'
пі́сля	genitive	after
по	locative	after; (a place)
	dative	through, all over
про	accusative	about, concerning
у/в	locative	place where (in, at)
	accusative	motion to
	genitive	at; possession
че́рез	accusative	through (a place); in (time)

Weeks and months

Days of the week			*Months*		
Time	*Time when*		*Time*	*Time when*	
понеді́лок	**у понеді́лок**	(M)	**сі́чень**	**у сі́чні**	(J)
вівто́рок	**у вівто́рок**	(T)	**лю́тий**	**у лю́тому**	(F)
середа́	**у се́реду**	(W)	**бе́резень**	**у бе́резні**	(M)
четве́р	**у четве́р**	(Th)	**кві́тень**	**у кві́тні**	(A)
п'я́тниця	**у п'я́тницю**	(F)	**тра́вень**	**у тра́вні**	(M)

субóта	**у субóту**	(Sa)	**чéрвень**	**у чéрвні**	(J)
неді́ля	**у неді́лю**	(Su)	**ли́пень**	**у ли́пні**	(J)
			сéрпень	**у сéрпні**	(A)
			вéресень	**у вéресні**	(S)
			жóвтень	**у жóвтні**	(O)
			листопáд	**у листопáді**	(N)
			грýдень	**у грýдні**	(D)

Adverbs of time and place

Place	*Place To*	*Place From*	*English Equivalents*	
де?	**куди́?**	**зві́дки?**	where?	(to . . .? from . . .?)
тут	**сюди́**	**зві́дси**	here	(to . . .? from . . .?)
там	**туди́**	**зві́дти**	there	(to . . .? from . . .?)

Miscellaneous adverbs of place

ось, ось тут	here, over here is/are
он, он там	there, over there is/are
скрі́зь	everywhere
нідé	nowhere
нікýди	(to) nowhere, not to any place
нізві́дки	(from) nowhere, not from any place
нізвідкиля́	"

Adverbs of time

чáсто	often	**врáнці**	in the morning
іноді, інколи	sometimes	**ввéчері**	in the evening
нікóли	never	**вночі́, уночі́**	at night
рі́дко	rarely		
щодня́	every day	**узи́мку**	in the winter
щовéчора	every evening	**навесні́**	in the spring
сьогóдні	today	**улі́тку**	in the summer
зáвтра	tomorrow	**восени́**	in the autumn
учóра	yesterday		
рані́ше, коли́сь	earlier, before		
пóтім	later (on), then		
тоді́	at that time		
якóсь	once, at one time		

Conjugation

The major verbal types are presented below in the non-past (imperfective and perfective), followed by the past tense, imperative and participles. Note how the infinitive always ends in -**ти**, preceded in the spelling either by a vowel or by a consonant; but do remember that it is crucial to know either the stem or the first person singular plus one or two other forms of the present tense, in order to create many of the forms of the verb and assign the correct stress. The infinitive is, however, the pointer to the forms of the past tense and, overall, to the conjugation class.

If the above is borne in mind, there are hardly any 'irregular' verbs in Ukrainian. The overall patterns may be conveyed by the following list, where we give the infinitive followed by the first person singular, the second person singular and the third person plural, as well as the masculine and feminine forms of the past if necessary (by 'necessary' we mean that you cannot derive the past tense by simply removing the -**ти** of the infinitive and adding -**в**, -**ла**, -**ло** or -**ли**).

The 'key' with which we accompany the verb infinitive in the vocabulary lists is basically the theme vowel: the vowel that marks which conjugation a verb follows, preceded as necessary by the end of the root. If the stress is marked on the 'key', then it is fixed there. If the stress is not marked, then look at the infinitive. A stress on the penultimate syllable will indicate a mobile stress (only the first personal singular end-stressed); earlier stress indicates the site of a fixed stress.

First conjugation

читá/ти, -ю, -єш, -ють	Ay-type
крá/яти, -ю, -єш, -ють	Ay-type
раді́/ти, -ю, -єш, -ють	Ay-type (Iy-type)
смі/я́тися, -ю́ся, -є́шся, -ю́ться	Ay-type (Iy-type)
чý/ти, -ю, -єш, -ють	Ay-type (Uy-type)
прац/ювáти, -ю́ю, -ю́єш, -ю́ють	Uva-type
пи/сáти, -шý, -шеш, -шуть	A-type
да/вáти, -ю́, -є́ш, -ю́ть	Avay-type
не/сти́, -сý, -се́ш, -сýть	consonantal type
ве/сти́, -дý, -де́ш, -дýть	consonantal type
вст́и/гнути, -гну, -гнеш, -гнуть, г(ла)	consonantal type

Second conjugation

хо/ди́ти, -джу́, -диш, -дять	Y/I-type
держ/а́ти, -у́, -иш, -ать	ZHa-type
сто/я́ти/ -ю́, -ї́ш, -я́ть	Ya-type

Note how, in the present tense, the stress either remains fixed on the stem or the ending (the very last vowel), or moves between the first person singular ending and the stem elsewhere. As regards the adjectival and adverbial participles, note that the stress of those formed from the third person plural of the present tense remains in the same place as in that form. Below we have one apparent exception, namely **сто́ячи**. Remember that the past passive participle with the ending -**о**, namely -**но**, -**то** (the impersonal) is very important.

Verbs of the first conjugation

(the A-type gives an example of a mobile-stress verb)

	Ay-type	Uva-type	Avay-type	A-type
	чита́ти	**будува́ти**	**дава́ти**	**писа́ти**
	читай-	**будуй-**	**дай-/давай-**	**пиш-**

Present tense

я	**чита́ю**	**буду́ю**	**даю́**	**пишу́**
ти	**чита́єш**	**буду́єш**	**дає́ш**	**пи́шеш**
він	**чита́є**	**буду́є**	**дає́**	**пи́ше**
ми	**чита́ємо**	**буду́ємо**	**даємо́**	**пи́шемо**
ви	**чита́єте**	**буду́єте**	**даєте́**	**пи́шете**
вони́	**чита́ють**	**буду́ють**	**даю́ть**	**пи́шуть**

Past tense

я,ти, він	**чита́в**	**будува́в**	**дава́в**	**писа́в**
я, ти, вона́	**чита́ла**	**будува́ла**	**дава́ла**	**писа́ла**
воно́	**чита́ло**	**будува́ло**	**дава́ло**	**писа́ло**
ми, ви, вони́	**чита́ли**	**будува́ли**	**дава́ли**	**писа́ли**

Imperative

ти:	**чита́й!**	**буду́й!**	**дава́й!**	**пиши́!**
ви:	**чита́йте!**	**буду́йте!**	**дава́йте!**	**пиші́ть!**
ми:	**чита́ймо!**	**буду́ймо!**	**дава́ймо!**	**пиші́мо!**

Past passive adjectival participle (most often perfective-based)

(прочита́ти)	**(збудува́ти)**	**- - -**	**(написа́ти)**
прочи́таний	**збудо́ваний**	**- - -**	**напи́саний**
прочи́тана	**збудо́вана**	**- - -**	**напи́сана**

We give them here as derived from perfective verbs.

Note how the **у** of **збудува́ти** becomes **о**; if we had a verb of the same type, but ending in -**ювати**, then **ю** would become **ьо**: **опрацюва́ти** 'to work out, elaborate' **опрацьо́ваний**.

Imperfective adverbial participle

чита́ючи	**буду́ючи**	**даючи́**	**–**

Perfective adverbial participle

прочита́вши	**збудува́вши**	**да́вши**	**написа́вши**

NB: in first conjugation verbs, remember that reflexive (**ся**) verbs have the 3rd sg. ending -**ться (здає́ться)**

Consonant stems (no stress shift in the non-past, end-stress throughout the past)

могти́	**нести́**	**жи́ти**	**бу́ти**	**пи́ти**
мож-	**нес-**	**жив-**	**буд-**	**п'й-**

Present tense (future of бу́ти)

мо́жу	**несу́**	**живу́**	**бу́ду**	**п'ю**
мо́жеш	**несе́ш**	**живе́ш**	**бу́деш**	**п'єш**
мо́же	**несе́**	**живе́**	**бу́де**	**п'є**
мо́жемо	**несемо́**	**живемо́**	**бу́демо**	**п'ємо́**
мо́жете	**несете́**	**живете́**	**бу́дете**	**п'єте́**
мо́жуть	**несу́ть**	**живу́ть**	**бу́дуть**	**п'ють**

Past tense:

міг	**ніс**	**жив**	**був**	**пив**
моглá	**неслá**	**жилá**	**булá**	**пилá**
моглó	**неслó**	**жилó**	**булó**	**пилó**
моглú	**неслú**	**жилú**	**булú**	**пилú**

Imperative:

- - -	**несú!**	**живú!**	**будь!**	**пий!**
- - -	**несíть!**	**живíть!**	**бýдьте!**	**пúйте!**
- - -	**несíмо!**	**живíмо!**	**бýдьмо!**	**пúймо!**

Past passive adjectival participle (most often perfective-based)

- - -	**(при)нéсений**	**(про)жúтий**	**(за)бýтий**	**(вú)пúтий**

Imperfective adverbial participle

- - -	**несучú**	**живучú**	**бýдучи**	- - -

Perfective adverbial participle

- - -	**принíсши**	**прожúвши**	**забýвши**	**вúпивши**

забýти 'to forget' is given just so as to provide certain forms of **бýти**. Forms omitted are doubtful or rare.

Verbs of the second conjugation

(if the stress is on **-úти**, then the stress is either fixed on the ending, **-ú-**, or is mobile)

Y- (or I-) type

бáчити	**говорúти**	**дивúтися**	**поспішúти**
бачи-	**говори-**	**диви-**	**поспіши-**

Present tense (future for the perfective поспіши́ти):

ба́чу	**говорю́**	**дивлю́ся**	**поспішу́**
ба́чиш	**гово́риш**	**ди́вишся**	**поспіши́ш**
ба́чить	**гово́рить**	**ди́виться**	**поспіши́ть**
ба́чимо	**гово́римо**	**ди́вимося**	**поспішимо́**
ба́чите	**гово́рите**	**ди́витеся**	**поспішите́**
ба́чать	**гово́рять**	**ди́вляться**	**поспіша́ть**

Past tense

ба́чив	**говори́в**	**диви́вся**	**поспіши́в**
ба́чила	**говори́ла**	**диви́лася**	**поспіши́ла**
ба́чило	**говори́ло**	**диви́лося**	**поспіши́ло**
ба́чили	**говори́ли**	**диви́лися**	**поспіши́ли**

Imperative

бач!*	**говори́!**	**диви́ся!**	**поспіши́!**
ба́чмо!	**говорі́м(о)!**	**диві́мося!**	**поспіші́м(о)!**
ба́чте!	**говорі́ть!**	**диві́ться!**	**поспіші́ть!**

Past passive adjectival participle (most often perfective-based)

поба́чений	—	—

Imperfective adverbial participle

ба́чачи	**гово́рячи**	**ди́влячись**	—

Perfective adverbial participle

побачи́вши	**поговори́вши**	**подиви́вшись**	**поспіши́вши**

*Replaced by **диви́сь**!

Диви́тися provides an example of a reflexive verb; remember that the particle **-ся** is simply attached – the verb's written forms are unaffected by it. One also comes across **-ся** in the form **-сь**; this option may be found in the adverbial participle, the infinitive, the past tense and the conditional mood of the verb. When the masculine form ends in a consonant other than **-в**, **-ся** is the only form: **хліб пі́кся в духо́вці** 'the bread was baking in the oven'.

In what follows, by 'ZHa-type' is meant second conjugation verbs whose infinitive ends in **-жати**, **-шати**, **-чати** or **-щати** (the stress may be fixed or mobile if the infinitive is **-а́ти**) while 'Ya-type' refers to **стоя́ти** and **боя́тися** 'to be afraid', where the ending **-яти** is preceded by **-о-** (the stress is fixed on the ending).

ZHa-type	**Ya**-type
лежа́ти	**стоя́ти**
лежа-/лежи-	**стоя-/стої-**

Present tense

лежу́	**стою́**
лежи́ш	**стоі́ш**
лежи́ть	**стоі́ть**
лежимо́	**стоїмо́**
лежите́	**стоїте́**
лежа́ть	**стоя́ть**

Past tense

лежа́в	**стоя́в**
лежа́ла	**стоя́ла**
лежа́ло	**стоя́ло**
лежа́ли	**стоя́ли**

Imperative

лежи́!	**стій!**
лежі́м(о)!	**сті́ймо!**
лежі́ть!	**сті́йте!**

Past passive adjectival participle (most often perfective-based):

– – –	– – –

Imperfective adverbial participle:

ле́жачи	**сто́ячи** (irregular stress)

Perfective adverbial participle:

полежáвши **постóявши**

Irregular verbs (including those whose conjugation differs from the infinitive)

дати	**(з’)ї́сти**	**(відпо)-ві́сти́**	**ї́хати**	**узя́ти**

Present or future tense

дам	**(з’)їм**	**-вім**	**ї́ду**	**візьму́**
даси́/даш	**(з’)їси́**	**-віси́**	**ї́деш**	**ві́зьмеш**
дасть	**(з’)їсть**	**-ві́сть**	**ї́де**	**ві́зьме**
дамó	**(з’)їмó**	**-вімó**	**ї́демо**	**ві́зьмемо**
дасте́	**(з’)їсте́**	**-вісте́**	**ї́дете**	**ві́зьмете**
даду́ть	**(з’)їдя́ть**	**-відя́ть**	**ї́дуть**	**ві́зьмуть**

Past tense

дав	**(з’)ї́в**	**-ві́в**	**ї́хав**	**узя́в**
далá	**(з’)ї́ла**	**-ві́ла**	**ї́хала**	**узялá**
далó	**(з’)ї́ло**	**-ві́ло**	**ї́хало**	**узялó**
дали́	**(з’)ї́ли**	**-ві́ли**	**ї́хали**	**узяли́**

Imperative

дай!	**(з’)їж!**	***- - -**	**(по)їдь!**	**візьми́!**
дáймо!	**(з’)ї́жмо!**	***- - -**	**(по)ї́дьмо!**	**візьмі́м(о)!**
дáйте!	**(з’)ї́жте!**	***- - -**	**(по)ї́дьте!**	**візьмі́ть!**

Past passive adjectival participle (most often perfective-based)

дáний	**з’ї́дений**	–	–	**узя́тий**

Imperfective adverbial participle

даючи́	–	–	**ї́дучи**	–

Perfective adverbial participle

дáвши	**з’ї́вши**	**відпові́вши**	**пої́хавши**	**узя́вши**

*The imperative forms of **відповісти́** 'to reply, answer' are rendered by periphrasis, for example: **Дай ві́дповідь!** 'Give an answer!', although some people use the imperfective, namely **відповіда́й(-мо/)те)**.

The future tense in Ukrainian may be rendered, for verbs of the perfective aspect, by their 'present-tense' forms. For imperfective verbs the choice is between (a) the future tense of the verb **бу́ти**, that is, **бу́ду** etc. together with the imperfective infinitive, for example:

Сього́дні уве́чері ми бу́демо дивитися телеба́чення.	This evening we'll watch TV.

and (b) the forms -**му**, -**меш**, -**ме** (reflexive: -**меться**), -**мемо**, -**мете**, -**муть** affixed to the imperfective infinitive, for example:

Щодня́ він писа́тиме до не́ї.	He'll write to her every day.

The conditional mood is conveyed by the past tense forms and the particle **би** (written **б** when it comes immediately after a vowel), for example:

Якби́ вона́ пого́дилася приї́хати зі мно́ю, я був би таки́й ра́дий.	If she agreed to come with me, I would be so glad.
Ми хоті́ли б поі́хати туди́ по́їздом.	We'd like to take the train there.

Selected further reading

Certain of the items are a little dated, but they do represent the genuine use of Ukrainian by different communities, and were all of considerable use.

Andrusyshen, C. H. and Crett, J. N. (1985) *Українсько-англійський словник/Ukrainian-English Dictionary*, Toronto: University of Saskatchewan (3rd printing).

Comrie, B. and Corbett, G.G. (eds) (1993) *The Slavonic Languages*. London and New York: Routledge (Contribution on Ukrainian by George Y. Shevelov, pp. 947–98.)

Kubijovyč, V. (ed.) (1963–71) *Ukraine. A Concise Encyclopedia. I-II*, Toronto: University of Toronto Press.

Palamar, L.M. and O.A. Bekh (1993) *Практичний курс української мови. Навчальний посібник*, Kyiv: Lybid'.

Podvez'ko, M.L. and Balla, M.I. (1988) *Англо-український словник/English-Ukrainian Dictionary*, Edmonton: Canadian Institute of Ukrainian Studies, University of Alberta (First published by *Radianska shkola*, Kyiv, 1974).

Rusanivskyi, V.M., M.M. Pylynskyi and S.Ya. Yermolenko (1991) *Українська мова*, Kyiv: Radianska shkola (5th edition).

Shevelov, G.Y. (1980) 'Ukrainian', in Schenker, A. M. and E. (eds) *The Slavic Literary Languages: Formation and Development*, New Haven: Yale Concilium on International and Area Studies.

Subtelny, Orest (1988) *Ukraine. A History*, Toronto, Buffalo, and London: University of Toronto Press and Canadian Institute of Ukrainian Studies.

Zhluktenko, Yu.O., N.I. Totska and T.K. Molodid (1978) *Ukrainian. A Textbook for Beginners*, Kiev; Vyshcha shkola (2nd edition).

1984–8 *Encyclopedia of Ukraine, I: A-F, II: G-K*, Toronto, Buffalo, and London: University of Toronto Press.

Key to the exercises

Lesson 1

1a

Examples: книжка студéнтки, кімнáта Мáрти, квартúра Марíї, книжка Микóли, квартúра жíнки.

1b

я живý, ти живéш, він живé, ми живемó, ви живетé, вонú живýть; я читáю, ти читáєш, вонá читáє, ми читáємо, ви читáєте, вонú читáють; я питáю, ти питáєш, він питáє, ми питáємо, ви питáєте, вонú питáють; я дýмаю, ти дýмаєш, вонá дýмає, ми дýмаємо, ви дýмаєте, вонú дýмають; я знáю, ти знáєш, він знáє, ми знáємо, ви знáєте, вонú знáють.

Lesson 2

2b

'Please tell me where the "Odessa" cinema is.'	(self)
'The "Odessa" cinema? I don't know.'	(stranger)
'You don't know?'	(self)
'No. I'm not from Odessa, I'm from Chernihiv.'	(stranger)
'I know: it's on Shevchenko Street.'	(bystander)
'Thanks!'	(self)
'Don't mention it.'	(bystander)

2c

(a) Я живý в Одéсі. (b) Чи ви живетé в квартúрі в Лóндоні? (c) В університéті ми дýмаємо, читáємо, питáємо. (d) Він студéнт, а вонá студéнтка. (e) Так, я з Áнглії; родúна живé в Лóндоні. (f) Вонú з Фрáнції; вонú живýть у Парúжі. (g) Я читáю в кімнáті. (h) Чи ти живéш тут?

2d

(a) живé; (b) де; (c) студéнтка; (d) украї́нець; (e) читáємо; (f) знáєте; (g) я живý; (h) він; (i) телеві́зор; (j) Украї́ни й Одéси.

2e

(a) лондон- + -(н)ець; (b) італій- + -ка; (c) америка- + -н- + -ка; (d) вчи- + -тель.

2f

(a) Дóбрий день! Я студéнт з Áнглії. (b) Ми живемó в Лóндоні. (c) Там є університéт. (d) Я Микóла, з Одéси. (e) В Одéсі такóж є університéт. (f) Чи ви знáєте, де він? (g) Ні, я не знáю. (h) А я знáю, де готéль «Украї́на». (i) Чи ти живéш тут у кімнáті? (j) Так. (k) Я живý в квартúрі; родúна такóж живé тут.

Lesson 3

3a

Examples: Це моя́ мáма, йогó тáто, її́ брат, твоя́ сестрá, наш готéль, ї́хній знайóмий, моє́ ім'я́, вáша кімнáта, її́ кнúжка, мій лист, твій президéнт, ї́хня родúна, йогó університéт, нáша фотогрáфія, вáша шкóла. Чия́ це сестрá? Чий це президéнт? Чиє́ це ім'я́?

3b

працю́єш, працю́ю; живéш, живý; сидúш, не стою́; стоїтé; люблю́, люблю́; рóбиш, пишý; йдéш/йдетé, йдý.

3c

Examples: у магазúні, у бібліотéці, у шкóлі, у музéї, на пóшті, на заводі, на вýлиці.

Lesson 4

4a

(a) Натáлка хóдить до шкóли. (b) Джон живé в Лóндоні. (c) Ми в квартúрі; вонá дýже приє́мна. (d) Вітáльня бі́ля вáнної. (e) Сьогóдні Микóла йдé в університéт. (f) Мій знайóмий читáє в вітáльні.

4b

(a) він стоя́в, вона́ стоя́ла; (b) він чита́в, вона́ чита́ла; (c) він ішо́в, вона́ йшла; (d) він жив, вона жила́; (e) він роби́в, вона́ роби́ла; (f) він ходи́в, вона́ ходи́ла; (g) він знав, вона́ зна́ла; (h) він працюва́в, вона́ працюва́ла; (i) none; (j) він диви́вся, вона́ диви́лася.

4c

(a) хо́дить/йде; (b) Ки́єві; (c) живу́ть, прие́мна; (d) розмовля́ють, ку́хні; (e) Чи ви; (f) сиди́ть, вікна́; (g) ди́виться; (h) відпочива́ємо; (i) ціка́ва; (j) стої́ть, кімна́ті, ду́має.

4e

(a) Ната́лка живе́ в це́нтрі мі́ста. (b) Ми не гово́римо по́льською; ми гово́римо українською. (c) Щодня́ я сні́даю та чита́ю. (d) Я не зна́ю, чому́ вона́ ще хо́дить до шко́ли. (e) Мій друг працю́є в Ло́ндонському Університе́ті. (f) Книжка он там, бі́ля ку́хні. (g) Петро́ з Полта́ви. (h) Лі́да сиди́ть право́руч, бі́ля вікна́. (i) Де Президе́нт і його́ жі́нка? (j) Куди́ ти йдеш?

Lesson 5

5a

студе́нти (студе́нтки), готе́лі, кварти́ри/поме́шкання, університе́ти, кімна́ти, сі́мї/роди́ни, театри, книга́рні, брати́, се́стри, листи́, імена́, заво́ди, інжене́ри, вчителі́/викладачі́ (вчительки/виклада́чки), магази́ни/ крамни́ці, вечори́, міста́, словники́, товариші́, дру́зі, краї́ни.

5b

(a) що, пе́рше занятття́; (b) профе́сора-украї́нця; (c) його́; (d) листи́; (e) none; (f) ва́ші га́рні міста́; (g) її́, Петра́; (h) none; (i) Киї́в, Оде́су, Львів; (j) ти́хий день, ти́ху ніч.

5d

буди́нок, бра́та, лист, маши́ну, кни́жку, О́льгу, дире́ктора, учи́тельку, ба́тька, Петра́, ву́лицю, читача́, ніч, си́на, день, лі́каря.

5e

мій, мого́, мій, мою́, мою́, мою́, мого́, мою́, мого́, мого́, мою́, могó, мою́, могó, мій, могó; наш, нáшого, наш, нáшу, нáшу, нáшу, нáшого, нáшу, нáшого, нáшого, нáшу, нáшого, нáшу, нáшого, наш, нáшого.

5f

Надíє Сергíївно! Мáрку! Пáне профéсоре! Михáйле Володи́мировичу! Ю́рію! Пéтре Семéновичу! Олéксо Григóровичу! Марíє Бори́сівно! Гáле/Гáлю! Тарáсе! Натáлко Михáйлівно! Лéсю!

5g

(a) either; (b) сидíла; (c) either, though написáв then прочитáв might be more likely; (d) дýмаємо; (e) диви́лися; (f) купи́ла; (g) зустрічáлися; (h) працю́ю.

5h

(a) Yesterday he read the book (ambiguous in English). Yesterday he was reading the book. (b) She sat there for a long time. (c) Oleksa wrote a letter, then read an article (ambiguous in English). (d) We're always thinking about him. (e) We watched the film all day. (f) Mother has already bought the bread. (g) Every day they met/would meet here. (h) I'm now working at the post office.

Lesson 6

6b

(a) Мáємо кварти́ру/дáчу/університéт/кáву/чай. У нас немáє кварти́ри/дáчі/університéту/кáви/чáю. (b) Чи ти не купýєш газéти/кни́жки/цýкру/словникá? (c) Я бáчу знайóмого/жíнку/демокрáта/винó. Я не бáчу знайóмого/жíнки/демокрáта/винá.

6c

Він дає́ менí кни́жку; Що вонá кáже íй?; Ти відповідáєш нам; Ви посилáєте йомý лист; Вони́ пи́шуть нам листíвку; Я показáла їм маши́ну.

6d

For example (you can use other foods, of course!): мáєте; немáє; свини́ни; кілогрáм свини́ни; капýсти; кóштує; будь лáска; я́ловичини.

Lesson 7

7a

(a) За́втра я дам ба́тькові ціка́ву кни́жку. (b) Я відпові́в ма́мі. (c) Профе́сор сказа́в студе́нтові, що екза́мена нема́є. (d) Лю́ди посла́ли листи́ в Украї́ну з А́нглії. (e) Вона́ нічо́го не купи́ла дити́ні. (f) Інжене́р пока́зував нам заво́д. (g) Кому́ ти пи́шеш лист? (h) Ма́ма за́вжди́ розповіда́ла йому́ про да́вню Украї́ну.

7b

(a) Ната́лка ча́сто ї́здить по мі́сті маши́ною. (b) Дя́дько та ті́тка живу́ть на да́чі. (c) Коли́ Окса́на була́ в ку́хні, Мико́ла накрива́в на стіл. (d) Това́ришеві здає́ться, що Іва́н ма́є вели́ку маши́ну. (e) Ба́тькові було́ приємно в кварти́рі Ната́лки.

7d

(a) накрива́є; (b) бу́дуть, Ки́єві; (c) мені́, голо́дний; (d) запроси́ла; (e) да́чі, хо́димо/ї́здимо; (f) йому́, знайшо́в; (g) було́; (h) говорю́ украї́нською.

7e

(a) Окса́на знайшла́ свій ключ, коли́ вона́ йшла́ по ву́лиці. (b) Ми ви́рішили за́втра поі́хати до Ки́єва. (c) Петро́ живе́ недале́ко, у це́нтрі мі́ста. (d) Уже́ час пої́сти, тому́ що мені́ ско́ро тре́ба піти́ до заво́ду. (e) Ї́м здає́ться, що мо́жна нічо́го не роби́ти; вони́ про́сто лежа́ть у па́рку. (f) Цьо́го́ ве́чора я хо́чу піти́ до ново́го рестора́ну. (g) Вона́ писа́ла листа́, коли́ він ви́рішив повече́ряти. (h) Навіщо́ мені́ сиді́ти вдо́ма? (i) Мені́ хо́лодно! (j) Тепе́р нам тре́ба пої́хати додо́му.

Lesson 8

8a

(a) Я розмовля́ю англі́йською мо́вою. (b) Я пишу́ ру́чкою. (c) Ми займа́ємося пра́цею. (d) Ти ціка́вишся му́зикою. (e) Я ї́ду маши́ною. (f) Я не працю́ю зимо́ю. (g) Я стою́ пе́ред буди́нком. (h) Я п’ю ка́ву з молоко́м.

8b

gen. sing.; gen. sing.; gen. sing.; nom. sing.; gen. sing. and nom. pl.; gen. sing.; nom. pl.; nom. sing.; nom. sing.; gen. sing.

8d

(a) однá кни́жка; (b) дві кни́жки; (c) три вікнá; (d) чоти́ри студéнти (чéтверо студéнтів); (e) однá студéнтка; (f) два буди́нки; (g) три мі́ста; (h) чоти́ри селá.

8e

(a) Люди́на ї́де до робóти маши́ною. (b) Йогó брати́ займáються математи́кою. (c) Два рóки тáто працю́є на завóді. (d) У вели́кому селі́ чоти́ри ву́лиці. (e) Ми цікáвимося украї́нською мóвою. (f) Мину́лого рóку студéнт ішóвціє́ю ву́лицею. (g) Я даю́ дру́гові три кни́жки. (h) Ми лю́бимо писáти олівцéм.

Lesson 9

9a

сáдом; сéрцем; телебáченням; банду́рою; ві́дповіддю; дощéм; дурни́цею; кінцéм; картóплею; кі́стю; конферéнцією; герóєм; папéром.

9b

(a) йдемó; (b) ходи́ла; (c) йдéш; (d) прихóдить; (e) ніс. There are other possibilities.

9c

In the bathroom Oksana turns on the light: she finds the switch by the wash-basin. There she sees the bath, the toilet, a mirror (over the wash-basin), and a towel rail; in the bathroom there is also a very new shower. Oksana tries everything, and it turns out that there is hot and cold water (everything works!). On the rail there are towels, but there is neither soap nor toilet paper: fortunately she brings her own soap, but the paper has to be got from the floor lady. Other things which Oksana takes from her suitcase are shampoo, toothpaste and brush, and deodorant, and she puts them alongside the soap. In his room John also unpacks his suitcase, and puts the same things on a shelf in the bathroom, plus his razor and shaving brush.

9d

(a) За мі́сяць ми прочита́ємо цю кни́жку, ко́жну сторі́нку. (b) Ця ва́нна мала́, а га́рна; мені́ подо́бається ра́ковина. (c) Чи ти спро́бувала гаря́чу во́ду? (d) Ні, але́ я подиви́вся телеві́зор; він працю́є! (e) Іва́н сказа́в, що че́рез ти́ждень він приї́де маши́ною. (f) Моя́ кімна́та не ду́же вели́ка: я ма́ю книжки́, валі́зки та й і́нші ре́чі. (g) По́руч з лі́жком є телефо́н; над лі́жком є ла́мпа. (h) Пе́ред вікно́м є мали́й стіл; на ньо́му я пишу́ листи́. (i) Чим ви ціка́витеся? Му́зикою? Істо́рією? Украї́нською мо́вою? (j) Що вам принести́? Ка́ви? Мінера́льної води́?

Lesson 10

10a

(a) украї́нців; (b) вели́ких міст; (c) мину́лих ро́ків, англі́йців; (d) пита́нь; (e) ві́дповідей, праць; (f) раз(і́в); (g) кімна́т; (h) ножі́в, виде́лок, ло́жо́к; (i) слів; (j) карбо́ванців.

10b

(a) покажи́/покажі́ть; (b) забу́дь(те); (c) іди́/іді́ть; (d) захо́дь; (e) дава́й(те); (f) пиши́/пиші́ть; (g) одяга́йся/одяга́йтеся; (h) прочита́й(те); (i) ви́ріш(те) (or вирі́шувай(те)); (j) знайди́ (possibly знайді́ть).

Lesson 11

11a

Examples: (a) Вона́ живе́ на да́чі, яка́ знахо́диться на Полта́вщині. (b) Джон телефону́є до ді́вчини, з яко́ю він познайо́мився вчо́ра. (c) Ось той чолові́к, яки́й до́бре зна́є Ната́лку. (d) Я чита́ю підру́чник, яки́й я купи́в у цій книга́рні. (e) У саду́, яки́й бі́ля рі́чки, стоя́ть дере́ва. (f) Мені́ подо́бається хло́пець, що йому́ я дав я́блуко. (g) Ми знайшли́ цю статтю́, яку́ вона́ шука́ла. (h) Покажі́ть мені́ кварти́ру, що в ній вони́ коли́сь жили́. (i) До Ха́ркова приї́хали два хло́пці, які́ купи́ли ба́тькові маши́ну. (j) Ви зроби́ли ма́йже всі впра́ви, які́ вона́ написа́ла до ціє́ї ле́кції.

11b

за де́сять дев'я́та; шо́ста; (о) пів на деся́ту; о дев'я́тій; о деся́тій.

11c
(a) за двáдцять одинáдцята вéчора; (b) чверть на дрýгу нóчі; (c) пів по дрýгій дня; (d) вóсьма рáнку; (e) сьóма вéчора; (f) двáдцять п'ять на одинáдцяту вéчора; (g) дéсять по п'ятій рáнку; (h) за чверть четвéрта дня; (i) п'ять по дев'ятій рáнку; (j) двáдцять на п'яту рáнку; (k) шістнáдцять по дванáдцятій дня; (l) за дéсять сьóма вéчора. And so on.

11e
These are quite straightforward if you follow the rules. Do watch out for that of **дочкá**, namely **доччи́н**:
Богдáнів, Макси́мів, Степáнів, Катери́нин, Тетя́нин, Катрýсін, Олéксин, Олéксів, Валенти́нин, Оксáнин, си́нів, Вáлін, Дми́трів вщт Дмитрóва, Пéтрів - Петрóва, Зінáїдин, Олéнин, доччи́н/-нá, Слáвин, Євгéнів, Семéнів, Іри́нин, Ярослáвин, мáмин, Зі́нин.

Lesson 12

12b
(a) Позавчóра ввéчері я зустрі́вся з Óльгою. (b) Минýлого рóку (мені́ здає́ться, що в сі́чні) я прочитáв цікáву кни́жку. (c) У ли́пні (це влі́тку) ми відпочивáємо. (d) Котрé числó булó вчóра? (e) Котрóго числá приї́хала Оксáна до Украї́ни з Áнглії? (f) Післязáвтра (мáбýть врáнці), абó мáбýть настýпного ти́жня, я зателефонýю до тéбе.

12c
(a) дрýге лю́того ти́сяча дев'ятсóт дев'янóсто четвéртого рóку (b) трéтє сéрпня ... сімдеся́т вóсьмого рóку (c) шістнáдцяте сі́чня дві ти́сячі пéршого рóку (d) двáдцять вóсьме вéресня ... дев'янóстого рóку (e) вóсьме грýдня ... шістдеся́т вóсьмого рóку (f) п'я́те ли́пня ... сóрок пéршого рóку (g) дев'я́те чéрвня ... дев'ятнáдцятого рóку (h) двáдцять сьóме трáвня ... п'ятдеся́того рóку (i) вісімнáдцяте бéрезня ... п'ятдеся́т сьóмого рóку (j) двáдцять пéрше кві́тня ... дев'янóсто п'я́того рóку (k) сьóме листопáда ... вісімдеся́т шóстого рóку (l) три́дцять пéрше жóвтня ... дев'янóсто вóсьмого рóку.

12d

Simply put the first ordinal into the genitive: дру́гого, тре́тього, шістна́дцятого, два́дцять во́сьмого, во́сьмого, п'я́того, дев'я́того, два́дцять сьо́мого, вісімна́дцятого, два́дцять пе́ршого, сьо́мого, три́дцять пе́ршого.

12e

(a) Я змо́жу купува́ти проду́кти за́втра. (b) Я му́шу поі́хати до Ки́єва, бо ті́льки там вони́ мо́жуть допомага́ти мені́. (c) Да́йте, будь ла́ска, ваш план мі́ста. Я зали́шив мій (свій) удо́ма. (d) Не ва́рто тут вече́ряти; несма́чно ва́рять/готу́ють. (e) Я так раді́ю, що ти знахо́диш кни́жку ціка́вою. (f) Я зго́ден, що він пови́нен поі́хати, але́ чи ти пе́вна, що його́ сестра́ кра́ще й шви́дше бу́де працюва́ти. (g) Я не вмі́ю друкува́ти на маши́нці, тому́ му́шу переда́ти доку́мент на́шій секрета́рці. (h) На жа́ль, нам довело́ся піти́ в кав'я́рню. (i) Скажі́ть, чи ви вмі́єте говори́ти украї́нською?

12f

(a) Ба́тько приї́хав з ма́мою до Ки́єва. (b) За́втра ввече́рі ході́мо до кі́но диви́тися фільм. (c) О́льга сиди́ть поза́ду, ліво́руч від вікна́. (d) Трина́дцятого жо́втня Петро́ поі́хав з Оде́си. (e) Яки́й він із се́бе? Він висо́кий, товсти́й. (f) Вона́ купи́ла бага́то книжо́к у книга́рні. (g) Мої́ батьки́ тепе́р ме́шкають на да́чі. (h) Ми зустрі́ли її́ сесте́р на база́рі. (i) Яко́го ко́льору цей телефо́н? Він жо́втий. (j) Я пе́вна, що він до нас за́йде.

Lesson 13

13a

(a) центра́льним, -ими, -их бульва́рам, -ами, -ах (b) і́ншим, -ими, -их райо́нам, -ами, -ах (c) незале́жним, -ими, -их держа́вам, -ами, -ах (d) вузьки́м, -и́ми, -и́х доро́гам, -ами, -ах (e) суча́сним, -ими, -их мі́стам, -ами, -ах (f) за́втрашнім, -іми, -ціх газе́там, -ами, -ах (g) цим, ци́ми, цих англі́йцям, -ями, -ях (h) цим, ци́ми, цих америка́нкам, -ами, -ах (i) нови́м, -и́ми, -и́х маши́нам, -ами, -ах (j) четве́ртим, -ими, -их ле́кціям, -ями, -ях

13c
(a) столі́в два; (b) книжо́к дві; (c) домі́в п'ять; (d) буди́нків три; (e) міст де́сять.

13e
готе́лі, самі́, потрі́бно було́, пішли́, вели́кий, Продаве́ць, нема́є, ву́лиці, знайшли́, купи́ли, звари́ли, до́вго, шука́ли, було́, шко́лу.

13f
(a) (най)бі́льший, -ше; (b) (най)кра́щий, -ще; (c) (най)ме́нший, -ше; (d) (най)міцні́ший, -ше.

13g
Ключі́, чергово́ї, показа́ла, кімна́ту, відійшла́, відчини́в, две́рі, свою́, столі́, була́, насті́льна, поба́чив, лі́жко, стіл, цій, кімна́ті, удо́ма, одна́, працю́є, ви́рішив, чергову́.

13h
ва́нній, увімкну́ла, сві́тло, ба́чила, ра́ковину, ві́шалку для рушникі́в, було́, ми́ла, туале́тного папе́ру, На, привезла́, свій, папі́р, валі́зки, ви́йняла, зубну́, щі́тку, свої́й, кімна́ті, розпакува́в, свою́, валі́зку.

13i
знахо́диться, Дніпро́м, Ки́єва, літако́м, по́їздом, маши́ною, мі́сті, аеропо́рт, авто́бусний, де, зупини́тися, це́нтрі, готе́ль, бли́зько, бага́то, готе́лів, напри́клад, суча́сним мі́стом, спра́вжньою, столи́цею, держа́ви.

13j
(a) прийти́, я прийду́, вони́ при́йдуть (b) попрацюва́ти, я попрацю́ю, вони́ попрацю́ють (c) відчиня́ти, я відчиня́ю, вони́ відчиня́ють (d) зрозумі́ти, я зрозумі́ю, вони́ зрозумі́ють (e) бра́ти, я беру́, вони́ беру́ть (f) дава́ти, я даю́, вони́ даю́ть (g) поба́чити, я поба́чу, вони́ поба́чать (h) відповіда́ти, я відповіда́ю, вони́ відповіда́ють (i) зготува́ти, я зготу́ю, вони́ зготу́ють (j) накрива́ти, я накрива́ю, вони накрива́ють.

13k

(a) пога́ний; (b) вимика́ти; (c) ма́ти; (d) відповіда́ти; (e) оде́ржати (or отри́мати); (f) вели́кий; (g) брат; (h) прихо́дити: (i) до́нька; (j) діду́сь; (k) чита́ти; (l) чолові́к; (m) гі́рше; (n) ді́ти; (o) найме́нш; (p) за́втра.

13l

For example (some are interchangeable): o, h, p, m, n, g, k, i, f, b, a, c, l, d, j, e.

13m

студе́нтки; англі́йських студе́нтів; голо́дних чолові́к; ві́льні мі́сця; склянки; тарі́лки; меню́; серве́тки; копі́йки; копі́йок; карбо́ванці; копі́йка; копі́йок; скля́нки; карбо́ванців.

Lesson 14

14a

(a) Якщо́ я піду́ на конце́рт, Зіна бу́де ду́же ра́да. (b) Якщо́ ді́ти вже прийшли́ з шко́ли, то батьки́ вече́ряють. (c) Якби́ вона́ не ме́шкала там, нам було́ б ду́же прие́мно. (d) Якщо́ Богда́н спита́є мене́, де я живу́, я не скажу́ йому́. (e) Якби́ Груше́вський не написа́в свої́х книжо́к, ми ме́нше зна́ли б про істо́рію Украї́ни. (f) Якщо́ в ме́не не бу́де вака́цій, я не змо́жу поїхати до Фра́нції. (g) Якщо́ Лі́да ще не поверну́лася додо́му, вона́ гра́є з і́ншими дітьми́. (h) Ми були́ б в Іспа́нії, якби́ ми ма́ли час на це. (i) Якщо́ він не зна́йде підру́чника, він не змо́же ви́йти сього́дні зі Сла́вою. (j) Якщо́ ми закінчимо́ впра́ву, ми бу́демо зо́всім уто́млені.

14b

– Я бу́ду вдо́ма о дев'я́тій.
– Але́ я хо́чу ви́йти на конце́рт. Чи ти встиѓнеш приготува́ти мою́ вече́рю?
– ... Ти жарту́єш. Ти не той чолові́к, яко́го я так до́бре зна́ю.
– Я зго́ден, бо я таки́й уто́млений.

14c

(a) Він сказа́в мені́, щоб я прочита́в кни́жку сього́дні вве́чері. (b) Я запита́в її́ пе́ред тим, як він прийшо́в додо́му. (c) Робі́ це так, щоб ми встúгли трóшки відпочúти пізнíше. (d) Я люблю́ Кúїв, бо це такé гáрне мíсто. (e) Незважáючи на те, що я хóчу вам повíрити, я прóсто не мóжу. (f) Хочá ти мій друг, я прóсто не згóдний з Тобóю. (g) Вонá вислóвлює своЇ дýмки, мов вонá наспрáвді розумíє стан справ. (h) Я знáю, що ти хóчеш сказáти. (i) Вона запізнúлася завдя́ки тóму, що її́ бáтько хотíв порозмовля́ти з нéю. (j) Чому вам трéба взя́ти такí книжкú, я прóсто не знáю.

14d

Where there are seven nannies, there is a child without a head.
(If) you hurry, you will make people laugh.
Don't say 'hop' until you jump over.
It did not happen (turn out) as it was desired.
Don't go chasing after two hares, for you will not catch any (either).

Lesson 15

15a

(a) A=Білорýсь; B=Словáччина; C=Молдóва; D=Росíя; E=Пóльща; F=Румýнія; G=Угóрщина.
(b) 1=Луцьк; 2=Рíвне; 3=Житóмир; 4=Кúїв; 5=Чернíгів; 6=Сýми; 7=Хáрків; 8=Лугáнськ; 9=Ýжгород; 10=Львів; 11=Тернóпіль; 12=Хмельнúцьк; 13=Вíнниця; 14=Черкáси; 15=Полтáва; 16=Івáно-Франкíвськ; 17=Чернівцí; 18=Кіровогрáд; 19=Дніпропетрóвськ; 20=Донéцьк; 21=Одéса; 22=Миколáїв; 23=Херсóн; 24=Запорíжжя; 25=Сімферóполь; 26=Севастóполь.
(c) a=Лýцька; b=Рíвненська; c=Житóмирська; d=Кúївська; e=Чернíгівська; f=Сýмська; g=Хáрківська; h=Лугáнська; j=Львíвська; k=Тернóпільська; l=Хмельнúцька; m= Вíнницька; n=Черкáська; o=Полтáвська; p=Закарпáтська; q=Івáно-Франкíвська; r=Чернівéцька; s=Кіровогрáдська; t=Дніпропетрóвська; u=Донéцька; v=Одéська; w= Миколáївська; x=Херсóнська; y=Запорíзька; z=Крим.
(d) I=Азóвське мóре; II=Чóрне мóре.
(e) i=Дніпрó; ii=Деснá; iii=Сейм; iv=Прúп'ять; v=Горúнь; vi=Півдéнний Буг; vii=Інгулéць; viii=Дон; ix=Кубáнь; x=Дунáй; xi=Прут; xii=Сірéт; xiii=Дністéр; xiv=Тúса; xv=Сíверний Донéць; xvi=Зáхідній Буг; xvii=Сулá; xviii=Псел; xix=Вóрскла.
(f) α=Кахóвське водосхóвище; β=Кременчýцьке водосхóвище; γ=Кúївське водосхóвище; δ=Печенíзьке водосхóвище.

15b

(a) Коли́ я прийшо́в до теа́тру, дру́зі вже ввійшли́. (b) Миха́йло сиди́ть удо́ма, бо він хворі́є. (c) О́ля купи́ла кни́жку, але́ ніхто́ не хо́че чита́ти її́. (d) Він живе́ в Ки́єві, бо він ду́же лю́бить це мі́сто. (e) Вона́ повече́ряла, по́тім вона́ пішла́ до о́перного теа́тру послу́хати о́перу. (f) Коли́ ми знайшли́ маши́ну, ми були́ ду́же ра́ді. (g) Була́ во́сьма годи́на, тому́ ми ви́рішили подиви́тися переда́чу. (h) Він пі́де в університе́т, хоча́ він не знайшо́в підру́чника вдо́ма.

15c

(a) Так, вона́ лежи́ть там. (b) Так, він дале́ко ві́дти. (c) Так, вони́ впада́ють туди́. (d) Так, вона́ прито́ка Дніпра́.

Lesson 17

17a

(a) double bass, (b) flute, (c) saxophone, (d) cymbals, (e) trumpet, (f) viola, (g) cello, (h) bandura, (i) sopilka, fife, (j) accordion, (k) mouth organ, harmonica, (l) hockey, (m) chess, (n) volleyball, (o) tig, (p) jacks, (q) football, (r) marbles, (s) baseball, (t) hide and seek, (u) draughts, checkers.

17b

(a) Щодня́ я вожу́ Га́лю до бібліоте́ки; ми ї́здимо маши́ною. (b) Він прилеті́в учо́ра; він приві́з мені́ нови́й украї́нський словни́к. (c) Чи ти но́сиш свою́ дити́ну, коли́ гуля́єш у па́рку? (d) Ні, вона́ вже хо́дить. (e) Уве́чері грузови́к в'ї́хав у мі́сто; у ньо́му був хліб для люде́й. (f) Чи А́нглія вво́зить газ? (g) Ні, ми на́віть виво́зимо газ!

Lesson 18

18a

(a) Окса́на розмовля́є з Бондарчука́ми, Олекса́ндром та Есфі́р. (b) Ї́х п'ять (п'я́теро). (c) У лі́сі. (d) Нічо́го! (e) (Мо́же) на поча́тку столі́ття. (f) У/в збідні́лого росі́йського аристокра́та. (g) Про приро́ду, про да́чу. (h) Так, я б хоті́в/хоті́ла...

18b

зро́блений, ви́питий, зна́йдений, пошу́каний, збудо́ваний, (піти́ is intransitive), ку́плений, прочи́таний, (розмовля́ти is intransitive), узя́тий, ви́словлений.

18c

(a) День незалéжності Украї́ни. (b) Сприя́тливі умо́ви для відпочи́нку. (c) На підприє́мствах, в устано́вах, організа́ціях. (d) День відпочи́нку. (e) Якщо́ робо́та компенсу́ється. (f) Або́ і́нший день відпочи́нку, або́ гро́ші.

18d

(a) Я розмовля́в з Іва́ном Сергі́йовичем. (b) Окса́на познайо́мила мене́ із свої́м викладаче́м, Га́нною Петрі́вною. (c) Я зо́всім не зна́ю па́ні Прокопо́вич. (d) Я така́ ра́да, що Мико́ли Савчука́ тут нема́є. (e) Люди́на з таки́м прі́звищем, як «Голубе́нко», ча́сто зі схі́дної Украї́ни. (f) Славко́ й Есфі́р Бондарчуки́, як Ні́на Прокопо́вич, з за́хідної Украї́ни. (g) Ната́лка Микола́єва тако́ж з за́хідної Украї́ни. (h) І́гор Свищу́к живе́ під Оде́сою, у півде́нній Украї́ні.

18e

(a) Знайшо́вши бра́та, він поверну́вся з ним додо́му. (b) Ми поїхали за мі́сто до села́, де ми провели́ ти́ждень. (c) Оскі́льки сестра́ бажа́є попрацюва́ти за кордо́ном, вона́ пови́нна порозмовля́ти з батька́ми про робо́ту там. (d) Коли́ ми пообі́дали, вона́ показа́ла мені́ свою кни́жку. (e) Прочита́вши про око́лиці Ки́єва, ви дізна́лися, що Пу́ща-Води́ця недале́ко. (f) Коли́ я зга́дую часи́ ві́льної Украї́ни, я роблю́ся тако́ю сумно́ю. (g) Проки́нувшись о сьо́мій, Петро́ шви́дко поми́вся та поголи́вся.

18f

What follows is a slightly edited version of an actual leaflet distributed just before the elections:

14 жовтня — Всі на вибори!
Кандидат у народні депутати України

ЮРІЙ ЩЕРБАК

українець, безпартійний. Письменник, доктор медичних наук. Голова української екологічної асоціації «Зелений світ».

Він потрібен Україні!

Lesson 19

19a

Колú я приї́хав до ї́хньої дáчі, Олексáндр сидíв там на верáнді та читáв. Він подивúвся на мéне та всміхнýвся. Я знав, що він дýже рáдий, що я вúрішив поговорúти з ним про питáння могó життя́ за кордóном. «Сідáй! – сказáв він. – Есфíр зі своїм брáтом в селí. Ми порозмовля́ємо, колú вонá повéрнеться.» На верáнді булú дві стільцí. Сíвши, я сказáв Олексáндрові про тих трьох чоловíків, які́ рáптом вúйшли з селá вчóра.

19b

(a) З далéких краї́н; з КНР та з Монгóлії. (b) Що ýряд КНР єдúний і закóнний ýряд Китáю. (c) Три дні. (d) Нúнішній стан та перспектúви розвúтку двосторóннього співробітнúцтва. (e) В Австрáлії.

Lesson 20

20a

(a) До Кúєва. (b) Відпочивáють, лежáть на травí, розмовля́ють. (c) Про настýпний етáп ї́хньої мандрíвки по Україні. (d) Вонú покáзують Джóнові кнúжку. (e) Дарýють їм квíти.

20b

(a) У двадцятú домáх. (b) Вісімнáдцять підрýчників. (c) Дáйте двáдцять три олівцí. (d) Вонá бáчить тридцятьóх сімóх студéнтів. (e) У тих восьмú магазúнах. (f) Усíм сорокá дев'ятьóм украї́нцям. (g) Тúсяча дев'ятсóт дев'янóсто трéтій рік. (h) До цéнтру пíдеш двомá вýлицями. (i) Там живé шістдеся́т дéв'ять інженéрів. (j) Цúми дня́ми я вчýся тíльки однóї мóви.

20c

(a) Чомý він нічóго не знáє про істóрію Украї́ни? (b) Якбú я міг, я був би там якнайскорíше. (c) Не вáрто читáти знáчно бíльше про Кúїв. (d) Розмовля́ючи з дрýгом, я дізнáвся, що ніхтó не хотíв повернýтися додóму. (e) Сьогóдні він почувáє себé трíшки крáще. (f) Захóдь, будь лáска, ти ж зáвждú кáжеш, що тобí нíколи. (g) Я нíколи не був у Чернівця́х. (h) Як далéко від Львóва до Івáна-Франкíвська? (i) Читáй цю кнúжку якнайповíльніше; вонá такá цікáва. (j) Усí хóчуть провестú лíто бíля óзера абó мóря.

Ukrainian–English glossary

The Ukrainian–English glossary is based on the words found in the dialogues, texts, and readings. It is far from being a complete list, and on the whole includes only those words that we felt might usefully be repeated here. Some useful words not included will be found grouped thematically, in individual lessons. Look up words in **в/у** in both sections. We have varied them on purpose.

The English–Ukrainian glossary is intended to be useful, if not exhaustively so, when doing the exercises.

а	and, but; and how about...?
а то	or else, because (in the sense: 'if you don't you'll...')
або́ ж... або́ ж...	either... or...
або́	or
авіапо́шта, -и	air mail (**авіапо́штою** 'by air mail')
авто́бус, -а	bus
авто́ма́т, -а для розмі́ну гро́шей	machine giving change
автомаши́на, -и	car
адре́са, -и	address
аеропо́рт, -у	airport
акредити́в, -а	traveller's cheque
але́	but
але́я, -ї	path, garden path
америка́нець, -нця	American (male)
америка́нка, -и	American (female)
англі́єць, -і́йця	Englishman
англі́йка, -и	Englishwoman
анке́та, -и	application form, questionnaire
ая́кже	of course!
бабу́ся, -і	grandmother
бага́тий	rich
бага́то	much, many (+gen. sing. or pl.)
бажа́ти, -а́є-	wish (perf. **побажа́ти, -а́є-**)
база́р, -у	market (cf. **ри́нок, -нку** 'market place/square')
байду́же	indifferent, not to care less (subject in the dat.)

батькѝ, -і́в	parents (pl. of **ба́тько**)
ба́тько, -а	father
ба́чити, -и-	see
бензѝн, -у	petrol, (Amer.) gasoline
бензоколо́нка, -и	petrol station/pump
без	without (prep. + gen.)
безсумні́вно	without doubt
бібліоте́ка, -и	library
бі́лий	white
бі́льше	more
бі́льше не, вже не	no longer, not any longer
бі́ля + gen.	about, approximately
бі́ля + gen.	near
блакѝтний	blue
близькѝй	near
блѝзько	near(by)
блискавѝця, -і	(flash of) lightning
блідѝй	pale
бо	because, for
Бог, -а	God
болі́ти, -ѝ-, imperf.	ache
борщ, -у́	borshch, borsht
брат, -а	brother
брѝтва, -и	razor
будѝнок, -нку	building
буді́вля, -і	building
будува́ти, -у́є, imperf.	build (perf. **збудува́ти, -у́є-**)
бульва́р, -у	boulevard
бу́ря, -і	storm
бу́ти	be
бу́ти в + loc.	be wearing
в час відпочѝнку	when not working, during rest-time
вага́тися, -а́є-, imperf.	hesitate
ва́жко	difficult (it is)
важлѝвий	important
вака́ції, -ій, pl.	holidays, vacation
валі́зка, и	suitcase
ва́нна, -ої	bathroom (declined like an adj.), bath (declined like a noun)
варе́ник, -а	dumpling with filling
ва́ртість, -ості	value, cost
ва́рто	it's worth (neg. 'there's no point in, it's not worth')
ваш	your
вважа́ти, -а́є-	consider
ввесь, все, вся (у-)	all; the whole
вве́чері, уве́чері	in the evening
вво́дити, -и-, imperf.	introduce, bring in (perf. **ввестѝ, -де́-**)
вдо́ма	at home
вдяга́ти, -а́є-, perf. **вдягну́ти, -не-**	put (something on) (followed by the accusative)
везтѝ, -зе́-	take by vehicle (det.)
Велѝкдень, Велико́дня	Easter
велѝкий	big
велосипе́д, -а	bicycle
вера́нда, -и	veranda
ве́село	pleasant, fun ('it's . . .')

веснá	spring
веснóю	in spring
вечéря, -і	supper, dinner
вечéряти, -яє-	have dinner/supper (perf. **повечéряти**)
вéчір, -чора	evening
вже	already
вжúти, -вé-, perf.	use, make use of (imperf. **уживáти, -áє-**)
взагалі́	in general, on the whole
взúмку	in winter
взя́ти, візьмý, ві́зьмеш, perf.	take (imperf. **брáти, берé-**)
ви	you (sing., polite; pl.)
вúбачте	excuse me, pardon
виглядáти	look (+ instr. 'sad, etc.'; + **на** + acc. of a noun 'like a . . .'; **дóбре** 'well')
вигравáти, -аé-, imperf.	win (perf. **вúграти, -ає-**)
видéлка, -и	fork
вúдужати, -ає-, perf.	get better, recover (from illness)
визначнúй	outstanding, eminent, excellent (person)
вúйняти, вúйме-, perf.	take out (imperf. **виймáти, -áє-**)
вúїхáти, -де-	leave, depart from (+ **з** + gen.)
викладáти, -áє-, imperf.	teach (higher/further education)
викладáч, -á	lecturer, teacher
вúникнути, -не-, perf.	emerge, crop up (imperf. **виникáти, -áє-**)
винó, -á	wine
вирі́шувати, -ує-, imperf.	discuss, (try to) decide (perf. **вúрішити, -и-**)
вúсіти, -и-/-ú-	hang (intrans.)
вислóвлювати, -ує-, imperf.	express (perf. **вúсловити, -и-**)
висóкий	tall, high
витрúмувати, -ує-, imperf.	bear, hold out (perf. **вúтримати, -ає-**)
вихóдити, вúйти (з + gen.)	get out/off
вúявитися, -и-, perf.	turn out
від + gen.	than
від... + gen. **до...** + gen.	from... to... (**з . . . до . . .** with verbs of motion)
відбýти, -де- пóдорож	make a journey (perf.)
відбýтися, -де-, perf.	take place (imperf. відбувáтися, -áє-)
відві́дати, -ає-, perf.	visit, call on (imperf. відві́дувати, -ує-)
ві́дділ, -у	department, section
ві́дділ, -у самообслугó-вування	self-service department
відкладáти, -áє-, imperf.	postpone (perf. **відклáсти, -дé-**)

відкри́ти, -и́є-, perf.	reveal (imperf. **відкрива́ти, -а́є-**)
відо́мий	famous
відповіда́ти, -а́є-, imperf.	reply (perf. **відпові́сти́**)
відпочива́ти, -а́є-, imperf.	rest (perf. **відпочи́ти, -и́не-**)
відправля́ти, -я́є-	send (perf. **відпра́вити, -и-**)
відсила́ти, -а́є-, imperf.	send (perf. **відісла́ти, -шле-**)
відчини́ти, -и-, perf.	open (imperf. **відчиня́ти, -я́є-**)
візи́тна ка́ртка	hotel room card (usually to be shown when requesting your key)
вік, -у	age
віко́нце, -я	window (for service)
ві́льний	free
він	he, it
ві́рити, -и-, imperf.	believe (+ dat.)
ві́рно	true (it is true)
вла́сний	own (one's own)
віта́льна листі́вка, -ої -и	greetings card
віта́льня, -і	sitting room, drawing room
віта́ю!	hello! (lit. 'I welcome'; also + acc. + **з** + instr.

	'congratulate someone on something')
ві́шалка, -и для рушникі́в	towel rod, rack
влі́тку	in summer
вночі́	during the night
водно́ча́с	simultaneously, at one and the same time
вокза́л, -у	railway station
воло́сся, -я, neut.	hair
вона́	she, it
вони́	they
воно́	it
восени́ (у восени́)	in autumn/fall
впе́рше	for the first time
вплива́ти, -а́є-, imperf. **на** + acc.	influence, have an influence on (perf. **вплинути, -не-**)
впра́ва, -и	exercise
вродли́вий	handsome, beautiful
вра́нці	in the morning
все	everything (nom/acc sing. neut. of **(у)весь, вся, все, всі** 'all')
все в поря́дку	everything's fine (lit. 'in order')
все́-таки	all the same, nonetheless
всміхну́тися, -не́-, perf.	smile (imperf. **всміха́тися, -а́є-**)
встига́ти, -а́є-, imperf.	manage to, succeed in

	(perf. **вcти́гнути, -не-**; past **-г-**)
вступа́ти, -а́є-, imperf.	join (perf. **вступи́ти, -и-**)
всіля́кий	every kind of
вся́кий	all sorts of
вто́млений	tired
вузьки́й	narrow
вча́сно	in time; just at the right time, timely (with negative, 'at the wrong time')
вчи́тель, -я	teacher
вчи́ти, -и-/-и́-, imperf.	teach (+ acc. + gen. 'someone something'; see **учи́тися**)
вчо́ра	yesterday
гада́ти, -а́є-, imperf.	(here) think, be of the opinion
газе́та, -и	newspaper
га́зова плита́, -ої -и́	gas cooker (Amer. gas stove)
га́лло́!	hello (on the telephone)
га́льба, -и	pint (actually 'half a litre')
гамане́ць, -нця́	purse
гара́зд	fine, OK, yes (also **до́бре**)
га́рний	fine, beautiful, nice
га́рно	nice
гаря́чий	hot (as in water)
геогра́фія, -ї	geography
геть	completely, utterly, a great deal
геть	away (interjection)
гість, го́стя	guest
годи́на, -и	hour
годи́нник, -а	clock
голи́тися, -и-, imperf.	shave (perf. **поголи́тися, -и-**)
голова́, -и́ (acc. **го́лову**)	head
головне́	principally, mainly, the main thing
головни́й	main, principal
голо́дний	hungry
голуби́й	light blue
гора́, -и́	mountain, hill
горо́д, -у	kitchen garden (note **на** + loc. 'in')
го́стрий	sharp
готе́ль, -ю	hotel
гото́в, -а, -е	ready, prepared
готува́ти, -у́є-, imperf.	prepare, cook (perf. **при-/з-готува́ти, -у́є-**)
гра́дус, -а	degree
грам, -а	gram
гра́ти, -а́є-, imperf.	play (perf. **зігра́ти, -а́є-** 'to have/finish a game (of)')
гри́вня, -і	hryvnia, future Ukrainian currency
гро́ші, -ей	money
грузови́к, -а́	lorry, truck
гру́ша, -і	pear tree, pear
гуля́ти, -я́є-, imperf.	walk, go for a walk

дава́ти, -ає́-, imperf.	give (perf. **да́ти, дам...** (irreg.))
да́вній	ancient
давно́	long ago
да́ча, -і	dacha
да́йте + product, adding **будь ла́ска**	give..., please
дале́ко	far (away)
да́лі	further
дарува́ти, -у́є-, imperf.	give (as a present) (perf. **подарува́ти, -у́є-**)
да́ти, дам, дасть, perf. irreg.	give (imperf. **дава́ти, -ає́-**)
дба́ти, -а́є-, imperf. **про** + acc.	care about, look after
две́рі, -е́й	door (plural form only in Ukrainian)
де	where
дебе́лий	stout, fat
де́кілька	several, a few (+gen. pl.)
де́куди	here and there
день, дня наро́дження	birthday
де́рево, -а	tree
держа́ва, -и	state, country
держа́ти, -и-, imperf.	keep, hold
десь	somewhere around, approximately, somewhere
де́який	some (kind of), a certain

де́хто, де́кого	some people
дзвіно́к, -нка́	call
дзе́ркало, а	mirror
диви́тися, -и-, imperf.	watch (+acc.), look at (+ **на** + acc.)
ди́вно	strange (it is strange)
діало́г, -у	dialogue
ді́вчина, -и	girl
діду́сь, -я́	grandfather
дізна́тися, -а́є-, perf.	find out (imperf. **дізнава́тися,** -ає́-)
діста́ти, діста́не-, perf.	receive (imperf. **дістава́ти, -ає́-**; + **наза́д** ‘get back, recover’)
ді́ти, -е́й	children (singular **дити́на, -и-**)
до + gen.	before (in time expressions)
до + gen.	to, up to, until, before
до запита́ння	poste restante
до зу́стрічі!	until we meet again!
до поба́чення	goodbye
до ре́чі	by the way
добра́тися, -бере́-, perf. **до** + gen.	get to, reach
до́бре	fine, good (adv.)
до́брий	good
до́вгий	long
до́вго	for a long time
довідко́ве бюро́, -ого -о́	information (office) (**бюро́** is indeclinable)
дові́дник, -а	information booklet,

	reference handbook
дово́дитися, -и-, imperf.	have to, happen to have to, fall to one's lot to (with the subject in the dative; perf. **довести́ся, -де́-**)
додо́му	home(wards) (i.e. movement towards home)
доі́хати, -ї́ду, -ї́деш, perf.	drive up to, as far as (imperf. **доїжджа́ти, -а́є-**)
до́лар, -а	dollar
домо́витися, -и-, perf.	arrange, agree (**про** + acc. '(about) something')
до́ня, -і; до́нька, -и; дочка́, -и́	daughter
допи́тливий	curious, inquisitive
допомага́ти, -а́є-, imperf.	help (perf. **допомогти́, -же-**) (+ dat.)
допомо́га, -и	help **за допомо́гою** + gen. 'with the help of'
доро́га, -и	way, trip, journey
дороги́й	expensive
до́сить	quite, enough
дощ, -у́	rain
дощи́ти, дощи́ть/дощи́ло, imperf.	rain
дрібні́ гро́ші, -и́х -ей	small change
друг, -а, pl. **дру́зі, -ів**	friend
дру́гий	second
дру́же	friend (masc.) (voc.)
дружи́на, -и	spouse (masc. or fem.)
друкува́ти, -у́є- (на маши́нці)	type (imperf.)
ду́же	very
ду́мати, -ає-, imperf.	think
ду́мка, -и	opinion, thought, idea
ду́шно	close, stifling
дя́кую	thanks
електри́чка, -и	train (suburban)
епо́ха, -и	epoch, period
ета́п, -у	stage
євре́йський	Jewish
ж	and, but (after a consonant we have же)
жа́рко	hot (weather)
жартува́ти, -у́є-, imperf.	joke (perf. **пожартува́ти, -у́є-**)
жи́ти, -ве́-	live
життя́, -я́ neut.	life
жі́нка, -и	wife, woman
жіно́чий	women's, female, feminine
жо́втий	yellow
з + gen.	from, out of (see **від**)
з + acc.	about, approximately

з + instr.	with
з ча́сом	gradually, lit. 'with time'
за + acc.	than
за + instr./acc.	behind
за кордо́н(ом)	abroad (motion + acc., no motion + instr.; from abroad **з-за кордо́ну**)
за мі́сто	out of town (movement; **за мі́стом** 'in the countryside, out of town' (no movement))
зава(д)жа́ти, -а́є-, imperf.	pester, prevent, get in the way of (perf. **зава́дити, -и-**) (+ dat.)
завести́, -де́-, perf. **поря́док**	tidy up (imperf. **заво́дити, -и-**) + expression of place
за́вжди́	always
заво́д, -у	factory, works
за́втра	tomorrow
загоря́ти, -я́є- imperf.	sunbathe, get sunburnt (perf. **загорі́ти, -і́є-**)
загорі́лий	sunburnt
задово́лений	satisfied
задово́лення, -я neut.	satisfaction, pleasure
за́здрити, -и-, imperf. + acc.	envy
займа́тися, -а́є-, imperf.	be occupied with (+ instr.)
зайня́ти, -йму́, -ймеш, perf.	take, rent, get
зайня́тий	occupied, busy
закінчи́ти, -и́-, perf.	finish (imperf. **кінча́ти, -а́є-**)
зал, -у чека́ння	waiting room
зал, а	hall, large room (also **примі́щення**, -я)
зале́жати, -и-, imperf.	depend (**від** + gen. 'on')
зале́жно від + gen.	depending on
залиша́тися, -а́є-, imperf.	stay (lit: 'leave oneself'!) (perf. **зали́шитися, -и-**)
зали́шити, -и-, perf.	leave (something somewhere) (imperf. **залиша́ти, -а́є-**)
залізни́ця, -і	railway
заміни́ти, -и-, perf.	replace (imperf. **despite замі́нювати, -ює-**)
за́мість + gen.	instead of
замовля́ти, imperf.	order (meal etc.; perf. **замо́вити, -и-**)
записа́тися, -ше-, perf. **на** + acc.	enrol for
записа́тися, -ше-, perf. **на зу́стріч**	make an appointment ('with' **у/в** + gen.)
запита́ння, -я, neut.	question(s)
запі́зно	(it is/was) too late; adverb
запо́внювати, -ює-, imperf. **бланк**	fill in a form (perf. **запо́внити, -и-**)
запропонува́ти, -ує-, perf.	propose, suggest (imperf.

	пропонува́ти, -у́є-)
запро́шувати, -ує-, imperf.	invite (perf. **запроси́ти, -и-**)
за́раз	right away; in a second
засмія́тися, -і́є-, perf.	burst out laughing, began to laugh
засмути́тися, -и-, perf.	become sad, be saddened
засну́ти, -не́-, perf.	fall asleep (imperf. **засипа́ти, -а́є-**)
за́соби, -ів ма́сової інформа́ції	mass media
зати́шни́й	cosy
затри́мка, -и	delay
заува́жити, -и-, perf.	notice (imperf. **заува́жувати, -ує-**; 'to bring something to someone's attention' + acc. + dat.)
захо́дити, -и-, imperf.	set (of the sun)
за́хід, за́ходу	west
захо́дити, -и, imperf.	call in at, drop in at (followed by **у/в** + acc. or **до** + gen.)
заходи́тися, -и- perf. (+ instr.)	be enraptured by, transported (imperf. **захо́плюватися, -ює-**)
захо́плений	enthusiastic
зберегти́ся, -же́-, perf.	be preserved (imperf. **зберіга́тися, -а́є-**)
збира́ти, -ає-, imperf.	collect, gather (perf. **зібра́ти, збере́-**)
звари́ти, -и-, perf.	cook, boil (imperf. **вари́ти, -и-**)
зва́тися, -ве́-, imperf.	be called (synonym of **назива́тися**)
зверта́тися, -а́є-, imperf. **до** + gen.	address, turn to, apply for (**зверну́тися, -не-** perf.; note the very common phrase **зверта́ти/зверну́ти ува́гу на** + acc. 'to pay attention to, take into account'
звича́йний	ordinary
звича́йно	of course, usually
зви́чка, -и	from where
зві́дки	custom
зві́дси	from there
зві́дти	from here
зв'язо́к, -зку́	link, connection
зв'я́зувати, -ує-, imperf.	connect
згада́ти, -а́є-, perf.	recall (imperf. **зга́дувати, -ує-**)
зго́ден/зго́дний /згі́дний	agree (useful alternatives here may be **я (не) хо́чу** 'I (don't) want' and **я за/ про́ти** 'I'm for/against' (**за** + acc., **про́ти** + gen. if you wish to say more!)

згуби́ти, -и-, perf.	lose, mislay (imperf. **губи́ти, -и-**)
здає́ться	it seems ('to...'=dative case)
зда́ча, і	change (what's given back to you)
здоро́в'я, -я, neut.	health
зеле́ний	green
земля́, -і́	land, earth, ground
з-за кордо́ну	from abroad
зима́	winter
зимо́ю	in winter
зійти, -де́-, perf.	get off (**з** + gen.; transport; imperf. **схо́дити, -и-**)
змі́нюватися, -ює-, imperf.	change ('to change something/someone', non-reflexive; perf. **зміни́тися**, **-и-**)
змогти́, -же-; perf.	be able; can (imperf. **могти́, -же**; note stress fixed not on ending, in spite of infinitive)
знайо́мий	acquaintance
знайти́, -де-, perf.	find (imperf. **знахо́дити, -и-**)
знахо́дити, -и-, imperf.	find (perf. **знайти́, -де-**)
знахо́дитися, -и-, imperf.	be located (perf. **знайти́ся, -де-**)
зна́чити, -и-, imperf.	mean, signify
зна́чно	much, significantly (+ comp.)
зна́ти, -а́є-, imperf.	know
зні́мок, -мка	photo, snapshot
зо́внішній	external ('internal' **уну́трішній**)
зо́всім не	not at all
зокре́ма́	particularly
золоти́й	gold(en)
зраді́ти, -і́є-, perf.	be happy/glad; (imperf. **раді́ти, -і́є-**)
зра́зу	first of all, at once, right away
зру́чни́й	comfortable
зупини́ти, -и-, perf. **ви́бір на** + loc.	choose (lit. 'to halt one's choice on...')
зупини́тися, -и-, perf.	stop, stay, spend some time (imperf. **зупиня́тися, -я́є-**)
зупи́нка, -и	stop, parking place
зустрі́ти, -не-, perf.	meet (imperf. **зустріча́ти, -а́є-**)
зустріча́тися, -а́є-, imperf.	meet (each other)
зу́стріч, -і	appointment
і/й	and
і... і...	both..., and...
ім'я́, і́мені, neut.	name (first name)

інжене́р, -а engineer
і́ноді sometimes
і́нший other
інститу́т, -у institute
інформа́ція, -ї information
іти́/йти, -де́-, imperf. det. go, be going/walking
їда́льня, -і refectory, canteen; Amer. cafeteria
ї́здити, -и-, imperf. indet. go (by some means of transport; indet.)
ї́ї her, possessive; see **вона́**
ї́сти, їм, їсть, imperf. irreg. eat (perf. **з'ї́сти**)
ї́хати, ї́де- й go (by some means of transport; det.)
ї́хній their, poss.
ка́ва, -и coffee
кав'я́рня, -і café (also **кафе́**)
каза́ти, -же- say (perf. **сказа́ти, -же-**)
ка́мера, -и схо́ву left luggage office
кані́кули, кані́кул holidays
карбо́ванець, -нця karbovanets, Ukrainian 'ruble'
карто́пля, -і potatoes
ка́са, -и ticket office, tickets
ката́тися, -а́є-, imperf. **на ковзана́х** skate
ка́чка, -и duck
ка́ша, -і porridge, kasha
кашне́, indecl. scarf
кварта́л, -у block
кварти́ра, -и apartment
квито́к, -тка́ ticket
кві́тка, -и flower
ке́лех, -а glass, chalice
ке́мпінґ, -у camp site
ке́пка, -и cap
керівни́к, -а́ leader
кефі́р, -у buttermilk
кіло́, -а́/кілогра́м, -а (**кіло́** usually indecl.) kilogram
кіломе́тр, -а kilometre
кі́лькість, -ості quantity
кімна́та, -и room
кінча́тися, -а́є- finish (perf. **закінчи́тися, -и́-**)
кіо́ск, -а kiosk (**книжко́вий, газе́тний**)
кла́сти, -де́-, imperf. place in a lying position (perf. **покла́сти, -де́-**)
ключ, -а́ key
клі́мат, -у climate
кни́жка, -и book
книжко́ва ша́фа, -ої -и bookcase
книга́рня, -і bookshop
ковбаса́, -и́ sausage
ко́жен (ко́жний) every
коли́ when, if
коли́сь once (not in the sense 'once, twice...'), sometime
коли́шній former

ко́ло	near (prep. + gen.)
ко́лір (ко́льору) обли́ччя	complexion (lit. 'colour of face')
комбінезо́н, -у	overalls
компо́т, -у	compote, stewed fruit
конве́рт, -а	envelope
конце́рт, -у	concert
копі́йка, -и	kopeck
кордо́н, -у	border
кори́сний	useful ('to, for' + dat.)
користува́тися, -у́є-, imperf.	use, make use of, 'enjoy' (+ instr.); profit from (+**з** + gen.) (perf. **скористува́тися, -у́є-**)
кори́чневий	brown
коро́ва, -и	cow
коро́ткий	short
костю́м, -а	suit
ко́шик, -а	wastepaper basket, rubbish basket
ко́штувути, -ує-	to cost
краї́на, -и	country
край, -ю	land
крамни́ця, -і	store, shop
краси́вий	handsome, beautiful
кра́ще	better
крім	besides, apart from (+gen.)
крі́сло, -а	armchair
кру́глий	round
куди́	to where, whither, which way
кульба́ба, -и	dandelion
культу́ра, -и	culture
культу́рний	cultural
купа́тися, -а́є-	bathe
купе́ (indecl.)	compartment
купи́ти, -и-, perf.	buy (imperf. **купува́ти, -у́є-**)
купо́н, -а	coupon
кури́ти, -и-, imperf.	smoke
ку́хня, -і	kitchen
ла́вка, -и	bench
ла́дний/ла́ден	capable of, ready, inclined
ла́мпа, -и	lamp; **насті́льна лампа** 'table/reading lamp'
ла́мпочка, -и	light bulb
ле́гше	easier, more easily
лежа́ть, -и́-, imperf.	lie, be in a lying position
ле́кція, -ї	lesson (rare these days), lecture
леті́ти, -и́-, imperf. det.	fly
лимона́д, -у	soft drink (can include British 'lemonade', but not American 'lemonade')
лист, -а́	letter
листоно́ша, -и, masc.	postman, mailman
листува́тися, -у́є-, imperf.	correspond (write letters) (**з** + instr. 'with')
листі́вка, -и	postcard
лише́	only, just
ліво́руч	to/on the left
лі́жко, -а	bed

ліс, -у	forest, woods
літа́к, -а́	aeroplane (airplane)
літа́ти, -а́є-, imperf. indet.	fly
лі́то	summer
лі́том	in summer
ліфт, -а	lift, elevator
лови́ти, -и-, imperf. **ри́бу**	fish (to)
ло́жечка, -и	(tea)spoon
ло́жка, -и	(table)spoon
Ло́ндон, -а	London
люби́ти, -и-, imperf.	like, love
люди́на, -и	person (note its feminine gender)
лягáти, -áє-, imperf.	lie down (perf. **лягти́, -же-**; NB **я ля́жу**: stress fixed not on ending, in spite of infinitive)
ма́бу́ть	perhaps, probably, I think
ма́йже	almost
майбу́тнє, -ього (adj. declension)	future
мале́нький	small, short
мали́й	little, small
мандрі́вка, -и	ramble, journey
ма́рка, -и	stamp
маршру́т, -у	route
ма́ти, -а́є-, imperf.	have, be supposed to, due to, intend
ма́ти, ма́тері; ма́ма, -и	mother
маши́на, -и	car
мене́ зва́ти + name	I am called, my name is...
метрополіте́н, -у (**метро́,** indecl.)	subway/underground
ме́шканець, -нця	inhabitant
ме́шкати, -ає-, imperf.	live
ме́шти, мешт	shoes (from **ме́шта, -и**; perhaps the general term; see *17*)
ми	we
ми́лий	nice, pleasant
ми́ло, а	soap
милува́тися, -у́є- imperf. (+ instr.)	admire
мину́лого ро́ку	last year (adv.)
мисте́цтво, -а	art
ми́тися, -и́є-, imperf.	wash, have a wash (perf. **поми́тися, -и́є-**)
ми́ттю	in an instant
між + instr.	between
між і́ншим	by the way
міліціоне́р, -а	policeman, militiaman
мінера́льна вода́	mineral water
мі́сто, -а	town, city
мі́сце, -я	place
мі́сяць, -я	month
міцни́й	strong
мо́дний	fashionable
можли́вість, -ості	possibility, opportunity
можли́во	perhaps, maybe, possibly
моде́рний	modern
могти́, -же-, imperf.	be able, can (see **змогти́**)
мо́жна	it is possible to, it is permissible to, one may

молоко́, -а́	milk
моро́з, -у	frost
моро́зиво, -а	ice-cream
мотоци́кл, -а	motorcycle
му́сити, му́сіти, -и-, imperf.	have to, must
м'яки́й	soft, gentle
м'я́со, -а	meat
на	at, in, on; to (prep. + loc.; acc. with motion)
на все до́бре	so long, all the best
на жаль	unfortunately
на мою́ ду́мку	in my opinion (**ду́мка, -и** 'opinion')
на ща́стя	happily, luckily
набага́то	much (used with comparatives)
навесні́	in spring
навколи́шнє середо́вище, -ього -а	environment
на́віть	even (adv.)
наві́що	why, what is the purpose of?
над + instr.	over, above
над усе́	above all
надво́рі	outside (adverb)
надзвича́йно	extremely
нага́дувати, -ує-, imperf.	remind (+ dat. + acc. 'someone of something')
наза́д	back (adverb)
найбі́льше	most (of all)
найбі́льший	biggest
найбли́жчий	nearest
найбли́жчим ча́сом	in the immediate future
наї́вний	ingenuous, naive
накри́ти, -и́є-, perf.	lay/set (the table) (followed by **стіл** or **на стіл**; imperf. **накрива́ти, -а́є-**)
нале́жати, -и-, imperf. **до** + gen.	belong to
напе́вно	certainly, for sure
напри́кінці́	finally (adv.); at the end of (prep. + gen.)
напро́ти	opposite, facing
наро́д, -у	people, nation
наре́шті	at last, finally
насе́лення, -я, neut.	population
наспра́вді	really, indeed
насті́йно вимага́ти, -а́є-, imperf.	insist (lit. 'demand insistently')
насту́пний	next, following (also **черго́ви́й**)
насту́пного ро́ку	next year
натра́пити, -и-, perf.	find by chance, come across (+ **на** + acc.)
нау́ка, -и	science
на́ш	our
ная́вність, -ості	evidence
не	not (compare with **ні**!)
не ка́жучи вже про	not to mention (+ acc.)
не зо́всім	not so . . . (supply: good, bad)
небага́то	a little (+ gen. sing.)
не́бо	sky

невжé	is it possible that? are you serious that?
невисóкий	not tall, short
незалéжний	independent
незважáючи на	in spite of (+ acc.)
незрýчно	uncomfortable, embarrassed
неймовíрний	incredible
немáє	there is no, is not present, there is not available (also the rarer **немá**, + gen.)
ненáвидіти, -и-, imperf. (+ acc.)	hate
непогáно	not bad(ly)
неподалíк від + gen.	near, not far from
несмáчно	not good/well, not tasty/tastily (of food)
несподíвано	unexpectedly
нести́, -сé-, imperf. det.	take by foot, carry
низьки́й	short
ни́ні	now, today
ни́нішній стан, -ього -у	the present situation
ні	no
ніж	than
ніж, ножá	knife
ніч, нóчі	night
нічнá сорóчка, -óї -и	nightdress
ніс, нóса	nose
нісенíтниця, -і	nonsense
ніхтó не (+ verb)	no-one, not anyone
ні́чого (often + inf.)	there is nothing, it is useless, there is no point [to do, in doing...]
нічóго не	nothing (direct object of verb)
нíщó не (+ verb)	nothing, not anything
нія́к не	not at all
нови́й	new
Нови́й рік, -óго рóку	New Year
ногá, -и́ (acc. **нóгу**)	leg, foot
нóжиці, -ць (pl. only)	scissors
нормáльний	normal
носи́ти, -и-, imperf. indet.	wear (habitually); carry
нуль, -я́	zero
обережно	carefully, cautiously
обвинувáчувати, -ує-, imperf.	accuse (+ acc. + **у/в** + loc. 'someone of something')
обговóрювати, -ює-, imperf.	disuss, talk over
обли́ччя, -я, neut.	face
обов'язкóво	without fail, obligatorily
обстанóв(к)а, -и	situation, setting
óвочі, -ів	vegetables (also **горóдина, -и**)
óгляд, -у	visit, sightseeing (note the following gen.)
огля́нути, -не-, perf.	look around (at), see the sights of (imperf. **оглядáти, -áє-**)

оде́ржати, -и-, perf.	receive (imperf. **оде́ржувати, -ує-**)
одне́ о́дного	each other (male/female); with two males **оди́н о́дного,** with two females **одна́ о́дну** (only the second component is declined, and any preposition comes before the second component, whose case it determines)
о́дяг, -у	clothes
одяга́ти, -а́є-, imperf.	dress (someone), put (something on) (followed by the acc.) (perf. **одягну́ти, -не-**)
одяга́тися/ удяга́тися	get dressed (perfectives and conjugation as **одяга́ти** and **вдяга́ти**)
о́зеро, -а	lake
око́лиця, -і	outskirts, environs (often in plural)
окре́мий	separate, individual
олі́ве́ць, -вця́	pencil
он	over there
о́перний теа́тр, -ого -у	opera (theatre) (**о́пера** ‘opera’)
опусти́ти моне́ту в ка́су-автома́т	put a coin in the ‘gate’ (**-и-**; perf.)
оскі́льки	since, as, because
особли́во	especially
оста́нній	last, final
оста́ннім ча́сом	recently, lately
ось	here is, there is (like French *voici, voilà*)
от	(t)here is
от чому́	that’s why
о́тже	and so, consequently
отри́мати, -ає-, perf.	receive, obtain (imperf. **отри́мувати, -ує-**)
о́чі, оче́й (instr. **очи́ма**)	eyes
паку́нок, -нка	parcel
пальто́, -а́	overcoat
па́м’ятник, -а	monument
папа́	bye’, ‘see you (later)’
папі́р, -е́ру (для листі́в)	writing paper
па́рк, -у	park
пе́вний/пе́вен, пе́вна	certain, sure
пе́вно	certain(ly), it’s certain
перебува́ння, -я, neut.	stay, sojourn
перева́га (віддава́ти(ся), -ає́-)	preference ((be) give(n) to), prefer (imperf.)
перева́жно	primarily
перегово́ри, -ів	negotiations
пе́ред тим, як	before (+ verb form; note the

	comma)
передавáти, -aє́- imperf.	hand over, pass; broadcast (perf. **передáти**, irreg.)
передплáчувати, -ує-, imperf.	subscribe to, lit. 'pre-pay' (**передплáта, -и** 'subscription, prepayment')
переодягáтися, -áє-, imperf.	change clothes (perfective and conjugation as **одягáти** and **вдягáти**)
перепрóшую	excuse me
пересі́сти, -ся́де- perf.	change (**на** + acc. 'onto'; transport) (imperf. **пересідáти**, **-áє-**)
перехі́д, -хóду	crossing, pedestrian crossing
перехрéстя, -я, neut.	crossroads
п'є́са, -и	play
пи́во, -а	beer
писáти, -ше-, imperf.	write (perf. **написáти, -ше-**)
питáння, -я, neut.	question, issue
питáти, -áє-, imperf.	ask (perf. **запитáти, -áє-** and **спитáти, -áє-**)
пи́ти, п'є́-, imperf.	drink (perf. **ви́пити, -п'є-**); **+ за** drink (a toast) to + acc.
пі́вдень, пі́вдня, masc.	south
пі́вніч, пі́вночі, fem.	north
пізні́ший	later, subsequent
під	under, near (+ instr./acc.; often used with place-names)
підвóзити, -и-, imperf.	give a lift, take (someone somewhere) (perf. **підвезти́, -зé-**)
підня́ти, підійму́, піді́йме-, perf.	raise (imperf. **піднімáти** or **підіймáти, -áє-**)
підру́чник, -а	textbook, manual
підстáвочка, -и	small plate, saucer
підтвéрджено	it was declared, affirmed, asserted
під чáс, prep. + gen.	during
пі́сля	after (prep. + gen.)
пі́сля полу́дня	in the afternoon
пі́сля тогó, як, conj.	after (+ verb)
післязáвтра	the day after tomorrow
пі́сня, -і	song
піти́, піду́, пі́деш, perf.	go, set off (see **іти́, іду́, ідéш**)
піти́, -де- в гóсті до + gen.	go and visit someone (see **піти́**)
пі́шки	on foot
план, -у	plan
плáвати, -ає-, imperf. indet.	swim (det. **плисти́, пливé-**)
плати́ти, -и-, imperf.	pay (perf. **заплати́ти, -и-**)

пло́ща, -і	square
пляж, -у	beach
по	around, all over (prep. + loc./dat., in this meaning)
по-дома́шньому	just like at home (adv.)
поблизу́	near
побу́ти, -де-, perf.	be for a while; 'spend' (imperf. **побува́ти, -а́є-**)
поверну́ти, -не-, perf.	turn (e.g. left and right)
поверну́тися, -не- perf.	return, come back
	give back (imperf. **поверта́тися, -а́є-**)
по́верх, -у	storey, floor (not what is under your feet)
повз, prep. + gen.	past
пови́нний/пови́нен	should, must, be obliged to
пові́льно	slowly
пові́рити, -и-, perf.	believe (imperf. **ві́рити, -и-**)
по́вний	full, stout
пово́лі	slowly
пога́ний	bad
пога́но	bad
поговори́ти, -и-, perf.	have a chat
пого́да, -и	weather
поді́я, -ї	event
подо́батися, -ає-, imperf.	be pleasing, like (perf. **сподо́батися, -ає-**)
по́дорож, -і, fem.	trip
по́друга, -и	friend (female)
подорожува́ти, -у́є-, imperf.	travel
поду́мати, -ає-, perf.	think
поза́втра (coll.)	day after tomorrow
позавчо́ра	day before yesterday
поза́ду	behind (adv.)
позича́ти, -а́є-, imperf.	lend (perf. **пози́чити, -и-**)
познайо́митися, -и-, perf.	get to know (**+ з** + instr.)
поїзд, -у	train (also **по́тяг, -а**)
поі́здити, -и-, perf.	drive/go around a little
поі́здка, -и	journey, trip
поі́сти, perf. irreg.	have something to eat (perf.; see **і́сти**)
поі́хати, -і́де-, perf.	go (by some means of transport; perf. of det. verb of motion **і́хати, і́де-**)
пока́зувати, -ує-, imperf.	show (perf. **показа́ти, -же-**)
по́кищо	for the time being, until now
по́ле, -я	field
полу́день, полу́дня	midday
поме́шкання, -я	flat, apartment
помі́рний	moderate
пообіця́ти, -я́є-, perf.	promise (imperf. **обіця́ти, -я́є-**; + dat.)
попроща́тися, -а́є-, perf.	say good-bye to (**з** + instr.; imperf.

	прощáтися, -áє-)
порáда, -и	advice
порівня́ти, -я́є-, perf.	compare (imperf. **порíвнювати, -ює-**)
порóжній	empty
порозмовля́ти, -я́є-, perf.	converse, chat (imperf. **розмовля́ти, -я́є-**)
портфéль, -ю	briefcase
пóруч	close by, nearby
пóруч з + instr.	side-by-side with
посилáти, -áє-, imperf.	send (perf. **післáти** or **послáти, -шлé-**)
посúлка, -и	package
поспáти, -и́-, perf.	have a (little) sleep (imperf. **спáти, -и́-**)
поспішáти, -áє-, imperf.	hurry, rush (perf. **поспіши́ти, -и́-**)
постáвити, -и-, perf.	place in a standing position (here: car) (imperf. **стáвити, -и**)
пóтім	then
потрíбен/ потрíбний	necessary; to be needed
потрíбно (бýти)	need
похóдити, -и-, perf.	walk around a little
почáток, -тку	beginning
починáти, -áє-, imperf.	begin (perf. **почáти, -нé-**)
починáтися, -áє-, imperf.	start, begin (intrans.; perf. **почáтися, -чнé-**)
почувáтися, -ýє-, imperf.	feel
поштáмт, -у; **пóшта, -и**	post office (larger; the latter word also means 'post')
поштóва мáрка, (-ої) -и	stamp
поштóве відділення	small, local, village post office
поясни́ти, -и́-, perf.	explain (imperf. **поясня́ти, -я́є-** or **поя́снювати, -ює-**)
прáвду кáжучи	tell the truth...
прáвильно	correct (adverb)
прáво	law
праворуч	to/on the right
прáгнути, -не-, imperf.	yearn, long, tend
працювáти, -ю́є-, imperf.	work
представити, -и-, perf.	introduce (imperf. **представля́ти, -я́є-**; used with dat. and acc.)
приблúзно	approximately
прибувáти, -áє-, imperf.	come, arrive
прибуття́, -я́	arrival
привáбливий	attractive
привáтний	private
привести́, -дé-, perf.	lead (imperf. **привóдити, -и-**)
привезти́, -зé, perf.	bring by vehicle (imperf. **привóзити, -и-**)
приє́мно	pleased (lit. 'pleasant'; from **приє́мний**)

приї́хати, -ї́де-, perf.	arrive by vehicle (imperf. **приїжджа́ти, -а́є-**)
при́кро	unpleasant, harsh
приміська́ зо́на, -ої -и	suburb
приміськи́й райо́н, -ого -у	suburb
примі́щення, -я, neut.	place, hall
принаймні	at least (adverb)
принести́, -се́-	bring (on foot), perf. (imperf. **прино́сити, -и-**)
припіка́ти, -а́є-, imperf.	to be very hot; scorch
припуска́ти, -а́є-, imperf.	admit, acknowledge
приро́да, -и	nature
притягува́ння, -я	attraction
про + acc.	about, concerning
проба́чте	excuse me, sorry
проби́ти, -б'є́- компо́стером тало́н	cancel a ticket (perf.; imperf. **пробива́ти, -а́є-**)
пробле́ма, -и	problem
пробу́ти, -де-, perf.	spend (time)
провести́, -де́-, perf.	spend (time) (imperf. **прово́дити, -и-**)
програва́ти, -ає́-, imperf.	lose (perf. **програ́ти, -а́є-**)
прогре́с, -у	progress
прогу́люватися, -ює-, imperf.	take a walk (perf. **прогуля́тися, -я́є-**)
продаве́ць, -вця́	salesman
продавчи́ця, -і	saleswoman
продо́вжувати(ся), -ає-, imperf.	continue (ref. is intrans.; perf. **продо́вжити, -и-**)
проду́кти, -ів	products (used with **купува́ти** to mean 'to do the shopping'; from **проду́кт, -у/-а**)
прожи́ти, -ве́-, perf.	live (a certain period of time)
проїзд, -у у метро́	journey on the metro
проїзни́й (квито́к, -тка́)	ticket
прої́хати, -ї́де-, perf. **до** + gen.	get (somewhere, by transport)
пройти́, -де-, perf.	get to, make one's way to; pass, go past (imperf. **прохо́дити, -и-**)
проки́нутися, -не-, perf.	wake up (imperf. **прокида́тися; -а́є-**)
проси́ти, -и- зу́стріч у + gen.	ask for an appointment (imperf.)
про́сто	simply, only
про́ти + gen.	than
прохоло́дно	it's cool, refreshing
про́шу	please; you're welcome
прошу́ проба́чення	excuse me
прями́й	straight
пря́мо	straight on
ра́дий	glad
ра́дити, -и-, imperf.	to advise (perf. **пора́дити, -и-;**

+ acc. of what you advise, or plus an infinitive (or both), and the dat. of the person(s) being advised)

радíсно joyful, gives joy

радíти, -íє-, imperf. be glad at (+dat. or **з** + gen.) (perf. **зрадíти, -íє-**)

рáзом together; (all) at once (adv.)

рáзом з + instr. together with, along with

райóн, -у region, area

ранíше earlier, formerly, before

рáнком in the morning

рáно early (adverb)

рáптом suddenly

ревнувáти, -ýє-, imperf. (+ acc.) be jealous of

регуля́рно regularly

респýбліка, -и republic

ресторáн, -у restaurant

ри́ба, -и fish

ри́бна лóвля, -ої -і fishing

рівно precisely, on the dot

рíг, рóгу corner

Різдвó, -á Christmas

різний various, different

рік, рóку year

рікá, -и́ river (also **річка, -и**)

річ, рéчі, fem. thing

річ у тім, що the fact is that... (also **спрáва в тóму, що**)

рóдич, -а relative

роби́ти, -и-, imperf. do, make (perf. **зроби́ти, -и-**)

роби́ти, -и-, imperf. **пересáдку** change (onto) (**на** + acc.; perf. **зроби́ти, -и-**)

роби́тися, -и-, imperf. happen (perf. **зроби́тися, -и-; з** + instr. 'to [me]')

роби́тися, -и-, imperf. become (perf. **зроби́тися, -и-** + instr.)

робóта, -и work (e.g., be at, go to work; **прáця, -і** 'labour')

роди́на, -и family

роздягáти(ся), -áє-, imperf. undress (get undressed) (perfective and conjugation as **одягáти** and **вдягáти**)

рóзклад, -у поїздíв train timetable (as displayed on a board; **таблó** is indeclinable)

рóзмір, -у size

розкривáти, -áє-, imperf. open (wide, of book etc.) (perf. **розкри́ти, -и́є-**)

розмóва, -и conversation

розмовля́ти, -я́є-, imperf. talk, chat (perf. **порозмовля́ти, -я́є-**)

розмíнювати, -ює-, imperf. (**грóші**) change (money) (perf. **розміня́ти, -я́є-**)

розпакувáти, -ýє- unpack (**пакувáти(ся), -ýє-** 'to pack

	(one's luggage)')
розповіда́ти, -а́є-, imperf.	recount, relate (perf. **розпові́сти́**, irreg.)
розташо́ваний	situated
розумі́ти, -і́є-, imperf.	understand (perf. **зрозумі́ти, -і́є-**)
розу́мний	clever, sensible
ро́ля, -і	rôle, part
рости́, -сте́-, imperf.	grow
рот, -а	mouth
роя́ль, -я	piano (grand)
рука́, -и́	arm, hand
рух, -у	traffic; movement
рушни́к, -а́	towel
са́д, -у	garden
сади́ти, -и-, imperf.	seat, place in a sitting position; plant (perf. **посади́ти, -и-**)
садовина́, -и́	fruit
сала́т, -у	salad
сам	itself (emphatic pron./adj.)
са́ме так	exactly! ('just so')
сами́й собо́ю, pron.	oneself
сантиме́тр, -а	centimetre
свій	one's (own)
світи́ти, -и-, imperf.	shine
сві́тлий (in compounds: **я́сно-**)	light
сві́тло, -а	light
світлове́ табло́, -о́го -о́	video display with information
світлофо́р, -а	traffic lights

or **-у**	
св'яти́й	holy, Saint
секрета́рка, -и	secretary
село́, -а́	village
серве́тка, -и	napkin
се́ред + prep. gen.	in the middle of
сере́дина, -и	middle
серйо́зний	serious
сестра́, -и́	sister
сиді́ння, -я, neut.	seat
сиді́ти, -и́-	sit, be sitting
си́льно	strongly
симпати́чний	nice, likeable
син, -а	son
си́ній	dark blue
сир, -у	cheese
сіда́ти, -а́є-, imperf.	sit down (perf. **сі́сти, ся́де-**)
сік, со́ку	juice
сіль, со́лі	salt
сільське́ господа́рство	agriculture
сім'я́, -ї́	family (a synonym is **роди́на**)
складни́й	complex, complicated
скла́сти, -де́-, perf.	compose (imperf. **склада́ти, -а́є-**)
скля́нка, -и	glass
ско́ро	soon (adv,)
скрізь	everywhere
скі́льки	how much, how many (+ gen. sg./pl.)
скі́льки з ме́не?	how much do I owe? (the answer: **з вас** + amount)
славе́тний	famous, renowned
слід	it is advisable to, one should, one

has to

словни́к, -á dictionary (derived from **сло́во, -а** 'word')

слу́хаю hello (on the telephone; from **слу́хати, -ає-** 'listen to' (+ acc.))

смагля́вий tanned

смачно́го! have a good meal!

сма́чно well, tastily

смета́на, -и smetana; sour cream

СНД (indecl.) **Співдру́жність Незале́жних Держа́в** Commonwealth of Independent States (CIS)

сніг, -у snow

сніда́нок, -нку breakfast

сні́дати, -ає-, imperf. have breakfast

сніжи́ти, сніжи́ть/сніжи́ло, imperf. snow (to snow)

собо́р, -у cathedral

сова́, -и́ owl

со́кіл, -ола hawk, falcon

со́нце, -я sun

сопі́лка, -и sopilka, fife (Ukrainian flute)

соро́чка, -и shirt

сосна́, -и́ pine tree

Софі́йська це́рква, -ої -и St. Sophia's Cathedral (several names)

сою́з, -у union, alliance

спаси́бі thanks (**за** + acc. 'for')

спа́ти, -и́-, imperf. sleep

спеко́тно it's really hot, a heatwave, sultry

спе́ка, -и hot weather, heatwave

спецви́пуск, -у special issue

співробі́тництво, -а collaboration

спідни́ця, -і skirt

спі́дня біли́зна, -ьої -и underclothes

спі́лка, -и association

сподо́батися, -ає-, perf. to please (imperf. **подо́батися, -ає-**)

сподіва́тися, -а́є-, imperf. hope

спокі́йний calm

спокі́йно calmly, peacefully

спорт, -у sport

споча́тку at first

спра́вжній real, genuine (a soft adjective)

спра́ва, -и affair

спра́вді really

спро́бувати, -уе-, perf. try, test (imperf. **про́бувати, -уе-**)

става́ти, -ає́-, imperf. go and stand, become (perf. **ста́ти, -ста́не-**)

ста́вити, -и-, imperf. place in a standing position (perf. **поста́вити, -и-**)

ста́вити запита́ння ask a question (see **ста́вити**; also **задава́ти кому́сь запита́ння**)

стан, -у справ situation, state of affairs

ста́нція, -ї метро́ subway/under-

	ground station
стари́й	old(-fashioned)
старі́тися, -і́є-, imperf.	get older(er)
старови́нний	old, ancient
ста́ти, -не-, perf.	become (imperf. **става́ти, -ає́-**; + instr.)
статтЯ́, -і́	article
стіл, стола́/сто́лу	table; **письмо́вий с.**; writing table, desk
стіле́ць, -льця́	chair
сті́льки	so much, so many (+ gen. sg./pl.)
стіна́, -и́	wall
сто́лик, -у	small table
столи́ця, -і	capital (city)
столі́ття, -я, neut.	century
сто́млений	tired
сторі́нка, -и	page
стоя́ти, -ої́- imperf.	stand, be standing
стра́ви	dishes, food (plural of **стра́ва, -и**)
стражда́ти, -а́є-, imperf. + **від** + gen.	suffer from
стри́маний	restrained
струнки́й	slim
студе́нт, -а	student (male)
студе́нтка, -и	student (female)
суво́рий	severe
сумніва́тися, -а́є-, imperf. (**у/в** + loc.)	doubt, have doubts about (something)
су́мно	sad
суспі́льство, -а	society
сусі́д, -а	neighbour
сухи́й	dry
суча́сний	modern
схвильо́ваний	excited, touched
схід, схо́ду	east
схо́дити, -и-, imperf.	get down/off, come down/off (perf.: **зійти́, -де-**)
схо́ванки, -нок	hide and seek (perf.: **схова́ти, -а́є-** ‘hide’; imperf. **хова́ти, -а́є-**)
сху́днути, -не-, perf.	grow thin
сього́дні	today
сього́дні вве́чері	this evening
та	and, but
та й	and (indeed)
таве́рна, -и	inn
так	yes
так	so, thus
таки́й	so, such (a)
таки́й же..., як	just as... as
тако́ж	also
таксі́	taxi
тало́н, -а	ticket
там	there
тарі́лка, -и	plate
та́то, -а	father, dad
те, що	the fact that...
теа́тр, -у	theatre
теж	also (less common than **тако́ж**)
текти́, -че́-, imperf.	flow
телефо́н, -а	telephone
телефонува́ти, -у́є-, imperf.	telephone (**до** + gen. ‘to someone’; perf.

по-/ за- телефонува́ти, -у́є-)
те́мний (in compounds: **те́мно-**) dark
температу́ра, -и temperature
тенді́тний soft, gentle, fine
тепе́р now
те́плий warm
теплохі́д, -хо́ду motor vessel, ship
террито́рія, -ї territory
ти you (sing., familiar)
ти́ждень, ти́жня week
тим ча́сом meanwhile
тимчасо́вий temporary, provisional
типо́вий typical
типо́во typically
ти́хий quiet, peaceful
ті́сно losely
ті́тка, -и aunt
то 'then' (it balances **коли́**, earlier in the sentence)
то́бто that is, in other words
това́р, -у product, (pl.) wares
това́риш, -а friend
той that (dem.)
той са́мий the same (also **цей са́мий**)
тому́ ago (placed after a time expression in the acc.); and so
тому́ що because
торби́нка, -и bag
торт, -а cream cake
то́чний precise, exact
то́що and so on
трава́, -и́ grass
тре́ба it is necessary, (I...) must (impers.; + dat. of person)
трива́лий lengthy
троле́йбус, -а trolleybus (a bus with an overhead cable)
тро́хи a little
тро́шки a little
туале́т, -у toilet
туди́ (to) there, to that place
турбува́ти, -у́є-, imperf. bother
тури́ст, -а tourist
тут here
тя́жко seriously

у/в + loc. in, at
у/в + acc. into (motion)
у/в + gen. at a person's home, *chez*
ува́жно attentively (adv. from the adjective **ува́жний**)
уве́сь all, everyone (**всі** nominative plural)
уве́чері in the evening
увімкну́ти, -не́-, perf. turn on (a light) (perf. **вмика́ти, -а́є-**); turn off: **ви́мкнути, -не-,** imperf. **вимика́ти, -а́є**
удава́тися, -ає́-, imperf. be successful, manage (impers.)
уздо́вж + gen. along
узя́ти, ві́зьме-, take on

perf. **на озбро́єння**	
украї́нець, -нця	Ukrainian (male)
украї́нка, -и	Ukrainian (female)
улашто́вувати, -ує-, imperf. + acc.	suit, be OK for (someone) (perf. **улаштува́ти, -у́є-**)
умі́ти, -і́є-, imperf.	be able to, know how to, can (perf. **зумі́ти, -і́є-**)
університе́т	university
ура́нці	in the morning
усього́ найкра́щого!	all the best!
уста́ти, -не-, perf.	get up, off (imperf. **устава́ти, -ає́-**)
утво́рення, -я, neut.	creation
утоми́тися, -и-, perf.	become tired, be tired out
уто́млений	tired
уче́ний, -ого	scholar, scientist (declined as adjective)
учи́тель, -я	teacher (man)
учи́телька, -и	teacher (woman)
учи́тися, -и-, imperf.	study (perf. **навчи́тися, -и́-**; + gen. of what studied)
учо́ра	yesterday
фантасти́чний	fantastic
фотогра́фія, -ї	photograph (also the indeclinable neuter noun **фо́то**)
фотоплі́вка, -и	film for a camera
фунт, -а	pound
футбо́л, -у	football
ха́та, -и	house, home
хворі́ти, -і́є-, imperf.	be ill
хліб, -а	bread
хло́пець, -пця	boy, lad, fellow
хма́ра, -и	cloud
хма́рно	cloudy
ходи́ти, -и-, imperf. indet.	go, walk
ходи́ти, -и-, imperf. + **у/в** + loc.	be wearing
холоди́льник, -а	refrigerator
хо́лод, -у	cold
хо́лодно	cold ('it is...') (from **холо́дний**)
харо́ший	good (weather)
хоті́ти, -че-, imperf. **сказа́ти**	mean, lit. 'wish to say' (an alternative is **ма́ти на ува́зі** 'have in mind')
хоті́ти, -че-, imperf.	want (perf. **схоті́ти, схо́че-**)
хоті́тися, -че-, imperf.	feel like (impers.; + dat. of person who 'feels like doing something')
хоч(а́)	although (note that it is preceded by a comma)
хто	who
худи́й	thin
це	this is.../these are...
цей	this
центр, -у/-а	centre
центра́льний	central
це́рква, -и	church

цим ра́зом	this time	**черво́ний**	red
ци́ми днями	recently, (during) these days	**че́рга́, -и́**	queue, line
цирк, -у	circus	**черго́ви́й, -а́**	person on duty for the day (not just in hotels)
ціка́вий	interesting (**ціка́во** 'it's interesting' may be used to render 'wonder': **йому́ ціка́во, чому́...** 'he wonders why...')	**череви́ки, -ів**	shoes (ankle high)
		че́рез + acc.	through; after, in (times)
		чи	interrogative particle; or
		чи не так?	isn't it so?
		чий, чия́, чиє́	whose
ціка́витися, -и-, imperf. **у/в** + gen.	ask (i.e. to show enough interest to ask someone something) (perf. **поціка́витися** or **зацікавитися**, **-и-**; also 'to be interested in', in which case the perf. is **за-** and it takes the instr.)	**чима́ло**	quite a lot of, a great deal of (+ gen.)
		чи́стий	pure, clean
		чита́ти, -а́є-, imperf.	read (perf. **прочита́ти, -а́є-**)
		чита́ч, -а́	reader
		член, -а	member
		чобітки́, чобітків	boots
		чо́боти, чобі́т	boots
		чого́сь	genitive of **щось**
ці́лий	whole, entire	**чолові́к, -а**	husband, man (the word for 'person' is **люди́на, -и**)
цілко́м	completely, 'emphatic "yes"'		
ціль, -и	aim, object(ive)		
ціна́, -и́	price	**чолові́чий**	men's, male, masculine
цу́кор, -кру	sugar		
цього́ ро́ку	this year (adv.)	**чому́?**	why?
чай, -ю	tea	**чо́рна сморо́дина, -ої -и**	blackberries
час, -у	time		
части́на, -и	part	**чо́рний**	black
ча́сом	sometimes (adverb)	**чудо́вий**	wonderful
ча́сто	often	**чу́ти, -у́є-,** imperf.	hear, feel
ча́шка, -и	cup	**шанува́ти, -у́є-,** imperf.	respect
чек, -а	cheque, receipt		
чека́ти, -а́є-	wait (for: **на** + acc.)	**ша́фа, -и**	cupboard (for

	dishes and cutlery: **для пóсуду**)
ширóкий	broad, wide
шкодá	too bad! (what) a pity; be sorry
шкóла, -и	school
шлях, -ý	way, path
шматóк, -ткá	piece
шофéр таксí	taxi driver
шоколáдні цукéрки, -их, -рок/ків	chocolates (from **цукéрка, -и** or **цукéрок, -рка**)
шукáти, -áє	look for (perf. **пошукáти, -áє-** 'have a little look for')
ще/іщé	still, yet; **ще оди́н** 'yet another'
ще раз	once again
щи́рий	sincere
що	that; what ('that' as in 'he says "that we..."')
що вам до душí?	what pleases you?
що нóвого?	what's new?
що такé?	'what is...?', asking for a definition or description
щоб	in order to (+ inf.); in order that, so that (+ past tense)
щодня́	every day
щóйно	just, just now
щось	something, anything
я	I
я́блуко, -а	apple
я́блуня, -і	apple tree
яйцé, -я́	egg
як	how
як	than (with comparatives)
якби́ conj. + p. t.	if (also **коли́ б**)
яки́й	who, which/that (relative pronoun), what kind of
яки́йсь	some, a (certain)
якнайчастíше	as often as possible
якнайскорíше	as soon as possible
якрáз	just, precisely
якщó	if
ясни́й	clear

English–Ukrainian glossary

a little	**тро́шки**
about, approximately	**бі́ля** + gen.
about, concerning	**про** (prep. + acc.)
abroad	**за кордо́н(ом)** (motion + acc., no motion + instr.; from abroad **з-за кордо́ну**)
acquaintance	**знайо́мий**
aeroplane	**літа́к, -а́**
after, in (time)	**че́рез** + acc.
agree	**зго́дний/згі́дний/зго́ден**
all	**ввесь, все, вся (у-)**
all, the whole	**уве́сь (всі,** ‘everyone’ nom. pl.)
almost	**ма́йже**
already	**вже**
also	**тако́ж, теж** (less common than **тако́ж**)
although	**хоч(а́)**
always	**за́вжди**
America	**Аме́рика, -и**
American (female)	**америка́нка, -и**
American (male)	**америка́нець, -нця**
ancient	**да́вній**
and (indeed)	**та й**
and so on	**то́що**
and	**і**
and, but	**ж** (it suggests a contrast, or introduces new information, and comes straight after the first stressed word in the sentence or phrase; after a consonant we have **же**)
and, but	**та**
apartment	**кварти́ра, -и; поме́шкання, -я**
apple	**я́блуко, -а**
application form, questionnaire	**анке́та, -и**
armchair	**крі́сло, -а**
arrive by vehicle	**прии́хати, -ї́де-,** perf. (imperf. **приїжджа́ти, -а́є-**)
article in a periodical	**стаття́, -і́**

ask	**питáти, -áє-,** imperf. (perf. **запитáти, -áє-** and **спитáти, -áє-)**
at a person's home, *chez*	**у/в** (prep. + gen.)
at home	**вдóма**
at last, finally	**нарéшті**
at least	**принáймні**
at, in, on	**на** (prep. + loc.)
aunt	**тíтка, -и**
bad	**погáний**
bad	**погáно**
bandura	**бандýра, -и**
bathroom	**вáнна, -ої** ('adj.'; 'bath', declined like a noun)
be able to, know how to, can	**умíти, -íє-,** imperf. (perf. **зумíти, -íє-)**
be able, can	**могти́, -же-,** imperf. (perf. **змогти́**, -же-)
be	**бýти**
be glad (at)	**радíти, -íє-,** imperf. (+ dat. or + **з** + gen.) (perf. **зрадíти, -íє-)**
be ill	**хворíти, -іє-,** imperf. (perf. **за-** 'fall ill')
be located	**знахóдитися, -и-,** imperf. (perf. **знайти́, -де-)**
be occupied/busy with	**займáтися, -áє-,** imperf. (+ instr.)
be pleasing, like	**подóбатися, -ає-,** imperf. (perf. **сподóбатися, -ає-)**
because	**томý що, бо**
become	**стáти, -не-,** perf. (imperf. **ставáти, -áє-;** + instr.)
become interested in	**зацікáвитися, -и-** (perf. of **цікáвитися, -и-** + instr.)
bed	**лíжко, -а**
before	**до** (+ gen.)
before (+ verb)	**пéред тим, як**
believe	**повíрити, -и-,** perf. (imperf. **вíрити, -и-)** + dat. 'someone'; + **у/в** 'in someone or something'
beside, side-by-side with	**пóруч з** + instr. (on its own 'near' (adv.)
better	**крáще**
bon appétit!	**смачнóго!**
book	**кни́жка, -и**
bookshop	**книгáрня, -і**
boy, lad, fellow	**хлóпець, -пця**
bread	**хліб, -а**
bring (on foot), perf.	**принести́, -сé-** (imperf. **принóсити, -и-)**
bring by vehicle	**привезти́, -зé,** perf. (imperf. **привóзити, -и-)**
bus, coach	**автóбусний**
but	**алé**
buy	**купи́ти, -и-,** perf. (imperf. **купувáти, -ýє-)**
by bicycle	**на велосипéді**

by bus	**авто́бусом**
by car	**маши́ною**
by taxi	**на таксі́**
by tram	**трамва́єм**
by trolleybus	**троле́йбусом**
by underground	**на метро́**
café	**кафе́,** indecl. (indecl. neut.) **кав'я́рня, -і**
call in at, drop in at	**захо́дити, -и,** imperf. (followed by **у/в** + acc. or **до** + gen.)
capital (city)	**столи́ця, -і**
car	**маши́на, -и**
centre	**центр, -у/-а**
certain(ly), it's certain	**пе́вно**
chair	**стіле́ць, -льця́**
chat	**порозмовля́ти, -я́є-,** perf. (imperf. **розмовля́ти, -я́є-)**
children	**ді́ти, -е́й** (sing. **дити́на, -и-)**
coffee	**ка́ва, -и**
cold	**хо́лод, -у**; 'it is...': **хо́лодно**
colour	**ко́лір, ко́льору**
concert	**конце́рт, -у**
consequently, and so	**о́тже**
continue	**продо́вжувати(ся), -ає-,** imperf. (refl., intrans); (perf. **продо́вжити, -и-)**
conversation	**розмо́ва, -и**
cook, boil	**звари́ти, -и-,** perf. (imperf. **вари́ти, -и-)** more often **при-/з-готува́ти, -у́є-**
correspond (write letters)	**листува́тися, -у́є-,** imperf. (**з** + instr. 'with')
country	**краї́на, -и**
dacha	**да́ча, -і**
daughter	**до́ня, -і; до́нька, -и; дочка́, -и**
dictionary	**словни́к, -а** (from **сло́во, -а** 'word')
difficult (it's difficult)	**ва́жко**
discuss, (try to) decide	**вирі́шувати, -ує-,** imperf. (perf. **ви́рішити, -и-)**
discuss, talk over	**обгово́рювати, -ює-,** imperf.
do, make	**роби́ти, -и-,** imperf. (perf. **зроби́ти, -и-)**
door	**две́рі, -е́й** (plural form only)
drink	**пи́ти, п'є́-,** imperf. (perf. **ви́пити, -п'є-)**
earlier, formerly, before	**рані́ше**
early (adv.)	**ра́но**
east(ern)	**схі́дний**
eat	**ї́сти, їм, їсть,** imperf. irreg. (perf. **з'ї́сти)**
engineer	**інжене́р, -а**
England	**А́нглія, -ї**
Englishman	**англі́єць, -і́йця**
Englishwoman	**англі́йка**
even (adv.)	**на́віть**
evening	**ве́чір, -чора**

every day	**щодня́**
every	**ко́жен (ко́жний)**
exercise	**впра́ва, -и**
express	**висло́влювати, -ує-**, imperf. (perf. **ви́словити, -и-)**
factory, works	**заво́д, -у**
family	**сім'я, -ї́; роди́на, -и**
far (away)	**дале́ко**
father	**ба́тько, -а; та́то, -а**
feel	**почува́тися, -у́є-**, imperf.
find out	**дізна́тися, -а́є-**, perf. (imperf. **дізнава́тися, -ає́-)**
fine, beautiful, nice	**га́рний**
fine, good (adv.)	**до́бре**
first	**пе́рший**
fly	**леті́ти, -и́-**, imperf. det. (**літа́ти, -а́є-**, imperf. indet.)
for a long time	**до́вго**
fork	**виде́лка, -и**
friend (female)	**по́друга, -и**
from, of	**з** + gen.
full, stout	**по́вний**
garden	**са́д, -у**
gas	**га́з, -а**
get dressed	**одяга́тися/удяга́тися, -а́є-**
get out/off (a vehicle)	**вихо́дити, ви́йти** (**з** + gen.)
get to know	**познайо́митися, -и-**, perf. (+**з** + instr.)
girl	**ді́вчина, -и**
give	**дава́ти, -ає́-**, imperf. (perf. **да́ти, дам. . .** (irreg.))
give..., please	**да́йте** + whatever, adding **будь ла́ска**
glad	**ра́дий**
glass	**скля́нка, -и**
go, set off (by vehicle)	**пої́хати, -ї́де-**, perf. (by some means of transport; perf. of det. verb of motion **ї́хати, ї́де-; ї́здити, -и-**, imperf. indet.)
go, be going/walking	**іти́/йти, -де́-**, imperf. det.
go, set off (by foot)	**піти́, піду́, пі́деш**, perf. (see **іти́, іду́, іде́ш)**
go, walk in general	**ходи́ти, -и-**, imperf. indet.
grandfather	**діду́сь, -я́**
grandmother	**бабу́ся, -і**
greetings card	**віта́льна листі́вка, -ої -и**
hand over, pass, broadcast	**передава́ти, -ає́** imperf. (perf. **переда́ти**, irreg.)
have a (little)	**поспа́ти, -и́-,**

sleep	perf. (imperf. **спа́ти, -и́-**)
have a good meal!	**смачно́го!**
have a little supper	**повече́ряти, -яє-,** perf.
have breakfast	**сні́дати, -ає-,** imperf.
have dinner/supper	**вече́ряти, -яє-**
have something to eat	**пої́сти,** perf. irreg. (perf.; see **ї́сти**)
have to, happen to have to, fall to one's lot to	**дово́дитися, -и-,** imperf. (with the subject in the dative; perf. **довести́ся, -де́-**)
have to, must	**му́сити, му́сіти, -и-,** imperf.
have to, be supposed to, due to, intend	**ма́ти, -а́є-,** imperf.
he, it	**він**
help	**допомага́ти, -а́є,** imperf. (perf. **допомогти́, -же-**) (+ dat.)
here	**тут**
here is, there is	**ось** (like French *voici*, *voilà*)
holidays (usually school)	**кані́кули, кані́кул; вака́ції, -ій; відпу́стка, -и**
hot	**гаря́чий** (as in 'water'); weather: **жа́рко**
hotel	**готе́ль, -ю**
house, home	**ха́та, -и**
how	**як**
hungry	**голо́дний**
husband, man	**чолові́к, -а** ('person' **люди́на, -и**)
I	**я**
if	**якщо́; якби́**
in, at	**у/в** (prep. + loc.)
in autumn/fall	**восени́** (у **восени́**)
in order to	**щоб** (+ inf.); in order that, so that (+ past tense)
in spite of	**незважа́ючи на** (+ acc.)
in spring	**навесні́, весно́ю**
in summer	**влі́тку, лі́том**
in the evening	**вве́чері, уве́чері**
in the morning	**вра́нці**
in winter	**взи́мку, зимо́ю**
interesting	**ціка́вий**
(interrogative particle) 'or'	**чи**
into, to	**у/в** (motion; prep. + acc.)
introduce	**предста́вити, -и-,** perf. (imperf. **представля́ти, -я́є-**; used with dat. and acc.)
invite	**запро́шувати, -ує-,** imperf. (perf. **запроси́ти, -и-**)
it	**воно́**
it is necessary, (I...) must	**тре́ба** (impers.; + dat. of person)
it seems	**здає́ться** ('to me...' dative case)
it's time for us to... (+ inf.)	**час нам**

it's worth	**ва́рто** (neg. 'there's no point in, it's not worth')	letter	**лист, -а́**
		library	**бібліоте́ка, -и**
		lie, be in a lying position	**лежа́ть, -и́-,** imperf.
		life	**життя́, -я́** neut.
karbovanets	**карбо́ванець, -нця**	light	**сві́тло, -а**
		like, love	**люби́ти, -и-,** imperf.
keep, hold	**трима́ти, -а́є-,** imperf.; **держа́ти, -и-,** imperf.	like, please	**сподо́батися, -ає-,** perf. (imperf. **подо́батися, -ає-**)
key	**ключ, -а́**		
kitchen	**ку́хня, -і**	listen to	**слу́хати, -ає-** (+ acc.)
knife	**ніж, ножа́**		
know	**зна́ти, -а́є-,** imperf.	little, small	**мали́й; мале́нький**
		live	**жи́ти, -ве́-; ме́шкати, -ає-,** imperf.
kopeck	**копі́йка, -и**		
lake	**о́зеро, -а**	look for	**шука́ти** (perf. **пошука́ти, -а́є-** 'have a little look for'))
lamp	**ла́мпа, -и; насті́льна ла́мпа** 'table/reading lamp'	lorry, truck	**грузови́к, -а́; ванта́жна маши́на**
last year (adv.)	**мину́лого ро́ку**		
lay/set (the table)	**накри́ти, -и́є-,** perf. (+ **стіл** or **на стіл;** imperf. **накрива́ти, -а́є-**)	lose, mislay	**згуби́ти, -и-,** perf. (imperf. **губи́ти, -и-**)
		lunch, dinner (midday meal)	**обі́д, -у**
lead	**привести́, -де́-** perf. (imperf. **приво́дити, -и-**)	manage to, succeed in, be in time for, catch (+ **на** + acc.)	**встига́ти, -а́є-,** imperf. (perf. **всти́гнути, -не-;** past **-г-**)
leave (something somewhere)	**залиши́ти, -и-,** perf. (imperf. **залиша́ти, -а́є-**)	market	**база́р, -у** (cf. **ри́нок, -нку** 'market place/square')
leave, depart from	**ви́їхати, -де-** (+з + gen.)		
lecturer, teacher	**виклада́ч, -а́**	matter, affair	**спра́ва, -и**
lesson	**заняття́, -я́; уро́к, -у**	mean, lit. 'wish to say'	**хоті́ти, -че-,** imperf.

	сказа́ти (an alternative is **ма́ти на ува́зі** 'have in mind')
meet	**зустріча́тися, -а́є-,** imperf.
milk	**молоко́, -а́**
mineral water	**мінера́льна вода́**
modern	**суча́сний**
more	**бі́льше**
mother	**ма́ти, ма́тері; ма́ма, -и**
much, many	**бага́то** (+ gen. sing. or pl.)
much, significantly	**зна́чно** (+ comp.)
name (first name)	**ім'я́, і́мені,** neut.
napkin	**серве́тка, -и**
near	**бі́ля** + gen.
near, not far from	**неподалі́к від** + gen.
necessary	**потрі́бний/потрі́бен**
need	**потрі́бно (бу́ти)**
never	**ніко́ли не** (+ verb form)
new	**нови́й**
newspaper	**газе́та, -и**
next, following	**насту́пний**
night	**ніч, но́чі**
no longer, not any longer	**бі́льше не, вже не**
no	**ні**
no-one, not anyone	**ніхто́ не** (+ verb form)
normal	**норма́льний**
not at all	**зо́всім не**
not bad(ly)	**непога́но**
not good/well, not tasty/tastily (of food)	**несма́чно**

not	**не** (compare with **ні**)
nothing	**нічо́го не** (direct object of verb); **ніщо́ не** (+ verb form)
now	**тепе́р**
October	**жо́втень, -тня**
old(-fashioned)	**стари́й**
once, sometime	**коли́сь** (not in the sense 'once, twice...')
once, one time	**раз**
one's (own)	**свій**
only, just	**лише́**
open	**відчини́ти, -и-,** perf. (imperf. **відчиня́ти, -я́є-**)
opera (theatre)	**о́перний теа́тр, -ого -у (о́пера** 'opera')
opinion, thought, idea	**ду́мка, -и**
or	**або́, чи**
other	**і́нший**
our	**на́ш**
out of town	**за мі́сто** (movement); **за мі́стом** (no movement)
outskirts, environs (often in plural)	**око́лиця, -і**
over there	**он**
paper (writing paper)	**папі́р, -е́ру (для листі́в)**
parents	**батьки́, -і́в** (pl. of **ба́тько**)
park	**па́рк, -у**
pencil	**оліве́ць, -вця́**
person	**люди́на, -и** (NB: fem.)

place	**мі́сце, -я**	real, genuine	**спра́вжній**
plate	**тарі́лка, -и**	really, indeed	**наспра́вді**
play	**гра́ти, -а́є-,** imperf. (perf. **зігра́ти, -а́є-**)	receive	**оде́ржати, -и-,** perf. (imperf. **оде́ржувати, -ує-**); **отри́мати, -ає-,** perf. (imperf. **отри́мувати, -ує-**)
pleased (lit. 'it's pleasant')	**прие́мно**		
Polish	**по́льський**		
Poltava region	**Полта́вщина, -и**		
post office	**пошта́мт, -у; по́шта, -и** (larger; the latter word also means 'post')	recently, (during) these days	**ци́ми дня́ми**
		recount, relate	**розповіда́ти, -а́є-,** imperf. (perf. **розпові́сти́,** irreg.)
postcard	**листі́вка, -и**		
potatoes	**карто́пля, -і**		
prepare, cook	**готува́ти, -у́є-,** imperf. (perf. **при-/з-готува́ти, -у́є-**)	reply	**відповіда́ти, -а́є-,** imperf. (perf. **відпові́сти́**)
		rest	**відпочива́ти, -а́є-,** imperf. (perf. **відпочи́ти, -и́не-**)
products	**проду́кти, -ів** (used with **купува́ти** to mean 'to do the shopping'; from **проду́кт, -у/-а**)	return, come back	**поверну́тися, -не-**
		river	**ріка́, -и́** (or **рі́чка, -и**)
question ('issue')	**пита́ння, -я; запита́ння, -я** (that which is asked)	room	**кімна́та, -и**
		salesman	**продаве́ць, -вця́**
		saleswoman	**продавщи́ця, -і**
quiet, peaceful	**ти́хий**	satisfied	**задово́лений**
quite a lot of, a great deal of	**чима́ло** (+ gen.)	say	**каза́ти, -же-** (perf. **сказа́ти, -же-**)
quite, enough	**до́сить**		
rain	**дощ, -у́**	secretary	**секрета́рка, -и**
read	**чита́ти, -а́є-,** imperf. (perf. **прочита́ти, -а́є-**)	see	**ба́чити, -и-**
		send	**посила́ти, -а́є-,** imperf. (perf. **післа́ти, пішлю́, пішле́** or **посла́ти...**)
reader	**чита́ч, -а́**		
ready, prepared	**гото́в, -а, -е**		

shave	**голи́тися, -и-,** imper. (perf. **поголи́тися, -и-**)
she, it	**вона́**
should, must, be obliged to	**пови́нний/пови́нен**
show	**пока́зувати, -ує-,** imperf. (perf. **показа́ти, -же-**)
simply, only	**про́сто**
sister	**сестра́, -и́**
sit down	**сіда́ти, -а́є-,** imperf. (perf. **сі́сти, ся́де-**)
sit, be sitting	**сиді́ти, -и́-**
sitting room, drawing room	**віта́льня, -і**
situated	**розташо́ваний**
situation, state of affairs	**стан, -у справ**
sleep	**спа́ти, -и́-,** imperf.
slim	**стру́нки́й**
slowly	**пові́льно**
small table	**сто́лик, -у**
small, short	**мале́нький**
smile	**всміхну́тися, -не́-,** perf. (imperf. **всміха́тися, -а́є-**)
so much, so many	**сті́льки** (+ gen. sg./pl.)
so, thus	**так**
soap	**ми́ло, а**
son	**син, -а**
soon	**ско́ро**
Spain	**Іспа́нія, -ї**
spend (time)	**провести́, -де́-,** perf. (imperf. **прово́дити, -и-**)
spoon, tablespoon	**ло́жка, -и**
stand, be standing	**стоя́ти, -і́-**
state, country	**держа́ва, -и; краї́на, -и**
still, yet	**ще/іще́** ('yet another' **ще оди́н**)
stop, stay, spend some time	**зупини́тися, -и-,** perf. (imperf. **зупиня́тися, -я́є-**)
store, shop	**магази́н, -у; крамни́ця, -і**
strong	**міцни́й**
student (female)	**студе́нтка, -и**
student (male)	**студе́нт, -а**
study	**учи́тися, -и-,** imperf. (perf. **навчи́тися, -и́-**; + gen. of what studied)
such (a), so	**таки́й**
suddenly	**ра́птом**
sugar	**цу́кор, -кру**
suitcase	**валі́зка, и**
summer	**лі́то, -а**
supper, dinner (evening meal)	**вече́ря, -і**
sure, certain	**пе́вний/пе́вен**
table	**стіл, стола́/сто́лу** (**письмо́вий стіл** 'writing table, desk')
take a walk	**прогу́люватися, -ює-,** imperf. (perf. **прогуля́тися, -я́є-**)
take by foot, carry	**нести́, -се́-,** imperf. det.
take out	**ви́йняти, ви́йме-,** perf. (imperf. **вийма́ти, -а́є-**)
take	**взя́ти, візьму́,**

	ві́зьмеш, perf. (imperf. **бра́ти, бере́-**)
talk, chat	**розмовля́ти, -я́є-,** imperf. (perf. **порозмовля́ти, -я́є-**)
tall	**висо́кого зро́сту**
tall, high	**висо́кий**
tea	**чай, -ю**
teacher (female)	**учи́телька, -и**
teacher	**вчи́тель, -я**
telephone	**телефонува́ти, -у́є-,** imperf. (**до** + gen. 'to someone'; perf. **по-/за-телефонува́ти, -у́є-**)
than	**ніж; як**
thanks	**дя́кую; спаси́бі** (**за** + acc. 'for')
that (dem.)	**той**
that's why	**от чому́**
that; what (conjunction)	**що** ('he says *that* we...')
theatre	**теа́тр, -у**
then (subsequently)	**по́тім**
then (*if...then*)	**то** (it balances **коли́**, earlier in the sentence)
there	**там**
there is no time	**ні́коли** (often + inf.)
there is no, is not present, there is not available	**нема́є** (also **нема́**, + gen.)
there is (pointing to something)	**от**
they	**вони́**
thing	**річ, ре́чі,** fem.
think	**ду́мати, -ає-,** imperf.; **по-,** perf.

third	**тре́тій**
this (dem.)	**цей**
this evening	**сього́дні вве́чері**
this year (adv.)	**цього́ ро́ку**
this, that, it (is)	**це**
through	**че́рез** + acc.
time	**час, -у**
tired	**уто́млений**
to, up to, until, before	**до** + gen.
to/on the left	**ліво́руч**
to/on the right	**право́руч**
today	**сього́дні**
together; (all) at once	**ра́зом**
together with, along with	**ра́зом з** + instr.
toilet	**туале́т, -у**
toilet tissue	**туале́тний папі́р, -пе́ру**
tomorrow	**за́втра**
toothbrush	**зубна́ щі́тка, -о́ї -и**
toothpaste	**зубна́ па́ста, -о́ї -и**
towel rod/rail	**ві́шалка, -и для рушникі́в**
town, city	**мі́сто, -а**
train	**по́їзд, -у** (also **по́тяг, -а**)
tree	**де́рево, -а**
try, test	**спро́бувати, -ує-,** perf. (imperf. **про́бувати, -ує-**)
turn off (a light, etc.)	**ви́мкнути, -не-** (imperf. **вимика́ти, -а́є-**)
turn on (a light, etc.)	**увімкну́ти, -не́-,** perf. (imperf. **вмика́ти, -а́є-**)
type	**друкува́ти, -у́є-,**

	imperf. (**на маши́нці**)
Ukraine	**Украї́на, -и**
Ukrainian (female)	**украї́нка, -и**
Ukrainian (male)	**украї́нець, -и, -я**
uncle	**дя́дько, -а**
under, near	**під** (+ instr./acc.; often used with place-names)
understand	**розумі́ти, -і́є-,** imperf. (perf. **зрозумі́ти, -і́є-)**
unfortunately	**на жаль**
university	**університе́т, -у**
unpack	**розпакува́ти, -у́є- (пакува́ти(ся), -у́є-** ‘pack (one’s luggage)’**)**
veranda, porch	**вера́нда, -и**
very	**ду́же**
village	**село́, -а́**
wait	**чека́ти, -а́є-** (for: **на** + acc.)
wake up	**проки́нутися, -не-,** perf. (imperf. **прокида́тися, -а́є-**)
want	**хоті́ти, -че-,** imperf. (perf. **схоті́ти, схо́че-)**
wash, have a wash	**ми́тися, -и́є-,** imperf. (perf. **поми́тися, -и́є-**)
watch	**диви́тися, -и-,** imperf. (+ acc.), look at (+ **на** + **acc.**)
we	**ми**
wear (habitually),	**носи́ти, -и-,**

carry	imperf. indet.
week	**ти́ждень, ти́жня**
well, tastily	**сма́чно**
western	**за́хідний**
when	**коли́**
where	**де**
white	**бі́лий**
who?	**хто**
who, which/that	**яки́й** (rel. pron.)
whole, entire	**ці́лий**
whose	**чий, чия́, чиє́**
why, what is the purpose of?	**наві́що** (+ inf.)
why?	**чому́?**
window	**вікно́, -а́**
wife, woman	**жі́нка, -и**
wine	**вино́, -а́**
winter	**зима́, -и́**
wish	**бажа́ти, -а́є-** (perf. **побажа́ти, -а́є-**)
work	**робо́та, -и** (e.g. ‘be at (**на** + loc.)’, ‘go to (**на** + acc.)’ ‘work’; **пра́ця,** ‘labour’)
write	**писа́ти, -ше-,** imperf. (perf. **написа́ти, -ше-**)
year	**рік, ро́ку**
yellow	**жо́втий**
yes	**так**
yesterday	**учо́ра**
you (sing., familiar)	**ти**
you (sing., polite; and pl.)	**ви**

Index

The numbers refer to lessons.